THE NATIONALISM READER

THE
NATIONALISM
READER

Edited by
Omar Dahbour
and
Micheline R. Ishay

Humanity
Books

an imprint of Prometheus Books
59 John Glenn Drive, Amherst, New York 14228-2119

Published by Humanity Books, an imprint of Prometheus Books

The Nationalism Reader. This collection copyright © 1995 Humanity Books. Introduction © 1995 Micheline R. Ishay. All rights reserved. No part of this publication may be reproduced, stored in a retrieval system, or transmitted in any form or by any means, digital, electronic, mechanical, photocopying, recording, or otherwise or conveyed via the Internet or a Web site without prior written permission of the publisher, except in the case of brief quotations embodied in critical articles and reviews.

Inquiries should be addressed to
Humanity Books
59 John Glenn Drive
Amherst, New York 14228–2119
VOICE: 716–691–0133, ext. 210
FAX: 716–691–0137
WWW.PROMETHEUSBOOKS.COM

19 18 17 16   20 19 18 17

Library of Congress Cataloging-in-Publication Data

The Nationalism Reader / edited by Omar Dahbour and Micheline R. Ishay.
    p.   cm.
    Originally published: Atlantic Highlands, NJ : Humanities Press International, Inc., 1995
    Includes index.
    ISBN 13: 978-1-57392-623-2
    ISBN 10: 1-57392-623-X (paper)

    1. Nationalism—History. 2. Political science—History. 3. I. Dahbour, Omar. II. Ishay, Micheline R.
JC311.N326   1995
320.5'4—dc20   94–12537
                                                    CIP

Printed in the United States of America on acid-free paper

CONTENTS

Acknowledgments   ix

Introduction   1
  Micheline R. Ishay

Part I   The Enlightenment Background of Internationalism and Nationalism

1   JEAN-JACQUES ROUSSEAU
    The Geneva Manuscript   22
    Judgment on Saint-Pierre's Project for Perpetual Peace   26
    The Government of Poland   30

2   EMMANUEL JOSEPH SIEYÈS
    What Is the Third Estate?   35

3   IMMANUEL KANT
    The Metaphysics of Morals   38

4   JOHANN GOTTFRIED VON HERDER
    Reflections on the Philosophy of the History of Mankind   48

Part II   Liberalism and Nationalism

5   JOHANN GOTTLIEB FICHTE
    The Foundations of Natural Law According to the
    Principles of the Theory of Science   60
    Addresses to the German Nation   62

6   GEORG WILHELM FRIEDRICH HEGEL
    The Philosophy of Right   71
    The Philosophy of World History   79

7   GIUSEPPE MAZZINI
    The Duties of Man   87

8   JOHN STUART MILL
    Considerations on Representative Government   98

9   LORD ACTON
    Nationality   108

10 MAX WEBER
    Economic Policy and the National Interest in Imperial
    Germany   119

11 THEODOR HERZL
    A Jewish State   125

Part III   Conservatism and Nationalism

12 EDMUND BURKE
    Reflections on the Revolution in France   134

13 ERNEST RENAN
    What Is a Nation?   143

14 LEOPOLD RANKE
    The Great Powers   156

15 ELIE KEDOURIE
    Nationalism   160

16 ALEKSANDR SOLZHENITSYN
    Rebuilding Russia   169

Part IV   Socialism, Nationalism, and Internationalism

17 KARL MARX AND FRIEDRICH ENGELS
    Manifesto of the Communist Party   178

18 OTTO BAUER
    The Nationalities Question and Social Democracy   183

19 JOSEPH STALIN
    Marxism and the National-Colonial Question   192

20 ROSA LUXEMBURG
    The National Question and Autonomy   198

21 VLADIMIR ILYICH LENIN
    The Right of Nations to Self-Determination   208

Part V   Integral Nationalism, Fascism, and Nazism

22 CHARLES MAURRAS
    The Future of French Nationalism   216

23 BENITO MUSSOLINI
   Fascism   222

24 ADOLF HITLER
   Mein Kampf   230

Part VI Anticolonialism and National Liberation
Movements

25 SUN YAT-SEN
   Three Principles of the People   240

26 JAWAHARLAL NEHRU
   The Discovery of India   248

27 SATI AL-HUSRI
   Muslim Unity and Arab Unity   255

28 AYATOLLAH KHOMEINI
   Islamic Government   260

29 LÉOPOLD SÉDAR SENGHOR
   On African Socialism   268

30 FRANTZ FANON
   The Wretched of the Earth   274

Part VII American Perspectives on Nationalism

31 ABRAHAM LINCOLN
   First Inaugural Address, March 1861   286

32 RANDOLPH BOURNE
   Trans-National America   292

33 MARCUS GARVEY
   The Resurrection of the Negro   302

34 WOODROW WILSON
   Address to a Joint Session of Congress, January 1918   306

35 REINHOLD NIEBUHR
   Moral Man and Immoral Society   312

Part VIII The Contemporary Debate on Nationalism

36 MICHAEL WALZER
   The New Tribalism: Notes on a Difficult Problem   322

37 JURGEN HABERMAS
    *Citizenship and National Identity: Some Reflections on the
    Future of Europe*   333

38 JEREMY BRECHER
    *"The National Question" Reconsidered from an Ecological
    Perspective*   344

39 ERIC HOBSBAWM
    Nationalism in the Late Twentieth Century   362

Index   373

ACKNOWLEDGMENTS

We would like to thank Keith Ashfield, Stephen Bronner, Mitchell Cohen, Nanette Funk, David Goldfischer, Carlangelo Liverani, and Cynthia Meyers for their helpful comments and suggestions, and Kristen Bornhorst, Michele Pietrowski, William Daniel, Paul Kan, and Cindy Nixon for their valuable assistance.

We would also like to thank those publishers and organizations listed below who generously granted us permission to reprint portions of this text. Material has been reprinted from the following sources:

Lord Acton, "Nationality," in *History of Freedom and Other Essays* (pp. 273–300). Salem, NH: Ayer Co. Pubs, Inc., 1907. Reprinted with permission.

Bauer, Otto, "The Nationalities Question and Social Democracy," in *Austro-Marxism*, ed. and trans. T. Bottomore and P. Goode (pp. 107–17). Oxford: Oxford University Press, 1978. Reprinted with the permission of Oxford University Press.

Bourne, Randolph, "Trans-National America," in *Radical Will: Selected Writings, 1911–1918* (pp. 266–84, 287–89, 295–97). Berkeley: University of California Press. Reprinted with the permission of University of California Press.

Brecher, Jeremy, "'The National Question' Reconsidered from an Ecological Perspective," *New Politics* (summer 1987): 95–111. Reprinted with permission.

Burke, Edmund, *Reflections on the Revolution in France*, ed. J. G. A. Pocock (pp. 29–31, 44–45, 72–73, 75–77, 79–81, 84–85). Indianapolis, IN: Hackett Publishing Company, 1987. Reprinted with the permission of Hackett Publishing Company.

Fanon, Frantz, from "The Wretched of the Earth," in *Nationalism in Asia and Africa*, ed. E. Kedourie (pp. 488–95, 497, 508–11, 535–36). New York: Meridian Books/New American Library, 1970.

Fichte, Johann Gottlieb, *Addresses to the German Nation* (pp. 130–50). La Salle, IL: Open Court Publishing Company, 1922. Reprinted with the permission of Open Court Publishing Company.

Fichte, Johann Gottlieb, "The Foundations of Natural Law According to the Principles of the Theory of Science," from "An Outline of International and Cosmopolitan Law," in *The Political Thought of the German Romantics*, ed. H. S. Reiss and P. Brown (pp. 73–84). Oxford: Blackwell Publishers, 1955. Reprinted with the permission of Blackwell Publishers.

Garvey, Marcus, "The Resurrection of the Negro," in *Nationalism in Asia and Africa*, ed. E. Kedourie (pp. 283–87, 293). New York: Meridian Books/New American Library, 1970.

Habermas, Jürgen, "Citizenship and National Identity; Some Reflections on the Future of Europe," *Praxis International* 12:1 (April 1992): 1–18. Reprinted with the permission of Blackwell Publishers.

Hegel, G. W. F., *Lectures on the Philosophy of World History*, ed. D. Forbes and H. B. Nisbet (pp. 51–56, 61–63, 80–83, 96–97). New York: Cambridge University Press, 1975. Reprinted with the permission of Cambridge University Press.

Hegel, G. W. F., *The Philosophy of Right*, trans. T. M. Knox (pp. 160–65, 208–19). Oxford: Oxford University Press, 1952. Reprinted with the permission of Oxford University Press.

Herder, Johann Gottfried von, *Reflections on the Philosophy of the History of Mankind* (pp. 3–13, 96–118). Chicago, IL: The University of Chicago Press. Reprinted with the permission of The University of Chicago Press.

Herzl, Theodor, *A Jewish State*, trans. S. D'Avigdor (pp. 16–19, 24–29, 97–102). Rev. ed. New York: Maccabaean Publishing Company, 1904.

Hitler, Adolf, *Mein Kampf*, trans. R. Manheim (pp. 121–33). Copyright 1943, © renewed 1991 by Houghton Mifflin Company. All rights reserved. Reprinted with the permission of Houghton Mifflin Company.

Hobsbawm, Eric, "Nationalism in the Late Twentieth Century," in *Nations and Nationalism since 1780* (pp. 163–83). New York: Cambridge University Press, 1990. Reprinted with the permission of Cambridge University Press.

Sati al-Husri, "Muslim Unity and Arab Unity," in *Arab Nationalism: An Anthology*, ed. S. Haim (pp. 147–53). Rev. ed. Berkeley: University of California Press, 1962. Reprinted with the permission of University of California Press.

Kant, Immanuel, "The Metaphysics of Morals," in *Kant's Political Writings*, ed. H. S. Reiss, trans. H. B. Nisbet (pp. 164–75). New York: Cambridge University Press, 1970. Copyright © Cambridge University Press, 1970. Reprinted with permission.

Kedourie, Elie, *Nationalism* (pp. 96–110, 113–17, 126–27, 138–40). London: Hutchinson. © Elie Kedourie, 1960, 1961, 1969, 1985.

Ayatollah Khomeni, "Islamic Government," in *Political and Social Thought in the Contemporary Middle East*, ed. K. H. Karpat (pp. 501–10). Rev. ed. New York and London: Praeger, 1982. Praeger is an imprint of Greenwood Publishing Group, Inc., Westport, CT.

Lenin, V. I. *The Right of Nations to Self-Determination* (pp. 10–14, 24–26, 34–36, 61–62, 64). New York: International Publishers, 1970. Reprinted with the permission of International Publishers.

Lincoln, Abraham, "First Inaugural Address, March 1861." Reprinted with the permission of Macmillan College Publishing Company from *The Political Thought of Abraham Lincoln* by R. N. Current (pp. 169, 171–79). Copyright © 1967 by Macmillan College Publishing Company, Inc.

Luxemburg, Rosa, "The National Question and Autonomy," in *The National Question: Selected Writings by Rosa Luxemburg*, ed. H. B. Davis (pp. 101–3, 110–14, 121–25, 129–30, 134–40, 143–49). New York: Monthly Review Press, 1976. Copyright © 1976 by Horace Davis. Reprinted by permission of Monthly Review Foundation.

Marx, Karl, and Friedrich Engels, "Manifesto of the Communist Party," from *The Portable Karl Marx*, ed. E. Kamenka (pp. 203–8, 224–26). New York: Penguin, 1983. Copyright © 1983 by Viking Penguin Inc. Used by permission of Viking Penguin, a division of Penguin Books USA Inc.

Maurras, Charles, "The Future of French Nationalism," in *The French Right*, ed. J. S. McClelland, trans. J. Frears (pp. 295–304). Copyright © 1970 by Jonathan Cape, Ltd. Reprinted by permission of HarperCollins Publishers Inc.

Mazzini, Giuseppe, "The Duties of Man," in *The Duties of Man and Other Essays* (pp. 8–19, 51–59). London: J. M. Dent and Co.; New York: E. P. Dutton and Co.

Mill, John Stuart, "Considerations on Representative Government" in *Three Essays* (pp. 380–88, 401–4, 408–12). New York: Oxford University Press, 1975.

Mussolini, Benito, *Fascism* (pp. 7–14, 18–26). New York: Howard Fertig, 1968; reprint.

Nehru, Jawaharlal, *The Discovery of India* (pp. 384–87, 391–95, 543–46). New York: Oxford University Press, 1990.

Niebuhr, Reinhold, *Moral Man and Immoral Society* (pp. 83–97, 110–12). Reprinted with the permission of Scribner's, an imprint of Simon & Schuster. Copyright 1932 Charles Scribner's Sons; copyright renewed © 1960 Reinhold Niebuhr.

Ranke, Leopold, "The Great Powers," in *Theory and Practice of History*, ed. G. Iggers and K. von Moltke, trans. W. Iggers (pp. 86, 88–89, 94, 98–101). New York: Irvington, 1983. Reprinted with permission.

Renan, Ernest, "What Is a Nation?" in *Modern Political Doctrines*, ed. A. Zimmern (pp. 187–205). Oxford: Oxford University Press, 1939.

Rousseau, Jean-Jacques, "The Geneva Manuscript," in *On the Social Contract, with Geneva Manuscript and Political Economy*, ed. R. D. Masters, trans. J. R.

Masters (pp. 49–50, 163–66). New York: St. Martin's Press. Copyright © 1978. Reprinted with the permission of St. Martin's Press.

Rousseau, Jean-Jacques, *The Government of Poland*, trans. W. Kendall (pp. 10–13, 19–20). Indianapolis, IN: Hackett Publishing Company, Inc., 1985. Reprinted with the permission of Hackett Publishing Company.

Rousseau Jean-Jacques, "Judgment on Saint-Pierre's Project for Perpetual Peace," in *The Theory of International Relations*, ed. M. G. Forsyth, H. M. A. Keens-Soper, and P. Savigaer (pp. 157–66). Englewood Cliffs, NJ: Prentice-Hall, 1970.

Senghor, Léopold Sédar, *On African Socialism*, trans. M. Cook (pp. 72–75, 78–84). New York and London: Praeger, 1964. © Léopold Sédar Senghor, 1964. Praeger is an imprint of Greenwood Publishing Group, Inc., Westport, CT.

Sieyès, Emmanuel Joseph, *What Is the Third Estate?* ed. S. E. Finer, trans. M. Blondel (pp. 53–58). New York and London: Praeger, 1963. Praeger is an imprint of Greenwood Publishing Group, Inc., Westport, CT. Reprinted with permission.

Solzhenitsyn, Aleksandr, *Rebuilding Russia*, trans. A. Klimoff (pp. 5–11, 41–43, 48–54). New York: Farrar, Straus and Giroux, 1991. Translation copyright © 1991 by Farrar, Straus & Giroux, Inc. Reprinted by permission of Farrar, Straus & Giroux, Inc.

Stalin, Joseph, *Marxism and the National and Colonial Question* (pp. 8–9, 26–35). New York: International Publishers. Reprinted with the permission of International Publishers.

Sun Yat-sen, from "Three Principles of the People," in *Nationalism in Asia and Africa*, ed. E. Kedourie (pp. 304–17). New York: Meridian Books/New American Library, 1970.

Walzer, Michael, "The New Tribalism: Notes on a Difficult Problem," *Dissent* (spring 1992): 164–71. Reprinted with permission.

Weber, Max, "Economic Policy and the National Interest in Imperial Germany," in *Selections in Translation*, ed. W. G. Runciman, trans. E. Matthews (pp. 263–68). New York: Cambridge University Press, 1978. © Cambridge University Press, 1978. Reprinted with permission.

Wilson, Woodrow, "Address to a Joint Session of Congress," in *Papers of Woodrow Wilson*, ed. A. Link (pp. 534–39). Princeton, NJ: Princeton University Press, 1966. Reprinted with the permission of Princeton University Press.

INTRODUCTION

The hailing of a "New World Order"[1] at the end of the Cold War coincided with an eruption of nationalism. The withering of the bipolar balance of power has created a vacuum which has been filled by a new tide of ethnic conflict in the former Soviet Union, Bosnia, Somalia, and elsewhere. The rampant spread of nationalism has become a frightening prospect in our nuclear age. A comprehensive and rigorous understanding of the problem of nationalism has become imperative.

Despite general recognition of this resurgent phenomenon, there is neither widespread awareness nor expert consensus on the meaning and origins of nationalism. Past and contemporary literature on nationalism shows that there are many conceptions and types of nationalism, and hence more than one way to understand the origins of this phenomenon. Although some scholars, such as John Amstrong and Anthony Smith, trace national loyalty to antiquity, others, such as Ernest Gellner and Benedict Anderson, distinguish the concept of nationalism from other historical forms of social identity and associate its origins with the seventeenth-century development of the modern apparatus of statehood.[2]

Modern state structures, combined with the eighteenth-century revolutionary call for popular participation in politics, created the potential for a qualitatively different tie between people and the state, which in critical circumstances evolved into nationalism. In the words of Carlton Hayes, nationalism is a "modern emotional effusion" aroused by the nation-state.[3] This book adopts this latter position by tracing the development of nationalism from the Enlightenment to our contemporary period.

This anthology depicts the historical evolution of nationalist thought in the words of leading political actors and thinkers. In that sense it can serve as a primary source supplement to historical interpretations of nationalism by such scholars as Hans Kohn, Ernest Gellner, Eric Hobsbawm, Liah Greenfeld,[4] and others. This reader, however, is more than merely a useful reference book for students. It also proposes to explain nationalism in *ideological* terms. The issue here is not whether nationalism is itself an ideology, as Elie Kedourie maintained, or a sentiment, as held by Benedict Anderson and Carlton Hayes.[5] What is crucial is how different historical manifestations of nationalism can be better understood by placing them in the context of major political traditions such as liberalism, conservatism, and socialism.

1

This approach does not suggest that all political ideologies are reducible to nationalism, but rather that each of these political ideologies oscillates between a universalist (or at least a quasi-universalist) conception of human rights and a particularist focus on the nation. Nineteenth-century liberals like Fichte, for example, advocated German national and cultural unity against Napoleon, in contrast to his own earlier promotion of equal political rights for all humankind.[6] Similarly, Stalin's call in the 1930s for "socialism in one country" differed sharply from the internationalist socialist ideals of the turn of the century. In a qualitatively different way from liberals and socialists, conservatives moved back and forth from a strong nationalist position during the world wars to support a relatively stable global order during the Cold War.

By organizing this reader to illustrate these fluctuations within contending ideological approaches, I hope to shed new theoretical light on the study of nationalism. Such an approach reveals that each political tradition contains both a universalist and a particularist component, and that its particularist element tends toward nationalism under the stress of war, crises, or internal struggles for power. Readers should therefore consider how liberals' embrace of cultural rights can degenerate into claims of national supremacy; how socialists' tactical use of nationalist fervor can become an end in itself; and how conservatives' visions of global order and stability can become a disguise for nationalist aspirations. In extreme circumstances, all these tendencies can culminate in the most extreme form of particularism: fascism.

With the exception of the section on fascism, which covers the writings of ultra-nationalist thinkers, this reader in effect presents a range of positive and negative responses to nationalism in the form of debates *within* particular ideological perspectives. It should be remembered that various historical crises (war, economic depression, ethnic or class conflicts, and so on) have prompted divergent reactions even from political thinkers and leaders who shared the same basic political ideology. For example, although the liberal Johann G. Fichte, appealed to German nationalism against Napoleon (1806), the liberal Woodrow Wilson proposed a League of Nations (1917) to countervail the threat of nationalism.

This reader thus acknowledges the importance of historical contingencies, systematically classifies the question of nationalism according to conflicting perspectives, and at the same time covers the writings of European, American, and non-European contributors to nationalism. Nationalist ideas originated during the growth of the European nation-state and imperial conquest; colonialism ensured their spread throughout the world. In their fight against European colonialism, national liberation movements revived indigenous cultures and often incorporated Western values, while claiming national self-determination. The fact that Third-World nationalism was shaped by colonialism constitutes an additional reason for beginning with European views on nationalism.

In short, this reader shows in a unique way the ideological transformation of nationalism in Europe, in the Third World, and in the federal framework of the United States. The selection among the great political writers was made according to the above qualifications, that is, according to the thinkers' political views, their writings on nationalism, and their geographical background. Their contributions are divided into the following sections: Part I, The Enlightenment Background of Internationalism and Nationalism; Part II, Liberalism and Nationalism; Part III, Conservatism and Nationalism; Part IV, Socialism, Nationalism, and Internationalism; Part V, Integral Nationalism, Fascism, and Nazism; Part VI, Anticolonialism and National Liberation Movements; Part VII, American Perspectives on Nationalism; and Part VIII, The Contemporary Debate on Nationalism.

I. THE ENLIGHTENMENT BACKGROUND OF INTERNATIONALISM AND NATIONALISM

Prior to the eighteenth century, European political unity was built on feudal and religious institutions such as the Catholic church. These institutions served to link each individual to the community. Successive events gradually destroyed medieval Christendom: The Protestants' attempt to replace the Catholic church led to prolonged religious wars; the rationalist postulates of the scientific revolution defied the revealed truths espoused by the church; and the development of autonomous mercantile nation-states challenged the centralized political expression of Christianity, represented by the Holy Roman Empire.[7] In the seventeenth century the nation-state gradually became the focal point of political activity.

The international nature of these events created conditions for the emergence of alternative forms of political allegiance. Political unity was now consolidated by absolute monarchs, who destroyed old feudal loyalties by weakening the ties of the church and by emphasizing the secular and commercial character of the nation-state. The growth of mercantilism strengthened the national economic unit and paved the way for the development of national solidarity. In the eighteenth century liberals identified national allegiance with the universal right of people to establish representative political institutions, in particular republican regimes. At the same time, the expansion of global trade provided the means for the dissemination of these internationalist and republican ideas throughout the world, especially in Western Europe and North America.

The parallel development of national and international solidarity can be examined in the works of major political thinkers such as Jean-Jacques Rousseau (1712–1778), Emmanuel Joseph Sieyès (1748–1836), Immanuel Kant (1724–1804), and Johann Gottfried von Herder (1744–1803). The French theorist and novelist Rousseau believed that the idea of a world federation launched by the Abbé de Saint-Pierre was a laudable project (1756). He was nevertheless skeptical about its viability. Rousseau argued that the development of international harmony could never be prompted merely by the extension of commercial trade and contractual agreement. Such harmony could be achieved only by the proliferation of self-sufficient agrarian states based on the "General Will," ideas he explicated in the *Geneva Manuscript* (1756) and *On the Social Contract* (1762). To forge national unity, he advised in *The Government of Poland* (1772) that Poles reduce domestic economic inequalities by cultivating their lands cooperatively, celebrate their civic rights with patriotic fervor, and take pride in their history and national character. It is therefore not surprising that his political treatise became a major source of inspiration for the leaders of the French Revolution and the Romantic generation.

Influenced by Rousseau's *On the Social Contract*, the French priest and constitutional theorist Sieyès guided the French bourgeoisie in its struggle against the monarchy and nobility during the opening months of the French Revolution. Following the ensuing public controversy over the Estates General, he published his pamphlet *What Is the Third Estate?* (1789). Sieyès drew on Rousseau's principles of the General Will by entrusting the unprivileged Third Estate, that is, the overwhelming majority of the French people, with the right to draft a new constitution and with the inalienable right to self-determination. This principle became a major legacy of the French Revolution.

Like Sieyès, the German philosopher Kant celebrated the French Revolution, yet he also warned against its excesses. In *The Metaphysics of Morals* (1797), he developed his republican project, which aimed to reconcile national loyalty with international solidarity. The republican state was the political structure in which individuals could preserve their freedom by remaining their own lawgivers. Yet he stated that since individuals had relinquished their lawless freedom for their own good in entering the republican state, so now the state needed to surrender some of its "lawless freedom" for the sake of global welfare. Kant argued that the family of nations could be maintained so long as each state recognized an authority above itself. A world confederation of states, he maintained, would ultimately emerge as commerce and republicanism expanded.

This vision of international harmony was challenged by Herder, who argued that the natural rights of all were to be superseded by the rights of cultural nations. In *Reflections on the Philosophy of the History of Mankind* (1784–1797), Herder acknowledged that all of humankind shared the same basic attributes. Yet various nations have modified their characters according to time, place, and their own internal nature. By loving the culture of one's country, asserted Herder in a Rousseauan voice, one loves humankind. That conception contributed to the development of the Romantic Sturm und Drang movement.

II. LIBERALISM AND NATIONALISM

Herder's work adumbrated the liberal tension between internationalism and Romantic nationalism. Liberalism was developed during the French Revolution as a doctrine which promoted individual liberties, such as the right to private property, freedom of speech, political participation, and equality before the law. It also advocated international cooperation based on commerce and on the spread of republican institutions. The French Revolution raised hopes but did not implement globally, let alone domestically, the internationalist and republican aspirations of the Enlightenment.

The Napoleonic conquests and the subsequent Congress of Vienna (1815), which restored the old dynastic balance of power, subverted the progress of liberal internationalism and incubated the outburst of nationalist movements in 1848. Citizens' rights were gradually superseded by cultural rights, individual rights by national interest, and republican institutions by whatever institutions were suited to the historical temperament or need of its people.

In countries such as Germany and Italy—where peoples of the same nationality were politically divided or subject to foreign rule—liberal political thinkers promulgated nationalist programs aimed at attaining political unity. Elsewhere, in already independent and unified European nations such as Britain and France, liberals invoked nationalist sentiments whenever they perceived that the interest of their country was at stake. Despite variations in the lyrics of their national anthems, liberals still believed that the spread of a liberal type of nationalism would lead to global cooperation.

Bearing in mind the various historical contexts, these ideas were evident in the works of Johann Gottlieb Fichte (1762–1864), G. W. F. Hegel (1770–1831), Giuseppe Mazzini (1805–1872), John Stuart Mill (1806–1873), Lord Acton (1834–1902), Max Weber (1864–1920), and Theodore Herzl (1860–1904).

In *The Foundations of Natural Law* (1796), the German political theorist Fichte affirmed his adherence to the concept of universal citizenship championed by the French Revolution. Yet, in his *Addresses to the German Nation* (1808), one can observe Fichte's disillusionment with the Revolution's unfulfilled promises of political emancipation. The universal slogan "liberty, equality, and fraternity" was seen as a disguise for France's expansionist aims. The Germans, he argued, should reassert their cultural uniqueness against the hegemony of the Napoleonic empire.

For the German philosopher Hegel, a key question remained unanswered after the restoration of the old balance of power in 1815: How could a commitment be maintained to the most progressive values of the French Revolution when the conditions for their realization had vanished? In other words, how could the Napoleonic reforms be secured within a national order? In *The Philosophy of Right* (1821), Hegel attempted to resolve the liberal tension between republicanism and Romantic nationalism. While retaining an Enlightenment concept of citizenship by endorsing individuals' subscription to the rule of law, he insisted that the state embodied a particular will, which bound individuals together through their participation in a national spirit. The nature of such national spirits, and the ways in which they received recognition throughout history, became a major focus of the *Philosophy of World History* (1822–1831). In short, he attempted to place the Romantic call for cultural and national rights in the framework of the state of law, the *Rechtsstaat*.

In a similar spirit, Mazzini—a major contributor to Italian unification—maintained that national culture and civic duty were the driving forces behind national unity. "A nation," he said, "which had been enslaved for centuries, can regenerate itself through virtue and sacrifice." Acknowledging in his *Duties of Man* (1861) that fervent nationalism often proved to be destructive, Mazzini advocated a united Europe of free peoples, in which national singularities would be transcended in a Pan-European harmony.

Like his liberal nationalist precursors, the renowned British political theorist Mill fused the concept of republican citizenship with the idea of nationality. In *Considerations on Representative Government* (1861), he argued that the homogeneity of national identity, of a "united public opinion," allowed the establishment of free political regimes. The nation, rather than the multinational states, formed the fundamental political unit. Its existence was a necessary precondition for free government. The other prerequisite was economic and social development, and those lagging behind were legitimate objects of an "enlightened" colonialism for which the British provided a model.

Lord Acton, a renowned British liberal historian and philosopher, challenged Mill's position by suggesting that individual freedom was better maintained in a state composed of diverse nationalities and multiple centers of power. In his essay "Nationality" (1862), Acton explained that national diversity led to the decentralization of power and therefore to the preservation of freedom. Yet, somehow like Mill, he believed that the British Empire "includ[ed] various distinct nationalities without oppressing them." Acton's cosmopolitan liberalism overlooked the oppression undertaken by British imperialism. Acton's view was not firmly rooted in universal reason, but in religion. "I fully admit," he wrote, "that political rights proceed directly from religious duties and hold this to be the true basis of liberalism."

In his early writings, the German sociologist Max Weber rejected Acton's denunciation of power, implicitly agreeing with Mill's justification for great-power unity.[8] If Germany hoped to match the colonial expansion of Britain, Weber maintained, the Germans would have to reach a new level of political maturity. In his "Economic Policy and the National Interest in Imperial Germany" (1895), Weber argued that neither the existing liberal parties nor the German working class was in a position to assume political power. Only the nation as a whole, ruled by an elite, trained in power politics, could bring Germany to a new international stature. It was important for the Germans, he proclaimed, to pave the way toward "a great period" by unifying themselves into a great power.

While Weber's view of nationalism was aimed at developing a great German power, other political thinkers asserted the right to self-determination of smaller nations. A notable example was Theodor Herzl's call for a Jewish homeland, which inspired the nationalist movement known as Zionism. As a German newspaper correspondent in Paris, Herzl witnessed the Dreyfus affair[9] of the 1890s and its accompanying outburst of anti-Semitism. These events led him to write *A Jewish State* (1896). Herzl regarded Jewish assimilation into European society as desirable but, because of anti-Semitism, impossible. Jews must therefore form their own nation. In his pamphlet Herzl contemplated the possible establishment of a Jewish state in Argentina or Palestine. Herzl's Zionism was liberal—the socialist strain prevalent at the founding of Israel a half century later had its origin in the plight and pogroms of the impoverished Jews of Eastern Europe. Herzl, by contrast, depicted Jewish life as he had known it among the liberal and assimilated Central European Jews. In his call for a Jewish national homeland, he rejected all forms of narrow nationalism, unchecked by moral standards of rights.

III. Conservatism and Nationalism

Whereas liberals or liberal nationalists strive to justify political practices in terms of moral rights, conservative nationalists disparage such "abstract" notions of rights. Conservatives have long believed that religious duties were an important source of allegiance to the state. Religion, the family, and tradition, they argue, ensure and legitimize the continuity of national loyalty. They regard inequality as congruent with natural order. They prefer invoking experience, stability, and the balance of power as the basis of prudent policy. At times, however, conservatives endeavor to use nationalist aspirations ad hoc to strengthen the role of existing regimes or to legitimize the creation of new ones, but rarely to justify principles of natural or human rights.

The relationship between nationalist ideas and conservative ideology has varied historically and geographically. These two perspectives were combined against liberalism and the French Revolution of 1789 by such thinkers as Edmund Burke (1729–1797). From the mid-nineteenth century, however, conservatives such as Ernest Renan (1823–1892) and Leopold Ranke (1795–1886) began to use nationalist rhetoric to promote other objectives: fostering the expansionist aims of great powers or countering the emergence of new working-class movements. In the twentieth century, the same attachment to stability and order produced antinationalist arguments—as conservatives such as Elie Kedourie (1926–1992) rejected claims of colonialized peoples' right to nationhood. Finally, the recent disintegration of the communist bloc has led conservatives like Aleksandr Solzhenitsyn (1918–) to reassert national claims based on historical and cultural rights rather than on democratic aspirations.

This worldview was already evident in the work of counter-Enlightenment thinkers such as Burke. Criticizing the revolutionary ideas in his *Reflections on the Revolution in France* (1790), Burke argued for preserving the authority of old regimes, not only in Britain but across Europe. The eloquent British politician justified his position by attacking the legitimacy of revolutionary political change, whatever its justification. Burke asserted the value of founding and maintaining regimes on the basis of tradition, religion, and prejudice. To reject these criteria meant, he thought, abandoning the only foundation for stable societies. He thus praised those nations which respected historical continuity and hierarchical authority. This should not suggest that Burke believed, like the liberals, that nations should possess equal rights to self-determination and action in the international community. Instead, inequality between nations should be supervised by the major Christian powers of Europe.

In his essay "What Is a Nation?" (1882), the French theologian Ernest Renan's definition of a nation challenged Burke's. It is not the qualifications of religion, state, civilization, or economic interest that constitute a nation, Renan argued, but "a common heroic past, great leaders and true glory." However it is constituted, "A nation is a soul, a spiritual principle." A nation is legitimized, wrote Renan, by great solidarities based on the consciousness of past sacrifice and the willingness to make future ones. A nation, he remarked, is a sort of plebiscite repeated daily. It is the existence of the nation alone which guarantees what liberties individuals would possess. Although Renan understood the shortcomings of such a "spiritual principle," he regarded the triumph of the nation as the "law of the age."

If it was not a "law," the question of nationhood was definitely a preoccupation of the age. In Germany, for instance, many thinkers like Ranke were hoping for a stronger role for German power in world affairs. In his essay "The Great Powers" (1833), the German historian Leopold Ranke sought to explain the success of dominant European states in different times. Only by developing a "sense of nationality," he maintained, could states truly become great powers on the world scene. Contrary to radical views of his time, he argued that the peaceful evolution of culture was definitively protected against the danger of revolution and that conflict between popular sovereignty and the monarchy had been settled once and for all in favor of the latter. Ranke's prescription reflected Prussia's ascendancy in the context of German disunity.

The aversion to abrupt change was echoed by Elie Kedourie in the twentieth century. In his classic study *Nationalism* (1960), written at the time of independence for many European colonies, particularly in Africa, Kedourie identified the nationalist aspirations of colonized peoples as subversive and destructive. Nationalist appeals for violent struggle undercut the spirit of compromise essential to political liberty. Moreover, self-determination for nations provided a way to rationalize despotism in terms of the "will of the individual." Finally, given the inevitable mixture of different national groups on the same territory, treating all citizens as members of a nation was invariably a disguise for the "tyranny of one group over another." Citing a variety of cases from the European experience to illustrate these claims, Kedourie argued that anticolonial nationalism could be even more dangerous—given the tradition of despotic rule in Africa and Asia that had preceded the "brief dominion" of the colonizers.

While Kedourie regarded nationalism as a source of tyranny and violence, other conservatives, such as Russian novelist and former dissident Alexsandr Solzhenitsyn, have regarded it as essential to the spiritual cohesion of society. In *Rebuilding Russia* (1990), he offers a nationalist alternative to both a rejected socialism and the unbridled greed associated with free market liberalism. In a challenge to the virulent political nationalism recently associated with Vladimir Zhirinovsky, Solzhenitsyn charges that the awakening of Russian "national self-awareness" has been ensnared in "imperial delusions." Instead, the revival of Russia as a cultural and spiritual entity required abandoning empire in favor of retreat to a "national core." The path toward consolidating a renewed Russia, Solzhenitsyn maintained, would depend on neither democratic political structures nor economic progress, but on an "inner development" of the Russian spirit, built on the home and family, religious values, and community life. These views, of course, stand in stark contrast to the understanding of nationalism espoused during seven decades of socialism in Russia and elsewhere.

IV. SOCIALISM, NATIONALISM, AND INTERNATIONALISM

By the mid-nineteenth century socialist thinkers had already elaborated an ideological platform designed to counter the rise of nationalist policies articulated by conservatives, liberals, and others. Socialist internationalism found a major impetus with the publication of the *Manifesto of the Communist Party* (1848). In this highly influential political pamphlet, the German political thinkers Karl Marx (1818–1883) and Friedrich Engels (1820–1895) contended that socialism was a call for political *and* economic equality for all members of the state, and for an international order based on class solidarity. "Working men have no country," they wrote, "national differences . . . are daily more and more vanishing."

These views were informed by the globalization of the market under capitalism, which was gradually lending a "cosmopolitan character to production and consumption in every country." The struggle to control markets, however, created conflicts among the capitalist powers, which intensified rather than diminished conflicts between nationalities. Moreover, Europe's weakening empires provided opportunities for national minorities to assert claims to self-determination. As nationalism threatened Austria with disintegration, and threatened to draw Germany and Russia into war, socialists in those countries confronted the theoretical and political task of reconsidering the relationship between socialism and nationalism. Otto Bauer (1881–1938) attempted to work out some form of socialist accommodation with the increasing pressure of nationalism; Joseph Stalin (1879–1953) and Rosa Luxemburg (1870–1919) rejected, on different grounds, nationalist forces; and Vladimir Ilyich Lenin (1870–1924) attempted to use these forces as a tactical tool to advance socialism.

In his *Nationalities Question and Social Democracy* (1907), Bauer was aware that workers' allegiance to the state could supersede class solidarity. The leader of the Austrian Social Democratic Party thus attempted to incorporate workers' cultural and national allegiance within a socialist framework. His view also called for preserving national cultures within a multinational state (such as Austria before World War II). Bauer defined the nation as "the totality of men bound together through a common destiny into a community of character." Those autonomous "communities of character" were ultimately compatible with the building of a socialist nation.

Bauer's case for reconciling socialism with national autonomy was vehemently rejected by Joseph Stalin in his influential pamphlet *Marxism and the National-Colonial Question* (1914). Stalin argued that history was bearing out Marx's prediction that national differences would vanish under capitalism. In the meantime, national rights should only be granted if a people shared a common character, language, territory, economic life, and psychic formation. It is only when all these characteristics are present that one nationality can claim autonomy. Bauer's case for national autonomy, Stalin maintained, amounted to a pernicious effort to spread mistrust and disinterest among workers of different nationalities, to destroy the unity of the world's working class.

As early as 1909 Rosa Luxemburg, the exiled Polish socialist leader in Germany, had already maintained in *The National Question and Autonomy* that socialist concessions to nationalist claims were usually pointless and counterproductive. Yet, unlike Stalin, she favored claims to self-determination by oppressed people, so long as their economies could survive independence. Embroiled in polemics against Polish nationalists, Luxemburg therefore argued that secession from Russia was unacceptable: It would undermine the interests of the Polish proletariat. Such claims were utopian for industrially backward countries, such as Poland and Czechoslovakia, whose economies and industrial growth depended on the market of the mother country (Russia). Luxemburg also warned that any alliance of the working class with the nationalist bourgeoisie of oppressed countries would subvert the future establishment of democratic and socialist regimes.

In *The Right of Nations to Self-Determination* (1914), the revolutionary Bolshevik Lenin embraced some of Luxemburg's views yet diverged from others. With Luxemburg, he argued against Stalin that nationalism from "above" was different from nationalism from "below," distinguishing the oppressive nationalism of tsarist Russia from the justifiable nationalism of oppressed Poland. Yet, unlike Luxemburg, he maintained that the right to national self-determination should not be determined only by economic factors.

Lenin further argued, against Luxemburg, that workers among the oppressed nationalities in their pursuit of secession should consider tactical alliances with elements of the bourgeoisie. These debates, however, were soon eclipsed by the rise of fascism.

V. Integral Nationalism, Fascism, and Nazism

Fascism, an extreme form of nationalism, can be traced to the late nineteenth century in Europe. The war between Germany and France in 1870–1871, and its aftermath in the Dreyfus affair, paved the way for intensifying nationalist fervor. Many army officers and church officials in France saw the dispute over Dreyfus as an opportunity to overthrow the republican government. They regarded the social activities of Freemasons, Protestants, and Jews as anti-French. These reactionary forces espoused a more aggressive version of nationalism which has come to be known as "integral" nationalism.[10] This form of ultra-nationalism repudiated republican and liberal institutions, called for individual sacrifice to the corporative state, and invoked relentless warfare and the superiority of one national culture at the expense of others.

Integral nationalism incorporated French exponents of predatorial nationalism and racism, such as Charles Maurras (1868–1952). It reached its zenith in the two decades following World War I, as the spread of unemployment and inflation in Europe allowed fascist and Nazi variants to become the dominant force in Europe under the leadership of Benito Mussolini (1885–1945) and Adolf Hitler (1889–1945). Despite their differences, all these thinkers emphasized with equal intensity the superiority and uniqueness of their own particular nations at the expense of the rights of other nationalities or groups.

Charles Maurras, an influential French political activist and journalist, described "The Future of French Nationalism" (1950) in royalist terms. In 1909 he founded *Action Française*, a review which became the daily newspaper of the Royalist Party. There, he advocated integral nationalism, emphasizing the supremacy of France and its interests over those of other nations. Contrary to conservative nationalists, who believed in a relatively stable balance of power, Maurras deplored cooperation between nations and repeatedly invoked the grandeur and heroism of France, where, he maintained, individual sacrifice and nationalist fervor should become an end in itself.

In *Fascism* (1932), Benito Mussolini's rejection of liberal democracy fused the radical conservatism of Maurras with the antirepublican socialism of the French syndico-anarchist Georges Sorel. From socialist theory Mussolini took the concept of permanent struggle; from "radical conservatism" he appropriated the importance of individual sacrifice for the sake of the national spirit. Fascism, argued the Italian leader, was an education for combat. Yet instead of maintaining in a socialist mode that history is an incessant struggle toward universal emancipation, Mussolini defined national (versus class) struggle as an ethical end in its own terms. Fascism, he proclaimed, glorified the nation as the source of all ethics. War alone could bring the nation to new heights and new glories.

Like his contemporary Mussolini, Adolf Hitler, the leader of the German National Socialist Party, saw the creation of a strong state as the basis for a revitalized nation. Yet Hitler and other Nazi theorists added a racial component to Mussolini's conception of the state. Hitler claimed that the Aryan race was the only source of human creativity, greatness, and progress. In *Mein Kampf* (1925–1927), he saw, in a future German empire, the highest expression of Aryanism and wrote that Germany's triumph required the purification of German "blood" from contamination by inferior races. This view led to the merciless genocide of Jews during World War II.

VI. ANTICOLONIALISM AND NATIONAL LIBERATION MOVEMENTS

Nazism may have fanned the flames of Third-World nationalism, at least in the Middle East. Yet this process had long been under way. The dissemination of nationalist ideas began during the late nineteenth century with the education of Arabs, Chinese, and Indians in European universities, and reached a new intensity with the consolidation of liberation movements in the twentieth century. There was an affinity between many of the ideas of the leading anticolonial thinkers and those of nineteenth-century European nationalists such as Fichte and Mazzini. Like their European precursors who fought against imperial dynasties or foreign invasion, proponents of nation-building or national unity were concerned with reviving an indigenous culture shaped by foreign presence or influence. These advocates included Sun Yat-sen (1866–1925), Jawaharlal Nehru (1889–1964), Sati al-Husri (1880–1968), the Ayatollah Khomeini (1902?–1989), Léopold Sédar Senghor (1906–), and Frantz Fanon (1925–1961).

Sun Yat-sen, the first president of the Chinese Republic, indicated in "Three Principles of the People" (1929) how the struggle against colonialism required the development of a nation premised on egalitarian principles. In this work Sun relied on China's ability to match European achievements. In the same vein as liberal German and Italian nationalists of the late nineteenth century, he believed that nationalism would become the driving force for Chinese modernization. Sun's belief in the reawakening of Chinese nationalism was blended with socialist principles: the regulation of private capital and the equalization of land rights.

Later, India would be faced with issues similar to those confronted by China in the process of its own nation-building. One of the leaders of India's rising independence movement (second only to Mahatma Gandhi) was Jawaharlal Nehru—later to become India's first prime minister. Nehru published one of his major works, *The Discovery of India*, in 1946, shortly before independence was achieved. Though inclined toward socialism, Nehru's views had not set into a definite mold. His major objective was to carry India into the modern age of scientific discovery and socioeconomic progress. He claimed that this "modern idea of nationhood," effectively realized in Britain and France, could be achieved in India. Nehru, however, fell short of preserving the overall unity of India in its struggle for independence: The growing Muslim separatist movement led to the creation of Pakistan.

The problem of unity was also an important concern of the nationalist movement in the Arab countries. In the early twentieth century the Ottoman Empire's control over the Arab countries was gradually supplanted by fragmented European spheres of domination. In "Muslim Unity and Arab Unity" (1944), the Arab nationalist thinker Sati' al-Husri saw the unification of the Arab world as a necessary means of resisting foreign domination. Inspired by Fichte and other German Romantic thinkers, al-Husri approached the unity of the Arab world on a cultural and Romantic plane.[11] The whole Arab world, he hoped, would be combined into one nationally conscious and politically assertive community, united by a common geography, language, history, and tradition.

Whereas al-Husri emphasized political unity among Arab-speaking countries in secular terms, the Ayatollah Khomeini stressed the spiritual and religious unity of the Islamic world. The Iranian Islamic leader was instrumental in the revival of Pan-Islamic militancy. Exiled in Paris, Khomeini called for resistance to the Shah, who had spurned "true" Islamic faith to embrace corrupt Western values. He returned to Iran during the 1979 revolution to lead the new Islamic "awakening." His book *Islamic Government* (1979) was a blueprint for institutionalizing Islam politically and economically by establishing a theocratic government. Iran, in Khomeini's view, was the springboard for Islamic expansion. Iran's inability to defeat Iraq and the rivalry between Sunnite and Shiite factions have now weakened the original Islamic impetus of the late Khomeini.

The radical concept of national liberation—as a combination of nationalist and socialist ideas—has been most apparent among African political thinkers. For instance, Léopold Sédar Senghor, the Senegalese poet and former president of that country, advocated both the cultural concept of "negritude" and the idea of "African socialism." In his work *On African Socialism* (1961), Senghor called for a struggle against colonialism and for cultural, political, and economic independence. A new African socialism, he believed, should be based on African realities, free of both atheism and excessive materialism.

Frantz Fanon, the West Indian psychoanalyst and social philosopher, shared to some extent Senghor's political views. Like Senghor, he also wrote about the necessity of creating or re-creating a national cultural consciousness as a means of achieving true independence. Yet, the development of a genuine national consciousness was difficult to achieve, as Fanon realized in the *Wretched of the Earth* (1963). For the forces of domination are internalized by the indigenous elites who perpetuate—even after decolonization—the unequal social and economic structures inherited from colonialism. The lessons of the Algerian war (1954–1962) taught Fanon the importance of violent struggle as a mean to empower colonized people. Violence, he believed, was "a cleansing force" that "frees the native from his inferiority complex and from his despair and inaction." Although acknowledging that independence would create new problems, Fanon nonetheless concentrated mainly on the actual battle for nationhood as a means of achieving true independence.

VII. AMERICAN PERSPECTIVES ON NATIONALISM

The first successful anticolonial revolt led to American national independence. The debates on nationality and nationalism continued to be shaped by internal struggle: the Civil War, the massive immigration influx of the early twentieth century, and the civil rights movement of the 1960s. The liberal president Abraham Lincoln (1809–1865), the pacifist and socialist writer Randolph Bourne (1886–1918), and the Pan-Africanist activist Marcus Garvey (1887–1940) each represent a different ideological position relating to national identity. The question of nationalism was also transformed by America's assumption of a global role in the twentieth century. This situation prompted intellectuals such as the liberal president Woodrow Wilson (1856–1924) and the conservative Reinhold Niebuhr (1892–1971) to reassess the role of the United States and the meaning of nationalism in the international context.

In the isolationist period of the middle nineteenth century, however, the United States was first drawn into violent conflict over whether national identity belonged to the union or to its separate states. In his 1861 inaugural address, just prior to the American Civil War, President Lincoln repudiated the southern states' proclaimed right to secession on several grounds. Legally, the United States had been formed as a contract by all the states, and as such it would require all parties to rescind it. Secession was unnecessary, since the Constitution of the United States allowed states to maintain slavery and to control their own domestic institutions. Secession would lead to anarchy; and finally, secession violated the genuine unifying spirit of the American nation: "The mystic chords of memory, stretching from every battlefield and patriot grave to every living heart and hearthstone all over this broad land, will yet swell the chorus of the Union."

In the early twentieth century, the social fabric of the American society was once again rent asunder by the massive wave of immigration. The American essayist Randolph Bourne maintained that the immigrants' claim to nationality should coincide with egalitarian principles, on both the international and the domestic levels. He thus denounced the explosion of nationalism in Europe in the wake of World War I as well as American liberal support for the war. Referring to the American domestic issue of nationality,

Bourne commented in "Trans-National America" (1916) that America's self-conception as a "melting pot" was in fact a myth. "The truth is," he wrote, "that no more tenacious cultural allegiance to the mother country has been shown by any alien nation than by the ruling class of Anglo-Saxons in these American states." In the same spirit as Bauer's internationalism regarding Austria, Bourne argued that immigration created new possibilities, such as the development of a "federation of culture" along egalitarian principles.

Yet the viability of such a federation was implicitly challenged by the speeches and writings of Marcus Garvey, who called for the revival of a distinct African culture identity. In *The Resurrection of the Negro*, Garvey advocated the separation of races and the "blending of all Negroes into one strong, healthy race." Later, in his New York speeches of 1921–1922, he disputed the illusion of freedom entertained after the Civil War. For "up to now," he maintained, "we are still industrial slaves, we are social slaves, we are political slaves and the new Negro desires a freedom that has no boundary, no limit." Just as French and Russian despots were overthrown by their own people, Africans could achieve freedom for Africa. Like those who worked to overturn French and Russian despotism, Africans can work for the freedom of Africa. The racial separatism he promoted as an important aspect of the resurgence of Africa was later echoed by anticolonialist African political thinkers.

While Garvey and Bourne focused their attention on the domestic question of nationality, Woodrow Wilson saw a new global role for the United States to temper the threat of conflicting nationalism, which had led to World War I. In his "Fourteen Points" address to Congress (1918), the liberal president proclaimed the right of ethnic groups to claim national self-determination. This type of liberal nationalism would be mitigated by an Actonian-type or, rather, a Mazzinian-type League of Nations, which would preserve cultural diversity. Even had he not been thwarted by domestic opposition, Wilson's League of Nations would not have been successful in controlling the reemergence of nationalism during World War II. The aspirations, on the basis of their perceived nationality, of a variety of "stateless" peoples around the globe remain a source of international instability, despite the "supervision" of the United Nations.

In his book *Moral Man and Immoral Society* (1932), the influential American theologian Niebuhr argued against Wilson's idealism. Modern nations, he maintained, were indicative of a selfishness that could not be reversed merely by the espousal of sentiments of equality within the community of nations. He proposed a "realist" and conservative view of international relations based on power politics as well as on theological premises. International harmony could be achieved, wrote Niebuhr later in his life, by a concerted Western coalition of power to counterbalance the "evil" forces of communism. Like Burke's condemnation of the French Revolution, Niebuhr, moving to a conservative position, would denounce the radical agenda of communism and praise the United

States for its engagement in a noble crusade. Patriotic fervor, he believed, should be used to galvanize national support to combat the "evil" Soviet empire.

VIII. THE CONTEMPORARY DEBATE ON NATIONALISM

With the dismantlement of the Soviet bloc and the partial withdrawal of American power from the international scene, a new wave of nationalism has engulfed the former communist world, has spilled into Western Europe, and is intensifying in the Third World. The resurgence of nationalism has kindled growing scholarly interest in this topic and in its solution. The recent debates on nationalism reflect the legacy of ideologies inherited from the pre-1989 period. Among other scholars, Michael Walzer, Jürgen Habermas, Jeremy Brecher, and Eric Hobsbawm have sought to find a solution to the international instability created by the explosion of nationalism after the Cold War.

In "The New Tribalism" (1992), the American political thinker Michael Walzer surveys the resurgent tribal identities, whether in the form of states or groups. While he supports self-determination, he concedes that unlimited rights based on national indentity can produce a "slippery slope" toward repression of minorities in newly formed states. Yet these dangers may be averted by a combination of federal governing arrangements and international pressure. Without judging the cultural claims of various groups against any universal principles, Walzer maintains, in the nineteenth-century liberal nationalist tradition, that an international atmosphere based on mutual tolerance could temper predatorial tribalism. Common humanity, he argues, will never mean the abandonment of distinct national identities. Thus, acceptance of particularism is an essential prerequisite for successful intertribal negotiations.

The German philosopher Jürgen Habermas reaches quite different conclusions in a 1992 article discussing the advent of the European Community. Unlike Walzer, Habermas legitimizes the political rather than the cultural or ethnic aspect of such claims. Habermas distinguishes between national identity formed by common ethnic and cultural properties, and a nation of citizens based on subscription to civil and constitutional rights. The latter provides the best hope of reconciling the differences between diverse cultural groups and should be instituted through an ongoing procedure of public and democratic communication. The European Community might well become the forum for an effective communicative "proceduralism." Habermas thus reaffirms the universalist definition of citizenship adopted by Kant and liberal thinkers of the eighteenth century, arguing for a "constitutional patriotism" that does not discriminate on the basis of particular identities.

Rather than relying on a communicative proceduralist conception of community, as does Habermas, the U.S. historian Brecher argues, in "'The National Question' Reconsidered" (1989), that the development of international law and ecological consciousness could exert a new, combined pressure on nationalist and predatory governments. The strengthening of trans-national nongovernmental organizations and a principled adherence to already existing tenets of international law provide a platform to address the problems of environmental degradation and economic underdevelopment that nations cannot solve. Although Brecher challenges the feasibility of a world state, he expresses hope that trans-national organizations will both exert pressure on undisciplined nations and operate in a spirit of cultural tolerance.

In his book *Nations and Nationalism since 1780*, Eric Hobsbawm, unlike Brecher, Habermas, or Walzer, does not offer a solution to the current problem of nationalism. In the spirit of Marx, he foresees the decline of nationalism coinciding with the weakening of the nation-state. Nationalist claims in nineteenth-century Europe and in the twentieth-century colonized world were associated with nation-building, serving as a major vehicle for modernization. Late-twentieth-century nationalism, by contrast, is expressed by ethnic groups' claim for secession and rejection of modernization. Hobsbawm maintains that the recent xenophobic, reactionary, and fundamentalist manifestations of ethnic groups are an "imaginary" form of pre–World War II nationalism, which will diminish as the states are weakened by the progressive globalization of the world economy.

These contemporary social thinkers have each offered important, yet partial approaches to counter the progress and recurrence of nationalist excesses. An alternative to nationalism should be tolerant of cultural diversity, as Michael Walzer proposes; be invigorated by rational discourse in the public realm, as Habermas argues; be constrained by international organizations, as Brecher suggests; and be understood in terms of the world global economy, as Hobsbawm claims.

Yet none of these scholars provides a comprehensive answer to the problem of nationalism. Walzer may be seen as offering a double standard of moral rights, one relative to the national culture and the other based on a liberal view of international cooperation. Habermas does not really show how his model of democratic public discourse can constrain the spread of nationalist expression in a Europe fragmented by different political and economic agendas. Brecher fails to show how international organization could acquire sufficient authoritative power to deter nationalist aggression by states; and finally, Hobsbawm seems to have left the fate of nationalism to the caprices of the market.

Their views, however, constitute an important step toward the development of a new comprehensive alternative. In the absence of such an approach, nationalist aggressions will continue to violate not only the human rights of Muslim Bosnians, Armenians, Azeris, and Kurds, but also the fundamental right to peace, based on democracy, of all humankind. In other words, democratic institutions, even if built on citizens' rights, cannot be sustained in a world plagued by nationalist agendas. A fundamental question remains thus to be answered: How can a viable human rights option be developed which could disseminate basic rights—political and economic equality both domestically and globally—and at the same time preserve cultural diversity within the limits of these rights? This answer should not be left to the "invisible hand" of the market, the strength of the sword, or the whims of history, but addressed by creative scholars and students interested in ending the bloodshed resulting from ethnic and nationalist conflicts.

MICHELINE R. ISHAY

NOTES

1. See George Bush's speech presented to Congress on 6 September 1990, cited in Richard Rose, *The Postmodern President: George Bush Meets the World*, 2d ed. (Chatham, N.J.: Chatham House, 1991), 336; also Mark Whitaker, "A Wrinkle in the New World Order," *Newsweek*, 4 Mar. 1991, 51; or "On the New World Order Changeth," *The Economist*, 22–28 June 1992, 13–14.

2. For the debate concerning the possible antiquity of nations, see John Armstrong, *Nations before Nationalism* (Chapel Hill: University of North Carolina Press, 1982), and Anthony Smith, *The Ethnic Origins of Nations* (Oxford: Basil Blackwell, 1986), arguing for the antiquity of nations; and Ernest Gellner, *Nations and Nationalism* (Oxford: Basil Blackwell, 1983), and Benedict Anderson, *Imagined Communities: Reflections on the Origin and Spread of Nationalism* (London: Verso, 1983), arguing against. In John Breuilly's book *Nationalism and the State* (Chicago: University of Chicago Press, 1985), emphasis is placed on the modernity and the explicitly political character of nationalist movements.

3. Carlton Hayes, *Essays on Nationalism* (New York: Macmillan, 1933), 6.

4. Hans Kohn, *The Idea of Nationalism* (Toronto, Canada: Collier-Macmillan Company, 1969); Ernest Gellner, *Nations and Nationalism* (Ithaca, N.Y.: Cornell University Press, 1983); Eric Hobsbawm, *Nations and Nationalism* (Cambridge and New York: Cambridge University Press, 1990); and Liah Greenfeld, *Nationalism: Five Roads to Modernity* (Cambridge and New York: Cambridge University Press, 1992).

5. To be more precise: Anderson associates nationalism with such emotional attachments as kinship and religion, whereas Hayes identifies nationalism as an emotion aroused by the nation-state. See Benedict Anderson, *Imagined Communities: Reflections on the Origin and Spread of Nationalism*, rev. ed. (London: Verso, 1991), 5; Hayes, *Essays on Nationalism*, 6. See also Elie Kedourie, *Nationalism*, 3d ed. (London: Hutchinson, 1966), 9.

6. For a study on the dynamic between liberalism and nationalism, see Micheline Ishay, *Internationalism and Its Betrayal* (Minneapolis: University of Minnesota Press, 1995).

7. See also Ishay, *Internationalism and Its Betrayal*.

8. In his later writings, Weber would subscribe to a more liberal position regarding the state and world affairs.

9. In 1894 Alfred Dreyfus, a Jewish French army officer, was unjustly accused of treason. The trial began a twelve-year controversy known as the Dreyfus affair, during which anti-Semitic riots spread throughout France. This event had a significant impact on the political and social history of the French Third Republic.

10. The term was first used by Charles Maurras; see Peter Alter, *Nationalism*, trans.

Stuart McKinnon-Evans (London: Edward Arnold, 1989), 37–38, on the history of the term, as well as the selection from Maurras in this volume.

11. See William L. Cleveland, *The Making of Arab Nationalism, Ottomanism, and Arabism in the Thought of Sati' al-Husri* (Princeton, N.J.: Princeton University Press, 1971), 86–88.

PART I

The Enlightenment Background of Internationalism and Nationalism

1

JEAN-JACQUES ROUSSEAU

The Geneva Manuscript

BOOK I, CHAPTER III: ON THE FUNDAMENTAL COMPACT

Man was/is born free, and nevertheless everywhere he is in chains. One who believes himself the master of others is nonetheless a greater slave than they. How did this change occur? No one knows. What can make it legitimate? It is not impossible to say. If I were to consider only force, as others do, I would say that as long as a people is constrained to obey and does so, it does well; as soon as it can shake off the yoke and does so, it does even better. For in recovering its freedom by means of the same right used to steal it, either a people is well justified in taking it back, or those who took it away were not justified in doing so. But the social order is a sacred right that serves as a basis for all the others. However, this right does not have its source in nature; it is therefore based on a convention. The problem is to know what this convention is and how it could have been formed.

As soon as man's needs exceed his faculties and the objects of his desire expand and multiply, he must either remain eternally unhappy or seek a new form of being from which he can draw the resources he no longer finds in himself. As soon as obstacles to our self-preservation prevail, by their resistance, over the force each individual can use to conquer them, the primitive state can no longer subsist and the human race would perish if art did not come to nature's rescue. Since man cannot engender new forces but merely unite and direct existing ones, he has no other means of self-preservation except to form, by aggregation, a sum of forces that can prevail over the resistance; set them to work by a single motivation; make them act conjointly; and direct them toward a single object. This is the fundamental problem which is solved by the institution of the State.

If, then, these conditions are combined and everything that is not of the essence of the social compact is set aside, one will find that it can be reduced to the following terms: "Each of us puts his will, his goods, his force, and his person in common, under the direction of the general will, and in a body we all receive each member as an inalienable part of the whole."

Instantly, in place of the private person of each contracting party, this act of association produces a moral and collective body, composed of as many members as there are voices in the assembly, and to which the common self gives formal unity, life, and will. This public person, formed thus by the union of all the others, generally assumes the name body politic, which its members call *State* when it is passive, *Sovereign* when active, *Power* when comparing it to similar bodies. As for the members themselves, they take the name *People* collectively, and individually are called *Citizens* as members of the City or participants in the sovereign authority, and *Subjects* as subject to the laws of the State. But these terms, rarely used with complete precision, are often mistaken for one another, and it is enough to know how to distinguish them when the meaning of discourse so requires.

This formula shows that the primitive act of confederation includes a reciprocal engagement between the public and private individuals, and that each individual, contracting with himself so to speak, finds that he is doubly engaged, namely toward private individuals as a member of the sovereign and toward the sovereign as a member of the State. But it must be noted that the maxim of civil right that no one can be held responsible for engagements toward himself cannot be applied here, because there is a great difference between being obligated to oneself, or to a whole of which one is a part. It must further be noted that the public deliberation that can obligate all of the subjects to the sovereign—due to the two different relationships in which each of them is considered—cannot for the opposite reason obligate the sovereign toward itself, and that consequently it is contrary to the nature of the body politic for the sovereign to impose on itself a law that it cannot break. Since the sovereign can only be considered in a single relationship, it is then in the situation of a private individual contracting with himself. It is apparent from this that there is not, nor can there be, any kind of fundamental law that is obligatory for the body of people. This does not mean that this body cannot perfectly well enter an engagement toward another, at least insofar as this is not contrary to its nature, because with reference to the foreigner, it becomes a simple being or individual.

As soon as this multitude is thus united in a body, one could not harm any of its members without attacking the body in some part of its existence, and it is even less possible to harm the body without the members feeling the effects. For in addition to the common life in question, all risk also that part of themselves which is not currently at the disposition of the sovereign and which they enjoy in safety only under public protection. Thus duty and interest equally obligate the two contracting parties to be of mutual assistance, and the same persons should seek to combine in this double relationship all the advantages that are dependent on it. But there are some distinctions to be made insofar as the sovereign, formed solely by the private individuals composing it, never has any interest contrary to theirs, and as a consequence the sovereign power could never need a guarantee toward the private individuals, because it is impossible for the body ever to want to harm its members. The same is not true of the private individuals with reference to the sovereign, for despite the common interest, nothing would answer for their engagements to the sovereign if it did not find ways to be assured of their fidelity. Indeed, each individual can, as a man, have a private will contrary to or differing from the general will he has as a citizen. His absolute and independent existence can bring him to view what he owes the common cause as a free contribution, the loss of which will harm others less than its payment burdens him; and considering the moral person of the State as an imaginary being because it is not a man, he might wish to enjoy the rights of the citizen without wanting to fulfill the duties of a subject, an injustice whose spread would soon cause the ruin of the body politic.

In order for the social contract not to be an ineffectual formula, therefore, the sovereign must have some guarantees, independent of the consent of the private individuals, of their engagements toward the common cause. The oath is ordinarily the first of such guarantees, but since it comes from a totally different order of things and since each man, according to his inner maxims, modifies to his liking the obligation it imposes on him, it is rarely relied on in political institutions; and it is with reason that more real assurances, derived from the thing itself, are preferred. So the fundamental compact tacitly includes this engagement, which alone can give force to all the others: that whoever refuses to obey the general will shall be constrained to do so by the entire body. But it is important here to remember carefully that the particular, distinctive character of this compact is that the body of people contracts only with itself; that is, the people in a body, as sovereign, with the private individuals composing it, as subjects—a condition that creates all the ingenuity and functioning of the political machine, and alone renders legitimate, reasonable, and without danger engagements that without it would be absurd, tyrannical, and subject to the most enormous abuse.

This passage from the state of nature to the social state produces a remarkable change in man, by substituting justice for instinct in his behavior and giving his actions moral relationships which they did not have before. Only then, when the voice of duty replaces physical impulse, and right replaces appetite, does man, who until that time only considered himself, find that he is forced to act upon other principles and to consult his reason before heeding his inclinations. But although in this state he deprives himself of several advantages given him by nature, he gains such great ones, his faculties are exercised and developed, his ideas broadened, his feelings ennobled, and his whole soul elevated to such a point that if the abuses of this new condition did not often degrade him even beneath the condition he left, he ought ceaselessly to bless the happy moment that tore him away from it forever, and that changed him from a stupid, limited animal into an intelligent being and a man.

Let us reduce the pros and cons to easily compared terms. What man loses by the social contract is his natural freedom and an unlimited right to everything he needs; what he gains is civil freedom and the proprietorship of everything he possesses. In order not to be mistaken in these estimates, one must distinguish carefully between natural freedom, which is limited only by the force of the individual, and civil freedom, which is limited by the general will; and between possession, which is only the effect of force or the right of the first occupant, and property, which can only be based on a legal title.

✧ ✧ ✧

CHAPTER IV: ON SLAVERY

Since no man has any natural authority over his fellow man, and since force produces no right, there remain only conventions as the basis of all legitimate authority among men.

If a private individual, says Grotius, can alienate his freedom and enslave himself to a master, why can't a whole people alienate its freedom and subject itself to a king? There are many equivocal words in this that need explaining, but let us limit ourselves to the word *alienate*. To alienate is to give or to sell. Now a man who makes himself another's slave does not give himself, he sells himself, at the least for his subsistence. But why does a people sell itself? Far from furnishing the subsistence of his subjects, a king derives his own only from them, and according to Rabelais a king does not live cheaply. Do the subjects give their persons, then, on condition that their goods will be taken too? I do not see what remains for them to preserve.

It will be said that the despot guarantees civil tranquillity to his subjects. Perhaps so, but what have they gained if the wars that his ambition brings on them, if his insatiable greed, if the harassment of his ministers are a greater torment than their dissensions would be? What have they gained, if this tranquillity is one of their miseries? Life is tranquil in jail cells, too. Is that reason enough to like them? The Greeks lived tranquilly shut up in the Cyclop's cave as they awaited their turn to be devoured.

To say that a man gives himself gratuitously is to say something absurd and inconceivable. Such an act is illegitimate and null, if only because he who does so is not in his right mind. To say the same thing about an entire people is to suppose a people of madmen. Madness does not make right.

Even if everyone could alienate himself, he could not alienate his children. They are born men and free. Their freedom belongs to them; no one but themselves has a right to dispose of it. Before they have reached the age of reason, their father can, in their name, stipulate conditions for their preservation, for their well-being; but he cannot give them irrevocably and unconditionally, because such a gift is contrary to the ends of nature and exceeds the rights of paternity. For an arbitrary government to be legitimate, it would therefore be necessary for the people in each generation to be master of its acceptance or rejection. But then this government would no longer be arbitrary.

To renounce one's freedom is to renounce one's status as a man, the rights of humanity and even its duties. There is no possible compensation for anyone who renounces everything. Such a renunciation is incompatible with the nature of man, and taking away all his freedom of will is taking away all morality from his actions. Finally, it is a vain and contradictory convention to stipulate absolute authority on one side and on the other unlimited obedience. Isn't it clear that one is in no way engaged toward a person from whom one has the right to demand everything, and doesn't this condition alone—without equivalent and without exchange—entail the nullification of the act? For what right would my slave have against me, since all he has belongs to me, and his right being mine, my right against myself is a meaningless word?

❖   ❖   ❖

Judgment on Saint-Pierre's Project for Perpetual Peace

The scheme of a lasting peace was of all others the most worthy to fascinate a man of high principle. Of all those which engaged the Abbé de Saint-Pierre, it was therefore that over which he brooded the longest and followed up with the greatest obstinacy. It is indeed hard to give any other name to the missionary zeal which never failed him in this enterprise: and that, in spite of the manifest impossibility of success, the ridicule which he brought upon himself day by day and the rebuffs which he had continually to endure. It would seem that his well-balanced spirit, intent solely on the public good, led him to measure his devotion to a cause purely by its utility, never letting himself be daunted by difficulties, never thinking of his own personal interest.

If ever moral truth were demonstrated, I should say it is the utility, national no less than international, of this project. The advantages which its realization would bring to each Prince, to each Nation, to the whole of Europe, are immense, manifest, incontestable; and nothing could be more solid or more precise than the arguments which the author employs to prove them. Realize his Commonwealth of Europe for a single day, and you may be sure it will last forever; so fully would experience convince men that their own gain is to be found in the good of all. For all that, the very Princes who would defend it with all their might, if it once existed, would resist with all their might any proposal for its creation; they will as infallibly throw obstacles in the way of its establishment as they would in the way of its abolition. Accordingly Saint-Pierre's book on *A Lasting Peace* seems to be ineffectual for founding it and unnecessary for maintaining it. "It is then an empty dream," will be the verdict of the impatient reader. No: It is a work of solid judgment, and it is of great importance for us to possess it.

Let us begin by examining the criticisms of those who judge of reasons not by reason, but by the event, and who have no objection to bring against the scheme except that it has never been put in practice. Well, such men will doubtless say, if its advantages are so certain, why is it that the Sovereigns of Europe have never adopted it? Why do they ignore their own interest, if that interest is demonstrated so clearly? Do we see them reject any other means of increasing their revenue and their power? And, if this means were as efficacious as you pretend, is it conceivable that they should be less eager to try it than any of the schemes they have pursued for all these centuries? That they should prefer a thousand delusive expedients to so evident an advantage?

Yes, without doubt, that is conceivable; unless it be assumed that their wisdom is equal to their ambition, and that the more keenly they desire their own interest, the more clearly do they see it. The truth is that the severest penalty of excessive self-love is that it always defeats itself, that the keener the passion the more certain it is to be cheated of its goal. Let us distinguish then, in politics as in morals, between real and apparent interest. The former will be secured by an abiding peace; that is demonstrated in the *Project*. The latter is to be found in the state of absolute independence which frees Sovereigns from the reign of Law only to put them under that of chance. They are, in fact, like a madcap pilot who, to show off his idle skill and his power over his sailors, would rather toss to and fro among the rocks in a storm than moor his vessel in safety.

The whole life of Kings, or of those on whom they shuffle off their duties, is devoted solely to two objects: to extend their rule beyond their frontiers and to make it more absolute within them. Any other purpose they may have is either subservient to one of these aims, or merely a pretext for attaining them. Such pretexts are "the good of the community," "the happiness of their subjects," or "the glory of the Nation": phrases forever banished from the council chamber, and employed so clumsily in proclamations that they are always taken as warnings of coming misery and that a people groans with apprehension when its masters speak to it of their "fatherly solicitude."

From these two fundamental maxims we can easily judge of the spirit in which Princes are likely to receive a proposal which runs directly counter to the one and is hardly more favourable to the other. Anyone can see that the establishment of the Diet of Europe will fix the constitution of each State as inexorably as its frontiers; that it is impossible to guarantee the Prince against the rebellion of his subjects without at the same time securing the subjects against the tyranny of the Prince; and that, without this, the Federation could not possibly endure. And I ask whether there is in the whole world a single Sovereign who, finding himself thus bridled forever in his most cherished designs, would endure without indignation the very thought of seeing himself forced to be just not only with the foreigner, but even with his own subjects?

Again, anyone can understand that war and conquest without and the encroachments of despotism within give each other mutual support; that money and men are habitually taken at pleasure from a people of slaves, to bring others beneath the same yoke; and that conversely war furnishes a pretext for exactions of money and another, no less plausible, for keeping large armies constantly on foot, to hold the people in awe. In a word, anyone can see that aggressive Princes wage war at least as much on their subjects as on their enemies, and that the conquering nation is left no better off than the conquered. "I have beaten the Romans," so Hannibal used to write to Carthage, "send me more troops. I have exacted an indemnity from Italy, send me more money." That is the real meaning of the *Te Deums*, the bonfires and rejoicings with which the people hail the triumphs of their masters.

As for disputes between Prince and Prince, is it reasonable to hope that we can force before a higher tribunal men who boast that they hold their power only by the sword, and who bring in the name of God solely because He "is in heaven"? Will Sovereigns ever submit their quarrels to legal arbitration, when all the rigour of the laws has never succeeded in forcing private individuals to admit the principle in theirs? A private gentleman with a grievance is too proud to carry his case before the Court of the Marshals of France; and you expect a King to carry his claims before the Diet of Europe? Not to mention that the former offends against the laws, so risking his life twice over, while the latter seldom risks anything but the life of his subjects; and that, in taking up arms, he avails himself of a right recognized by all the world—a right for the use of which he claims to be accountable to God alone.

A Prince who stakes his cause on the hazards of war knows well enough that he is running risks. But he is less struck with the risks than with the gains on which he reckons, because he is much less afraid of fortune than he is confident in his own wisdom. If he is strong, he counts upon his armies; if weak, upon his allies. Sometimes he finds it useful to purge ill humours, to weaken restive subjects, even to sustain reverses; and the wily statesman knows how to draw profit even from his own defeats. I trust it will be remembered that it is not I who reason in this fashion, but the court sophist, who would rather have a large territory with few subjects, poor and submissive, than that unshaken rule over the hearts of a happy and prosperous people, which is the reward of a Prince who observes justice and obeys the laws.

It is on the same principle that he meets in his own mind the argument drawn from the interruption of commerce, from the loss of life, from the financial confusion and the real loss which result from an unprofitable conquest. It is a great miscalculation always to estimate the losses and gains of Princes in terms of money; the degree of power they aim at is not to be reckoned by the millions in their coffers. The Prince always makes his schemes rotate; he seeks to command in order to enrich himself, and to enrich himself in order to command. He is ready by turns to sacrifice the one aim to the other, with a view to obtaining whichever of the two is most wanting at the moment. But it is only in the hope of winning them both in the long run that he pursues each of them apart. If he is to be master of both men and things, he must have empire and money at the same time.

Let us add finally that, though the advantages resulting to commerce from a general and lasting peace are in themselves certain and indisputable, still, being common to all States, they will be appreciated by none. For such advantages make themselves felt only by contrast, and he who wishes to increase his relative power is bound to seek only such gains as are exclusive.

So it is that, ceaselessly deluded by appearances, Princes would have nothing to do with peace on these terms, even if they calculated their interests for themselves. How will it be, when the calculation is made for them by their ministers, whose interests are always opposed to those of the people and almost always to the Princes'? Ministers are in perpetual need of war, as a means of making themselves indispensable to their master, of throwing him into difficulties from which he cannot escape without their aid, of ruining the State, if things come to the worst as the price of keeping their own office. They are in need of it, as a means of oppressing the people on the plea of national necessity, of finding places for their creatures, of rigging the market and setting up a thousand odious monopolies. They are in need of it, as a means of gratifying their passions and driving their rivals out of favour. They are in need of it, as a means of controlling the Prince and withdrawing him from court whenever a dangerous plot is formed against their power. With a lasting peace, all these resources would be gone. And the world still persists in asking why, if such a scheme is practicable, these men have not adopted it. Is it not obvious that there is nothing impracticable about it, except its adoption by these men? What then will they do to oppose it? What they have always done: They will turn it into ridicule.

Again, even given the goodwill that we shall never find either in Princes or their ministers, we are not to assume, with the Abbé de Saint-Pierre, that it would be easy to find the right moment for putting the project into act. For this, it would be essential that all the private interests concerned, taken together, should not be stronger than the general interest, and that everyone should believe himself to see in the good of all the highest good to which he can aspire for himself. But this requires a concurrence of wisdom in so many heads, a fortuitous concourse of so many interests, such as chance can hardly be expected ever to bring about. But, in default of such spontaneous agreement, the one thing left is force; and then the question is no longer to persuade but to compel, not to write books but to raise armies.

Accordingly, though the scheme in itself was wise enough, the means proposed for its execution betray the simplicity of the author. He fairly supposed that nothing was needed but to convoke a Congress and lay the Articles before it; that they would be signed directly and all be over on the spot. It must be admitted that, in all his projects, this good man saw clearly enough how things would work, when once set going, but that he judged like a child of the means for setting them in motion.

To prove that the project of the Christian Commonwealth is not utopian, I need do no more than name its original author. For no one will say that Henry IV was a madman, or Sully a dreamer. The Abbé de Saint-Pierre took refuge behind these great names, to revive their policy. But what a difference in the time, the circumstances, the scheme itself, the manner of bringing it forward and, above all, in its author! [...]

Let us not say, then, if his system has not been adopted, that is because it was not good. Let us rather say that it was too good to be adopted. Evils and abuses, by which so many men profit, come in of themselves. Things of public utility, on the other hand, are seldom brought in but by force, for the simple reason that private interests are almost always ranged against them. Beyond doubt, a lasting peace is, under present circumstances, a project ridiculous enough. But give us back Henry IV and Sully, and it will become once more a reasonable proposal. Or rather, while we admire so fair a project, let us console ourselves for its failure by the thought that it could only have been carried out by violent means from which humanity must needs shrink.

No Confederation could ever be established except by a revolution. That being so, which of us would dare to say whether the League of Europe is a thing more to be desired or feared? It would perhaps do more harm in a moment that it would guard against for ages.

✧ ✧ ✧

The Government of Poland

III. THE FOREGOING APPLIED TO POLAND

Poland is a large state, surrounded by yet larger states whose military discipline and despotic forms of government give them great offensive power. In sharp contrast to them, Poland is weak from anarchy, so that, despite the bravery of its citizens, it must accept any outrages its neighbors choose to inflict upon it. It has no fortified places to prevent their incursions into its territory. It is underpopualted, and is therefore well-nigh incapable of defending itself. It has no proper economic system. It has few troops, or rather none at all. It lacks military discipline. It is disorganized. Its people do not obey. Constantly divided within, constantly threatened from without, it has in itself no stability whatever and is at the mercy of its neighbors' whims.

As matters now stand, I see only one means of giving Poland the stability it lacks, namely, to infuse into the entire nation, so to speak, the spirit of your confederates, and to establish the republic in the Poles' own hearts, so that it will live on in them despite anything your oppressors may do. Those hearts are, to my mind, the republic's only place of refuge: There force can neither destroy it nor even reach it. Of this you have just seen a proof that will be remembered forever; Poland was in Russian irons, but the Poles themselves remained free—a great object lesson, which teaches you how you can defy the power and ambition of your neighbors. You cannot possibly keep them from swallowing you; see to it, at least, that they shall not be able to digest you. Whatever you do, your enemies will crush you a hundred times before you have given Poland what it needs in order to be capable of resisting them. There is one rampart, however, that will always be readied for its defense, and that no army can possibly breach; and that is the virtue of its citizens, their patriotic zeal, in the distinctive cast that national institutions are capable of impressing upon their souls. See to it that every Pole is incapable of becoming a Russian, and I answer for it that Russia will never subjugate Poland.

I repeat: *national* institutions. That is what gives form to the genius, the character, the tastes, and the customs of a people; what causes it to be itself rather than some other people; what arouses in it that ardent love of fatherland that is founded upon habits of mind impossible to uproot; what makes unbearably tedious for its citizens every moment spent away from home—even when they find themselves surrounded by delights that are denied them in their own country. Remember the Spartan at the court of the Great King: They chided him when, sated with sensual pleasures, he hungered for the taste of black broth. "Ah!" he sighed to the satrap, "I know your pleasures; but you do not know ours!"

Say what you like, there is no such thing nowadays as Frenchmen, Germans, Spaniards, or even Englishmen—only Europeans. All have the same tastes, the same passions, the same customs, and for good reason: Not one of them has ever been formed *nationally*, by distinctive legislation. Put them in the same circumstances and, man for man, they will do exactly the same things. They will all tell you how unselfish they are, and act like scoundrels. They will all go on and on about the public good, and think only of themselves. They will all sing the praises of moderation, and each will wish himself a modern Croesus. They all dream only of luxury, and know no passion except the passion for money; sure as they are that money will fetch them everything they fancy, they will all sell themselves to the first man who is willing to pay them. What do they care what master's bidding they do, or what country's laws they obey? Their fatherland is any country where there is money for them to steal and women for them to seduce.

Give a different bent to the passions of the Poles; in doing so, you will shape their minds and hearts in a national pattern that will set them apart from other peoples, that will keep them from being absorbed by other peoples, or finding contentment among them, or allying themselves with them. You will give the Poles a spiritual vigor that will end all this iniquitous bandying-about of idle precepts, and will cause them to do by inclination and passionate choice the things that men motivated by duty or interest never do quite well enough. Upon souls like that, a wisely conceived legislation will take firm hold. They will obey, not elude, the laws, because the laws will suit them, and will enjoy the inward assent of their own wills. They will love their fatherland; they will serve it zealously and with all their hearts. Where love of fatherland prevails, even a bad legislation would produce good citizens. And nothing except good citizens will ever make the state powerful and prosperous.

I shall describe below a system of administration that, leaving the deeper levels of your laws virtually untouched, seems to me what you need in order to raise the patriotism of the Poles, as also the virtues that invariably accompany patriotism, to their highest possible level of intensity. But whether you adopt that system or not, you must still begin by giving the citizens of Poland a high opinion of themselves and of their fatherland. That opinion, in view of the manner in which they have just shown themselves, will not be unfounded, which is to say: Seize the opportunity afforded by the events of the present moment, and raise souls to the pitch of the souls of the ancients. The Confederation of Bar saved your fatherland at a moment when it was about to expire; so much is certain. Now: The story of that glorious episode should be carved in sacred characters upon each Polish heart. I should like you to erect, to the Confederation's memory, a monument inscribed with the name of every one of its members, including, since so great a deed should wipe out the transgressions of an entire lifetime, even those who may subsequently have betrayed the common cause. I should also like you to establish the custom of celebrating the confederates' deeds every ten years in solemn ceremonies—with the pomp appropriate to a republic: simple and proud rather than ostentatious and vain; and in them, with dignity and in language free from exaggeration, let praise be bestowed upon the virtuous citizens who had the honor to suffer for their country in the toils of the enemy. And finally, I should like some honorific distinction, one that would constantly remind the public of this noble heritage from the past, to be conferred even upon the confederates' families. During these solemnities I should not, however, like you to permit any invective against the Russians, or even any mention of them. That would be to honor them too much; besides which your silence about them at the very moment of remembering their cruelty, and your praise for the men who resisted them, will say about the Russians all that needs be said. You should despise them too much ever to hate them.

I should like you, by means of honors and public prizes, to shed luster on all the patriotic virtues, to keep the Poles' minds constantly on the fatherland, making it their central preoccupation, and to hold it up constantly before their eyes. This, I admit, would give them less opportunity and leave them less time for getting rich, but they would also have less desire and less need for riches: Their hearts would come to know happiness of another kind than that which wealth confers. There you have the secret for ennobling men's souls and for making of their ennoblement an incentive more powerful than gold. [. . .]

IV. EDUCATION

Here we have the important topic: It is education that you must count on to shape the souls of the citizens in a national pattern and so to direct their opinions, their likes, and dislikes that they shall be patriotic by inclination, passionately, of necessity.

The newly born infant, upon first opening his eyes, must gaze upon the fatherland, and until his dying day should behold nothing else. Your true republican is a man who imbibed love of the fatherland, which is to say love of the laws and of liberty, with his mother's milk. That love makes up his entire existence: He has eyes only for the fatherland, lives only for his fatherland; the moment he is alone, he is a mere cipher; the moment he has no fatherland, he is no more; if not dead, he is worse off than if he were dead.

Truly national education belongs exclusively to men who are free; they and they only enjoy a common existence; they and they only are genuinely bound together by laws. Your Frenchman, your Englishman, your Spaniard, your Italian, your Russian, are all pretty much the same man; and that man emerges from school already well-shaped for license, which is to say for servitude. When the Pole reaches the age of twenty, he must be a Pole, not some other kind of man. I should wish him to learn to read by reading literature written in his own country. I should wish him, at ten, to be familiar with everything Poland has produced; at twelve, to know all its provinces, all its roads, all its towns; at fifteen, to have mastered his country's entire history, and at sixteen, all its laws; let his mind and heart be full of every noble deed, every illustrious man, that ever was in Poland, so that he can tell you about them at a moment's notice. I do not, as that should make clear, favour putting the youngsters through the usual round of studies, directed by foreigners and priests. The content, the sequence, even the method of their studies should be specified by Polish law. They should have only Poles for teachers—all of them married men, if that were possible, all men of distinction, alike for their conduct, their probity, their good sense, and their lights, and all destined, after a certain number of years of creditable service as teachers, to fill not more important posts, for there is none more important, but more prestigious and less-exacting ones. Above all, do not make the mistake of turning teaching into a career. A public servant in Poland should have no permanent status other than that of citizen; each post he fills, especially if it be an important one like that of teacher, should be thought of merely as one further testing-ground, one further rung on a ladder, from which to climb, when he deserves to, yet higher. I urge the Poles to give heed to this principle, upon which I shall often insist; I believe it to be a key with which the state can unlock a great storehouse of energy. And the reader will see below how, in my opinion, it can be made workable in all cases.

2

EMMANUEL JOSEPH SIEYÈS

What Is the Third Estate?

What does a nation require to survive and prosper? It needs *private* activities and *public* services.

These private activities can all be comprised within four classes of persons:

1. Since land and water provide the basic materials for human needs, the first class, in logical order, includes all the families connected with work on the land.

2. Between the initial sale of goods and the moment when they reach the consumer or user, goods acquire an increased value of a more or less compound nature through the incorporation of varying amounts of labour. In this way human industry manages to improve the gifts of nature and the value of the raw material may be multiplied twice, or ten-fold, or a hundred-fold. Such are the activities of the second class of persons.

3. Between production and consumption, as also between the various stages of production, a variety of intermediary agents intervene, to help producers as well as consumers; these are the dealers and the merchants. Merchants continually compare needs according to place and time and estimate the profits to be obtained from warehousing and transportation; dealers undertake, in the final stage, to deliver the goods on the wholesale and retail markets. Such is the function of the third class of persons.

4. Besides these three classes of useful and industrious citizens who deal with *things* fit to be consumed or used, society also requires a vast number of special activities and of services *directly* useful or pleasant to the *person*. This fourth class embraces all sorts of occupations, from the most distinguished liberal and scientific professions to the lowest of menial tasks.

Such are the activities which support society. But who performs them? The Third Estate.

Public services can also, at present, be divided into four known categories, the army, the law, the Church, and the bureaucracy. It needs no detailed analysis to show that the Third Estate everywhere constitutes nineteen-twentieths of them, except that it is loaded with all the really arduous work, all the tasks which the privileged order refuses to perform. Only the well-paid and honorific posts are filled by members of the privileged

35

order. Are we to give them credit for this? We could do so only if the Third Estate was unable or unwilling to fill these posts. We know the answer. Nevertheless, the privileged have dared to preclude the Third Estate. "No matter how useful you are," they said, "no matter how able you are, you can go so far and no further. Honours are not for the like of you." The rare exceptions, noticeable as they are bound to be, are mere mockery, and the sort of language allowed on such occasions is an additional insult.

If this exclusion is a social crime, a veritable act of war against the Third Estate, can it be said at least to be useful to the commonwealth? Ah! Do we not understand the consequences of monopoly? While discouraging those it excludes, does it not destroy the skill of those it favours? Are we unaware that any work from which free competition is excluded will be performed less well and more expensively?

When any function is made the prerogative of a separate order among the citizens, has nobody remarked how a salary has to be paid not only to the man who actually does the work, but to all those of the same caste who do not, and also to the entire families of both the workers and the non-workers? Has nobody observed that as soon as the government becomes the property of a separate class, it starts to grow out of all proportion and that posts are created not to meet the needs of the governed but of those who govern them? Has nobody noticed that while on the one hand, we basely and I dare say *stupidly* accept this situation of ours, on the other hand, when we read the history of Egypt or stories of travels in India, we describe the same kind of conditions as despicable, monstrous, destructive of all industry, as inimical to social progress, and above all as debasing to the human race in general and intolerable to Europeans in particular . . .? But here we must leave considerations which, however much they might broaden and clarify the problem, would nevertheless slow our pace.

It suffices to have made the point that the so-called usefulness of a privileged order to the public service is a fallacy; that, without help from this order, all the arduous tasks in the service are performed by the Third Estate; that without this order the higher posts could be infinitely better filled; that they ought to be the natural prize and reward of recognized ability and service; and that if the privileged have succeeded in usurping all well-paid and honorific posts, this is both a hateful iniquity towards the generality of citizens and an act of treason to the commonwealth.

Who is bold enough to maintain that the Third Estate does not contain within itself everything needful to constitute a complete nation? It is like a strong and robust man with one arm still in chains. If the privileged order were removed, the nation would not be something less but something more. What then is the Third Estate? All; but an "all" that is fettered and oppressed. What would it be without the privileged order? It would be all; but free and flourishing. Nothing will go well without the Third Estate; everything would go considerably better without the two others.

It is not enough to have shown that the privileged, far from being useful to the nation, can only weaken and injure it; we must prove further that the nobility is not part of our society at all: it may be a *burden* for the nation, but it cannot be part of it.

First, it is impossible to find what place to assign to the caste of nobles among all the elements of a nation. I know that there are many people, all too many, who, from infirmity, incapacity, incurable idleness, or a collapse of morality, perform no functions at all in society. Exceptions and abuses always exist alongside the rule, and particularly in a large commonwealth. But all will agree that the fewer these abuses, the better organized a state is supposed to be. The most ill-organized state of all would be the one where not just isolated individuals but a complete class of citizens would glory in inactivity amidst the general movement and contrive to consume the best part of the product without having in any way helped to produce it. Such a class, surely, is foreign to the nation because of its *idleness*.

The nobility, however, is also a foreigner in our midst because of its *civil and political* prerogatives.

What is a nation? A body of associates living under *common* laws and represented by the same *legislative assembly*, etc.

Is it not obvious that the nobility possesses privileges and exemptions which it brazenly calls its rights and which stand distinct from the rights of the great body of citizens? Because of these special rights, the nobility does not belong to the common order, nor is it subjected to the common laws. Thus its private rights make it a people apart in the great nation. It is truly *imperium in imperio*.

As for its *political* rights, it also exercises these separately from the nation. It has its own representatives who are charged with no mandate from the People. Its deputies sit separately, and even if they sat in the same chamber as the deputies of ordinary citizens they would still constitute a different and separate representation. They are foreign to the nation first because of their origin, since they do not owe their powers to the People; and secondly because of their aim, since this consists in defending, not the general interest, but the private one.

The Third Estate then contains everything that pertains to the nation while nobody outside the Third Estate can be considered as part of the nation. What is the Third Estate? *Everything.*

3

IMMANUEL KANT

The Metaphysics of Morals

SECTION II: INTERNATIONAL RIGHT

§ 53 The human beings who make up a nation can, as natives of the country, be represented as analogous to descendants from a common ancestry (*congeniti*) even if this is not in fact the case. But in an intellectual sense or for the purposes of right, they can be thought of as the offspring of a common mother (the republic), constituting, as it were, a single family (*gens, natio*) whose members (the citizens) are all equal by birth. These citizens will not intermix with any neighbouring people who live in a state of nature, but will consider them ignoble, even though such savages for their own part may regard themselves as superior on account of the lawless freedom they have chosen. The latter likewise constitute national groups, but they do not constitute states.

What we are now about to consider under the name of international right or the right of nations is the right of *states* in relation to one another (although it is not strictly correct to speak, as we usually do, of the *right of nations*; it should rather be called the *right of states ins publicum civitatum*). The situation in question is that in which one state, as a moral person, is considered as existing in a state of nature in relation to another state, hence in a condition of constant war. International right is thus concerned partly with the right to make war, partly with the right of war itself, and partly with questions of right after a war, i.e., with the right of states to compel each other to abandon their warlike condition and to create a constitution which will establish an enduring peace. A state of nature among individuals or families (in their relations with one another) is different from a state of nature among entire nations, because international right involves not only the relationship between one state and another within a larger whole, but also the relationship between individual persons in one state and individuals in the other or between such individuals and the other state as a whole. But this difference between international right and the right of individuals in a mere state of nature is easily deducible from the latter concept without need of any further definitions.

§ 54 The elements of international right are as follows. Firstly, in their external relationships with one another, states, like lawless savages, exist in a condition devoid of right. Secondly, this condition is one of war (the right of the stronger), even if there is no actual war or continuous active fighting (i.e., hostilities). But even although neither of two states is done any injustice by the other in this condition, it is nevertheless in the highest degree unjust in itself, for it implies that neither wishes to experience anything better. Adjacent states are thus bound to abandon such a condition. Thirdly, it is necessary to establish a federation of peoples in accordance with the idea of an original social contract, so that states will protect one another against external aggression while refraining from interference in one another's internal disagreements. And fourthly, this association must not embody a sovereign power as in a civil constitution, but only a partnership or confederation. It must therefore be an alliance which can be terminated at any time, so that it has to be renewed periodically. This right is derived in subsidium from another original right, that of preventing oneself from lapsing into a state of actual war with one's partners in the confederation (foedus Amphictyonam).

§ 55 If we consider the original right of free states in the state of nature to make war upon one another (for example, in order to bring about a condition closer to that governed by right), we must first ask what right the state has as against its own subjects to employ them in a war on other states, and to expend or hazard their possessions or even their lives in the process. Does it not then depend upon their own judgment whether they wish to go to war or not? May they simply be sent thither at the sovereign's supreme command?

This right might seem an obvious consequence of the right to do what one wishes with one's own property. Whatever someone has himself substantially made is his own undisputed property. These are the premises from which a mere jurist would deduce the right in question.

A country may yield various natural products, some of which, because of their very abundance, must also be regarded as artefacts of the state. For the country would not yield them in such quantities if there were no state or proper government in control and if the inhabitants still lived in a state of nature. For example, domestic poultry (the most useful kind of fowl), sheep, pigs, cattle, etc. would be completely unknown in the country I live in (or would only rarely be encountered) if there were no government to guarantee the inhabitants their acquisitions and possessions. The same applies to the number of human beings, for there can only be few of them in a state of nature, as in the wilds of America, even if we credit them with great industry (which they do not have). The inhabitants would be very sparsely scattered, for no one could spread very far afield with his household in a land constantly threatened with devastation by other human beings, wild animals, or beasts of prey. There would thus be no adequate support for so large a population as now inhabits a country.

Now one can say that vegetables (e.g., potatoes) and domestic animals, in quantity at least, are *made* by human beings, and that they may therefore be used, expended, or consumed (i.e., killed) at will. One might therefore appear justified in saying that the supreme power in the state, the sovereign, has the right to lead his subjects to war as if on a hunt, or into battle as if on an excursion, simply because they are for the most part produced by the sovereign himself.

But while this legal argument (of which monarchs are no doubt dimly aware) is certainly valid in the case of animals, which can be the *property* of human beings, it is absolutely impermissible to apply it to human beings themselves, particularly in their capacity as citizens. For a citizen must always be regarded as a co-legislative member of the state (i.e., not just as a means, but also as an end in himself), and he must therefore give his free consent through his representatives not only to the waging of war in general, but also to every particular declaration of war. Only under this limiting condition may the state put him to service in dangerous enterprises.

We shall therefore have to derive the right under discussion from the *duty* of the sovereign towards the people, not vice versa. The people must be seen to have given their consent to military action, and although they remain passive in this capacity (for they allow themselves to be directed), they are still acting spontaneously and they represent the sovereign himself.

§ 56 In the state of nature, the *right to make war* (i.e., to enter into hostilities) is the permitted means by which one state prosecutes its rights against another. Thus if a state believes that it has been injured by another state, it is entitled to resort to violence, for it cannot in the state of nature gain satisfaction through *legal proceedings*, the only means of settling disputes in a state governed by right. Apart from an actively inflicted injury (the first aggression, as distinct from the first hostilities), a state may be subjected to *threats*. Such threats may arise either if another state is the first to make *military preparations*, on which the right of *anticipatory attack* (ins praeventionis) is based, or simply if there is an alarming increase of power (*potentia tremenda*) in another state which has acquired new territories. This is an injury to the less powerful state by the mere fact that the other state, even without offering any active offense, is *more powerful*; and any attack upon it is legitimate in the state of nature. On this is based the right to maintain a balance of power among all states which have active contact with one another.

Those *active injuries* which give a state the *right to make war* on another state include any unilateral attempt to gain satisfaction for an affront which the people of one state have offered to the people of the other. Such an act of *retribution* (retorsio) without any attempt to obtain compensation from the other state by peaceful means is similar in form to starting war without prior declaration. For if one wishes to find any rights in wartime, one must assume the existence of something analogous to a contract; in other words, one must assume that the other party has *accepted* the declaration of war and that both parties therefore wish to prosecute their rights in this manner.

§ 57 The most problematic task in international right is that of determining rights in wartime. For it is very difficult to form any conception at all of such rights and to imagine any law whatsoever in this lawless state without involving oneself in contradictions (*inter arma silent leges*). The only possible solution would be to conduct the war in accordance with principles which would still leave the states with the possibility of abandoning the state of nature in their external relations and of entering a state of right.

No war between independent states can be a *punitive* one (*bellum punitivum*). For a punishment can only occur in a relationship between a superior (*imperantis*) and a subject (*subditum*), and this is not the relationship which exists between states. Nor can there be a *war of extermination* (*bellum internecinum*) or a *war of subjugation* (*bellum subiugatorium*); for these would involve the moral annihilation of a state, and its people would either merge with those of the victorious state or be reduced to bondage. Not that this expedient, to which a state might resort in order to obtain peace, would in itself contradict the rights of a state. But the fact remains that the only concept of antagonism which the idea of international right includes is that of an antagonism regulated by principles of external freedom. This requires that violence be used only to preserve one's existing property, but not as a method of further acquisition; for the latter procedure would create a threat to one state by augmenting the power of another.

The attacked state is allowed to use any means of defense except those whose use would render its subjects unfit to be citizens. For if it did not observe this condition, it would render itself unfit in the eyes of international right to function as a person in relation to other states and to share equal rights with them. It must accordingly be prohibited for a state to use its own subjects as spies, and to use them, or indeed foreigners, as poisoners or assassins (to which class the so-called sharpshooters who wait in ambush on individual victims also belong), or even just to spread false reports. In short, a state must not use such treacherous methods as would destroy that confidence which is required for the future establishment of a lasting peace.

It is permissible in war to impose levies and contributions on the conquered enemy, but not to plunder the people, i.e., to force individual persons to part with their belongings (for this would be robbery, since it was not the conquered people who waged the war, but the state of which they were subjects which waged it *through them*). Bills of receipt should be issued for any contributions that are exacted, so that the burden imposed on the country or province can be distributed proportionately when peace is concluded.

§ 58 The right which applies *after* a war, i.e., with regard to the peace treaty at the time of its conclusion and also to its later consequences, consists of the following elements. The victor sets out the conditions, and these are drawn up in a *treaty* on which agreement is reached with the defeated party in order that peace may be concluded. A treaty of this kind is not determined by any pretended right which the victor possesses over his opponent because of an alleged injury the latter has done him; the victor should not concern himself with such questions, but should rely only on his own power for support. Thus he cannot claim compensation for the costs of the war, for he would then have to pronounce his opponent unjust in waging it. And even if this argument should occur to him, he could not make use of it, or else he would have to maintain that the war was a punitive one, which would in turn mean that he had committed an offense in waging it himself. A peace treaty should also provide for the exchange of prisoners without ransom, whether the numbers on both sides are equal or not.

The vanquished state and its subjects cannot forfeit their civil freedom through the conquest of the country. Consequently, the former cannot be degraded to the rank of a colony or the latter to the rank of bondsmen. Otherwise, the war would have been a punitive one, which is self-contradictory.

A *colony* or province is a nation which has its own constitution, legislation, and territory, and all members of any other state are no more than foreigners on its soil, even if the state to which they belong has supreme *executive* power over the colonial nation. The state with executive power is called the *mother state*. The daughter state is *ruled* by it, although it *governs* itself through its own parliament, which in turn functions under the presidency of a viceroy (*civitas hybrida*). The relationship of Athens to various islands was of this kind, as is that of Great Britain towards Ireland at the present moment.

It is even less possible to infer the rightful existence of *slavery* from the military conquest of a people, for one would then have to assume that the war had been a punitive one. Least of all would this justify hereditary slavery, which is completely absurd, for the guilt of a person's crime cannot be inherited.

It is implicit in the very concept of a peace treaty that it includes an *amnesty*.

§ 59 The *rights of peace* are as follows: firstly, the right to remain at peace when nearby states are at war (i.e., the right of *neutrality*); secondly, the right to secure the continued maintenance of peace once it has been concluded (i.e., the right of *guarantee*); and thirdly, the right to form *alliances* or confederate leagues of several states for the purpose of communal defense against any possible attacks from internal or external sources—although these must never become leagues for promoting aggression and internal expansion.

§ 60 The rights of a state against an *unjust enemy* are unlimited in quantity or degree, although they do have limits in relation to quality. In other words, while the threatened state may not employ *every* means to assert its own rights, it may employ any intrinsically permissible means to whatever degree its own strength allows. But what can the expression "an unjust

enemy" mean in relation to the concepts of international right, which requires that every state should act as judge of its own cause just as it would
do in a state of nature? It must mean someone whose publicly expressed
will, whether expressed in word or in deed, displays a maxim which would
make peace among nations impossible and would lead to a perpetual state
of nature if it were made into a general rule. Under this heading would
come violations of public contracts, which can be assumed to affect the
interests of all nations. For they are a threat to their freedom, and a challenge
to them to unite against such misconduct and to deprive the culprit of the
power to act in a similar way again. But this does *not* entitle them *to divide
up the offending state among themselves* and to make it disappear, as it were,
from the face of the earth. For this would be an injustice against the people,
who cannot lose their original right to unite into a commonwealth. They
can only be made to accept a new constitution of a nature that is unlikely
to encourage their warlike inclinations.

Besides, the expression "an unjust enemy" is a *pleonasm* if applied to any
situation in a state of nature, for this state is itself one of injustice. A just
enemy would be one whom I could not resist without injustice. But if this
were so, he would not be my enemy in any case.

§ 61 Since the state of nature among nations (as among individual human beings) is a state which one ought to abandon in order to enter a state
governed by law, all international rights, as well as all the external property
of states such as can be acquired or preserved by war, are purely *provisional*
until the state of nature has been abandoned. Only within a universal *union
of states* (analogous to the union through which a nation becomes a state)
can such rights and property acquire *peremptory* validity and a true *state of
peace* be attained. But if an international state of this kind extends over
too wide an area of land, it will eventually become impossible to govern it
and thence to protect each of its members, and the multitude of corporations this would require must again lead to a state of war. It naturally follows that *perpetual peace*, the ultimate end of all international right, is an
idea incapable of realization. But the political principles which have this
aim, i.e., those principles which encourage the formation of international
alliances designed to *approach* the idea itself by a continual process, are not
impracticable. For this is a project based upon duty, hence also upon the
rights of man and of states, and it can indeed be put into execution.

Such a *union of several states* designed to preserve peace may be called a
permanent congress of states, and all neighbouring states are free to join it. A
congress of this very kind (at least as far as the formalities of international
right in relation to the preservation of peace are concerned) found expression in the assembly of the States General at The Hague in the first half of
this century. To this assembly, the ministers of most European courts and
even of the smallest republics brought their complaints about any aggression suffered by one of their number at the hands of another. They thus

thought of all Europe as a single federated state, which they accepted as an arbiter in all their public disputes. Since then, however, international right has disappeared from cabinets, surviving only in books, or it has been consigned to the obscurity of the archives as a form of empty deduction after violent measures have already been employed.

In the present context, however, a *congress* merely signifies a voluntary gathering of various states which can be *dissolved* at any time, not an association which, like that of the American states, is based on a political constitution and is therefore indissoluble. For this is the only means of realizing the idea of public international right as it ought to be instituted, thereby enabling the nations to settle their disputes in a civilized manner by legal proceedings, not in a barbaric manner (like that of the savages) by acts of war.

Section III: Cosmopolitan Right

§ 62 The rational idea, as discussed above, of a *peaceful* (if not exactly amicable) international community of all those of the earth's peoples who can enter into active relations with one another, is not a philanthropic principle of ethics, but a principle of *right*. Through the spherical shape of the planet they inhabit (*globus terraquens*), nature has confined them all within an area of definite limits. Accordingly, the only conceivable way in which anyone can possess habitable land on earth is by possessing a part within a determinate whole in which everyone has an original right to share. Thus all nations are *originally* members of a community of the land. But this is not a *legal community* of possession (*communio*) and utilization of the land, nor a community of ownership. It is a community of reciprocal action (*commercium*), which is physically possible, and each member of it accordingly has constant relations with all the others. Each may *offer* to have commerce with the rest, and they all have a right to make such overtures without being treated by foreigners as enemies. This right, insofar as it affords the prospect that all nations may unite for the purpose of creating certain universal laws to regulate the intercourse they may have with one another, may be termed *cosmopolitan* (*ins cosmopoliticum*).

The oceans may appear to cut nations off from the community of their fellows. But with the art of navigation, they constitute the greatest natural incentive to international commerce, and the greater the number of neighbouring coastlines there are (as in the Mediterranean), the livelier this commerce will be. Yet these visits to foreign shores, and even more so, attempts to settle on them with a view to linking them with the motherland, can also occasion evil and violence in one part of the globe with ensuing repercussions which are felt everywhere else. But although such abuses are possible, they do not deprive the world's citizens of the right to *attempt* to enter into a community with everyone else and to *visit* all regions of the earth with this intention. This does not, however, amount to a right to *settle* on another nation's territory (*ins incolatus*), for the latter would require a special contract.

But one might ask whether a nation may establish a *settlement alongside another nation* (*accolatus*) in newly discovered regions, or whether it may take possession of land in the vicinity of a nation which has already settled in the same area, even without the latter's consent. The answer is that the right to do so is incontestable, so long as such settlements are established sufficiently far away from the territory of the original nation for neither party to interfere with the other in their use of the land. But if the nations involved are pastoral or hunting peoples (like the Hottentots, the Tunguses, and most native American nations) who rely upon large tracts of wasteland for their sustenance, settlements should not be established by violence, but only by treaty; and even then, there must be no attempt to exploit the ignorance of the natives in persuading them to give up their territories. Nevertheless, there are plausible enough arguments for the use of violence on the grounds that it is in the best interests of the world as a whole. For on the one hand, it may bring culture to uncivilized peoples (this is the excuse with which even Büsching tries to extenuate the bloodshed which accompanied the introduction of Christianity into Germany); and on the other, it may help us to purge our country of depraved characters, at the same time affording the hope that they or their offspring will become reformed in another continent (as in New Holland). But all these supposedly good intentions cannot wash away the stain of injustice from the means which are used to implement them. Yet one might object that the whole world would perhaps still be in a lawless condition if men had had any such compunction about using violence when they first created a law-governed state. But this can as little annul the above condition of right as can the plea of political revolutionaries that the people are entitled to reform constitutions by force if they have become corrupt, and to act completely unjustly for once and for all, in order to put justice on a more secure basis and ensure that it flourishes in the future.

CONCLUSION

If a person cannot prove that a thing exists, he may attempt to prove that it does not exist. If neither approach succeeds (as often happens), he may still ask whether it is *in his interest to assume* one or other possibility as a hypothesis, either from theoretical or from practical considerations. In other words, he may wish on the one hand simply to explain a certain phenomenon (as the astronomer, for example, may wish to explain the sporadic movements of the planets), or on the other, to achieve a certain end which may itself be either *pragmatic* (purely technical) or *moral* (i.e., an end which it is our duty to take as a maxim). It is, of course, self-evident that no one is duty-bound to make an *assumption* (*suppositio*) that the end in question can be realized, since this would involve a purely theoretical and indeed problematic judgment; for no one can be obliged to accept a given belief. But we can have a duty to act in accordance with the idea of such an end, even if there is not the slightest theoretical probability of its realization, provided that there is no means of demonstrating that it cannot be realized either.

Now, moral-practical reason within us pronounces the following irresistible veto: *There shall be no war*, either between individual human beings in the state of nature, or between separate states, which, although internally law-governed, still live in a lawless condition in their external relationships with one another. For war is not the way in which anyone should pursue his rights. Thus it is no longer a question of whether perpetual peace is really possible or not, or whether we are not perhaps mistaken in our theoretical judgment if we assume that it is. On the contrary, we must simply act as if it could really come about (which is perhaps impossible), and turn our efforts towards realizing it and towards establishing that constitution which seems most suitable for this purpose (perhaps that of republicanism in all states, individually and collectively). By working towards this end, we may hope to terminate the disastrous practice of war, which up till now has been the main object to which all states, without exception, have accommodated their internal institutions. And even if the fulfillment of this pacific intention were forever to remain a pious hope, we should still not be deceiving ourselves if we made it our maxim to work unceasingly towards it, for it is our duty to do so. To assume, on the other hand, that the moral law within us might be misleading, would give rise to the execrable wish to dispense with all reason and to regard ourselves, along with our principles, as subject to the same mechanism of nature as the other animal species.

It can indeed be said that this task of establishing a universal and lasting peace is not just a part of the theory of right within the limits of pure reason, but its entire ultimate purpose. For the condition of peace is the only state in which the property of a large number of people living together as neighbours under a single constitution can be guaranteed by *laws*. The rule on which this constitution is based must not simply be derived from the experience of those who have hitherto fared best under it, and then set up as a norm for others. On the contrary, it should be derived *a priori* by reason from the absolute ideal of a rightful association of men under public laws. For all particular examples are deceptive (an example can only illustrate a point, but does not prove anything), so that one must have recourse to metaphysics. And even those who scorn metaphysics admit its necessity involuntarily when they say, for example (as they often do): "The best constitution is that in which the power rests with laws instead of with men." For what can be more metaphysically sublime than this idea, although by the admission of those who express it, it also has a well-authenticated objective reality which can easily be demonstrated from particular instances as they arise. But no attempt should be made to put it into practice overnight by revolution, i.e., by forcibly overthrowing a defective constitution which has existed in the past; for there would then be an interval of time during which the condition of right would be nullified. If we try instead to give it reality by means of gradual reforms carried out in accordance with definite principles, we shall see that it is the only means of continually approaching the supreme political good—perpetual peace.

4

JOHANN GOTTFRIED
VON HERDER

Reflections on the Philosophy of the History of Mankind

NATIONAL GENIUS AND THE ENVIRONMENT
(BOOK VII)

The picture of nations hitherto sketched must be considered only as the foreground, serving as a basis to farther observations: while its groups answer the purpose of the *templa* of the augurs in the skies, forming definite spaces for our contemplation, and aids to our memory. Let us see what they afford towards a philosophy of our species.

CHAPTER 1: NOTWITHSTANDING THE VARIETIES OF THE HUMAN FORM, THERE IS BUT ONE AND THE SAME SPECIES OF MAN THROUGHOUT THE WHOLE OF OUR EARTH

No two leaves of any one tree in nature are to be found perfectly alike; and still less do two human faces, or human frames, resemble each other. Of what endless variety is our artful structure susceptible! Our solids are decomposable into such minute and multifariously interwoven fibres, as no eye can trace; and these are connected by a gluten of such a delicate composition, as the utmost skill is insufficient to analyze. Yet these constitute the least part of us: They are nothing more than the containing vessels and conduits of the variously compounded, highly animated fluid, existing in much greater quantity, by means of which we live and enjoy life. "No man," says Haller, "is exactly similar to another in his internal structure: the courses of the nerves and blood vessels differ in millions and millions of cases, so that amid the variations of these delicate parts, we are scarcely able to discover in what they agree."[1] But if the eye of the anatomist can perceive this infinite variety, how much greater must that be, which dwells in the invisible powers of such an artful organization! So that every man is ultimately a world, in external appearance indeed similar to others, but internally an individual being, with whom no other coincides. [...]

As the human intellect, however, seeks unity in every kind of variety, and the divine mind, its prototype, has stamped the most innumerable multiplicity upon the Earth with unity, we may venture from the vast realm of change to revert to the simplest position: *All mankind are only one and the same species.*

How many ancient fables of human monsters and prodigies have already disappeared before the light of history! And where tradition still repeats remnants of these, I am fully convinced, more accurate inquiry will explain them into more beautiful truths. We are now acquainted with the ourang-outang, and know, that he has no claim to speech, or to be considered as man: And when we have a more exact account of the ourang-kubub, and ourang-guhu, the tailed savages of the woods in Borneo, Sumatra, and the Nicobar Islands will vanish. The men with reverted feet in Malacca, the probably rickety nation of dwarfs in Madagascar, the men habited like women in Florida, and some others, deserve such an investigation as has already been bestowed on the albinoes, the dondoes, the Patagonians, and the aprons of the Hottentot females.[2] Men, who succeed in removing wants from the creation, falsehoods from our memory, and disgraces from our nature, are to the realms of truth, what the heroes of mythology were to the primitive world; they lessen the number of monsters on the Earth. [. . .]

For each genus Nature has done enough, and to each has given its proper progeny. The ape she has divided into as many species and varieties as possible, and extended these as far as she could: but thou, O man, honour thyself: neither the pongo nor the gibbon is thy brother: the American and the Negro are: these therefore thou shouldst not oppress, or murder, or steal; for they are men, like thee: with the ape thou canst not enter into fraternity.

Lastly, I could wish the distinctions between the human species, that have been made from a laudable zeal for discriminating science, not carried beyond due bounds. Some for instance have thought fit, to employ the term of *races* for four or five divisions, originally made in consequence of country or complexion: but I see no reason for this appellation. Race refers to a difference of origin, which in this case either does not exist, or in each of these countries, and under each of these complexions, comprises the most different races. For every nation is one people, having its own national form, as well as its own language: the climate, it is true, stamps on each its mark, or spreads over it a slight veil, but not sufficient to destroy the original national character. This originality of character extends even to families, and its transitions are as variable as imperceptible. In short, there are neither four or five races, nor exclusive varieties, on this Earth. Complexions run into each other: forms follow the genetic character: and upon the whole, all are at last but shades of the same great picture, extending through all ages, and over all parts of the Earth. They belong not, therefore, so properly to systematic natural history, as to the physico-geographical history of man.

CHAPTER 2: THE ONE SPECIES OF MAN HAS NATURALIZED ITSELF IN EVERY
CLIMATE UPON EARTH

Observe you locusts of the Earth, the Kalmuc and Mungal: they are fitted
for no region but their own hills and mountains.[3] The light rider flies on
his little horse over immense tracts of the desert; he knows how to invig-
orate his fainting courser, and by opening a vein in his neck, to restore his
own powers, when he sinks with fatigue. No rain falls on many parts of
these regions, which are refreshed solely by the dew, while inexhaustible
fertility clothes the earth with continually renovated verdure. Throughout
many extensive tracts no tree is to be seen, no spring of fresh water to be
discovered. Here these wild tribes, yet preserving good order among themselves, wander about among the luxuriant grass, and pasture their herds:
the horses, their associates, know their voices, and live like them in peace.
With thoughtless indifference sits the indolent Kalmuc, contemplating the
undisturbed serenity of his sky, while his ear catches every sound, that per-
vades the desert his eye is unable to scan. In every other region of the
Earth the Mungal has either degenerated or improved: in his own country
he is what he was thousands of years ago, and such will he continue, as
long as it remains unaltered by Nature or by art.

The Arab of the desert belongs to it, as much as his noble horse, and his
patient, indefatigable camel.[4] As the Mungal wanders over his heights, and
among his hills, so wanders the better-formed Bedouin over his extensive
Asiatic-African deserts; also a nomad, but a nomad of *his own* region. With
this his simple clothing, his maxims of life, his manners, and his character,
are in unison; and, after the lapse of thousands of years, his tent still preserves the wisdom of his forefathers. A lover of liberty, he despises wealth
and pleasure, is fleet in the course, a dextrous manager of his horse, of
whom he is as careful as of himself, and equally dextrous in handling the
javelin. His figure is lean and muscular; his complexion brown; his bones
strong. He is indefatigable in supporting labour, bold and enterprising, faithful
to his word, hospitable and magnanimous, and, connected with his fellows
by the desert, he makes one common cause with all. From the dangers of
his mode of life he has imbibed wariness and shy mistrust; from his solitary
abode, the feelings of revenge, friendship, enthusiasm, and pride. Wherever
an Arab is found, on the Nile or the Euphrates, on Libanus or in Senegal,
nay even in Zanguebar or the islands of the Indian Ocean, if a foreign
climate has not by length of time changed him into a colonist, he will
display his original Arabian character.

The Californian, on the verge of the earth, in his barren country, exposed as he is to want, and amid the vicissitudes of his climate, complains
not of heat or cold, eludes the force of hunger, though with the utmost
difficulty, and enjoys happiness in his native land. "God alone can tell," says
a missionary,

how many thousand miles a Californian, that has attained the age of eighty, must have wandered over before he finds a grave. Many of them change their quarters perhaps a hundred times in a year, sleeping scarcely three nights together on the same spot, or in the same region. They lie down wherever night overtakes them, without paying the least regard to the filthiness of the soil, or endeavouring to secure themselves from noxious vermin. Their dark brown skin serves them instead of coat and cloak. Their furniture consists of a bow and arrows, a stone for a knife, a bone or sharp stake to dig up roots, the shell of a tortoise for a cradle, a gut or a bladder to carry water, and, if they be peculiarly fortunate, a pouch made of the fibres of the aloe, somewhat in the fashion of a net, to contain their utensils and provision. They feed on roots, and all sorts of small seeds, even those of grass, which they collect with great labour; nay, when pressed by want, they pick them out of their own dung. Every thing that can be called flesh, or barely resembles it, even to bats, grubs, and worms, is to be reckoned among the dainties, on which they feast; and the leaves of certain shrubs, with their young shoots, leather, and spungy bones, are not excluded from their list of provision, when urged by hunger. Yet these poor creatures are healthy: they live to a great age, and are strong; so that it is uncommon to see a man grayheaded, and never but at a late period. They are always cheerful; forever jesting and laughing; well made, straight, and active; they can lift stones and other things from the ground with their two foremost toes; they walk as erect as a dart to the extreme of old age; and the children go alone before they are a year old. When weary of talking, they lie down and sleep, till awakened by hunger, or the desire of eating: and as soon as they are awake, the laugh, the talk, and the jest, recommence. Thus they go on, till worn out by old age, when they meet death with calm indifference. [. . .]

In the first place it is obvious why all sensual people, fashioned to their country, are so much attached to the soil, and so inseparable from it. The constitution of their body, their way of life, the pleasures and occupations to which they have been accustomed from their infancy, and the whole circle of their ideas, are climatic. Deprive them of their country, you deprive them of everything. [. . .]

No words can express the sorrow and despair of a bought or stolen negro slave, when he leaves his native shore, never more to behold it while he has breath. "Great care must be taken," says Römer,

> that the slaves do not get hold of a knife, either in the fort, or aboard the ship. To keep them in good humour on their passage to the West Indies requires the utmost exertion. For this purpose violins are provided, with fifes and drums; they are permitted to dance; and they are assured, that they are going to a pleasant country, where they may have as many wives as they please, and plenty of good food. Yet many deplorable instances have been known of their falling upon the crew, murdering them, and letting the ship drive ashore.[5]

But how many more deplorable instances have been known of these poor stolen wretches destroying themselves in despair! Sparmann informs us, from the mouth of a slavedealer, that at night they are seized with a kind of frenzy, which prompts them to commit murder, either on themselves or others; "for the painful recollection of the irreparable loss of their country and their freedom commonly awakes by night, when the bustle of the day ceases to engage their attention."[6] And what right have you, monsters! even to approach the country of these unfortunates, much less to tear them from it by stealth, fraud, and cruelty? For ages this quarter of the Globe has been theirs, and they belong to it: their forefathers purchased it at a dear rate, at the price of the Negro form and complexion. In fashioning them the African sun has adopted them as its children, and impressed on them its own seal: wherever you convey them, this brands you as robbers, as stealers of men.

Secondly. Thus the wars of savages for their country, or on account of its children, their brethren, torn from it, or degraded and oppressed, are extremely cruel. Hence, for instance, the lasting hatred of the natives of America toward Europeans, even when these behave to them with tenderness: they cannot suppress the feeling: "This land is ours; you have no business here." Hence the treachery of all savages, as they are called, even when they appear altogether satisfied with the courtesy of European visitors. The moment their hereditary national feelings awake, the flame they have long with difficulty smothered breaks out, rages with violence, and frequently is not appeased, till the flesh of the stranger has been torn by the teeth of the native. To us this seems horrible; and it is so, no doubt: yet the Europeans first urged them to this misdeed: for why did they visit their country? why did they enter it as despots, arbitrarily practicing violence and extortion?[7] For ages it had been to its inhabitants the universe: they had inherited it from their fathers, and from them too they had inherited the barbarous practice of destroying in the most savage manner all, who would deprive them of their territory, tear them from it, or encroach upon their rights. Thus to them an enemy and a stranger are the same: they resemble the *muscipula*, which, rooted to its soil, attacks every insect that approaches it: the right of devouring an unbidden or unfriendly guest is the tribute they exact; as *Cyclopical* a tribute as any in Europe. [. . .]

HUMANITY, THE END OF HUMAN NATURE (BOOK XV)

CHAPTER 3: THE HUMAN RACE IS DESTINED TO PROCEED THROUGH VARIOUS DEGREES OF CIVILIZATION, IN VARIOUS MUTATIONS; BUT THE PERMANENCY OF ITS WELFARE IS FOUNDED SOLELY AND ESSENTIALLY ON REASON AND JUSTICE

First natural law. It is demonstrated in physical mathematics, that *to the permanent condition of a thing a sort of perfection is requisite, a maximum or* minimum, *arising out of the mode of action of the powers of that thing.* Thus, for example, our Earth could not possess durability, if its centre of gravity did not lie deep within it, and all its powers act to and from this, in equiponderating harmony. Every stable being, therefore, bears in itself, according to this beautiful law of nature, its physical truth, goodness, and necessity, as the grounds of its stability.

Second natural law. It is in like manner demonstrated, *that all perfection and beauty of compound, limited things, or systems of them, rest on such a maximum.* Thus similitude and difference, simplicity in means and diversity in effects, the slightest application of power to attain the most certain or profitable end, form a kind of symmetry and harmonious proportion, universally observed by Nature, in her laws of motion, in the form of her creatures, in the greatest things and in the least; and imitated by the art of man, as far as his powers extend. In this, many rules limit each other, so that what would be greater according to one is diminished by another, till the compound whole attains the most beautiful form, with the greatest economy, and at the same time internal consistency, goodness, and truth. An excellent law, which banishes from Nature everything arbitrary, and all disorder; and displays to us, even in every variable and limited part of the creation, a rule of the highest beauty.

Third natural law. It is equally proved, that, *if a being, or system of beings, be forced out of this permanent condition of its truth, goodness, and beauty, it will again approach it by its internal powers, either in vibrations, or in an asymptote; as out of this state it finds no stability.* The more active and multifarious the powers, the less is the imperceptible straight course of the asymptote possible, and the more violent the vibrations and oscillations, till the disturbed subject attain an equilibrium of its powers, or harmony in their movements, and therewith the permanent condition essential to it.

Now as mankind, both taken as a whole, and in its particular individuals, societies, and nations, is a permanent natural system of the most multifarious living powers; let us examine, wherein its stability consists; in what point its highest beauty, truth, and goodness, unite; and what course it takes, in order to reapproach its permanent condition, on every aberration from it, of which many are exhibited to us by history and experience.

1. The human species is such a copious scheme of energies and capacities, that, as everything in nature rests on the most determinate individuality, its great and numerous capacities could not appear on our planet otherwise than *divided among millions.* Everything has been born, that could be born upon it; and everything has maintained itself, that could acquire a state of permanence according to the laws of Nature. Thus every individual bears within himself that symmetry, for which he is made, and to which he must mould himself, both in his bodily figure, and mental capacities. Human existence appears in every shape and kind, from the most sickly deformity, that can scarcely support life, to the superhuman form of a Grecian demi-

god; from the passionate ardour of the Negro brain, to the capacity for consummate wisdom. Through faults and errors, through education, necessity, and exercise, every mortal seeks the symmetry of his powers; as in this alone the most complete enjoyment of his existence lies: yet few are sufficiently fortunate, to attain it in the purest, happiest manner.

2. As an individual man can subsist of himself but very imperfectly, *a superior maximum of cooperating powers* is formed with every society. These powers contend together in wild confusion, till, agreeably to the unfailing laws of Nature, opposing regulations limit each other, and a kind of equilibrium and harmony of movement takes place. Thus nations modify themselves, according to time, place, and their internal character; each bears in itself the standard of its perfection, totally independent of all comparison with that of others. Now the more pure and fine the maximum on which a people hit, the more useful the objects to which it applied the exertions of its nobler powers, and, lastly, the more firm and exact the bond of union, which most intimately connected all the members of the state, and guided them to this good end; the more stable was the nation itself, and the more brilliant the figure it made in history. The course that we have hitherto taken through certain nations shows how different, according to place, time, and circumstances, was the object for which they strove. With the Chinese it was refined political morality; with the Hindoos, a kind of retired purity, quiet assiduity in labour, and endurance; with the Phenicians, the spirit of navigation, and commercial industry. The culture of the Greeks, particularly at Athens, proceeded on the maximum of sensible beauty, both in arts and manners, in science and in political institutions. In Sparta, and in Rome, men emulated the virtues of the patriot and hero; in each, however, in a very different mode. Now as in all these most depended on time and place, the ancients will scarcely admit of being compared with each other in the most distinguished features of national fame.

3. In all, however, we see the operation of *one principle*, namely *human reason*, which endeavours to produce unity out of multiplicity, order out of disorder, and out of variety of powers and designs one symmetrical and durably beautiful whole. From the shapeless artificial rocks, with which the Chinese ornaments his garden, to the Egyptian pyramid, or the ideal beauty of Greece, the plan and design of a reflecting understanding are everywhere observable, though in very different degrees. The more refined the reflections of this understanding were, and the nearer it came to the point, which is the highest in its kind, and admits no deviation to the right or to the left; the more were its performances to be considered as models, for they contain eternal rules for the human understanding in all ages. Thus nothing of the kind can be conceived superior to an Egyptian pyramid, or to several Greek and Roman works of art. They are simple solutions of certain problems of the understanding, which admit no arbitrary supposition, that the problems are perhaps not yet solved, or might be solved in a

better way; for in them the simple idea of what they ought to be is displayed in the easiest, fullest, and most beautiful manner. Every deviation from them would be a fault; and were they to be repeated and diversified in a thousand modes, we must still return to that single point, which is the highest of its kind.

4. Thus through all the polished nations, that we have hitherto considered, or shall hereafter consider, *a chain of cultivation* may be drawn, flying off in extremely divergent curves. In each it designates increasing and decreasing greatness, and has maximums of every kind. Many of these exclude or limit one another, till at length a certain symmetry takes place in the whole; so that were we to reason from one perfection of any nation concerning another, we should form very treacherous conclusions. Thus, because Athens had exquisite orators, it does not follow, that its form of government must likewise have been the best possible; or that, because the Chinese moralize so excellently, their state must be a pattern for all others. Forms of government refer to a very different maximum, from that of beautiful morals, or a pathetic oration; notwithstanding, at bottom, all things in any nation have a certain connexion, if it be only that of exclusion and limitation. No other maximum, but that of the most perfect bond of union, produces the most happy states; even supposing the people are in consequence obliged to dispense with many shining qualities.

5. But in one and the same nation every maximum of its commendable endeavours ought not and cannot endure forever; since it is but one point in the progress of time. This incessantly moves on; and the more numerous the circumstances, on which the beautiful effect depends, the sooner is it liable to pass away. Happy if its masterpieces remain as rules for future ages; since those that immediately succeed approach them too near, and will probably obliterate by attempting to excel them. Even the most active people frequently sink most speedily from the boiling to the freezing point. [...]

8. Thus the propagation of families and traditions, connected human reason: not as if it were in each individual no more than a fragment of the whole, a whole existing nowhere in one subject, and therefore by no means the end of the Creator; but because the disposition and concatenation of the whole species led to this. As men are propagated, so are animals; yet no general animal reason arises from their generations: but as reason alone gives permanency to mankind, it must be propagated, as the characteristic of the species; for without it the species would cease to be.

9. In the species, as a whole, reason has experienced the same fate, as in its individual members; for of individual members the whole consists. It has often been disturbed by the wild passions of men, acting with still more violence from conjunction, turned out of its way for centuries, and lain as if dormant beneath its ashes. To all these disorders Providence has applied no other remedy, than what she administers to individuals; namely, that each fault should be followed by its correspondent evil, and every act of

indolence, folly, malice, rashness, and injustice, be its own punishment. But as the species appears in collective bodies in such circumstances, children must suffer for the faults of their parents, the people for the folly of their rulers, and posterity for the indolence of their ancestors; and if they will not, or cannot, correct the evil, they may suffer under it for ages.

10. Thus the weal of the whole is the greatest good of each individual: for it is the inherent right and duty of everyone, who suffers under its evils, to ward off these evils from himself, and diminish them for his fellows. Nature has not calculated for sovereigns and states, but for the welfare of men. The former suffer not so speedily for their vices and follies as individuals, because they always reckon only with the whole, in which the miseries of the poor are long suppressed; but the state ultimately suffers, and with so much more violent a concussion. In all these things the laws of retaliation display themselves, as do the laws of motion on the shock of the slightest physical substance; and the greatest sovereign of Europe is not less subject to the natural laws of the human species, than the least of his people. This condition merely binds him, to be an economist of these natural laws; and, by that power, which he enjoys only through the means of other men, to be for other men a wise and good terrestrial divinity.

11. In general history, too, as in the lives of careless individuals, all the follies and vices of mankind are exhausted; till at length they are compelled by necessity, to learn reason and justice. Whatever can happen, happens; and produces, what from its nature it can produce. This law of Nature hinders not even the most eccentric power in its operation; but it confines all by the rule, that one opposing effect destroys another, and what is useful alone ultimately remains. The evil, that destroys another, must submit to order, or destroy itself. The rational and virtuous are uniformly happy in the kingdom of God; for virtue requires external reward, no more than reason covets it. If their works are not accompanied by external success, not to them, but to their age will be the loss: yet neither the discord nor folly of man can forever counteract them; they will succeed, when their time arrives.

12. Still human Reason pursues her course in the species in general: she invents, before she can apply; she discovers, though evil hands may long abuse her discoveries. Abuse will correct itself; and, through the unwearied zeal of ever-growing Reason, disorder will in time become order. By contending against passions, she strengthens and enlightens herself: from being oppressed in this place, she will fly to that, and extend the sphere of her sway over the Earth. There is nothing enthusiastical in the hope, that, wherever men dwell, at some future period will dwell men rational, just, and happy: happy, not through the means of their own reason alone, but of the common reason of their whole fraternal race.

I bend before this lofty sketch of the general wisdom of Nature with regard to the whole of my fellow creatures the more willingly, as I perceive, that it is Nature's universal plan. The law that sustained the mundane system, and formed each crystal, each worm, each flake of snow, formed and sustained also the human species: it made its own nature the basis of its continuance, and progressive action, as long as men shall exist. All the works of God have their stability in themselves, and in their beautiful consistency: for they all repose, within their determinate limits, on the equilibrium of contending powers, by their intrinsic energy, which reduces these to order. [. . .]

The problem of humanity has been solved a thousand ways around me, yet everywhere the result of man's endeavours is the same: "The essence, the object, and the fate of our species, rest on understanding and justice." There is no nobler use of history than this: it unfolds to us as it were the counsels of Fate, and teaches us, insignificant as we are, to act according to God's eternal laws. By teaching us the faults and consequences of every species of irrationality, it assigns us our short and tranquil scene on that great theatre, where Reason and Goodness, contending indeed with wild powers, still, from their nature, create order, and hold on in the path of victory.

Hitherto we have been wandering through the obscure field of ancient nations: we now joyfully advance to approaching day, and view the harvest, that the seed of antiquity has produced for succeeding ages. Rome destroyed the balance of nations; and under her a World bled to death: What new state will arise from this balance destroyed? What new creature will spring from the ashes of so many nations?

NOTES

1. Preface to Buffon's *Nat. Hist.*, vol. III.
2. See Sparmann's *Voyage*, 177.
3. The account given by G. Opitz of his life and imprisonment among a Kalmuc horde at Yaik would be a very descriptive picture of their mode of living, if it were not embellished with so many of the editor's remarks, which give it an air of romance.
4. Besides the many ancient travels in Arabia see those of Pagès, vol. II, 62–87.
5. Römer's *Nachrichten von der Küste Guinea* (Account of the Coast of Guinea), 279.
6. Sparmann's *Voyages*, 73. This humane traveler has interspersed through his work many melancholy accounts of the capture and treatment of slaves (see pp. 195, 612, etc.).
7. See the editor's remarks on the unfortunate Marion's *Voyage à la Mer du Sud* (Voyage to the South Sea): also R. Forster's preface to the *Journal of Cook's Last Voyage* (Berlin, 1781) and the accounts of the conduct of the Europeans.

PART II

Liberalism and Nationalism

5

JOHANN GOTTLIEB FICHTE

The Foundations of Natural Law According to the Principles of the Theory of Science

INTERNATIONAL LAW

1. Every individual has, according to what has been said previously, the right to compel every individual he meets to enter the state with him or else to leave his sphere of activity. If one of them is already within the state whilst the other is not, then the first will compel the other to join his state. If neither of them is a member of the state, then they at least join together to form the beginning of a state. From this the proposition follows: Anyone who is not in a state can be legally compelled by the first state that encounters him either to become a subject within it or to leave its territory.

As a result of this proposition all men who dwell on the earth's surface would eventually be compelled to become united in one single state.

2. It would, however, be just as possible for separate groups of human beings who knew nothing of each other's existence to unite in states in different places. In one place in the world the need for a state would be felt and the remedy taken and in another place the same would be felt and the same remedy taken without the former knowing of the latter or the latter knowing of the former. In this manner several states would arise in the world.

It is a proof that the state is not an arbitrary invention, but is demanded by nature and reason if in all places where human beings live together for a period and become educated to a certain extent, a state is established by them, without their knowing that other men too, outside their sphere, are doing or have done the same.

Since the earth's surface is divided into areas by seas, rivers, and mountains, which also separate men, it was inevitable that several states would arise.

3. The men in these various states know nothing of one another and they therefore do not stand in any real legal relationship to one another since, according to what has been said above, the possibility of all legal relationship is conditioned by real mutual influence consciously exerted.

4. Two citizens from these different states, which have been formed independently of one another, may meet; each will demand from the other guarantee of his security in their existence together, as a result of his complete right which has been proved; each will do this by demanding that the other should subject himself immediately to his sovereign. This demand: "subject yourself immediately to my sovereign" is made by each of them with the same right; for each is in a legal organization. Neither of them, therefore, has a right: for their rights cancel each other out.

But it is still necessary for each to give the other a guarantee. Since this cannot now be given in the manner we have proposed, how can it be given?—They must both subject themselves to a common judge; but each one of them already has his own particular judge.—Their judges must themselves unite and in any matter which affects both men the two judges must become one common legislator to both men: i.e., both their states must pledge mutually to one another to punish any injustice which befalls a citizen of the other state through the fault of a citizen of their own state, and to compensate for it just as if the injustice had been committed against one of their own citizens. [. . .]

16. Several states unite and mutually guarantee themselves their independence and the inviolability of the treaty just described in respect of one another and also against any state which is not a member of their association. The formula of this association would be as follows: We all promise to exterminate with our united might any state, whether it be a member of our association or not, which does not recognize the independence of any one of us, or which breaks a treaty existing between any one of us and itself.

I say the formula of this *association*; for what I have described would be a *federation of nations*, and not an *international state*. The difference exists in the following: An individual can be compelled to enter a state, because outside a state no legal relationship with him is possible. But no state can be compelled to enter this association, since it can also have a legal relationship with others outside this association. It enters such a relationship with its neighbouring states by recognizing them and by concluding with them the treaty which was described above. No state has a right to compel men for the purpose of the *positive protection* of another state.—It is therefore a voluntary association which is in no way founded by compulsion; and such an association is called a federation. [. . .]

20. As this federation extends wider and wider and gradually embraces the whole world, *eternal peace* commences, the only lawful relationship of states; for if war is waged even by states which are their own judges of their cause, injustice can as easily be victorious as right can, or if war is waged under the leadership of a just federation of nations it is merely a means to the ultimate end, the preservation of peace, and in no way the ultimate end itself.

✧ ✧ ✧

Addresses to the German Nation

EIGHTH ADDRESS: WHAT IS A PEOPLE IN THE HIGHER MEANING OF THE WORD, AND WHAT IS LOVE OF FATHERLAND?

[. . .] What is a people? This question is similar to another, and when it is answered the other is answered too. The other question, which is often raised and the answers to which are very different, is this: What is love of fatherland, or, to express it more correctly, what is the love of the individual for his nation?

If we have hitherto proceeded correctly in the course of our investigation, it must here be obvious at once that only the German—the original man, who has not become dead in an arbitrary organization—really has a people and is entitled to count on one, and that he alone is capable of real and rational love for his nation.

The problem having been thus stated, we prepare the way for its solution by the following observation, which seems at first to have no connection with what has preceded it. [. . .]

111. Religion, as we have already remarked in our third address, is able to transcend all time and the whole of this present sensuous life, without thereby causing the slightest detriment to the righteousness, morality, and holiness of the life that is permeated by this belief. Even if one is firmly persuaded that all our effort on this earth will not leave the slightest trace behind it nor yield the slightest fruit, nay more, that the divine effort will even be perverted and become an instrument of evil and of still deeper moral corruption, one can nonetheless continue the effort, solely in order to maintain the divine life that has manifested itself in us, and with a view to a higher order of things in a future world, in which no deed that is of divine origin is lost. Thus the apostles, for example, and the primitive Christians in general, because of their belief in heaven had their hearts entirely set on things above the earth even in their lifetime; and earthly affairs—the State, their earthly fatherland, and nation—were abandoned by them so entirely that they no longer deemed them worthy of attention. [. . .] Although it is true that religion is, for one thing, the consolation of the unjustly oppressed slave, yet this above all is the mark of a religious disposition, viz., to fight against slavery and, as far as possible, to prevent religion from sinking into a mere consolation for captives. [. . .]

112. The natural impulse of man, which should be abandoned only in case of real necessity, is to find heaven on this earth, and to endow his daily work on earth with permanence and eternity; to plant and to culti-

vate the eternal in the temporal—not merely in an incomprehensible fashion or in a connection with the eternal that seems to the mortal eye an impenetrable gulf, but in a fashion visible to the mortal eye itself.

Let me begin with an example that everyone will understand. What man of noble mind is there who does not earnestly wish to relive his own life in a new and better way in his children and his children's children, and to continue to live on this earth, ennobled and perfected in their lives, long after he is dead? Does he not wish to snatch from the jaws of death the spirit, the mind, and the moral sense by virtue of which, perchance, he was in the days of his life a terror to wrongdoing and corruption, and by which he supported righteousness, aroused men from indolence, and lifted them out of their depression? Does he not wish to deposit these qualities, as his best legacy to posterity, in the souls of those he leaves behind, so that they too, in their turn, may someday hand them on again, increased and made more beautiful? What man of noble mind is there who does not want to scatter, by action or thought, a grain of seed for the unending progress in perfection of his race, to fling something new and unprecedented into time, that it may remain there and become the inexhaustible source of new creations? Does he not wish to pay for his place on this earth and the short span of time allotted to him with something that even here below will endure forever, so that he, the individual, although unnamed in history (for the thirst for posthumous fame is contemptible vanity), may yet in his own consciousness and his faith leave behind him unmistakable memories that he, too, was a dweller on the earth? What man of noble mind is there, I said, who does not want this? But only according to the needs of noble-minded men is the world to be regarded and arranged; as they are, so all men ought to be, and for their sake alone does a world exist. They are its kernel, and those of other mind exist only for their sake, being themselves only a part of the transitory world so long as they are of that mind. Such men must conform to the wishes of the noble-minded until they have become like them.

113. Now, what is it that could warrant this challenge and this faith of the noble-minded man in the permanence and eternity of his work? Obviously nothing but an order of things which he can acknowledge as in itself eternal and capable of taking up into itself that which is eternal. Such an order of things, however, is the special spiritual nature of human environment which, although indeed it is not to be comprehended in any conception, nevertheless truly exists, and from which he himself, with all his thoughts and deeds and with his belief in their eternity, has proceeded—the people from which he is descended and among which he was educated and grew up to be what he now is. [. . .] So long as this people exists, every further revelation of the divine will appear and take shape in that people in accordance with the same natural law. But this law itself is further determined by the fact that this man existed and worked as he did, and his

influence has become a permanent part of this law. Hence, everything that
follows will be bound to submit itself to, and connect itself with, the law.
So he is sure that the improvement achieved by him remains in his people
so long as the people itself remains, and that it becomes a permanent determining factor in the evolution of his people.

114. This, then, is a people in the higher meaning of the word, when
viewed from the standpoint of a spiritual world: the totality of men continuing to live in society with each other and continually creating themselves naturally and spiritually out of themselves, a totality that arises together
out of the divine under a certain special law of divine development. It is
the subjection in common to this special law that unites this mass in the
eternal world, and therefore in the temporal also, to a natural totality permeated by itself. The significance of this law itself can indeed be comprehended as a whole, as we have comprehended it by the instance of the
Germans as an original people; it can even be better understood in many of
its further provisions by considering the manifestations of such a people;
but it can never be completely grasped by the mind of anyone, for everyone
continually remains under its influence unknown to himself, although, in
general, it can be clearly seen that such a law exists. This law is "something more" of the world of images, that coalesces absolutely in the phenomenal world with the "something more" of the world of originality that
cannot be imaged; hence, in the phenomenal world neither can be separated again from the other. That law determines entirely and completes
what has been called the national character of a people—that law of the
development of the original and divine. From this it is clear that men who,
as is the case with what we have described as the foreign spirit, do not
believe at all in something original nor in its continuous development, but
only in an eternal recurrence of apparent life, and who by their belief become what they believe, are in the higher sense not a people at all. As
they in fact, properly speaking, do not exist, they are just as little capable
of having a national character.

115. The noble-minded man's belief in the eternal continuance of his
influence even on this earth is thus founded on the hope of the eternal
continuance of the people from which he has developed, and on the characteristic of the people as indicated in the hidden law of which we have
spoken, without admixture of, or corruption by, any alien element which
does not belong to the totality of the function of that law. This characteristic is the eternal thing to which he entrusts the eternity of himself and of
his continuing influence, the eternal order of things in which he places his
portion of eternity; he must will its continuance, for it alone is to him the
means by which the short span of his life here below is extended into continuous life here below. His belief and his struggle to plant what is permanent, his conception in which he comprehends his own life as an eternal
life, is the bond which unites first his own nation, and then, through his

nation, the whole human race, in a most intimate fashion with himself, and brings all their needs within his widened sympathy until the end of time. This is his love for his people, respecting, trusting, and rejoicing in it, and feeling honoured by descent from it. The divine has appeared in it, and that which is original has deemed this people worthy to be made its vesture and its means of directly influencing the world; for this reason there will be further manifestations of the divine in it. Hence, the noble-minded man will be active and effective, and will sacrifice himself for his people. Life merely as such, the mere continuance of changing existence, has in any case never had any value for him; he has wished for it only as the source of what is permanent. But this permanence is promised to him only by the continuous and independent existence of his nation. In order to save his nation he must be ready even to die that it may live, and that he may live in it the only life for which he has ever wished.

116. [. . .] Man is not able to love even himself unless he conceives himself as eternal; apart from that he cannot even respect, much less approve of, himself. Still less can he love anything outside himself without taking it up into the eternity of his faith and of his soul and binding it thereto. He who does not first regard himself as eternal has in him no love of any kind, and, moreover, cannot love a fatherland, a thing which for him does not exist. He who regards his invisible life as eternal, but not his visible life as similarly eternal, may perhaps have a heaven and therein a father-land, but here below he has no fatherland, for this, too, is regarded only in the image of eternity—eternity visible and made sensuous—and for this reason also he is unable to love his fatherland. If none has been handed down to such a man, he is to be pitied. But he to whom a fatherland has been handed down, and in whose soul heaven and earth, visible and invis-ible meet and mingle, and thus, and only thus, create a true and enduring heaven—such a man fights to the last drop of his blood to hand on the precious possession unimpaired to his posterity. [. . .]

117. People and fatherland in this sense, as a support and guarantee of eternity on earth and as that which can be eternal here below, far tran-scend the State in the ordinary sense of the word, viz., the social order as comprehended by mere intellectual conception and as established and main-tained under the guidance of this conception. The aim of the State is posi-tive law, internal peace, and a condition of affairs in which everyone may by diligence earn his daily bread and satisfy the needs of his material exis-tence, so long as God permits him to live. All this is only a means, a condition, and a framework for what love of fatherland really wants, viz., that the eternal and the divine may blossom in the world and never cease to become more and more pure, perfect, and excellent. That is why this love of fatherland must itself govern the State and be the supreme, final, and absolute authority. Its first exercise of this authority will be to limit the State's choice of means to secure its immediate object—internal peace.

To attain this object, the natural freedom of the individual must, of course, be limited in many ways. If the only consideration and intention in regard to individuals were to secure internal peace, it would be well to limit that liberty as much as possible, to bring all their activities under a uniform rule, and to keep them under unceasing supervision. Even supposing such strictness were unnecessary, it could at any rate do no harm, if this were the sole object. It is only the higher view of the human race and of peoples which extends this narrow calculation. Freedom, including freedom in the activities of external life, is the soil in which higher culture germinates; a legislation which keeps the higher culture in view will allow to freedom as wide a field as possible, even at the risk of securing a smaller degree of uniform peace and quietness, and of making the work of government a little harder and more troublesome.

118. [. . .] [I]f a nation could exist in which there were not even a few men of noble mind to make an exception to the general rule [it] would in fact need no freedom at all, for this is needed only for the higher purposes that transcend the State. [. . .] Whether this can be said with truth of any nation at all we may leave undecided; this much is clear, that an original people needs freedom, that this is the security for its continuance as an original people, and that, as it goes on, it is able to stand an ever-increasing degree of freedom without the slightest danger. This is the first matter in respect of which love of fatherland must govern the State itself.

119. Then, too, it must be love of fatherland that governs the State by placing before it a higher object than the usual one of maintaining internal peace, property, personal freedom, and the life and well-being of all. For this higher object alone, and with no other intention, does the State assemble an armed force. When the question arises of making use of this, when the call comes to stake everything that the State, in the narrow conception of the word, sets before itself as object, viz., property, personal freedom, life, and well-being, nay, even the continued existence of the State itself; when the call comes to make an original decision with responsibility to God alone, and without a clear and reasonable idea that what is intended will surely be attained—for this is never possible in such matters—then, and then only, does there live at the helm of the State a truly original and primary life, and at this point, and not before, the true sovereign rights of government enter, like God, to hazard the lower life for the sake of the higher. In the maintenance of the traditional constitution, the laws, and civil prosperity there is absolutely no real true life and no original decision. Conditions and circumstances, and legislators perhaps long since dead, have created these things; succeeding ages go on faithfully in the paths marked out, and so in fact they have no public life of their own; they merely repeat a life that once existed. In such times there is no need of any real government. But, when this regular course is endangered, and it is a question of making decisions in new and unprecedented cases, then there is need of a

life that lives of itself. What spirit is it that in such cases may place itself at the helm, that can make its own decisions with sureness and certainty, untroubled by any hesitation? What spirit has an undisputed right to summon and to order everyone concerned, whether he himself be willing or not, and to compel anyone who resists, to risk everything including his life? Not the spirit of the peaceful citizen's love for the constitution and the laws, but the devouring flame of higher patriotism, which embraces the nation as the vesture of the eternal, for which the noble-minded man joyfully sacrifices himself, and the ignoble man, who only exists for the sake of the other, must likewise sacrifice himself. It is not that love of the citizen for the constitution; that love is quite unable to achieve this, so long as it remains on the level of understanding. Whatever turn events may take, since it pays to govern they will always have a ruler over them. Suppose the new ruler even wants to introduce slavery (and what is slavery if not the disregard for, and suppression of, the characteristics ... of an original people?—but to that way of thinking such qualities do not exist). Then, since it is profitable to preserve the life of slaves, to maintain their numbers and even their well-being, slavery under him will turn out to be bearable if he is anything of a calculator. Their life and their keep, at any rate, they will always have. Then what is there left that they should fight for? After those two things it is peace which they value more than anything. But peace will only be disturbed by the continuance of the struggle. They will, therefore, do anything just to put an end to the fighting, and the sooner the better; they will submit, they will yield; and why should they not? All they have ever been concerned about, and all they have ever hoped from life, has been the continuation of the habit of existing under tolerable conditions. The promise of a life here on earth extending beyond the period of life here on earth—that alone it is which can inspire men even unto death for the fatherland. [. . .]

121. In this belief our earliest common forefathers, the original stock of the new culture, the Germans, as the Romans called them, bravely resisted the on-coming world-dominion of the Romans. Did they not have before their eyes the greater brilliance of the Roman provinces next to them and the more refined enjoyments in those provinces, to say nothing of laws and judges' seats and lictors' axes and rods in superfluity? Were not the Romans willing enough to let them share in all these blessings? In the case of several of their own princes, who did no more than intimate that war against such benefactors of mankind was rebellion, did they not experience proofs of the belauded Roman clemency? To those who submitted the Romans gave marks of distinction in the form of kingly titles, high commands in their armies, and Roman fillets; and if they were driven out by their countrymen, did not the Romans provide for them a place of refuge and a means of subsistence in their colonies? Had they no appreciation of the advantages of Roman civilization *e.g.*, of the superior organization of their

armies, in which even an Arminius did not disdain to learn the trade of war? They cannot be charged with ignorance or lack of consideration of any one of these things. Their descendants, as soon as they could do so without losing their freedom, even assimilated Roman culture, so far as this was possible without losing their individuality. Why, then, did they fight for several generations in bloody wars, that broke out again and again with every renewed force? A Roman writer puts the following expression into the mouth of their leaders: "What was left for them to do, except to maintain their freedom or else to die before they became slaves." Freedom to them meant just this: remaining Germans and continuing to settle their own affairs independently and in accordance with the original spirit of their race, going on with their development in accordance with the same spirit, and propagating this independence in their posterity. All those blessings which the Romans offered them meant slavery to them, because then they would have to become something that was not German, they would have to become half Roman. They assumed as a matter of course that every man would rather die than become half a Roman, and that a true German could only want to live in order to be, and to remain, just a German and to bring up his children as Germans. [. . .]

122. These men, and all others of like mind in the history of the world, won the victory because eternity inspired them, and this inspiration always does, and always must, defeat him who is not so inspired. It is neither the strong right arm nor the efficient weapon that wins victories, but only the power of the soul. He who sets a limit to his sacrifices, and has no wish to venture beyond a certain point, ceases to resist as soon as he finds himself in danger at this point, even though it be one which is vital to him and which ought not to be surrendered. He who sets no limit whatever for himself, but on the contrary stakes everything he has, including the most precious possession granted to dwellers here below, namely, life itself, never ceases to resist, and will undoubtedly win the victory over an opponent whose goal is more limited. A people that is capable of firmly beholding the countenance of that vision from the spiritual world, independence, even though it be only its highest representatives and leaders who are capable of perceiving it—a people capable of being possessed by love of this vision, as our earliest forefathers were, will undoubtedly win the victory over a people that is used, as were the Roman armies, only as the tool of foreign ambition to bring independent people under the yoke; for the former have everything to lose, and the latter merely something to gain. But the way of thinking which regards war as a game of chance, where the stakes are temporal gain or loss, and which fixes the amount to be staked on the cards even before it begins the game—such a way of thinking is defeated even by a whim. [. . .]

123. From all this it follows that the State, merely as the government of human life in its progress along the ordinary peaceful path, is not some-

thing which is primary and which exists for its own sake, but is merely the means to the higher purpose of the eternal, regular, and continuous development of what is purely human in this nation. It follows, too, that the vision and the love of this eternal development, and nothing else, should have the higher supervision of State administration at all times, not excluding periods of peace, and that this alone is able to save the people's independence when it is endangered. In the case of the Germans, among whom as an original people this love of fatherland was possible and, as we firmly believe, did actually exist up to the present time, it has been able up to now to reckon with great confidence on the security of what was most vital to it. As was the case with the ancient Greeks alone, with the Germans the State and the nation were actually separated from each other, and each was represented for itself, the former in the separate German realms and principalities, the latter represented visibly in the imperial connection and invisibly by virtue of a law, not written, but living and valid in the minds of all, a law whose results struck the eye everywhere—in a mass of customs and institutions. Wherever the German language was spoken, everyone who had first seen the light of day in its domain could consider himself as in a double sense a citizen, on the one hand, of the State where he was born and to whose care he was in the first instance commended, and, on the other hand, of the whole common fatherland of the German nation. To everyone it was permitted to seek out for himself in the whole length and breadth of this fatherland the culture most congenial to him or the sphere of action to which his spirit was best adapted; and talent did not root itself like a tree in the place where it first grew up, but was allowed to seek out its own place. Anyone who, because of the turn taken by his own development, became out of harmony with his immediate environment, easily found a willing reception elsewhere, found new friends in place of those he had lost, found time and leisure to make his meaning plainer and perhaps to win over and to reconcile even those who were offended with him, and so to unite the whole. No German-born prince ever took upon himself to mark out for his subjects as their fatherland, with mountains or rivers as boundaries, the territory over which he ruled, and to regard his subjects as bound to the soil. A truth not permitted to find expression in one place might find expression in another, where it might happen that those truths were forbidden which were permitted in the first. So, in spite of the many instances of one-sidedness and narrowness of heart in the separate States, there was nevertheless in Germany, considered as a whole, the greatest freedom of investigation and publication that any people has ever possessed. Everywhere the higher culture was, and continued to be, the result of the interaction of the citizens of all German States: And then this higher culture gradually worked its way down in this form to the people at large, which thus never ceased, broadly speaking, to educate itself by itself. This essential security for the continuance of a German nation was, as we have said, not impaired by any man of German spirit seated at the helm of government; and though with respect to other original decisions things may not always have happened as the higher German love of fatherland could not but wish, at any rate there has been no act in direct opposition to its interests; there has been no attempt to undermine that love or to extirpate it and put a love of the opposite kind in its place.

124. But what if the original guidance of that higher culture, as well as the national power which may not be used except to serve that culture and its continuance, the utilization of German property and blood—what if this should pass from the control of the German spirit to that of another? What would then be the inevitable results?

This is the place where there is special need of the disposition which we invoked in our first address—the disposition not to deceive ourselves wilfully about our own affairs, and the courage to be willing to behold the truth and confess it to ourselves. Moreover, it is still permitted to us, so far as I know, to speak to each other in the German language about the fatherland, or at least to sigh over it, and, in my opinion, we should not do well if we anticipated of our own accord such a prohibition, or if we were ready to restrain our courage, which without doubt will already have taken counsel with itself as to the risk to be run, with the chains forged by the timidity of some individuals.

Picture to yourselves, then, the new power, which we are presupposing, as well-disposed and as benevolent as ever you may wish; make it as good as God Himself; will you be able to impart to it divine understanding as well? Even though it wishes in all earnestness the greatest happiness and well-being of everyone, do you suppose that the greatest well-being it is able to conceive will be the same thing as German well-being? In regard to the main point which I have put before you today, I hope I have been thoroughly well understood by you. I hope that several, while they listened to me, thought and felt that I was only expressing in plain words what has always lain in their minds; I hope that the other Germans who will someday read this will have the same feeling—indeed, several Germans have said practically the same thing before I did, and the unconscious basis of the resistance that has been repeatedly manifested to a purely mechanical constitution and policy of the State has been the view of things which I have presented to you.

6

GEORG WILHELM FRIEDRICH HEGEL

The Philosophy of Right

A. CONSTITUTIONAL LAW

260. The state is the actuality of concrete freedom. But concrete freedom consists in this, that personal individuality and its particular interests not only achieve their complete development and gain explicit recognition for their right (as they do in the sphere of the family and civil society) but, for one thing, they also pass over of their own accord into the interest of the universal, and, for another thing, they know and will the universal; they even recognize it as their own substantive mind; they take it as their end and aim and are active in its pursuit. The result is that the universal does not prevail or achieve completion except along with particular interests and through the cooperation of particular knowing and willing; and individuals likewise do not live as private persons for their own ends alone, but in the very act of willing these they will the universal in the light of the universal, and their activity is consciously aimed at none but the universal end. The principle of modern states has prodigious strength and depth because it allows the principle of subjectivity to progress to its culmination in the extreme of self-subsistent personal particularity, and yet at the same time brings it back to the substantive unity and so maintains this unity in the principle of subjectivity itself.

261. In contrast with the spheres of private rights and private welfare (the family and civil society), the state is from one point of view an external necessity and their higher authority; its nature is such that their laws and interests are subordinate to it and dependent on it. On the other hand, however, it is the end immanent within them, and its strength lies in the unity of its own universal end and aim with the particular interest of individuals, in the fact that individuals have duties to the state in proportion as they have rights against it.

Duty is primarily a relation to something which from my point of view is substantive, absolutely universal. A right, on the other hand, is simply the embodiment of this substance and thus is the particular aspect of it and enshrines my particular freedom. Hence at abstract levels, right and duty appear parcelled out on different sides or in different persons. In the state, as something ethical, as the inter-penetration of the substantive and the particular, my obligation to what is substantive is at the

71

same time the embodiment of my particular freedom. This means that in the state duty and right are united in one and the same relation. But further, since nonetheless the distinct moments acquire in the state the shape and reality peculiar to each, and since therefore the distinction between right and duty enters here once again, it follows that while implicitly, i.e., in form, identical, they at the same time differ in content. In the spheres of personal rights and morality, the necessary bearing of right and duty on one another falls short of actualization; and hence there is at that point only an abstract similarity of content between them, i.e., in those abstract spheres, what is one man's right ought also to be another's, and what is one man's duty ought also to be another's. The absolute identity of right and duty in the state is present in these spheres not as a genuine identity but only as a similarity of content, because in them this content is determined as quite general and is simply the fundamental principle of both right and duty, i.e., the principle that men, as persons, are free. Slaves, therefore, have no duties because they have no rights, and vice versa. (Religious duties are not here in point.)

In the course of the inward development of the concrete Idea, however, its moments become distinguished and their specific determinacy becomes at the same time a difference of content. In the family, the content of a son's duties to his father differs from the content of his rights against him; the content of the rights of a member of civil society is not the same as the content of his duties to his prince and government.

This concept of the union of duty and rights is a point of vital importance and in it the inner strength of states is contained.

Duty on its abstract side goes no farther than the persistent neglect and proscription of a man's particular interest, on the ground that it is the inessential, even the discreditable, moment in his life. Duty, taken concretely as Idea, reveals the moment of particularity as itself essential and so regards its satisfaction as indisputably necessary. In whatever way an individual may fulfil his duty, he must at the same time find his account therein and attain his personal interest and satisfaction. Out of his position in the state, a right must accrue to him whereby public affairs shall be his own particular affair. Particular interests should in fact not be set aside or completely suppressed; instead, they should be put in correspondence with the universal, and thereby both they and the universal are upheld. The *isolated* individual, so far as his duties are concerned, is in subjection; but as a member of *civil society* he finds in fulfilling his duties to it protection of his person and property, regard for his private welfare, the satisfaction of the depths of his being, the consciousness and feeling of himself as a member of the whole; and, insofar as he completely fulfils his duties by performing tasks and services for the *state*, he is upheld and preserved. Take duty abstractly, and the universal's interest would consist simply in the completion as duties of the tasks and services which it exacts.

262. The actual Idea is mind, which, sundering itself into the two ideal spheres of its concept, family and civil society, enters upon its finite phase, but it does so only in order to rise above its ideality and become explicit as infinite actual mind. It is therefore to these ideal spheres that the actual Idea assigns the material of this its finite actuality, viz, human beings as a mass, in such a way that the function assigned to any given individual is visibly mediated by circumstances, his caprice and his personal choice of his station in life.

263. In these spheres in which its moments, particularity and individuality, have their immediate and reflected reality, mind is present as their objective universality glimmering in them as the power of reason in necessity, i.e., as the institutions considered above.

264. Mind is the nature of human beings *en masse* and their nature is

therefore twofold: (1) at one extreme, explicit individuality of consciousness and will, and (2) at the other extreme, universality which knows and wills what is substantive. Hence they attain their right in both these respects only insofar as both their private personality and its substantive basis are actualized. Now in the family and civil society they acquire their right in the first of these respects directly and in the second indirectly, in that (1) they find their substantive self-consciousness in social institutions which are the universal implicit in their particular interests, and (2) the Corporation supplies them with an occupation and an activity directed on a universal end.

265. These institutions are the components of the constitution (i.e., of rationality developed and actualized) in the sphere of particularity. They are, therefore, the firm foundation not only of the state but also of the citizen's trust in it and sentiment towards it. They are the pillars of public freedom since in them particular freedom is realized and rational, and therefore there is *implicitly* present even in them the union of freedom and necessity.

266. But mind is objective and actual to itself not merely as this necessity and as a realm of appearance, but also as the ideality and the heart of this necessity. Only in this way is this substantive universality *aware* of itself as its own object and end, with the result that the necessity appears to itself in the shape of freedom as well.

267. This necessity in ideality is the inner self-development of the Idea. As the substance of the individual subject, it is his political sentiment [patriotism]; in distinction therefrom, as the substance of the objective world, it is the organism of the state, i.e., it is the strictly political state and its constitution.

268. The political sentiment, patriotism pure and simple, is assured conviction with truth as its basis—mere subjective assurance is not the outcome of truth but is only opinion—and a volition which has become habitual. In this sense it is simply a product of the institutions subsisting in the state, since rationality is *actually* present in the state, while action in conformity with these institutions gives rationality its practical proof. This sentiment is, in general, trust (which may pass over into a greater or lesser degree of educated insight), or the consciousness that my interest, both substantive and particular, is contained and preserved in another's (i.e., in the state's) interest and end, i.e., in the other's relation to me as an individual. In this way, this very other is immediately not an other in my eyes, and in being conscious of this fact, I am free.

Patriotism is often understood to mean only a readiness for exceptional sacrifices and actions. Essentially, however, it is the sentiment which, in the relationships of our daily life and under ordinary conditions, habitually recognizes that the community is one's substantive groundwork and end. It is out of this consciousness, which during life's daily round stands the test in all circumstances, that there subsequently also arises the readiness for extraordinary exertions. But since men would often rather be magnanimous than law-abiding, they readily persuade themselves that they possess this exceptional patriotism in order to be sparing in the expression of a genuine patriotic sentiment or to excuse their lack of it. If again this genuine patriotism is looked upon as that which may begin of itself and arise from subjective ideas and thoughts, it is being confused with opinion, because so regarded patriotism is deprived of its true ground, objective reality.

269. The patriotic sentiment acquires its specifically determined content from the various members of the organism of the state. This organism is the development of the Idea to its differences and their objective actuality. Hence these different members are the various powers of the state with their functions and spheres of action, by means of which the universal continually engenders itself, and engenders itself in a necessary way because their specific character is fixed by the nature of the concept. Throughout this process the universal maintains its identity, since it is itself the presupposition of its own production. This organism is the constitution of the state.

270. (1) The abstract actuality or the substantiality of the state consists in the fact that its end is the universal interest as such and the conservation therein of particular interests since the universal interest is the substance of these. (2) But this substantiality of the state is also its *necessity*, since its substantiality is divided into the distinct spheres of its activity which correspond to the moments of its concept, and these spheres, owing to this substantiality, are thus actually fixed determinate characteristics of the state, i.e., its *powers*. (3) But this very substantiality of the state is mind, knowing and willing itself after passing through the forming process of education. The state, therefore, knows what it wills and knows it in its universality, i.e., as something thought. Hence it works and acts by reference to consciously adopted ends, known principles, and laws which are not merely implicit but are actually present to consciousness; and further, it acts with precise knowledge of existing conditions and circumstances, inasmuch as its actions have a bearing on these. [. . .]

322. [. . .] Those who talk of the "wishes" of a collection of people constituting a more or less autonomous state with its own centre, of its "wishes" to renounce this centre and its autonomy in order to unite with others to form a new whole, have very little knowledge of the nature of a collection or of the feeling of selfhood which a nation possesses in its independence.

Thus the dominion which a state has at its first entry into history is this bare autonomy, even if it be quite abstract and without further inner development. For this reason, to have an individual at its head—a patriarch, a chieftain, &c.—is appropriate to this original appearance of the state. [. . .]

324. This destiny whereby the rights and interests of individuals are established as a passing phase, is at the same time the positive moment, i.e., the positing of their absolute, not their contingent and unstable, individuality. This relation and the recognition of it is therefore the individual's substantive duty, the duty to maintain this substantive individuality, i.e., the independence and sovereignty of the state, at the risk and the sacrifice of property and life, as well as of opinion and everything else naturally comprised in the compass of life.

An entirely distorted account of the demand for this sacrifice results from regarding the state as a mere civil society and from regarding its final end as only the security of individual life and property. This security cannot possibly be obtained by the sacrifice of what is to be secured—on the contrary.

The ethical moment in war is implied in what has been said in this Paragraph. War is not to be regarded as an absolute evil and as a purely external accident, which itself therefore has some accidental cause, be it injustices, the passions of nations or the holders of power, &c., or in short, something or other which ought not to be. It is to what is by nature accidental that accidents happen, and the fate whereby they happen is thus a necessity. Here as elsewhere, the point of view from which things seem pure accidents vanishes if we look at them in the light of the concept and philosophy, because philosophy knows accident for a show and sees in it its essence, necessity. It is necessary that the finite—property and life—should be definitely established as accidental, because accidentality is the concept of the finite. From one point of view this necessity appears in the form of the power of nature, and everything is mortal and transient. But in the ethical substance, the state, nature is robbed of this power, and the necessity is exalted to be the work of freedom, to be something ethical. The transience of the finite becomes a willed passing away, and the negativity lying at the roots of the finite becomes the substantive individuality proper to the ethical substance.

War is the state of affairs which deals in earnest with the vanity of temporal goods and concerns—a vanity at other times a common theme of edifying sermonizing. This is what makes it the moment in which the ideality of the particular attains its right and is actualized. War has the higher significance that by its agency, as I have remarked elsewhere, "the ethical health of peoples is preserved in their indifference to the stabilization of finite institutions; just as the blowing of the winds preserves the sea from the foulness which would be the result of a prolonged calm, so also corruption in nations would be the product of prolonged, let alone "perpetual," peace. This, however, is said to be only a philosophic idea, or, to use another common expression, a "justification of Providence," and it is maintained that actual wars require some other justification. On this point, see below.

The ideality which is in evidence in war, i.e., in an accidental relation of a state to a foreign state, is the same as the ideality in accordance with which the domestic powers of the state are organic moments in a whole. This fact appears in history in various forms, e.g., successful wars have checked domestic unrest and consolidated the power of the state at home. Other phenomena illustrate the same point: e.g., peoples unwilling or afraid to tolerate sovereignty at home have been subjugated from abroad, and they have struggled for their independence with the less glory and success the less they have been able previously to organize the powers of the state in home affairs—their freedom has died from the fear of dying; states whose autonomy has been guaranteed not by their armed forces but in other ways (e.g., by their disproportionate smallness in comparison with their neighbours) have been able to subsist with a constitution of their own which by itself would not have assured peace in either home or foreign affairs. [. . .]

B. INTERNATIONAL LAW

331. The nation-state is mind in its substantive rationality and immediate actuality and is therefore the absolute power on earth. It follows that every state is sovereign and autonomous against its neighbours. It is entitled in the first place and without qualification to be sovereign from their point of view, i.e., to be recognized by them as sovereign. At the same time,

however, this title is purely formal, and the demand for this recognition of the state, merely on the ground that it is a state, is abstract. Whether a state is in fact something absolute depends on its content, i.e., on its constitution and general situation; and recognition, implying as it does an identity of both form and content, is conditional on the neighbouring state's judgment and will. [. . .]

333. The fundamental proposition of international law (i.e., the universal law which ought to be absolutely valid between states, as distinguished from the particular content of positive treaties) is that treaties, as the ground of obligations between states, ought to be kept. But since the sovereignty of a state is the principle of its relations to others, states are to that extent in a state of nature in relation to each other. Their rights are actualized only in their particular wills and not in a universal will with constitutional powers over them. This universal proviso of international law therefore does not go beyond an ought-to-be, and what really happens is that international relations in accordance with treaty alternate with the severance of these relations.

There is no Praetor to judge between states; at best there may be an arbitrator or a mediator, and even he exercises his functions contingently only, i.e., in dependence on the particular wills of the disputants. Kant had an idea for securing "perpetual peace" by a League of Nations to adjust every dispute. It was to be a power recognized by each individual state, and was to arbitrate in all cases of dissension in order to make it impossible for disputants to resort to war in order to settle them. This idea presupposes an accord between states; this would rest on moral or religious or other grounds and considerations, but in any case would always depend ultimately on a particular sovereign will and for that reason would remain infected with contingency.

334. It follows that if states disagree and their particular wills cannot be harmonized, the matter can only be settled by war. A state through its subjects has widespread connexions and many-sided interests, and these may be readily and considerably injured; but it remains inherently indeterminable which of these injuries is to be regarded as a specific breach of treaty or as an injury to the honour and autonomy of the state. The reason for this is that a state may regard its infinity and honour as at stake in each of its concerns, however minute, and it is all the more inclined to susceptibility to injury the more its strong individuality is impelled as a result of long domestic peace to seek and create a sphere of activity abroad. [. . .]

337. The substantial welfare of the state is its welfare as a particular state in its specific interest and situation and its no less special foreign affairs, including its particular treaty relations. Its government therefore is a matter of particular wisdom, not of universal Providence (compare Remark to Paragraph 324). Similarly, its aim in relation to other states and its principle for justifying wars and treaties is not a universal thought (the thought of philanthropy) but only its actually injured or threatened welfare as something specific and peculiar to itself.

At one time the opposition between morals and politics, and the demand that the latter should conform to the former, were much canvassed. On this point only a general remark is required here. The welfare of a state has claims to recognition totally different from those of the welfare of the individual. The ethical substance, the state, has its determinate being, i.e., its right, directly embodied in something existent, something not abstract but concrete, and the principle of its conduct and behaviour can only be this concrete existent and not one of the many universal thoughts supposed to be moral commands. When politics is alleged to clash with morals and so to be always wrong, the doctrine propounded rests on superficial ideas about morality, the nature of the state, and the state's relation to the moral point of view.

338. The fact that states reciprocally recognize each other as states remains, even in war—the state of affairs when rights disappear and force and chance hold sway—a bond wherein each counts to the rest as something absolute. Hence in war, war itself is characterized as something which ought to pass away. It implies therefore the proviso of the *jus gentium* that the possibility of peace be retained (and so, for example, that envoys must be respected), and, in general, that war be not waged against domestic institutions, against the peace of family and private life, or against persons in their private capacity.

339. Apart from this, relations between states (e.g., in wartime, reciprocal agreements about taking prisoners; in peacetime, concessions of rights to subjects of other states for the purpose of private trade and intercourse, &c.) depend principally upon the customs of nations, custom being the inner universality of behaviour maintained in all circumstances.

340. It is as particular entities that states enter into relations with one another. Hence their relations are on the largest scale a maelstrom of external contingency and the inner particularity of passions, private interests and selfish ends, abilities and virtues, vices, force, and wrong. All these whirl together, and in their vortex the ethical whole itself, the autonomy of the state, is exposed to contingency. The principles of the national minds are wholly restricted on account of their particularity, for it is in this particularity that, as existent individuals, they have their objective actuality and their self-consciousness. Their deeds and destinies in their reciprocal relations to one another are the dialectic of the finitude of these minds, and out of it arises the universal mind, the mind of the world, free from all restriction, producing itself as that which exercises its right—and its right is the highest right of all—over these finite minds in the "history of the world which is the world's court of judgment."

C. WORLD HISTORY

347. The nation to which is ascribed a moment of the Idea in the form of a natural principle is entrusted with giving complete effect to it in the advance of the self-developing self-consciousness of the world mind. This nation is dominant in world history during this one epoch, and it is only once that it can make its hour strike. In contrast with this its absolute right of being the vehicle of this present stage in the world mind's develop-

ment, the minds of the other nations are without rights, and they, along with those whose hour has struck already, count no longer in world history.

The history of a single world-historical nation contains (1) the development of its principle from its latent embryonic stage until it blossoms into the self-conscious freedom of ethical life and presses in upon world history; and (2) the period of its decline and fall, since it is its decline and fall that signalizes the emergence in it of a higher principle as the pure negative of its own. When this happens, mind passes over into the new principle and so marks out another nation for world-historical significance. After this period, the declining nation has lost the interest of the absolute; it may indeed absorb the higher principle positively and begin building its life on it, but the principle is only like an adopted child, not like a relative to whom its ties are immanently vital and vigorous. Perhaps it loses its autonomy, or it may still exist, or drag out its existence, as a particular state or a group of states and involve itself without rhyme or reason in manifold enterprises at home and battles abroad. [. . .]

349. A nation does not begin by being a state. The transition from a family, a horde, a clan, a multitude, &c., to political conditions is the realization of the Idea in the form of that nation. Without this form, a nation, as an ethical substance—which is what it is implicitly, lacks the objectivity of possessing in its own eyes and in the eyes of others, a universal and universally valid embodiment in laws, i.e., in determinate thoughts, and as a result it fails to secure recognition from others. So long as it lacks objective law and an explicitly established rational constitution, its autonomy is formal only and is not sovereignty. [. . .]

351. The same consideration justifies civilized nations in regarding and treating as barbarians those who lag behind them in institutions which are the essential moments of the state. Thus a pastoral people may treat hunters as barbarians, and both of these are barbarians from the point of view of agriculturists, &c. The civilized nation is conscious that the rights of barbarians are unequal to its own and treats their autonomy as only a formality.

When wars and disputes arise in such circumstances, the trait which gives them a significance for world history is the fact that they are struggles for recognition in connexion with something of specific intrinsic worth.

352. The concrete Ideas, the minds of the nations, have their truth and their destiny in the concrete Idea which is absolute universality, i.e., in the world mind. Around its throne they stand as the executors of its actualization and as signs and ornaments of its grandeur. As mind, it is nothing but its active movement towards absolute knowledge of itself and therefore towards freeing its consciousness from the form of natural immediacy and so coming to itself. [. . .]..world mind. Around its throne they stand as the executors of its actualization and as signs and ornaments of its grandeur. As mind, it is nothing but its active movement towards absolute knowledge of itself and therefore towards freeing its consciousness from the form of natural immediacy and so coming to itself. [. . .]

◇ ◇ ◇

The Philosophy of World History

The spirit is essentially individual, but in the field of world history, we are not concerned with particulars and need not confine ourselves to individual instances or attempt to trace everything back to them. The spirit in history is an individual which is both universal in nature and at the same time determinate: In short, it is the nation in general, and the spirit we are concerned with is the spirit of the nation. But the spirits of nations differ in their own conceptions of themselves, in the relative superficiality or profundity with which they have comprehended and penetrated the nature of spirit. The right which governs the ethical existence of nations is the spirit's consciousness of itself; the nations are the concepts which the spirit has formed of itself. Thus it is the conception of the spirit which is realized in history. The national consciousness varies according to the extent to which the spirit knows itself; and the ultimate phase of its consciousness, on which everything depends, is the recognition that man is free. The spirit's own consciousness must realize itself in the world; the material or soil in which it is realized in none other than the general consciousness, the consciousness of the nation. This consciousness encompasses and guides all the aims and interests of the nation, and it is on it that the nation's rights, customs, and religion depend. It is the substance which underlies the spirit of the nation, even if individual human beings are unaware of it and simply take its existence for granted. It is a form of necessity, for the individual is brought up within its atmosphere and does not know anything else. But it is not to be identified with education or with the results of education; for this consciousness emanates from the individual himself and is not instilled into him by others: The individual exists within this substance. This universal substance is not of a wordly nature and no worldly agency can successfully oppose it. No individual can transcend it, and although the individual may be able to distinguish between himself and others of his kind, he can make no such distinction between himself and the spirit of the nation. He may surpass many others in resourcefulness, but he cannot surpass the spirit of the nation. Only those who know the spirit of the nation and shape their actions in accordance with it can be described as truly resourceful.[1] They are the great ones of the nation; they lead it in accordance with the dictates of the universal spirit. Thus, individuality falls outside our province, except in the case of those individuals who translate the will of the national spirit into reality. If we wish to treat history philosophically, we must avoid such expressions as "this state would not have collapsed if there had been someone

who . . ." etc. Individuals fade into insignificance beside the universal substance, and it creates for itself the individuals it requires to carry out its
ends. But no individuals can prevent the preordained from happening.

On the one hand, the spirit of the nation is in essence particular, yet on
the other, it is identical with the absolute universal spirit—for the latter is
One. The world spirit is the spirit of the world as it reveals itself through
the human consciousness; the relationship of men to it is that of single
parts to the whole which is their substance. And this world spirit corresponds to the divine spirit, which is the absolute spirit. Since God is omnipresent, he is present in everyone and appears in everyone's consciousness;
and this is the world spirit. The particular spirit of a particular nation may
perish; but it is a link in the chain of the world spirit's development, and
this universal spirit cannot perish. The spirit of the nation is therefore the
universal spirit in a particular form; the world spirit transcends this particular form, but it must assume it insofar as it exists, for it takes on a particular
aspect as soon as it has actual being or existence. The particular character
of the national spirit varies according to the kind of awareness of spirit it
has attained. In everyday parlance, we say: "This nation had such and such
a conception of God, such and such a religion or system of justice, and
such and such views on ethics." We treat all these things as if they were
external objects which a nation had in its possession. But we can tell even
at a superficial glance that they are of a spiritual nature, so that the only
kind of reality they can have is a spiritual one, i.e., through the spirit's
consciousness of spirit.

But this, as already mentioned, is equivalent to self-consciousness, which
can easily give rise to a misunderstanding, for I may wrongly imagine that,
in the act of self-consciousness, it is my temporal individuality that I am
conscious of. One of the difficulties of philosophy is that most people think
it deals only with the particular and empirical existence of the individual.
But spirit, in its consciousness of itself, is free; in this realization, it has
overcome the limits of temporal existence and enters into relationship with
pure being, which is also its own being. If the divine being were not the
essence of man and nature, it would not in fact be a being at all. Self-
consciousness, then, is a philosophical concept, which can only attain its
full determinate character in philosophical discourse. If we take this as established, we may further conclude that the determinate national consciousness is the nation's consciousness of its own being. The spirit is primarily its
own object; but as long as it is this only in our eyes, and has not yet
recognized itself in its object, it is not yet its own object in the true sense.
Its ultimate aim, however, is the attainment of knowledge; for the sole endeavour of spirit is to know what it is in and for itself, and to reveal itself
to itself in its true form. It seeks to create a spiritual world in accordance
with its own concept, to fulfil and realize its own true nature, and to produce religion and the state in such a way that it will conform to its own

concept and be truly itself or become its own Idea. (The Idea is the reality of the concept, of which it is merely a reflection or expression.) This, then, is the universal goal of the spirit and of history; and just as the seed bears within it the whole nature of the tree and the taste and form of its fruits, so also do the first glimmerings of spirit contain virtually the whole of history.

Given this abstract definition, *we can say that world history is the record of the spirit's efforts to attain* **knowledge** *of what it is* **in itself**. *The Orientals do not know that the spirit or man as such is free in themselves. And because they do not know this, they are not themselves free. They only know that One is free; but for this very reason, such freedom is mere arbitrariness, savagery, and brutal passion, or a milder and tamer version of this which is itself only an accident of nature, and equally arbitrary. This One is therefore merely a despot, not a free man and a human being. The consciousness of freedom first awoke among the* **Greeks**, *and they were accordingly free; but, like the Romans, they only knew that* **Some**, *and not all men as such, are free. Plato and Aristotle did not know this either; thus the Greeks not only had slaves, on which their life and the continued existence of their estimable freedom depended, but their very freedom itself was on the one hand only a fortuitous, undeveloped, transient, and limited efflorescence, and, on the other, a harsh servitude of all that is humane and proper to man. The* **Germanic** *nations, with the rise of Christianity, were the first to realize that man is by nature free, and that freedom of the spirit is his very essence. This consciousness first dawned in religion, in the innermost region of the spirit; but to incorporate the same principle into secular existence was a further problem, whose solution and application require long and arduous cultural exertions. For example, slavery did not immediately [come to an end] with the adoption of Christianity; still less did freedom at once predominate in states, or governments and constitutions become rationally organized and founded upon the principle of freedom. This* **application** *of the principle to secular affairs, the penetration and transformation of secular life by the principle of freedom, is the long process of which history itself [is made up]. I have already drawn attention to this* **distinction** *between the* **principle** *as such and its application—i.e., its* **introduction** *and* **execution** *in the actual world of the spirit and of life—and we shall return to it again shortly. It is one of the basic articles of philosophical science, and its vital importance must not be overlooked. The same distinction applies not only to the* **Christian** *principle of the self-consciousness of freedom which I have mentioned provisionally here, it applies just as essentially to the principle of* **freedom** *in general. World history is the progress of the consciousness of freedom— a progress whose necessity it is our business to comprehend.*

These general remarks on the different degrees of knowledge of freedom—firstly, that of the Orientals, who knew only that **One** *is free, then that of the Greek and Roman world, which knew that* **Some** *are free, and finally,* **our own** *knowledge that* **All** *men as such are free, and that* **man** *is by nature free—supply us with the divisions we shall observe in our survey of world history and which will help* *us to organize our discussion of it. But these are only provisional remarks thrown out in passing; several other concepts must first be explained.*

The spirit's consciousness of its freedom (which is the precondition of the reality of this **freedom**) has been defined as spiritual reason in its determinate form, hence as the destiny of the spiritual world, and—since the latter is the substantial world and the physical world [is] subordinated to it (or, in speculative terminology, has no truth in comparison with it)—as the ultimate end of the world in general. But that this freedom, as defined above, still remains an indefinite term which is capable of infinite interpretations, and that, since it is the highest concept of all, it is open to an infinite number of misunderstandings, confusions, and errors and covers every possible kind of extravagance—all this has never been known and experienced so fully as in the present age; but we must make do for the moment with this general definition. We have also stressed the importance of the infinite difference between the principle—i.e., that which exists only *in itself*—and its realization. For freedom in itself carries with it the infinite necessity of attaining consciousness—for freedom, by definition, is self-knowledge—and hence of realizing itself: It is itself the end of its own operations, and the sole end of the spirit.

The substance of the spirit is freedom. From this, we can infer that its end in the historical process is the freedom of the subject to follow its own conscience and morality, and to pursue and implement its own universal ends; it also implies that the subject has infinite value and that it must become conscious of its supremacy. The end of the world spirit is realized in substance through the freedom of each individual.

The spirits of the nations are the links in the process whereby the spirit arrives at free recognition of itself. Nations, however, exist for themselves—for we are not concerned here with spirit in itself—and as such, they have a natural existence. Insofar as they are nations, their principles are natural ones; and since their principles differ, the nations themselves are also naturally different. Each has its own principle which it seeks to realize as its end; if it has attained this end, it has no further task to perform in the world.

The spirit of a nation should thus be seen as the development of a principle; this principle is at first bound up with an indistinct impulse which gradually works its way out and seeks to attain objective reality. A natural spirit of this kind is a determinate spirit, a concrete whole; it must gain recognition in its determinate form. Since it is a spirit, it can only be understood in spiritual terms, by means of thought, and it is we who understand it in this way; the next step is for the national spirit to understand itself in turn by the same means. We must therefore examine the determinate concept or principle of the spirit in question. This principle is extremely rich in content, and it assumes many forms in the course of its development; for the spirit is living and active, and is concerned only with it own productions. The spirit, as it advances towards its realization, towards self-satisfaction and self-knowledge, is the sole motive force behind all the deeds and aspirations of the nation. Religion, knowledge, the arts, and the destinies and events of history are all aspects of its evolution. This, and not the natural influences at work upon it (as the derivation of the word *natio* from *nasci* might suggest), determines the nation's character. In its active operations, the national spirit at first knows only the ends of its determinate reality, but not its own nature. But it is nevertheless endowed with an impulse to formulate its thoughts. Its supreme activity is thought, so that when it reaches the height of its powers, its aim is to comprehend itself. The ultimate aim of the spirit is to know itself, and to comprehend itself not merely intuitively but also in terms of thought. It must and will succeed in its task; but this very success is also its downfall, and this in turn heralds the emergence of a new phase and a new spirit. The individual national spirit fulfils itself by merging with the principle of another nation, so that we can observe a progression, growth and succession from one national principle to another. The task of philosophical world history is to discover the continuity within this movement. [. . .]

As we trace the passage of one national spirit into the other, we should note that the universal spirit as such does not die; it dies only in its capacity as a national spirit. As a national spirit, it belongs to world history, and its task is to attain knowledge of its own function and to comprehend itself by means of thought. This thought or reflection eventually ceases to respect its immediate existence, for it realizes that the principle behind it is a particular one; and as a result, the subjective spirit becomes divorced from the universal spirit. Individuals withdraw into themselves and pursue their own ends, and this, as already remarked, is the nation's undoing: Each individual sets himself his own ends as his passions dictate. But as the spirit withdraws into itself, thought emerges as a reality in its own right, and the learned disciplines flourish. Thus learning and the degeneration or downfall of a nation always go hand in hand.

But at the same time, a new and higher principle emerges. Division contains and carries with it the need for unification, because the spirit is itself one. It is a living thing, and is powerful enough to create the unity it requires. The opposition or contradiction between the spirit and the lower principle gives rise to a higher factor. For example, when their culture was at its height, the Greeks, for all the untroubled serenity of their manners, had no concept of universal freedom; they did have their own καθῆκον, their idea of propriety, but they had no real morality or conscience. Morality, which rests on a reflexive movement of the spirit, a turning in of the spirit upon itself, did not yet exist; it dates only from the time of Socrates. But as soon as reflection supervened and individuals withdrew into themselves and dissociated themselves from established custom to live their own lives according to their own wishes, degeneration and contradiction arose. But the spirit cannot remain in a state of opposition. It seeks unification, and in this unification lies the higher principle. History is the process whereby the spirit discovers itself and its own concept. Thus division contains within it the higher principle of consciousness; but this higher principle also has another side to it which does not enter the consciousness at all. For there can be no consciousness of opposition until the principle of personal freedom is already present. [. . .]

The spirit is free; and the aim of the world spirit in world history is to realize it essence and to obtain the prerogative of freedom. Its activity is that of knowing and recognizing itself, but it accomplishes this in gradual stages rather than at a single step. Each new individual national spirit represents a new stage in the conquering march of the world spirit as it wins its way to consciousness and freedom. The death of a national spirit is a transition to new life, but not as in nature, where the death of one individual gives life to another individual of the same kind. On the contrary, the world spirit progresses from lower determinations to higher principles and concepts of its own nature, to more fully developed expressions of its Idea. [. . .]

The worth of individuals is measured by the extent to which they reflect and represent the national spirit, and have adopted a particular station within the affairs of the state as a whole. And one of the conditions of freedom in a state is that this decision should be left to the individual, and that the occupation he takes up should not be laid down in advance by any kind of caste system. The individual's morality will then consist in fulfilling the duties imposed upon him by his social station; these can be recognized without difficulty, and their particular form will depend on the particular class to which the individual belongs. The substantial nature of such relationships, i.e., the rational element they embody, is universally known, and its expression is what we call duty. [. . .]

The great individuals of world history . . . are those who seize upon this higher universal and make it their own end. It is they who realize the end appropriate to the higher concept of the spirit. To this extent, they may be called heroes. They do not find their aims and vocation in the calm and regular system of the present, in the hallowed order of things as they are. Indeed, their justification does not lie in the prevailing situation, for they draw their inspiration from another source, from that hidden spirit whose hour is near but which still lies beneath the surface and seeks to break out without yet having attained an existence in the present. [. . .]

The spiritual individual, the nation—insofar as it is internally differentiated so as to form an organic whole—is what we call the state. This term is ambiguous, however, for the state and the laws of the state, as distinct from religion, science, and art, usually have purely political associations. But in this context, the word "state" is used in a more comprehensive sense, just as we use the word "realm" to describe spiritual phenomena. A nation should therefore be regarded as a spiritual individual, and it is not primarily its external side that will be emphasized here, but rather what we have previously called the spirit of the nation, i.e., its self-consciousness in relation to its own truth and being, and what it recognizes as truth in the absolute sense—in short, those spiritual powers which live within the nation and rule over it. The universal which emerges and becomes conscious within the state, the form to which everything in it is assimilated, is what we call in general the nation's culture. But the determinate content which this universal form acquires and which is contained in the concrete reality which constitutes the state is the national spirit itself. The real state is animated by this spirit in all its particular transactions, wars, institutions, etc. This spiritual content is a firm and solid nucleus which is completely removed from the world of arbitrariness, particularities, caprices, individuality, and contingency; whatever is subject to the latter is not part of the nation's character: It is like the dust which blows over a town or a field or hangs above it without changing it in any essential way. Besides, this spiritual content is the essential being of each individual, as well as constituting the spirit of the nation. It is the sacred bond which links men and spirits together. It remains one and the same life, one great object, one great end, and one great content, on which all private happiness and all private volition depend.

Thus, the state is the more specific object of world history in general, in which freedom attains its objectivity and enjoys the fruits of this objectivity. For the law is the objectivity of the spirit, and the will in its true expression; and only that will which obeys the law is free: for it obeys itself and is self-sufficient and therefore free. When the state or fatherland constitutes a community of existence, and when the subjective will of men subordinates itself to laws, the opposition between freedom and necessity disappears. The rational, as the substance of things, is necessary, and we are free insofar as we recognize it as law and follow it as the substance of our own being; the objective and the subjective will are then reconciled, forming a single, undivided whole. For the ethical character of the state is not that of individual morality, which is a product of reflection and subject to personal conviction; reflective morality is more accessible to the modern world, whereas the true ethics of antiquity are rooted in the fact that everyone adhered to his prescribed duty. An Athenian citizen did virtually by instinct what was expected of him; if I reflect on the object of my activity, however, I must be conscious that my will has assented to it. But ethical life is duty, the substantial right, or second nature (as it has justly been called); for man's first nature is his immediate animal existence.

NOTE

1. Hegel's term is *geistreich* (literally, "rich in spirit"). It is impossible to reproduce in English the relationship between *geistreich* and *Geist* ("spirit"), which Hegel is here exploiting.

7

GIUSEPPE MAZZINI

The Duties of Man

I: TO THE ITALIAN WORKING-MEN

[. . .] For the last fifty years whatever has been done for the cause of progress and of good against absolute governments and hereditary aristocracies has been done in the name of the Rights of Man; in the name of liberty as the means, and of *well-being* as the object of existence. All the acts of the French Revolution and of the revolutions which followed and imitated it were consequences of a Declaration of the Rights of Man. All the works of the philosophers who prepared it were based upon a theory of liberty, and upon the need of making known to every individual his own rights. All the revolutionary schools preached that man is born for happiness, that he has the right to seek it by all the means in his power, that no one has the right to impede him in this search, and that he has the right of overthrowing all the obstacles which he may encounter on his path. And the obstacles were overthrown; liberty was conquered. It endured for years in many countries; in some it still endures. Has the condition of the people improved? Have the millions who live by the daily labour of their hands gained the least fraction of the well-being hoped for and promised to them?

No; the condition of the people has not improved; rather it has grown and grows worse in nearly every country, and especially here where I write the price of the necessaries of life has gone on continually rising, the wages of the working-man in many branches of industry falling, and the population multiplying. In nearly every country the lot of workers has become more uncertain, more precarious, and the labour crises which condemn thousands of working-men to idleness for a time have become more frequent. The yearly increase of emigration from one country to another, and from Europe to other parts of the world, and the ever-growing number of beneficent institutions, the increase of poor rates and provisions for the destitute, are enough to prove this. The latter prove also that public attention is waking more and more to the ills of the people; but their inability to lessen those ills to any visible extent points to a no less continual increase of poverty among the classes which they endeavour to help.

And nevertheless, in these last fifty years, the sources of social wealth and the sum of material blessings have steadily increased. Production has doubled.

Commerce, amid continual crises, inevitable in the utter absence of organization, has acquired a greater force of activity and a wider sphere for its operations. Communication has almost everywhere been made secure and rapid, and the price of commodities has fallen in consequence of the diminished cost of transport. And, on the other hand, the idea of rights inherent in human nature is today generally accepted; accepted in word and, hypocritically, even by those who seek to evade it in deed. Why, then, has the condition of the people not improved? Why is the consumption of products, instead of being divided equally among all the members of the social body in Europe, concentrated in the hands of a small number of men forming a new aristocracy? Why has the new impulse given to industry and commerce produced, not the well-being of the many, but the luxury of the few?

The answer is clear to those who will look a little more closely into things. Men are creatures of education, and act only according to the principle of education given to them. The men who have promoted revolutions hitherto have based them upon the idea of the rights belonging to the individual: The revolutions conquered liberty—individual liberty, liberty of teaching, liberty of belief, liberty of trade, liberty in everything and for everybody. But of what use was the recognition of their rights to those who had no means of exercising them? What did liberty of teaching mean to those who had neither time nor means to profit by it, or liberty of trade to those who had nothing to trade with, neither capital nor credit? In all the countries where these principles were proclaimed society was composed of a small number of individuals who possessed the land, the credit, the capital, and of vast multitudes of men who had nothing but their own hands and were forced to give the labour of them to the former class, on any terms, in order to live, and forced to spend the whole day in material and monotonous toil. For these, constrained to battle with hunger, what was liberty but an illusion and a bitter irony? To make it anything else it would have been necessary for the men of the well-to-do classes to consent to reduce the hours of labour, to increase the remuneration, to institute free and uniform education for the masses, to make the instruments of labour accessible to all, and to provide a bonus fund for the working-man endowed with capacity and good intentions. But why should they do it? Was not *well-being* the supreme object in life? Were not material blessings desirable before all other things? Why should they lessen their own enjoyment for the advantage of others? Let those who could, help themselves. When society has secured to everybody who can use them the free exercise of the rights belonging to human nature, it does all that is required of it. If there be anyone who is unable from the fatality of his own circumstances to exercise any of these rights, he must resign himself and not blame others.

It was natural that they should say thus, and thus, in fact, they did say. And this attitude of mind towards the poor in the classes privileged by fortune soon became the attitude of every individual towards every other.

Each man looked after his own rights and the improvement of his own condition without seeking to provide for others; and when his rights clashed with those of others, there was war; not a war of blood, but of gold and of cunning; a war less manly than the other, but equally destructive; cruel war, in which those who had the means and were strong relentlessly crushed the weak or the unskilled. In this continual warfare, men were educated in egoism and in greed for material welfare exclusively. Liberty of belief destroyed all community of faith. Liberty of education produced moral anarchy. Men without a common tie, without unity of religious belief and of aim, and whose sole vocation was enjoyment, sought every one his own road, not heeding if in pursuing it they were trampling upon the heads of their brothers—brothers in name and enemies in fact. To this we are come today, thanks to the theory of *rights.*

Certainly rights exist; but where the rights of an individual come into conflict with those of another, how can we hope to reconcile and harmonize them, without appealing to something superior to all rights? And where the rights of an individual, or of many individuals, clash with the rights of the Country, to what tribunal are we to appeal? If the right to *well-being*, to the greatest possible well-being, belongs to every living person, who will solve the difficulty between the working-man and the manufacturer? If the right to existence is the first and inviolable right of every man, who shall demand the sacrifice of that existence for the benefit of other men? Will you demand it in the name of Country, of Society, of the multitude of your brothers? What is Country, in the opinion of those of whom I speak, but the place in which our individual rights are most secure? What is Society but a collection of men who have agreed to bring the strength of the many in support of the rights of each? And after having taught the individual for fifty years that Society is established for the purpose of *assuring to him the exercise of his rights*, would you ask him to sacrifice them all to Society, to submit himself, if need be, to continuous toil, to prison, to exile, for the sake of improving it? After having preached to him everywhere that the object of life is *well-being*, would you all at once bid him give up well-being and life itself to free his country from the foreigner, or to procure better conditions for a class which is not his own? After having talked to him for years of *material* interests, how can you maintain that, finding wealth and power in his reach, he ought not to stretch out his hand to grasp them even to the injury of his brothers? [. . .]

[. . .] The vital question agitating our century is a question of education. What we have to do is not to establish a new order of things by violence. An order of things so established is always tyrannical even when it is better than the old. *We have to overthrow by force the brute force which opposes itself today to every attempt at improvement,* and then propose for the approval of the nation, free to express its will, what we believe to be the best order of things and by every possible means educate men to develop it and act in conformity with it. The theory of *rights* enables us to rise and overthrow obstacles, but not to found a strong and lasting accord between all the elements which compose the nation. With the theory of happiness, of *well-being*, as the primary aim of existence we shall only form egoistic men, worshipers of the material, who will carry the old passions into the new order of things and corrupt it in a few months. We have therefore to find a principle of education superior to any such theory, which shall guide men to better things, teach them constancy in self-sacrifice, and link them with their fellow men without making them dependent on the ideas of a single man or on the strength of all. And this principle is Duty. We must convince men that they, sons of one only God, must obey one only law, here on earth; that each one of them must live, not for himself, but for others; that the object of their life is not to be more or less happy, but to make themselves and others better; that to fight against injustice and error for the benefit of their brothers is not only a *right*, but a *duty*; a duty not to be neglected without sin,—the duty of their whole life.

Italian Working-men, my Brothers! understand me fully. When I say that the knowledge of their *rights* is not enough to enable men to effect any appreciable or lasting improvement, I do not ask you to renounce these rights; I only say that they cannot exist except as a consequence of duties fulfilled, and that one must begin with the latter in order to arrive at the former. And when I say that by proposing *happiness, well-being*, or *material* interest as the aim of existence, we run the risk of producing egoists, I do not mean that you should never strive after these things. I say that material interests pursued alone, and not as a means, but as an end, lead always to this most disastrous result. [. . .] Material improvement is essential, and we shall strive to win it for ourselves; but not because the one thing necessary for man is to be well fed and housed, but rather because you cannot have a sense of your own dignity or any moral development while you are engaged, as at the present day, in a continual duel with want. [. . .] You have not the rights of citizens, nor any participation, by election or by vote, in the laws which regulate your actions and your life: How should you feel the pride of citizenship or have any zeal for the State, or sincere affection for the laws? Justice is not dealt out to you with the same equal hand as to the other classes: Whence, then, are you to learn respect and love for justice? Society treats you without a shadow of sympathy: Whence are you to learn sympathy with society? You need, then, a change in your material conditions to enable you to develop morally; you need to work less so as to have some hours of your day to devote to the improvement of your minds; you need a sufficient remuneration of your labour to put you in a position to accumulate savings, and so set your minds at rest about the future, and to purify yourselves above all of every sentiment of *retaliation*, every impulse of revenge, every thought of injustice towards those who have been unjust to you. You must strive, then, for this change, and you will obtain it, but you must strive for it as a *means*, not as an *end*; strive for it from a sense of *duty*, not only as a *right*; strive for it in order to make yourselves better, not only to make yourselves *materially* happy. If not, what difference would there be between you and your tyrants? They are tyrants precisely because they do not think of anything but *well-being*, pleasure, and power.

To make yourselves better; this must be the aim of your life. You cannot make yourselves permanently less unhappy except by improving yourselves. Tyrants will arise by the thousand among you, if you fight only in the name of material interests, or of a particular organization. [. . .]

[. . .] All possible theories of rights and of material *well-being* can only lead you to attempts which, so long as they remain isolated and dependent on your strength only, will not succeed, but can only bring about the worst of social crimes, a civil war between class and class.

Italian Working-men, my Brothers! When Christ came and changed the face of the world, He did not speak of rights to the rich, who had no need to conquer them; nor to the poor, who would perhaps have abused them, in imitation of the rich. He did not speak of utility or of self-interest to a people whom utility and self-interest had corrupted. He spoke of Duty, He spoke of Love, of Sacrifice, of Faith: He said that *they only should be first among all who had done good to all by their work*. And these thoughts, breathed into the ear of a society which had no longer any spark of life, reanimated it, conquered the millions, conquered the world, and caused the education of the human race to progress a degree. Italian Working-men! we live in an epoch like Christ's. We live in the midst of a society rotten as that of the Roman Empire, and feel in our souls the need of reviving and transforming it, of associating all its members and its workers in one single faith, under one single law, and for one purpose; the free and progressive development of all the faculties which God has planted in His creatures. We seek the reign of God upon earth as in heaven, or better, that the earth shall be a preparation for heaven, and society an endeavour towards a progressive approach to the Divine Idea. [. . .]

V. Duties to Country

Your first Duties—first, at least, in importance—are, as I have told you, to Humanity. You are *men* before you are *citizens* or *fathers*. If you do not embrace the whole human family in your love, if you do not confess your faith in its unity—consequent on the unity of God—and in the brotherhood of the Peoples who are appointed to reduce that unity to fact—if wherever one of your fellow men groans, wherever the dignity of human nature is violated by falsehood or tyranny, you are not prompt, being able, to succour that wretched one, or do not feel yourself called, being able, to fight for the purpose of relieving the deceived or oppressed—you disobey your law of life, or do not comprehend the religion which will bless the future.

But what can *each* of you, with his isolated powers, *do* for the moral improvement, for the progress of Humanity? You can, from time to time, give sterile expression to your belief; you may, on some rare occasion, perform an act of *charity* to a brother not belonging to your own land, no more. Now, *charity* is not the watchword of the future faith. The watchword of the future faith is *association*, fraternal cooperation towards a common aim, and this is as much superior to *charity* as the work of many uniting to raise with one accord a building for the habitation of all together would be superior to that which you would accomplish by raising a separate hut each for himself, and only helping one another by exchanging stones and bricks and mortar. But divided as you are in language, tendencies, habits, and capacities, you cannot attempt this common work. The *individual* is too weak, and Humanity too vast. *My God*, prays the Breton mariner as he puts out to sea, *protect me, my ship is so little, and Thy ocean so great!* And this prayer sums up the condition of each of you, if no means is found of multiplying your forces and your powers of action indefinitely. But God gave you this means when he gave you a Country, when, like a wise overseer of labour, who distributes the different parts of the work according to the capacity of the workmen, he divided Humanity into distinct groups upon the face of our globe, and thus planted the seeds of nations. Bad governments have disfigured the design of God, which you may see clearly marked out, as far, at least, as regards Europe, by the courses of the great rivers, by the lines of the lofty mountains, and by other geographical conditions; they have disfigured it by conquest, by greed, by jealousy of the just sovereignty of others; disfigured it so much that today there is perhaps no nation except England and France whose confines correspond to this design. They did not, and they do not, recognize any country except their own families and dynasties, the egoism of caste. But the divine design will infallibly be fulfilled. Natural divisions, the innate spontaneous tendencies of the peoples will replace the arbitrary divisions sanctioned by bad governments. The map of Europe will be remade. The Countries of the People will rise, defined by the voice of the free, upon the ruins of the Countries of Kings and privileged castes. Between these Countries there will be harmony and brotherhood. And then the work of Humanity for the general amelioration, for the discovery and application of the real law of life, carried on in association and distributed according to local capacities, will be accomplished by peaceful and progressive development; then each of you, strong in the affections and in the aid of many millions of men speaking the same language, endowed with the same tendencies, and educated by the same historic tradition, may hope by your personal effort to benefit the whole of Humanity.

To you, who have been born in Italy, God has allotted, as if favouring you specially, the best-defined country in Europe. In other lands, marked by more uncertain or more interrupted limits, questions may arise which the pacific vote of all will one day solve, but which have cost, and will yet perhaps cost, tears and blood; in yours, no. God has stretched round you sublime and indisputable boundaries; on one side the highest mountains of Europe, the Alps; on the other the sea, the immeasurable sea. Take a map of Europe and place one point of a pair of compasses in the north of Italy on Parma; point the other to the mouth of the Var, and describe a semicircle with it in the direction of the Alps; this point, which will fall, when the semicircle is completed, upon the mouth of the Isonzo, will have marked the frontier which God has given you. As far as this frontier your language is spoken and understood; beyond this you have no rights. Sicily, Sardinia, Corsica, and the smaller islands between them and the mainland of Italy belong undeniably to you. Brute force may for a little while contest these frontiers with you, but they have been recognized from of old by the tacit general consent of the peoples; and the day when, rising with one accord for the final trial, you plant your tricoloured flag upon that frontier, the whole of Europe will acclaim re-risen Italy, and receive her into the community of the nations. To this final trial all your efforts must be directed.

Without Country you have neither name, token, voice, nor rights, no admission as brothers into the fellowship of the Peoples. You are the bastards of Humanity. Soldiers without a banner, Israelites among the nations, you will find neither faith nor protection; none will be sureties for you. Do not beguile yourselves with the hope of emancipation from unjust social conditions if you do not first conquer a Country for yourselves; where there is no Country there is no common agreement to which you can appeal; the egoism of self-interest rules alone, and he who has the upper hand keeps it, since there is no common safeguard for the interests of all. Do not be led away by the idea of improving your material conditions without first solving the national question. You cannot do it. Your industrial associations and mutual help societies are useful as a means of educating and disciplining yourselves; as an economic fact they will remain barren until you have an Italy. The economic problem demands, first and foremost, an increase of capital and production; and while your Country is dismembered into separate fragments—while shut off by the barrier of customs and artificial difficulties of every sort, you have only restricted markets open to you—you cannot hope for this increase. Today—do not delude yourselves—you are not the working-class of Italy; you are only fractions of that class; powerless, unequal to the great task which you propose to yourselves. Your emancipation can have no practical beginning until a National Government, understanding the signs of the times, shall, seated in Rome, formulate a Declaration of Principles to be the guide for Italian progress, and shall insert into it these words, *Labour is sacred, and is the source of the wealth of Italy.*

Do not be led astray, then by hopes of material progress which in your present conditions can only be illusions. Your Country alone, the vast and rich Italian Country, which stretches from the Alps to the farthest limit of Sicily, can fulfil these hopes. You cannot obtain your *rights* except by obeying the commands of *Duty*. Be worthy of them, and you will have them. O my Brothers! love your Country. Our Country is our home, the home which God has given us, placing therein a numerous family which we love and are loved by, and with which we have a more intimate and quicker communion of feeling and thought than with others; a family which by its concentration upon a given spot, and by the homogeneous nature of its elements, is destined for a special kind of activity. Our Country is our field of labour; the products of our activity must go forth from it for the benefit of the whole earth; but the instruments of labour which we can use best and most effectively exist in it, and we may not reject them without being unfaithful to God's purpose and diminishing our own strength. In labouring according to true principles for our Country we are labouring for Humanity; our Country is the fulcrum of the lever which we have to wield for the common good. If we give up this fulcrum we run the risk of becoming useless to our Country and to Humanity. Before *associating* ourselves with the Nations which compose Humanity we must exist as a Nation. There can be no association except among equals; and you have no recognized collective existence.

Humanity is a great army moving to the conquest of unknown lands, against powerful and wary enemies. The Peoples are the different corps and divisions of that army. Each has a post entrusted to it; each a special operation to perform; and the common victory depends on the exactness with which the different operations are carried out. Do not disturb the order of the battle. Do not abandon the banner which God has given you. Wherever you may be, into the midst of whatever people circumstances may have driven you, fight for the liberty of that people if the moment calls for it; but fight as Italians, so that the blood which you shed may win honour and love, not for you only, but for your Country. And may the constant thought of your soul be for Italy, may all the acts of your life be worthy of her, and may the standard beneath which you range yourselves to work for Humanity be Italy's. Do not say *I*; say *we*. Be every one of you an incarnation of your Country, and feel himself and make himself responsible for his fellow-countrymen; let each one of you learn to act in such a way that in him men shall respect and love his Country.

Your Country is one and indivisible. As the members of a family cannot rejoice at the common table if one of their number is far away, snatched from the affection of his brothers, so you should have no joy or repose as long as a portion of the territory upon which your language is spoken is separated from the Nation.

Your Country is the token of the mission which God has given you to fulfil in Humanity. The faculties, the strength of *all* its sons should be united for the accomplishment of this mission. A certain number of common duties and rights belongs to every man who answers to the *Who are you?* of the other peoples, *I am an Italian*. Those duties and those rights cannot be represented except by one *single* authority resulting from your votes. A Country must have, then, a single government. The politicians who call themselves federalists, and who would make Italy into a brotherhood of different states, would dismember the Country, not understanding the idea of Unity. The States into which Italy is divided today are not the creation of our own people; they are the result of the ambitions and calculations of princes or of foreign conquerors, and serve no purpose but to flatter the vanity of local aristocracies for which a narrower sphere than a great Country is necessary. What you, the people, have created, beautified, and consecrated with your affections, with your joys, with your sorrows, and with your blood, is the City and the Commune, not the Province or the State. In the City, in the Commune, where your fathers sleep and where your children will live, where you exercise your faculties and your personal rights, you live out your lives as *individuals*. It is of your City that each of you can say what the Venetians say of theirs: *Venesia la xe nostra: l'avemo falla nu* (Venice is our own: We have made her). In your City you have need of *liberty* as in your Country you have need of *association*. The Liberty of the Commune and the Unity of the Country—let that, then, be your faith. Do not say Rome and Tuscany, Rome and Lombardy, Rome and Sicily; say Rome and Florence, Rome and Siena, Rome and Leghorn, and so through all the Communes of Italy. Rome for all that represents Italian life; your Commune for whatever represents the *individual* life. All the other divisions are artificial and are not confirmed by your national tradition.

A Country is a fellowship of free and equal men bound together in a brotherly concord of labour towards a single end. You must make it and maintain it such. A Country is not an aggregation, it is an *association*. There is no true Country without a uniform right. There is no true Country where the uniformity of that right is violated by the existence of caste, privilege, and inequality—where the powers and faculties of a large number of individuals are suppressed or dormant—where there is no common principle accepted, recognized, and developed by all. In such a state of things there can be no Nation, no People, but only a multitude, a fortuitous agglomeration of men whom circumstances have brought together and different circumstances will separate. In the name of your love for your Country you must combat without truce the existence of every privilege, every inequality, upon the soil which has given you birth. One privilege only is lawful—the privilege of Genius when Genius reveals itself in brotherhood with Virtue; but it is a privilege conceded by God and not by men, and when you acknowledge it and follow its inspirations, you acknowledge it freely by the exercise of your own reason and your own choice. Whatever privilege claims your submission in virtue of force or heredity, or any right which is not a common right, is a usurpation and a tyranny, and you ought to combat it and annihilate it. Your Country should be your Temple. God at the summit, a People of equals at the base. Do not accept any other formula, any other moral law, if you do not want to dishonour your Country and yourselves. Let the secondary laws for the gradual regulation of your existence be the progressive application of this supreme law.

And in order that they should be so, it is necessary that *all* should contribute to the making of them. The laws made by one fraction of the citizens only can never by the nature of things and men do otherwise than reflect the thoughts and aspirations and desires of that fraction; they represent, not the whole country, but a third, a fourth part, a class, a zone of the country. The law must express the general aspiration, promote the good of all, respond to a beat of the nation's heart. The whole nation therefore should be, directly or indirectly, the legislator. By yielding this mission to a few men, you put the egoism of one class in the place of the Country, which is the union of *all* the classes.

A Country is not a mere territory; the particular territory is only its foundation. The Country is the idea which rises upon that foundation; it is the sentiment of love, the sense of fellowship which binds together all the sons of that territory. So long as a single one of your brothers is not represented by his own vote in the development of the national life—so long as a single one vegetates uneducated among the educated—so long as a single one able and willing to work languishes in poverty for want of work—you have not got a Country such as it ought to be, the Country of all and for all. *Votes, education, work* are the three main pillars of the nation; do not rest until your hands have solidly erected them.

And when they have been erected—when you have secured for every one of you food for both body and soul—when freely united, entwining your right hands like brothers round a beloved mother, you advance in beautiful and holy concord towards the development of your faculties and the fulfilment of the Italian mission—remember that that mission is the moral unity of Europe; remember the immense duties which it imposes upon you. Italy is the only land that has twice uttered the great word of unification to the disjoined nations. Twice Rome has been the metropolis, the temple, of the European world; the first time when our conquering eagles traversed the known world from end to end and prepared it for union by introducing civilized institutions; the second time when, after the Northern conquerors had themselves been subdued by the potency of Nature, of great memories and of religious inspiration, the genius of Italy incarnated itself in the Papacy and undertook the solemn mission—abandoned four centuries ago—of preaching the union of souls to the peoples of the Christian world. Today a third mission is dawning for our Italy; as much vaster than those of old as the Italian People, the free and united Country which you are going to found, will be greater and more powerful than Caesars or Popes. The presentiment of this mission agitates Europe and keeps the eye and the thought of the nations chained to Italy.

Your duties to your Country are proportioned to the loftiness of this mission.

You have to keep it pure from egoism, uncontaminated by falsehood and by the arts of the political Jesuitism which they call diplomacy.

The government of the country will be based through your labours upon the worship of principles, not upon the idolatrous worship of interests and of opportunity. There are countries in Europe where Liberty is sacred within, but is systematically violated without; peoples who say, *Truth is one thing, utility another: Theory is one thing, practice another.* Those countries will have inevitably to expiate their guilt in long isolation, oppression, and anarchy. But you know the mission of our Country, and will pursue another path. Through you Italy will have, with one only God in the heavens, one only truth, one only faith, one only rule of political life upon earth. Upon the edifice, sublimer than Capitol or Vatican, which the people of Italy will raise, you will plant the banner of Liberty and of Association, so that it shines in the sight of all the nations, nor will you lower it ever for terror of despots or lust for the gains of a day. You will have boldness as you have faith. You will speak out aloud to the world, and to those who call themselves the lords of the world, the thought which thrills in the heart of Italy. You will never deny the sister nations. The life of the Country shall grow through you in beauty and in strength, free from servile fears and the hesitations of doubt, keeping as its *foundation* the people, as its *rule* the consequences of its principles logically deduced and energetically applied, as its *strength* the strength of all, as its *outcome* the amelioration of all, as its *end* the fulfilment of the mission which God has given it. And because you will be ready to die for Humanity, the life of your Country will be immortal.

JOHN STUART MILL

Considerations on Representative Government

CHAPTER XVI: OF NATIONALITY, AS CONNECTED WITH REPRESENTATIVE GOVERNMENT

A portion of mankind may be said to constitute a Nationality, if they are united among themselves by common sympathies, which do not exist between them and any others—which make them cooperate with each other more willingly than with other people, desire to be under the same government, and desire that it should be government by themselves or a portion of themselves, exclusively. This feeling of nationality may have been generated by various causes. Sometimes it is the effect of identity of race and descent. Community of language, and community of religion, greatly contribute to it. Geographical limits are one of its causes. But the strongest of all is identity of political antecedents; the possession of a national history, and consequent community of recollections; collective pride and humiliation, pleasure and regret, connected with the same incidents in the past. None of these circumstances however are either indispensable, or necessarily sufficient by themselves. Switzerland has a strong sentiment of nationality, though the cantons are of different races, different languages, and different religions. Sicily has, throughout history, felt itself quite distinct in nationality from Naples, notwithstanding identity of religion, almost identity of language, and a considerable amount of common historical antecedents. The Flemish and the Walloon provinces of Belgium, notwithstanding diversity of race and language, have a much greater feeling of common nationality, than the former have with Holland, or the latter with France. Yet in general the national feeling is proportionally weakened by the failure of any of the causes which contribute to it. Identity of language, literature, and, to some extent, of race and recollections, has maintained the feeling of nationality in considerable strength among the different portions of the German name, though they have at no time been really united under the same government; but the feeling has never reached to making the separate States desire to get rid of their autonomy. Among Italians an identity far from complete, of language and literature, combined with a geographical position which

98

separates them by a distinct line from other countries, and, perhaps more than everything else, the possession of a common name, which makes them all glory in the past achievements in arts, arms, politics, religious primacy, science, and literature, of any who share the same designation, give rise to an amount of national feeling in the population, which, though still imperfect, has been sufficient to produce the great events now passing before us, notwithstanding a great mixture of races, and although they have never, in either ancient or modern history, been under the same government, except while that government extended or was extending itself over the greater part of the known world.

Where the sentiment of nationality exists in any force, there is a prima facie case for uniting all the members of the nationality under the same government, and a government to themselves apart. This is merely saying that the question of government ought to be decided by the governed. One hardly knows what any division of the human race should be free to do, if not to determine, with which of the various collective bodies of human beings they choose to associate themselves. But, when a people are ripe for free institutions, there is a still more vital consideration. Free institutions are next to impossible in a country made up of different nationalities. Among a people without fellow-feeling, especially if they read and speak different languages, the united public opinion, necessary to the working of representative government, cannot exist. The influences which form opinions and decide political acts, are different in the different sections of the country. An altogether different set of leaders has the confidence of one part of the country and of another. The same books, newspapers, pamphlets, speeches, do not reach them. One section does not know what opinions, or what instigations, are circulating in another. The same incidents, the same acts, the same system of government, affect them in different ways; and each fears more injury to itself from the other nationalities, than from the common arbiter, the State. Their mutual antipathies are generally much stronger than jealousy of the government. That any one of them feels aggrieved by the policy of the common ruler, is sufficient to determine another to support that policy. Even if all are aggrieved, none feel that they can rely on the others for fidelity in a joint resistance; the strength of none is sufficient to resist alone, and each may reasonably think that it consults its own advantage most by bidding for the favour of the government against the rest. Above all, the grand and only effectual security in the last resort against the despotism of the government, is in that case wanting: the sympathy of the army with the people. The military is the part of every community in whom, from the nature of the case, the distinction between their fellow countrymen and foreigners is the deepest and strongest. To the rest of the people, foreigners are merely strangers; to the soldier, they are men against whom he may be called, at a week's notice, to fight for life or death. The difference to him is that between friends and foes—we may almost say between fellow men and another kind of animal: for as respects the enemy, the only law is that of force, and the only mitigation, the same as in the case of other animals—that of simple humanity. Soldiers to whose feelings half or three-fourths of the subjects of the same government are foreigners, will have no more scruple in mowing them down, and no more desire to ask the reason why, than they would have in doing the same thing against declared enemies. An army composed of various nationalities has no other patriotism than devotion to the flag. Such armies have been the executioners of liberty through the whole duration of modern history. The sole bond which holds them together is their officers, and the government which they serve; and their only idea, if they have any, of public duty, is obedience to orders. A government thus supported, by keeping its Hungarian regiments in Italy and its Italian in Hungary, can long continue to rule in both places with the iron rod of foreign conquerors.

If it be said that so broadly marked a distinction between what is due to a fellow countryman and what is due merely to a human creature, is more worthy of savages than of civilized beings and ought, with the utmost energy, to be contended against, no one holds that opinion more strongly than myself. But this object, one of the worthiest to which human endeavour can be directed, can never, in the present state of civilization, be promoted by keeping different nationalities of anything like equivalent strength, under the same government. In a barbarous state of society, the case is sometimes different. The government may then be interested in softening the antipathies of the races, that peace may be preserved, and the country more easily governed. But when there are either free institutions, or a desire for them, in any of the peoples artificially tied together, the interest of the government lies in an exactly opposite direction. It is then interested in keeping up and envenoming their antipathies; that they may be prevented from coalescing, and it may be enabled to use some of them as tools for the enslavement of others. The Austrian Court has now for a whole generation made these tactics its principal means of government; with what fatal success, at the time of the Vienna insurrection and the Hungarian contest, the world knows too well. Happily there are now signs that improvement is too far advanced, to permit this policy to be any longer successful.

For the preceding reasons, it is in general a necessary condition of free institutions, that the boundaries of governments should coincide in the main with those of nationalities. But several considerations are liable to conflict in practice with this general principle. In the first place, its application is often precluded by geographical hindrances. There are parts even of Europe, in which different nationalities are so locally intermingled, that it is not practicable for them to be under separate governments. The population of Hungary is composed of Magyars, Slovacks, Croats, Serbs, Roumans, and in some districts, Germans, so mixed up as to be incapable of local separation; and there is no course open to them but to make a virtue of necessity, and reconcile themselves to living together under equal rights and laws. Their community of servitude, which dates only from the destruction of Hungarian independence in 1849, seems to be ripening and disposing them for such an equal union. The German colony of East Prussia is cut off from Germany by part of the ancient Poland, and being too weak to maintain separate independence, must, if geographical continuity is to be maintained, be either under a non-German government, or the intervening Polish territory must be under a German one. Another considerable region in which the dominant element of the population is German, the provinces of Courland, Esthonia, and Livonia, is condemned by its local situation to form part of a Slavonian state. In Eastern Germany itself there is a large Slavonic population: Bohemia is principally Slavonic, Silesia and other districts partially so. The most united country in Europe, France, is far from being homogeneous: Independently of the fragments of foreign nationalities at its remote extremities, it consists, as language and history prove, of two portions, one occupied almost exclusively by a Gallo-Roman population, while in the other the Frankish, Burgundian, and other Teutonic races form a considerable ingredient.

When proper allowance has been made for geographical exigencies, another more purely moral and social consideration offers itself. Experience proves, that it is possible for one nationality to merge and be absorbed in another: And when it was originally an inferior and more backward portion of the human race, the absorption is greatly to its advantage. Nobody can suppose that it is not more beneficial to a Breton, or a Basque of French Navarre, to be brought into the current of the ideas and feelings of a highly civilized and cultivated people—to be a member of the French nationality, admitted on equal terms to all the privileges of French citizenship, sharing the advantages of French protection, and the dignity and prestige of French power—than to sulk on his own rocks, the half-savage relic of past times, revolving in his own little mental orbit, without participation or interest in the general movement of the world. The same remark applies to the Welshman or the Scottish Highlander, as members of the British nation.

Whatever really tends to the admixture of nationalities, and the blending of their attributes and peculiarities in a common union, is a benefit to the human race. Not by extinguishing types, of which, in these cases, sufficient examples are sure to remain, but by softening their extreme forms, and filling up the intervals between them. The united people, like a crossed breed of animals (but in a still greater degree, because the influences in operation are moral as well as physical), inherits the special aptitudes and excellences of all its progenitors, protected by the admixture from being exaggerated into the neighbouring vices. But to render this admixture possible, there must be peculiar conditions. The combinations of circumstances which occur, and which affect the result, are various.

The nationalities brought together under the same government, may be about equal in numbers and strength, or they may be very unequal. If unequal, the least numerous of the two may either be the superior in civilization, or the inferior. Supposing it to be superior, it may either, through that superiority, be able to acquire ascendancy over the other, or it may be overcome by brute strength, and reduced to subjection. This last is a sheer mischief to the human race, and one which civilized humanity with one accord should rise in arms to prevent. The absorption of Greece by Macedonia was one of the greatest misfortunes which ever happened to the world: That of any of the principal countries of Europe by Russia would be a similar one.

If the smaller nationality, supposed to be the more advanced in improvement, is able to overcome the greater, as the Macedonians, reinforced by the Greeks, did Asia, and the English India, there is often a gain to civilization; but the conquerors and the conquered cannot in this case live together under the same free institutions. The absorption of the conquerors in the less advanced people would be an evil: These must be governed as subjects, and the state of things is either a benefit or a misfortune, according as the subjugated people have or have not reached the state in which it is an injury not to be under a free government, and according as the conquerors do or do not use their superiority in a manner calculated to fit the conquered for a higher stage of improvement. This topic will be particularly treated of in a subsequent chapter.

When the nationality which succeeds in overpowering the other, is both the most numerous and the most improved; and especially if the subdued nationality is small, and has no hope of reasserting its independence; then, if it is governed with any tolerable justice, and if the members of the more powerful nationality are not made odious by being invested with exclusive privileges, the smaller nationality is gradually reconciled to its position, and becomes amalgamated with the larger. No Bas-Breton, nor even any Alsatian, has the smallest wish at the present day to be separated from France. If all Irishmen have not yet arrived at the same disposition towards England, it is partly because they are sufficiently numerous to be capable of constituting a respectable nationality by themselves; but principally because, until of late years, they had been so atrociously governed, that all their best feelings combined with their bad ones in rousing bitter resentment against the Saxon rule. This disgrace to England, and calamity to the whole empire, has, it may be truly said, completely ceased for nearly a generation. No Irishman is now less free than an Anglo-Saxon, nor has a less share of every benefit either to his country or to his individual fortunes, than if he were sprung from any other portion of the British dominions. The only remaining real grievance of Ireland, that of the State Church, is one which half, or nearly half, the people of the larger island have in common with them. There is now next to nothing, except the memory of the past, and the difference in the predominant religion, to keep apart two races, perhaps the most fitted of any two in the world to be the completing counterpart of one another. The consciousness of being at last treated not only with equal justice but with equal consideration, is making such rapid way in the Irish nation, as to be wearing off all feelings that could make them insensible to the benefits which the less numerous and less wealthy people must necessarily derive, from being fellow citizens instead of foreigners to those who are not only their nearest neighbours, but the wealthiest, and one of the freest, as well as most civilized and powerful, nations of the earth.

The cases in which the greatest practical obstacles exist to the blending of nationalities, are when the nationalities which have been bound together are nearly equal in numbers, and in the other elements of power. In such cases, each, confiding in its strength, and feeling itself capable of maintaining an equal struggle with any of the others, is unwilling to be merged in it: Each cultivates with party obstinacy its distinctive peculiarities; obsolete customs, and even declining languages, are revived, to deepen the separation; each deems itself tyrannized over if any authority is exercised within itself by functionaries of a rival race; and whatever is given to one of the conflicting nationalities, is considered to be taken from all the rest. When nations, thus divided, are under a despotic government which is a stranger to all of them, or which, though sprung from one, yet feeling greater interest in its own power than in any sympathies of nationality, assigns no privilege to either nation, and chooses its instruments indifferently from all; in the course of a few generations, identity of situation often produces harmony of feeling, and the different races come to feel towards each other as fellow countrymen; particularly if they are dispersed over the same tract of country. But if the era of aspiration to free government arrives before this fusion has been effected, the opportunity has gone by for effecting it. From that time, if the unreconciled nationalities are geographically separate, and especially if their local position is such that there is no natural fitness or convenience in their being under the same government (as in the case of an Italian province under a French or German yoke), there is not only an obvious propriety, but, if either freedom or concord is cared for, a necessity, for breaking the connexion altogether. There may be cases in which the provinces, after separation, might usefully remain united by a federal tie: But it generally happens that if they are willing to forgo complete independence, and become members of a federation, each of them has other neighbours with whom it would prefer to connect itself, having more sympathies in common, if not also greater community of interest. [. . .]

CHAPTER XVIII: OF THE GOVERNMENT OF DEPENDENCIES BY A FREE STATE

Free States, like all others, may possess dependencies, acquired either by conquest or by colonization; and our own is the greatest instance of the kind in modern history. It is a most important question, how such dependencies ought to be governed.

It is unnecessary to discuss the case of small posts, like Gibraltar, Aden, or Heligoland, which are held only as naval or military positions. The military or naval object is in this case paramount, and the inhabitants cannot, consistently with it, be admitted to the government of the place; though they ought to be allowed all liberties and privileges compatible with that restriction, including the free management of municipal affairs; and as a compensation for being locally sacrificed to the convenience of the governing State, should be admitted to equal rights with its native subjects in all other parts of the empire.

Outlying territories of some size and population, which are held as dependencies, that is, which are subject, more or less, to acts of sovereign power on the part of the paramount country, without being equally represented (if represented at all) in its legislature, may be divided into two classes. Some are composed of people of similar civilization to the ruling country; capable of, and ripe for, representative government: such as the British possessions in America and Australia. Others, like India, are still at a great distance from that state.

In the case of dependencies of the former class, this country has at length realized, in rare completeness, the true principle of government. England has always felt under a certain degree of obligation to bestow on such of her outlying populations as were of her own blood and language, and on some who were not, representative institutions formed in imitation of her own: But until the present generation, she has been on the same bad level with other countries as to the amount of self-government which she allowed them to exercise through the representative institutions that she conceded to them. She claimed to be the supreme arbiter even of their purely internal concerns, according to her own, not their, ideas of how those concerns could be best regulated. This practice was a natural corollary from the vicious theory of colonial policy—once common to all Europe, and not yet completely relinquished by any other people—which regarded colonies as valuable by affording markets for our commodities, that could be kept entirely to ourselves: a privilege we valued so highly, that we thought it worth purchasing by allowing to the colonies the same monopoly of our market for their own productions, which we claimed for our commodities in theirs. This notable plan for enriching them and ourselves, by making each pay enormous sums to the other, dropping the greatest part by the way, has been for some time abandoned. But the bad habit of meddling in the internal government of the colonies, did not at once terminate when we relinquished the idea of making any profit by it. We continued to torment them, not for any benefit to ourselves, but for that of a section or faction among the colonists: And this persistence in domineering cost us a Canadian rebellion, before we had the happy thought of giving it up. England was like an ill-brought-up elder brother, who persists in tyrannizing over the younger ones from mere habit, till one of them, by a spirited resistance, though with unequal strength, gives him notice to desist. We were wise enough not to require a second warning. A new era in the colonial policy of nations began with Lord Durham's Report; the imperishable memorial of that nobleman's courage, patriotism, and enlightened liberality, and of the intellect and practical sagacity of its joint authors, Mr. Wakefield and the lamented Charles Buller.[1]

It is now a fixed principle of the policy of Great Britain, professed in theory and faithfully adhered to in practice, that her colonies of European race, equally with the parent country, possess the fullest measure of internal self-government. They have been allowed to make their own free representative constitutions, by altering in any manner they thought fit, the already very popular constitutions which we had given them. Each is governed by its own legislature and executive, constituted on highly democratic principles. The veto of the Crown and of Parliament, though nominally reserved, is only exercised (and that very rarely) on questions which concern the empire, and not solely the particular colony. How liberal a construction has been given to the distinction between imperial and colonial questions, is shown by the fact, that the whole of the unappropriated lands in the regions behind our American and Australian colonies, has been given up to the uncontrolled disposal of the colonial communities; though they might, without injustice, have been kept in the hands of the Imperial Government, to be administered for the greatest advantage of future emigrants from all parts of the empire. Every colony has thus as full power over its own affairs, as it could have if it were a member of even the loosest federation; and much fuller than would belong to it under the Constitution of the United States, being free even to tax at its pleasure the commodities imported from the mother country. Their union with Great Britain is the slightest kind of federal union; but not a strictly equal federation, the mother country retaining to itself the powers of a Federal Government, though reduced in practice to their very narrowest limits. This inequality is, of course, as far as it goes, a disadvantage to the dependencies, which have no voice in foreign policy, but are bound by the decisions of the superior country. They are compelled to join England in war, without being in any way consulted previous to engaging in it. [. . .]

Thus far, of the dependencies whose population is in a sufficiently advanced state to be fitted for representative government. But there are others which have not attained that state, and which, if held at all, must be governed by the dominant country, or by persons delegated for that purpose by it. This mode of government is as legitimate as any other, if it is the one which in the existing state of civilization of the subject people, most facilitates their transition to a higher stage of improvement. There are, as we have already seen, conditions of society in which a vigorous despotism is in itself the best mode of government for training the people in what is specifically wanting to render them capable of a higher civilization. There are others, in which the mere fact of despotism has indeed no beneficial effect, the lessons which it teaches having already been only too completely learnt; but in which, there being no spring of spontaneous improvement in the people themselves, their almost only hope of making any steps in advance depends on the chances of a good despot. Under a native despotism, a good despot is a rare and transitory accident: But when the dominion they are under is that of a more civilized people, that people ought to be able to supply it constantly. The ruling country ought to be able to do for its subjects all that could be done by a succession of absolute monarchs, guaranteed by irresistible force against the precariousness of tenure attendant on barbarous despotisms, and qualified by their genius to anticipate all that experience has taught to the more advanced nation. Such is the ideal rule of a free people over a barbarous or semi-barbarous one. We need not expect to see that ideal realized; but unless some approach to it is, the rulers are guilty of a dereliction of the highest moral trust which can devolve upon a nation: And if they do not even aim at it, they are selfish usurpers, on a par in criminality with any of those whose ambition and rapacity have sported from age to age with the destiny of masses of mankind.

As it is already a common, and is rapidly tending to become the universal, condition of the more backward populations, to be either held in direct subjection by the more advanced, or to be under their complete political ascendancy; there are in this age of the world few more important problems, than how to organize this rule, so as to make it a good instead of an evil to the subject people; providing them with the best attainable present government, and with the conditions most favourable to future permanent improvement. But the mode of fitting the government for this purpose is by no means so well understood, as the conditions of good government in a people capable of governing themselves. We may even say, that it is not understood at all. [. . .]

It is always under great difficulties, and very imperfectly, that a country can be governed by foreigners; even when there is no extreme disparity, in habits and ideas, between the rulers and the ruled. Foreigners do not feel with the people. They cannot judge, by the light in which a thing appears to their own minds, or the manner in which it affects their feelings, how it will affect the feelings or appear to the minds of the subject population. What a native of the country, of average practical ability, knows as it were by instinct, they have to learn slowly, and after all imperfectly, by study and experience. The laws, the customs, the social relations, for which they have to legislate, instead of being familiar to them from childhood, are all strange to them. [. . .] The utmost they can do is to give some of their best men a commission to look after it; to whom the opinion of their own country can neither be much of a guide in the performance of their duty, nor a competent judge of the mode in which it has been performed.

NOTE

1. I am speaking here of the *adoption* of this improved policy, not, of course, of its original suggestion. The honour of having been its earliest champion belongs unquestionably to Mr. Roebuck.

9

LORD ACTON

Nationality

In the old European system, the rights of nationalities were neither recognized by governments nor asserted by the people. The interest of the reigning families, not those of the nations, regulated the frontiers; and the administration was conducted generally without any reference to popular desires. Where all liberties were suppressed, the claims of national independence were necessarily ignored, and a princess, in the words of Fénelon, carried a monarchy in her wedding portion. The eighteenth century acquiesced in this oblivion of corporate rights on the Continent, for the absolutists cared only for the State, and the liberals only for the individual. The Church, the nobles, and the nation had no place in the popular theories of the age; and they devised none in their own defense, for they were not openly attacked. The aristocracy retained its privileges, and the Church her property; and the dynastic interest, which overruled the natural inclination of the nations and destroyed their independence, nevertheless maintained their integrity. The national sentiment was not wounded in its most sensitive part. To dispossess a sovereign of his hereditary crown, and to annex his dominions, would have been held to inflict an injury upon all monarchies, and to furnish their subjects with a dangerous example, by depriving royalty of its inviolable character. In time of war, as there was no national cause at stake, there was no attempt to rouse national feeling. The courtesy of the rulers towards each other was proportionate to the contempt for the lower orders. Compliments passed between the commanders of hostile armies; there was no bitterness, and no excitement; battles were fought with the pomp and pride of a parade. The art of war became a slow and learned game. The monarchies were united not only by a natural community of interests, but by family alliances. A marriage contract sometimes became the signal for an interminable war, whilst family connections often set a barrier to ambition. After the wars of religion came to an end in 1648, the only wars were those which were waged for an inheritance or a dependency, or against countries whose system of government exempted them from the common law of dynastic States, and made them not only unprotected but obnoxious. These countries were England and Holland, until Holland ceased to be a republic, and until, in England, the defeat of the Jacobites in the forty-five terminated the struggle for the Crown. There was one country, however, which still continued to be an exception; one monarch whose place was not admitted in the comity of kings.

Poland did not possess those securities for stability which were supplied by dynastic connections and the theory of legitimacy, wherever a crown could be obtained by marriage or inheritance. A monarch without royal blood, a crown bestowed by the nation, were an anomaly and an outrage in that age of dynastic absolutism. The country was excluded from the European system by the nature of its institutions. It excited a cupidity which could not be satisfied. It gave the reigning families of Europe no hope of permanently strengthening themselves by intermarriage with its rulers, or of obtaining it by bequest or by inheritance. The Habsburgs had contested the possession of Spain and the Indies with the French Bourbons, of Italy with the Spanish Bourbons, of the empire with the house of Wittelsbach, of Silesia with the house of Hohenzollern. There had been wars between rival houses for half the territories of Italy and Germany. But none could hope to redeem their losses or increase their power in a country to which marriage and descent gave no claim. Where they could not permanently inherit they endeavoured, by intrigues, to prevail at each election, and after contending in support of candidates who were their partisans, the neighbours at last appointed an instrument for the final demolition of the Polish State. Till then no nation had been deprived of its political existence by the Christian Powers, and whatever disregard had been shown for national interests and sympathies, some care had been taken to conceal the wrong by a hypocritical perversion of law. But the partition of Poland was an act of wanton violence, committed in open defiance not only of popular feeling but of public law. For the first time in modern history a great State was suppressed, and a whole nation divided among its enemies.

This famous measure, the most revolutionary act of the old absolutism, awakened the theory of nationality in Europe, converting a dormant right into an aspiration, and a sentiment into a political claim. "No wise or honest man," wrote Edmund Burke, "can approve of that partition, or can contemplate it without prognosticating great mischief from it to all countries at some future time."[1] Thenceforward there was a nation demanding to be united in a State,—a soul, as it were, wandering in search of a body in which to begin life over again; and, for the first time, a cry was heard that the arrangement of States was unjust—that their limits were unnatural, and that a whole people was deprived of its right to constitute an independent community. Before that claim could be efficiently asserted against the overwhelming power of its opponents,—before it gained energy, after the last partition, to overcome the influence of long habits of submission, and of the contempt which previous disorders had brought upon Poland,—the ancient European system was in ruins, and a new world was rising in its place.

The old despotic policy which made the Poles its prey had two adversaries,—the spirit of English liberty, and the doctrines of that revolution which destroyed the French monarchy with its own weapons; and these two contradicted in contrary ways the theory that nations have no collective rights. At the present day, the theory of nationality is not only the most powerful auxiliary of revolution, but its actual substance in the movements of the last three years. This, however, is a recent alliance, unknown to the first French Revolution. The modern theory of nationality arose partly as a legitimate consequence, partly as a reaction against it. As the system which overlooked national division was opposed by liberalism in two forms, the French and the English, so the system which insists upon them proceeds from two distinct sources, and exhibits the character either of 1688 or of 1789. When the French people abolished the authorities under which it lived, and became its own master, France was in danger of dissolution: for the common will is difficult to ascertain, and does not readily agree. "The laws," said Vergniaud, in the debate on the sentence of the king, "are obligatory only as the presumptive will of the people, which retains the right of approving or condemning them. The instant it manifests its wish the work of the national representation, the law, must disappear." This doctrine resolved society into its natural elements, and threatened to break up the country into as many republics as there were communes. For true republicanism is the principle of self-government in the whole and in all the parts. In an extensive country, it can prevail only by the union of several independent communities in a single confederacy, as in Greece, in Switzerland, in the Netherlands, and in America; so that a large republic not founded on the federal principle must result in the government of a single city, like Rome and Paris, and, in a less degree, Athens, Berne, and Amsterdam; or, in other words, a great democracy must either sacrifice self-government to unity, or preserve it by federalism.

[. . .] The substance of the ideas of 1789 is not the limitation of the sovereign power, but the abrogation of intermediate powers. These powers, and the classes which enjoyed them, come in Latin Europe from a barbarian origin; and the movement which calls itself liberal is essentially national. If liberty were its object, its means would be the establishment of great independent authorities not derived from the State, and its model would be England. But its object is equality; and it seeks, like France in 1789, to cast out the elements of inequality which were introduced by the Teutonic race. This is the object which Italy and Spain have had in common with France, and herein consists the natural league of the Latin nations.

This national element in the movement was not understood by the revolutionary leaders. At first, their doctrine appeared entirely contrary to the idea of nationality. They taught that certain general principles of government were absolutely right in all States; and they asserted in theory the unrestricted freedom of the individual, and the supremacy of the will over every external necessity or obligation. This is in apparent contradiction to the national theory, that certain natural forces ought to determine the character, the form, and the policy of the State, by which a kind of fate is put in the place of freedom. Accordingly the national sentiment was not developed directly out of the revolution in which it was involved, but was exhibited first in resistance to it, when the attempt to emancipate had been absorbed in the desire to subjugate, and the republic had been succeeded by the empire. [. . .]

The first liberal movement, that of the Carbonari in the south of Europe, had no specific national character, but was supported by the Bonapartists both in Spain and Italy. In the following years the opposite ideas of 1813 came to the front, and a revolutionary movement, in many respects hostile to the principles of revolution, began in defense of liberty, religion, and nationality. All these causes were united in the Irish agitation, and in the Greek, Belgian, and Polish revolutions. Those sentiments which had been insulted by Napoleon, and had risen against him, rose against the governments of the restoration. They had been oppressed by the sword, and then by the treaties. The national principle added force, but not justice, to this movement, which, in every case but Poland, was successful. A period followed in which it degenerated into a purely national idea, as the agitation for repeal succeeded emancipation, and Panslavism and Panhellenism arose under the auspices of the Eastern Church. This was the third phase of the resistance to the settlement of Vienna, which was weak, because it failed to satisfy national or constitutional aspirations, either of which would have been a safeguard against the other, by a moral if not by a popular justification. At first, in 1813, the people rose against their conquerors, in defense of their legitimate rulers. They refused to be governed by usurpers. In the period between 1825 and 1831, they resolved that they would not be misgoverned by strangers. The French administration was often better than that which it displaced, but there were prior claimants for the authority exercised by the French, and at first the national contest was a contest for legitimacy. In the second period this element was wanting. No dispossessed princes led the Greeks, the Belgians, or the Poles. The Turks, the Dutch, and the Russians were attacked, not as usurpers, but as oppressors,—because they misgoverned, not because they were of a different race. Then began a time when the text simply was, that nations would not be governed by foreigners. Power legitimately obtained, and exercised with moderation, was declared invalid. National rights, like religion, had borne part in the previous combinations, and had been auxiliaries in the struggles for freedom, but now nationality became a paramount claim, which was to assert itself alone, which might put forward as pretexts the rights of rulers, the liberties of the people, the safety of religion, but which, if no such union could be formed, was to prevail at the expense of every other cause for which nations make sacrifices. [. . .]

Beginning by a protest against the dominion of race over race, its mildest and least-developed form, it grew into a condemnation of every State that included different races, and finally became the complete and consistent theory, that the State and the nation must be co-extensive. "It is," says Mr. Mill, "in general a necessary condition of free institutions, that the boundaries of governments should coincide in the main with those of nationalities."[2] [. . .]

[. . .] In supporting the claims of national unity, governments must be subverted in whose title there is no flaw, and whose policy is beneficent and equitable, and subjects must be compelled to transfer their allegiance to an authority for which they have no attachment, and which may be practically a foreign domination. Connected with this theory in nothing except in the common enmity of the absolute state, is the theory which represents nationality as an essential, but not a supreme element in determining the forms of the State. It is distinguished from the other, because it tends to diversity and not to uniformity, to harmony and not to unity; because it aims not at an arbitrary change, but at careful respect for the existing conditions of political life, and because it obeys the laws and results of history, not the aspirations of an ideal future. While the theory of unity makes the nation a source of despotism and revolution, the theory of liberty regards it as the bulwark of self-government, and the foremost limit to the excessive power of the State. Private rights, which are sacrificed to the unity, are preserved by the union of nations. No power can so efficiently resist the tendencies of centralization, of corruption, and of absolutism, as that community which is the vastest that can be included in a State, which imposes on its members a consistent similarity of character, interest, and opinion, and which arrests the action of the sovereign by the influence of a divided patriotism. The presence of different nations under the same sovereignty is similar in its effect to the independence of the Church in the State. It provides against the servility which flourishes under the shadow of a single authority, by balancing interests, multiplying associations, and giving to the subject the restraint and support of a combined opinion. In the same way it promotes independence by forming definite groups of public opinion, and by affording a great source and centre of political sentiments, and of notions of duty not derived from the sovereign will. Liberty provokes diversity, and diversity preserves liberty by supplying the means of organization. All those portions of law which govern the relations of men with each other, and regulate social life, are the varying result of national custom and the creation of private society. In these things, therefore, the several nations will differ from each other; for they themselves have produced them, and they do not owe them to the State which rules them all. This diversity in the same State is a firm barrier against the intrusion of the government beyond the political sphere which is common to all into the social department which escapes legislation and is ruled by spontaneous laws. This sort of interference is characteristic of an absolute government, and is sure to provoke a reaction, and finally a remedy. That intolerance of social freedom which is natural to absolutism is sure to find a corrective in the national diversities, which no other force could so efficiently provide. The coexistence of several nations under the same State is a test, as well as the best security of its freedom. It is also one of the chief instruments of civilization; and, as such, it is in the natural and providential order, and indicates a state of greater advancement than the national unity which is the ideal of modern liberalism.

The combination of different nations in one State is as necessary a condition of civilized life as the combination of men in society. Inferior races are raised by living in political union with races intellectually superior. Exhausted and decaying nations are revived by the contact of a younger vitality. Nations in which the elements of organization and the capacity for government have been lost, either through the demoralizing influence of despotism, or the disintegrating action of democracy, are restored and educated anew under the discipline of a stronger and less corrupted race. This fertilizing and regenerating process can only be obtained by living under one government. It is in the cauldron of the State that the fusion takes place by which the vigour, the knowledge, and the capacity of one portion of mankind may be communicated to another. Where political and national boundaries coincide, society ceases to advance, and nations relapse into a condition corresponding to that of men who renounce intercourse with their fellow men. The difference between the two unites mankind not only by the benefits it confers on those who live together, but because it connects society either by a political or a national bond, gives to every people an interest in its neighbours, either because they are under the same government or because they are of the same race, and thus promotes the interests of humanity, of civilization, and of religion.

Christianity rejoices at the mixture of races, as paganism identifies itself with their differences, because truth is universal, and errors various and particular. In the ancient world idolatry and nationality went together, and the same term is applied in Scripture to both. It was the mission of the Church to overcome national differences. The period of her undisputed supremacy was that in which all Western Europe obeyed the same laws, all literature was contained in one language, and the political unity of Christendom was personified in a single potentate, while its intellectual unity was represented in one university. As the ancient Romans concluded their conquests by carrying away the gods of the conquered people, Charlemagne overcame the national resistance of the Saxons only by the forcible destruction of their pagan rites. Out of the medieval period, and the combined action of the German race and the Church, came forth a new system of nations and a new conception of nationality. Nature was overcome in the nation as well as in the individual. In pagan and uncultivated times, nations were distinguished from each other by the widest diversity, not only in religion, but in customs, language, and character. Under the new law

they had many things in common; the old barriers which separated them
were removed, and the new principle of self-government, which Christianity imposed, enabled them to live together under the same authority, without necessarily losing their cherished habits, their customs, or their laws.
The new idea of freedom made room for different races in one State. A
nation was no longer what it had been to the ancient world,—the progeny
of a common ancestor, or the aboriginal product of a particular region,—a
result of merely physical and material causes,—but a moral and political
being; not the creation of geographical or physiological unity, but developed in the course of history by the action of the State. It is derived from
the State, not supreme over it. A State may in course of time produce a
nationality; but that a nationality should constitute a State is contrary to
the nature of modern civilization. The nation derives its rights and its power
from the memory of a former independence.

The Church has agreed in this respect with the tendency of political
progress, and discouraged wherever she could the isolation of nations; ad-
monishing them of their duties to each other, and regarding conquest and
feudal investiture as the natural means of raising barbarous or sunken nations
to a higher level. But though she has never attributed to national independence an immunity from the accidental consequences of feudal law, of
hereditary claims, or of testamentary arrangements, she defends national
liberty against uniformity and centralization with an energy inspired by perfect
community of interests. For the same enemy threatens both; and the State
which is reluctant to tolerate differences, and to do justice to the peculiar
character of various races, must from the same cause interfere in the internal government of religion. The connection of religious liberty with the
emancipation of Poland or Ireland is not merely the accidental result of
local causes; and the failure of the Concordat to unite the subjects of Austria
is the natural consequence of a policy which did not desire to protect the
provinces in their diversity and autonomy, and sought to bribe the Church
by favours instead of strengthening her by independence. From this influence
of religion in modern history has proceeded a new definition of patriotism.

The difference between nationality and the State is exhibited in the nature
of patriotic attachment. Our connection with the race is merely natural or
physical, whilst our duties to the political nation are ethical. One is a community of affections and instincts infinitely important and powerful in savage
life, but pertaining more to the animal than to the civilized man; the other
is an authority governing by laws, imposing obligations, and giving a moral
sanction and character to the natural relations of society. Patriotism is in
political life what faith is in religion, and it stands to the domestic feelings
and to homesickness as faith to fanaticism and to superstition. It has one
aspect derived from private life and nature, for it is an extension of the
family affections, as the tribe is an extension of the family. But in its real
political character, patriotism consists in the development of the instinct

of self-preservation into a moral duty which may involve self-sacrifice. Self-preservation is both an instinct and a duty, natural and involuntary in one respect, and at the same time a moral obligation. By the first it produces the family; by the last the State. If the nation could exist without the State, subject only to the instinct of self-preservation, it would be incapable of denying, controlling, or sacrificing itself; it would be an end and a rule to itself. But in the political order moral purposes are realized and public ends are pursued to which private interests and even existence must be sacrificed. The great sign of true patriotism, the development of selfishness into sacrifice, is the product of political life. That sense of duty which is supplied by race is not entirely separated from its selfish and instinctive basis; and the love of country, like married love, stands at the same time on a material and a moral foundation. The patriot must distinguish between the two causes or objects of his devotion. The attachment which is given only to the country is like obedience given only to the State—a submission to physical influences. The man who prefers his country before every other duty shows the same spirit as the man who surrenders every right to the State. They both deny that right is superior to authority. [. . .]

The nationality formed by the State, then, is the only one to which we owe political duties, and it is, therefore, the only one which has political rights. The Swiss are ethnologically either French, Italian, or German; but no nationality has the slightest claim upon them, except the purely political nationality of Switzerland. The Tuscan or the Neapolitan State has formed a nationality, but the citizens of Florence and of Naples have no political community with each other. There are other States which have neither succeeded in absorbing distinct races in a political nationality, nor in separating a particular district from a larger nation. Austria and Mexico are instances on the one hand, Parma and Baden on the other. The progress of civilization deals hardly with the last description of States. In order to maintain their integrity they must attach themselves by confederations, or family alliances, to greater Powers, and thus lose something of their independence. Their tendency is to isolate and shut off their inhabitants, to narrow the horizon of their views, and to dwarf in some degree the proportions of their ideas. Public opinion cannot maintain its liberty and purity in such small dimensions, and the currents that come from larger communities sweep over a contracted territory. In a small and homogeneous population there is hardly room for a natural classification of society, or for inner groups of interests that set bounds to sovereign power. The government and the subjects contend with borrowed weapons. The resources of the one and the aspirations of the other are derived from some external source, and the consequence is that the country becomes the instrument and the scene of contests in which it is not interested. These States, like the minuter communities of the Middle Ages, serve a purpose, by constituting partitions and securities of self-government in the larger States; but they are impediments to the progress of society, which depends on the mixture of races under the same governments. [. . .]

[. . .] When different races inhabit the different territories of one Empire composed of several smaller States, it is of all possible combinations the most favourable to the establishment of a highly developed system of freedom. In Austria there are two circumstances which add to the difficulty of the problem, but also increase its importance. The several nationalities are at very unequal degrees of advancement, and there is no single nation which is so predominant as to overwhelm or absorb the others. These are the conditions necessary for the very highest degree of organization which government is capable of receiving. They supply the greatest variety of intellectual resource; the perpetual incentive to progress, which is afforded not merely by competition, but by the spectacle of a more advanced people; the most abundant elements of self-government, combined with the impossibility for the State to rule all by its own will; and the fullest security for the preservation of local customs and ancient rights. In such a country as this, liberty would achieve its most glorious results, while centralization and absolutism would be destruction.

The problem presented to the government of Austria is higher than that which is solved in England, because of the necessity of admitting the national claims. The parliamentary system fails to provide for them, as it presupposes the unity of the people. Hence in those countries in which different races dwell together, it has not satisfied their desires, and is regarded as an imperfect form of freedom. It brings out more clearly than before the differences it does not recognize, and thus continues the work of the old absolutism, and appears as a new phase of centralization. In those countries, therefore, the power of the imperial parliament must be limited as jealously as the power of the crown, and many of its functions must be discharged by provincial diets, and a descending series of local authorities.

The great importance of nationality in the State consists in the fact that it is the basis of political capacity. The character of a nation determines in great measure the form and vitality of the State. Certain political habits and ideas belong to particular nations, and they vary with the course of the national history. A people just emerging from barbarism, a people effete from the excesses of a luxurious civilization, cannot possess the means of governing itself; a people devoted to equality, or to absolute monarchy, is incapable of producing an aristocracy; a people averse to the institution of private property is without the first element of freedom. Each of these can be converted into efficient members of a free community only by the contact of a superior race, in whose power will lie the future prospects of the State. A system which ignores these things, and does not rely for its support on the character and aptitude of the people, does not intend that they should administer their own affairs, but that they should simply be obedient to the supreme command. The denial of nationality, therefore, implies the denial of political liberty.

The greatest adversary of the rights of nationality is the modern theory of nationality. By making the State and the nation commensurate with each other in theory, it reduces practically to a subject condition all other nationalities that may be within the boundary. It cannot admit them to an equality with the ruling nation which constitutes the State, because the State would then cease to be national, which would be a contradiction of the principle of its existence. According, therefore, to the degree of humanity and civilization in that dominant body which claims all the rights of the community, the inferior races are exterminated, or reduced to servitude, or outlawed, or put in a condition of dependence.

If we take the establishment of liberty for the realization of moral duties to be the end of civil society, we must conclude that those states are substantially the most perfect which, like the British and Austrian Empires, include various distinct nationalities without oppressing them. Those in which no mixture of races has occurred are imperfect; and those in which its effects have disappeared are decrepit. A State which is incompetent to satisfy different races condemns itself; a State which labours to neutralize, to absorb, or to expel them, destroys its own vitality; a State which does not include them is destitute of the chief basis of self-government. The theory of nationality, therefore, is a retrograde step in history. It is the most advanced form of the revolution, and must retain its power to the end of the revolutionary period, of which it announces the approach. Its great historical importance depends on two chief causes.

First, it is a chimera. The settlement at which it aims is impossible. As it can never be satisfied and exhausted, and always continues to assert itself, it prevents the government from ever relapsing into the condition which provoked its rise. The danger is too threatening, and the power over men's minds too great, to allow any system to endure which justifies the resistance of nationality. It must contribute, therefore, to obtain that which in theory it condemns,—the liberty of different nationalities as members of one sovereign community. This is a service which no other force could accomplish; for it is a corrective alike of absolute monarchy, of democracy, and of constitutionalism, as well as of the centralization which is common to all three. Neither the monarchical, nor the revolutionary, nor the parliamentary system can do this; and all the ideas which have excited enthusiasm in past times are impotent for the purpose except nationality alone.

And secondly, the national theory marks the end of the revolutionary doctrine and its logical exhaustion. In proclaiming the supremacy of the rights of nationality, the system of democratic equality goes beyond its own extreme boundary, and falls into contradiction with itself. [. . .] [N]ationality does not aim either at liberty or prosperity, both of which it sacrifices to the imperative necessity of making the nation the mould and measure of the State. Its course will be marked with material as well as moral ruin, in order that a new invention may prevail over the works of God and the interests of mankind. There is no principle of change, no phase of political speculation conceivable, more comprehensive, more subversive, or more arbitrary than this. It is a confutation of democracy, because it sets limits to the exercise of the popular will, and substitutes for it a higher principle. It prevents not only the division, but the extension of the State, and forbids to terminate war by conquest, and to obtain a security for peace. Thus, after surrendering the individual to the collective will, the revolutionary system makes the collective will subject to conditions which are independent of it, and rejects all law, only to be controlled by an accident.

Although, therefore, the theory of nationality is more absurd and more criminal than the theory of socialism, it has an important mission in the world, and marks the final conflict, and therefore the end, of two forces which are the worst enemies of civil freedom,—the absolute monarchy and the revolution.

NOTES

1. "Observations on the Conduct of the Minority," *Works*, vol. 112.
2. *Considerations on Representative Government*, 298.

10

MAX WEBER

Economic Policy and the National Interest in Imperial Germany

It has always been the case that, when a class has achieved *economic* power, it begins to think of its expectations of *political* leadership. It is dangerous and, in the long run, contrary to the national interest for an economically declining class to retain political dominance. But it is even more dangerous when economic strength and so the hope of political power come the way of classes which are not yet sufficiently mature in political terms for the leadership of the state. Both these menaces threaten Germans at the present time and are in reality the key to the present dangers of our situation. Furthermore, the shifts in the social structure of the East, with which the phenomena discussed in the first part of this lecture are connected, belong in this wider context.

Right up to the present day, the dynasty in Prussia has been politically dependent on the Prussian *Junker* Estate. It is only in cooperation with it (though admittedly also in opposition to it) that it has been able to build the Prussian state. I am well aware that, to South German ears, the word "Junker" has a joyless ring. Perhaps it will be felt that I am speaking in too "Prussian" a fashion if I say a word in their favour. I do not know. Even today in Prussia that Estate has many opportunities for achieving power and influence, or for reaching the ear of the monarch, which are not open to every citizen. It has not always used this power in a way which could be defended before History, and I do not see why a bourgeois scholar should feel any love for it. Nevertheless, and for all that, the strength of its political instincts used to be one of the most important sources of capital for promoting the interests of the state and its power. It has done its job and lies today in its economic death-agony, from which no state economic policy can restore it to its former place in society. Moreover, the tasks of the present are not those which it could perform. For a quarter of a century, the highest office in Germany was in the hands of the last and greatest of the Junkers. Future generations will find in his career as a statesman, not only incomparable grandeur, but also an inherent element of tragedy which at present increasingly escapes many people's notice. The tragic element in his career will be seen in the fact that under his rule his own creation, the nation, to which he gave its unity, slowly and inevitably changed in its economic structure, to the point where it became a different kind of people, requiring other institutions than those which he had given it and in which his imperious nature could find a place. In the end, it was precisely this which brought about the partial shipwreck of his life's work. For this life's work should have led, not only to the external unity of the nation, but also to an inner unification, and we all know that that was not what was achieved. It could not be achieved by this means. And when in the winter of that last year, trapped in the snare of his monarch's favour, he entered the Imperial capital, decked out as it was in all its finery, there were many (as I am well aware) who felt as if the Sachsenwald were opening up its innermost secrets like a latter-day Kyffhaüser. However, not everyone shared this feeling. For it seemed as if in the air of that January day could be sniffed the chilling breeze of historical transience. We were overcome by a peculiarly oppressive feeling—as if a ghost had come down among us from a distant past and was wandering amidst a new generation and through a world which had become strange to him.

The estates of the East were the bases of the Prussian ruling class, scattered as it was over the region: They were the point of contact between officialdom and society. But inevitably, as that class declined and as the old landed nobility began to lose its special social character, the center of gravity of the political intelligentsia shifted to the towns. This shift was the decisive *political* factor in the agrarian development of the East.

But whose are the hands into which the political function of the Junkers is passing, and what kind of political vocation do they have?

I am a member of the bourgeois class: I feel myself to be such and have been brought up on its opinions and ideals. But it is the solemn vocation of our science to say things which people will not like to hear—alike to those above one, below one, and of one's own class. When I ask myself, therefore, whether the German bourgeoisie is at present ready to be the dominant political class in the nation, I cannot *at present* answer "Yes." It was not from the special resources of the bourgeoisie that the German state was created; and when it was created there stood at the head of the nation that Caesar-like figure who was not from bourgeois stock. Grandiose exercises in power-politics were not again imposed on the nation; it was only much later that bashfully and half unwillingly there began to be pursued overseas a "power-politics" which was not worthy of the name.

After the unity of the nation had been achieved in this way and political "satisfaction" was assured, the growing tribe of the German bourgeoisie, intoxicated with success and thirsty for peace, was overcome by a peculiarly "unhistorical" and unpolitical mood. German history seemed at an end. The present represented the complete fulfilment of the preceding millennia: Who cared to ask whether posterity might reach a different conclusion? World history—or so it seemed—could not, in all modesty, move on from these successes of the German nation to the minutiae of its everyday course. Nowadays we have become more sober: We ought to try to lift the veil of illusions which cloaks the true position of our generation in the historical development of our fatherland. I think we shall then judge differently. History has bestowed on us as a baptismal gift the most burdensome curse which it could give to any people: the harsh fate of *following* the period of political greatness.

Wherever we look in our country, are we not even now confronted by its wretched countenance? In the events of recent months, for which bourgeois politicians are mainly answerable, in all too many remarks made in the last few days both in and to the German Parliament, we could recognize with passionate anger and sorrow—those of us who retain the capacity to hate what is petty—the paltry maneuverings of political *epigoni*. The blazing sun which shone at Germany's zenith, and which caused the name of Germany to shine in the furthest corners of the earth—this sun was, so it almost seemed, *too* strong for us; it had burned away the bourgeoisie's slowly growing capacity for political judgment. For what do we see?

A section of the *haute bourgeoisie* longs, all too frankly, for the appearance of a new Caesar to protect it: to protect it from below, against the rising popular masses, and from above, against the social and political assaults which they suspect the German dynasties of making against them.

Yet another section has long sunk into that political philistinism from which the mass of the *petite bourgeoisie* has never stirred. Even early on, in the time after the wars of unification, when they were confronted with the first of the positive political tasks facing the nation, the idea of overseas expansion, they lacked even such an elementary grasp of *economics* as would have enabled them to see what it might mean for German trade in distant seas if the German flag were to be planted on their shores.

The blame for the political immaturity of large sections of the German bourgeoisie does not lie with economic factors, nor even with the much-criticized "politics of interest," with which other nations are as familiar as we are. The source of its immaturity lies in its unpolitical past: A century's work in political education could not be made good in a decade, and the dominance of a great man is not always a means of political education. The serious question for the political future of the German bourgeoisie is now whether it may already be too *late* to make good the deficiency. No *economic* factor can compensate.

Will other classes be the bearers of a politically greater future? Proudly, the modern proletariat presents itself as the heir to bourgeois ideals. How do things stand with its aspirations towards the political leadership of the nation?

Anyone who would today say to the German working class that it was politically mature or on the way to political maturity would be indulging in flattery in an attempt to gain the dubious crown of popularity.

Economically, the upper strata of the German working class are much more mature than the egoism of the property-owning classes might admit. Justifiably, therefore, they demand freedom, even by means of organized and open struggles for economic power to defend their interests. *Politically*, the working class is infinitely less mature than the clique of journalists who aspire to monopolize its leadership would have it believe. Much play is made with memories of a century ago in the circle of these *déclassés* bourgeois: The result is that here and there the more timid souls see in them the spiritual descendants of the men of the Convention. However, they are infinitely more harmless than they appear to themselves: There is in them no glimmer of that Catilinarian energy of the *act*, nor certainly does there breathe in them any of that storm of *national* passion which blew through the halls of the Convention. They are pathetic experts in political triviality: They lack the deep instincts for *power* of a class which has been called to political leadership. It is not only the vested interests of capital, as the workers are led to believe, which are today behind the political opposition to granting them a share in power in the state. They would find few signs of any community of interests with capital if they were to investigate German academic circles. Nevertheless, we ask *them too* about their *political maturity*. If we are the political opponents of the working class, it is because there is no greater disaster that can befall a great nation than leadership by a *politically* uneducated *philistine class*, and because the German proletariat has not yet lost this character. Why is the proletariat of England and France to some extent differently constituted? The reason is to be found not only in a longer period of *economic* education, resulting from the organized struggle of the English working class for its interests. It is rather a matter of the reverberations of world-power status, which constantly confronts the state with great problems of power-politics and which provides the individual with continuous political schooling. This kind of schooling only becomes pressing for the individual in our case when our frontiers are threatened. It is also crucial for *our* development whether the pursuit of policies on the grand scale would again be able to bring before our eyes the meaning of the great questions of political power. We must grasp that the unification of Germany was a youthful spree, indulged in by the nation in its old age; it would have been better if it had never taken place, since it would have been a costly extravagance, if it was the conclusion rather than the starting point for German power-politics on a global scale.

The *menacing* feature of our situation, however, is this: that the bourgeois classes, as bearers of the interests of the nation as a *power*, seem to be declining and that there is as yet no sign that the working class is ready to take their place.

The danger does *not* lie in the *masses*, as those who stare transfixed into the depths of society believe. The nub of the social and political problem is not the *economic* situation of the *ruled*, but rather the *political* qualifications of the *ruling* classes and those classes which are *rising* to power. The aim of our social and political work is not universal charity, but the *social unification* of that nation which modern economic development has created, in preparation for the difficult struggles of the future. Should it ever come about that a "labour aristocracy" should be created to be the bearer of the political intelligence which is missing from the present-day labour movement, then it might be possible to lay on those broad shoulders the spear which the arms of the bourgeoisie have become too feeble to carry. But it seems we still have a long way to travel before we reach that point.

For the moment, however, one thing is clear, that we must carry out a colossal programme of *political* education. We have no more solemn obligation than this, that each of us, in his own sphere, should become aware of the need to work together on the political education of our nation. This must remain the ultimate goal, too, of our science in particular. The economic development of transitional periods threatens the natural political instincts with atrophy; it would be unfortunate if even economic science were to lead to the same result, by cultivating a feeble eudaemonism, in however ethereal a form, behind the illusion of independent "sociopolitical" ideals.

To be sure, we should also for this reason remember that it is the opposite of political education to seek to embody in legal formulae a vote of no confidence in the peaceful social future of the nation; or for the secular arm to grasp the hand of the Church in order to support the temporal authorities. But there are also other obstacles to political education, such as the mechanical yapping of the steadily swelling chorus of (if you will excuse the expression) "backwoods" social politicians; or that soft-headed attitude, so agreeable and even admirable from the human point of view, but nevertheless so unutterably philistine, which thinks it possible to replace political with "ethical" ideals and innocently imagines that this is the same as optimistically hoping for the best.

Moreover, in view of the profound distress of the masses in our nation, which is so burdensome to the more acute social conscience of the new generation, we must frankly accept that today there weighs upon us still more heavily our answerability *before history*. It is not given to our generation to see whether the struggle in which we are engaged bears fruit, whether posterity will acknowledge us as its forerunners. We shall not succeed in exorcising the curse laid upon us, the curse of being born *after* a period of political greatness. It is essential therefore that we should know how to become something else, the forerunners of a greater period. Will that be our place in history? I do not know: I can only say that it is the right of youth to be true to itself and its ideals. And it is not years which make a man a greybeard: He remains young as long as he is capable of experiencing the *grand* passions which nature has implanted in us. So (and here I must draw to a close) it is not through carrying the burden of thousands of years of glorious history that a great nation grows old. It remains young, as long

as it has the capacity and the heart to be true to itself and the great instincts with which it has been endowed; as long as its dominant classes are
able to raise themselves up into the hard clear air in which the sober work
of German politics prospers but which is pervaded by the stern magnifi-
cence of our national feelings.

11

THEODOR HERZL

A Jewish State

THE JEWISH QUESTION

No one can deny the gravity of the Jews' situation. Wherever they live in perceptible numbers, they are more or less persecuted. Their equality before the law, granted by statute, has become practically a dead letter. They are debarred from filling even moderately high positions, either in the army, or in any public or private capacity. And attempts are made to crowd them out of business also. "No dealing with Jews!"

Attacks in Parliaments, in assemblies, in the press, in the pulpit, in the streets, on journeys—for example, their exclusion from certain hotels—even in places of recreation, become daily more numerous, the forms of persecution varying according to the countries in which they occur. In Russia, impositions are levied on Jewish villages; in Roumania, a few human beings are put to death; in Germany, they get a good beating when the occasion serves; in Austria, anti-Semites exercise terrorism over all public life; in Paris, they are shut out of the so-called best social circles and excluded from clubs. Shades of anti-Jewish feeling are innumerable. But this is not to be an attempt to make out a doleful category of Jewish hardships; it is futile to linger over details, however painful they may be.

I do not intend to awaken sympathetic emotions on our behalf. That would be a foolish, futile, and undignified proceeding. I shall content myself with putting the following questions to the Jews: Is it true that, in countries where we live in perceptible numbers, the position of Jewish lawyers, doctors, men of science, teachers, and officials of all descriptions, becomes daily more intolerable? True, that the Jewish middle classes are seriously threatened? True, that the passions of the mob are incited against our wealthy representatives? True, that our poor endure greater sufferings than any other proletariat?

I think that this external pressure makes itself felt everywhere. In our upper classes it causes unpleasantness, in our middle classes continual and grave anxieties, in our lower classes absolute despair.

Everything tends, in fact, to one and the same conclusion, which is clearly enunciated in that classic Berlin phrase: "*Juden raus!*" (Out with the Jews!)

I shall now put the Jewish Question in the curtest possible form: Are we to "get out" now? And if so, to what place?

Or, may we yet remain? And if so, how long?

Let us first settle the point of staying where we are. Can we hope for better days, can we possess our souls in patience, can we wait in pious resignation till the princes and peoples of this earth are more mercifully disposed towards us? I say that we cannot hope for a change in the current of feeling. And why not? Were we as near to the hearts of princes as are their other subjects, even so they could not protect us. They would only feed popular hatred of Jews by showing us too much favour. By "too much," I really mean less than is claimed as a right by every ordinary citizen, and by every tribe.

Every nation in whose midst Jews live is, either covertly or openly, anti-Semitic.

The common people have not, and indeed cannot have, any historic comprehension. They do not know that the sins of the Middle Ages are now being visited on the nations of Europe. We are what the Ghetto made us. We have doubtless attained pre-eminence in finance, because medieval conditions drove us to it. The same process is now being repeated. Modern conditions force us again into finance, now the stock exchange, by keeping us out of all other branches of industry. Being on the stock exchange, we are therefore again considered contemptible. At the same time we continue to produce an abundance of mediocre intellects which finds no outlet, and this endangers our social position as much as does our increasing wealth. Educated Jews without means are now fast becoming socialists. Hence we are certain to suffer very severely in the struggle between classes, because we stand in the most exposed position in the camps of both socialists and capitalists.

PREVIOUS ATTEMPTS AT A SOLUTION

The artificial means heretofore employed to overcome the troubles of Jews have been either too petty—such as attempts at colonization, or mistaken in principle—such as attempts to convert the Jews into peasants in their present homes.

What is the result of transporting a few thousand Jews to another country? Either they come to grief at once, or prosper, and then their prosperity creates anti-Semitism. We have already discussed these attempts to divert poor Jews to fresh districts. This diversion is clearly inadequate and futile, if it does not actually defeat its own ends; for it merely protracts and postpones a solution, and perhaps even aggravates difficulties.

Whoever were to attempt a conversion of the Jew into a husbandman would be making an extraordinary mistake. For a peasant is a historical category, as is proved by his costume, which in some countries he has worn for centuries; and by his tools, which are identical with those used by his earliest forefathers. His plough is unchanged; he carries the seed in his apron; mows with the historical scythe, and threshes with the time-honoured flail. But we know that all this can be done by machinery. The agrarian question is only a question of machinery. America must conquer Europe, in the same way as large landed possessions absorb small ones. [. . .]

Is it worthwhile pointing out the sentimental folly of this view? He who would found his hope for improved conditions on the ultimate perfection of humanity, would indeed be painting a Utopia!

I referred previously to our "assimilation"; I do not for a moment wish to imply that I desire such an end. Our national character is too historically famous, and, in spite of every degradation, too fine, to make its annihilation desirable. We might perhaps be able to merge ourselves entirely into surrounding races, if these were to leave us in peace for a space of two generations. But they will not leave us in peace. For a little period they manage to tolerate us, and then their hostility breaks out again and again. The world is provoked by our prosperity, because it has for many centuries been accustomed to consider us as the most contemptible among the poverty-stricken. It forgets, in its ignorance and narrowness of heart, that prosperity weakens our Judaism and extinguishes our peculiarities. It is only pressure that forces us back to the parent stem; it is only hatred encompassing us that makes us strangers once more.

Thus, whether we like it or not, we are now, and shall henceforth remain, a historic group with unmistakable characteristics common to us all.

We are one people—our enemies have made us one in our despite, as repeatedly happens in history. Distress binds us together, and, thus united, we suddenly discover our strength. Yes, we are strong enough to form a State, and a model State. We possess all human and material resources necessary for the purpose.

This is the strictly appropriate place for an account of what has been somewhat rudely termed our human material. But it would not be appreciated till the broad lines of the plan, on which everything depends, had first been marked out.

THE PLAN

[. . .] If we wish to found a State today, we shall not do it in the way which would have been the only possible one a thousand years ago. It is foolish to revert to old stages of civilization, as many Zionists would like to do. Supposing, for example, we were obliged to clear a country of wild beasts, we should not set about the business in the fashion of Europeans of the fifth century. We should not take spear and lance and go out singly in pursuit of bears; we should organize a large and active hunting party, drive the animals together, and throw a melinite bomb into their midst.

If we wish to conduct building operations, we shall not plant a mass of stakes and piles on the shore of a lake, but we shall build as men build now.

Indeed, we shall build in a bolder and more stately style than was ever adopted before, for we now possess means which men never yet possessed.

The emigrants standing lowest in the economic scale will be slowly followed by those of a higher grade. Those who at this moment are living in despair will go first. They will be led by the mediocre intellects which we produce so superabundantly, and which are persecuted everywhere.

This pamphlet will open a general discussion on the Jewish Question, avoiding, if possible, the creation of an opposition party. Such a result would ruin the cause from the outset, and dissentients must remember that allegiance or opposition is entirely voluntary. Who will not come with us, may remain.

Let all who are willing to join us, fall in behind our banner and fight for our cause with voice and pen and deed.

Those Jews who fall in with our idea of a State will attach themselves to the Society, which will thereby be authorized to confer and treat with Governments in the name of our people. The Society will thus be acknowledged in its relations with Governments as a State-creating power. This acknowledgment will practically create the State.

Should the Powers declare themselves willing to admit our sovereignty over a neutral piece of land, then the Society will enter into negotiations for the possession of this land. Here two territories come under consideration, Palestine and Argentina. In both countries important experiments in colonization have been made, though on the mistaken principle of a gradual infiltration of Jews. An infiltration is bound to end in disaster.

PALESTINE OR ARGENTINA?

Shall we choose Palestine or Argentina? We shall take what is given us, and what is selected by Jewish public opinion. The Society will settle both these points.

Argentina is one of the most fertile countries in the world, extends over a vast area, has a sparse population and a mild climate. The Argentine Republic would derive considerable profit from the cession of a portion of its territory to us. The present infiltration of Jews has certainly produced some friction, and it would be necessary to enlighten the Republic on the intrinsic difference of our new movement.

Palestine is our ever-memorable historic home. The very name of Palestine would attract our people with a force of marvelous potency. Supposing His Majesty the Sultan were to give us Palestine, we could in return pledge ourselves to regulate the whole finances of Turkey. We should there form a portion of the rampart of Europe against Asia, an outpost of civilization as opposed to barbarism. The sanctuaries of Christendom would be safeguarded by assigning to them an extra-territorial status, such as is well known to the law of nations. We should form a guard of honour about these sanctuaries, answering for the fulfilment of this duty with our existence. This guard of honour would be the great symbol of the solution of the Jewish Question after eighteen centuries of Jewish suffering. [. . .]

CONCLUSION

How much has been left unexplained, how many defects, how many regrettable signs of carelessness, how many useless repetitions, in the pamphlet which I have so long considered and so carefully revised!

But a fair-minded reader, who has sufficient understanding to grasp the spirit of my words, will not be repelled by these defects. He will rather be roused thereby to devote his intelligence and energy to the improvement of a work which is not one man's task alone.

Have I not explained obvious things and overlooked important considerations?

I have tried to meet certain objections; but I know that many more will be made based on high grounds and low.

To the first class of objections belongs the remark, that the Jews are not the only people in the world who are in a condition of distress. Here I would reply that we may as well begin by removing some of this misery, even if it should at first be no more than our own.

It might further be said that we ought not to create distinctions between people; we ought not to raise fresh barriers; we should rather make the old disappear. But men who think in this way are amiable visionaries; and the idea of a native land will still flourish when the dust of their bones will have vanished tracelessly in the winds. Universal brotherhood is not even a beautiful dream. Antagonism is essential to man's greatest efforts.

But the Jews, once settled in their own State, would probably have no more enemies, and since prosperity enfeebles and causes them to diminish, they would soon disappear altogether. I think the Jews will always have sufficient enemies, much as every other nation has. But once fixed on their own land, it will no longer be possible for them to scatter all over the world. The diaspora cannot take place again, unless the civilization of the whole earth is destroyed; and such a consummation could be feared by none but foolish men. Our present civilization possesses weapons powerful enough for its self-defense.

Innumerable objections will be based on low grounds, for there are more low men than noble in this world. I have tried to remove some of these narrow-minded notions; and whoever is willing to fall in behind our white flag with its seven golden stars must assist in this campaign of enlightenment. Perhaps we shall have to fight first of all against many an evil-disposed, narrow-hearted, short-sighted member of our own race.

Again, people will say that I am furnishing the anti-Semites with weapons. Why so? Because I admit the truth? Because I do not maintain that there are none but excellent men amongst us?

Again, people will say that I am showing our enemies the way to injure us. This I absolutely dispute. My proposal could only be carried out with the free consent of a majority of Jews. Individuals or even powerful bodies of Jews might be attacked, but Governments will take no action against the collective nation. The equal rights of Jews before the law cannot be withdrawn where they have once been conceded; for the first attempt at withdrawal would immediately drive all Jews, rich and poor alike, into the ranks of the revolutionary party. The first official violation of Jewish liberties invariably brings about an economic crisis. Therefore no weapons can be effectually used against us, because these cut the hands that wield them. Meantime hatred grows apace. The rich do not feel it much, but our poor do. Let us ask our poor, who have been more severely persecuted since the last renewal of anti-Semitism than ever before.

Our prosperous men may say that the pressure is not yet severe enough to justify emigration, and that every forcible expulsion shows how unwilling our people are to depart. True, because they do not know where to go; because they only pass from one trouble into another. But we are showing them the way to the Promised Land; and the splendid force of enthusiasm must fight against the terrible force of habit.

Persecutions are no longer so malignant as they were in the Middle Ages. True, but our sensitiveness has increased, so that we feel no diminution in our sufferings; endless persecution has overstrained our nerves.

Will people say, again, that our enterprise is hopeless, because even if we obtained the land with supremacy over it, the poor only would go with us? It is precisely the poorest whom we need at first. Only desperadoes make good conquerors.

Will someone say, were it feasible, it would have been done long ago?

It has never yet been possible; now it is possible. A hundred, or even fifty years ago, it would have been nothing more than a dream. Today it may become a reality. Our rich, who have a pleasurable acquaintance with all our technical acquisitions, know full well how much money can do. And thus it will be: just the poor and simple, who do not know what power man already exercises over the forces of nature, just these will have firmest faith in the new message; for these have never lost their hope of the Promised Land.

Here it is, fellow Jews! Neither fable nor fraud! Every man may test its reality for himself, for every man will carry with him a portion of the Promised Land—one in his head, another in his arms, another in his acquired possessions.

Now all this may appear to be an interminably long affair. Even under favourable circumstances many years might elapse before the commencement of the foundation of the State. Meantime, Jews in a hundred different places would suffer insults, mortification, abuse, blows, depredation, and death. Not so, the initial steps towards the execution of the plan would stop anti-Semitism at once and forever. Ours is a treaty of peace.

The news of the formation of our Jewish Company will be carried in a single day to the remotest ends of the earth by the lightning speed of our telegraph wires.

And immediate relief will ensue. The mediocre intellects which we produce so superabundantly in our middle classes will find an outlet in our first organizations, as our first scientists, officers, professors, officials, lawyers, and doctors, and thus the movement will continue in swift but smooth progression.

Prayers will be offered up for the success of our work in temples and in churches also; for it will bring ease from a burden which has long weighed on all men.

But we must first bring enlightenment to men's minds. The idea must make its way into the most distant, miserable holes where our people dwell. They will awaken from gloomy brooding, for into their lives will come a new significance. If every man thinks only of himself, what vast proportions the movement will assume!

And what glory awaits those who fight unselfishly for the cause!

Therefore I believe that a wondrous generation of Jews will spring into existence. The Maccabaeans will rise again.

Let me repeat once more my opening words: The Jews wish to have a State, and they shall have one.

We shall live at last as free men on our own soil, and die peacefully in our own home.

The world will be freed by our liberty, enriched by our wealth, magnified by our greatness.

And whatever we attempt there to accomplish for our own welfare will react with beneficent force for the good of humanity.

PART III

Conservatism and Nationalism

12

EDMUND BURKE

Reflections on the Revolution in France

You will observe that from Magna Charta to the Declaration of Right it has been the uniform policy of our constitution to claim and assert our liberties as an *entailed inheritance* derived to us from our forefathers, and to be transmitted to our posterity—as an estate specially belonging to the people of this kingdom, without any reference whatever to any other more general or prior right. By this means our constitution preserves a unity in so great a diversity of its parts. We have an inheritable crown, an inheritable peerage, and a House of Commons and a people inheriting privileges, franchises, and liberties from a long line of ancestors.

This policy appears to me to be the result of profound reflection, or rather the happy effect of following nature, which is wisdom without reflection, and above it. A spirit of innovation is generally the result of a selfish temper and confined views. People will not look forward to posterity, who never look backward to their ancestors. Besides, the people of England well know that the idea of inheritance furnishes a sure principle of conservation and a sure principle of transmission, without at all excluding a principle of improvement. It leaves acquisition free, but it secures what it acquires. Whatever advantages are obtained by a state proceeding on these maxims are locked fast as in a sort of family settlement, grasped as in a kind of mortmain forever. By a constitutional policy, working after the pattern of nature, we receive, we hold, we transmit our government and our privileges in the same manner in which we enjoy and transmit our property and our lives. The institutions of policy, the goods of fortune, the gifts of providence are handed down to us, and from us, in the same course and order. Our political system is placed in a just correspondence and symmetry with the order of the world and with the mode of existence decreed to a permanent body composed of transitory parts, wherein, by the disposition of a stupendous wisdom, molding together the great mysterious incorporation of the human race, the whole, at one time, is never old or middle-aged or young, but, in a condition of unchangeable constancy, moves on through the varied tenor of perpetual decay, fall, renovation, and progression. Thus, by preserving the method of nature in the conduct of the state, in what we improve we are never wholly new; in what we retain we are never wholly obsolete. By adhering in this manner and on those principles to our forefathers, we are guided not by the superstition of antiquarians, but the spirit of philosophic analogy. In this choice of inheritance we have given to our frame of polity the image of a relation in blood, binding up the constitution of our country with our dearest domestic ties, adopting our fundamental laws into the bosom of our family affections, keeping inseparable and cherishing with the warmth of all their combined and mutually reflected charities our state, our hearths, our sepulchres, and our altars.

Through the same plan of a conformity to nature in our artificial institutions, and by calling in the aid of her unerring and powerful instincts to fortify the fallible and feeble contrivances of our reason, we have derived several other, and those not small, benefits from considering our liberties in the light of an inheritance. Always acting as if in the presence of canonized forefathers, the spirit of freedom, leading in itself to misrule and excess, is tempered with an awful gravity. This idea of a liberal descent inspires us with the sense of habitual native dignity which prevents that upstart insolence almost inevitably adhering to and disgracing those who are the first acquirers of any distinction. By this means our liberty becomes a noble freedom. It carries an imposing and majestic aspect. It has a pedigree and illustrating ancestors. It has its bearings and its ensigns armorial. It has its gallery of portraits, its monumental inscriptions, its records, evidences, and titles. We procure reverence to our civil institutions on the principle upon which nature teaches us to revere individual men: on account of their age and on account of those from whom they are descended. All your sophisters cannot produce anything better adapted to preserve a rational and manly freedom than the course that we have pursued, who have chosen our nature rather than our speculations, our breasts rather than our inventions, for the great conservatories and magazines of our rights and privileges.

You might, if you pleased, have profited of our example and have given to your recovered freedom a correspondent dignity. Your privileges, though discontinued, were not lost to memory. Your constitution, it is true, whilst you were out of possession, suffered waste and dilapidation; but you possessed in some parts the walls and in all the foundations of a noble and venerable castle. You might have repaired those walls; you might have built on those old foundations. Your constitution was suspended before it was perfected, but you had the elements of a constitution very nearly as good as could be wished. In your old states you possessed that variety of parts corresponding with the various descriptions of which your community was happily composed; you had all that combination and all that opposition of interests; you had that action and counteraction which, in the natural and in the political world, from the reciprocal struggle of discordant powers, draws out the harmony of the universe. These opposed and conflicting interests which you considered as so great a blemish in your old and in our present constitution interpose a salutary check to all precipitate resolutions. They render deliberation a matter, not of choice, but of necessity; they make all change a subject of *compromise*, which naturally begets moderation; they produce *temperaments* preventing the sore evil of harsh, crude, unqualified reformations, and rendering all the headlong exertions of arbitrary power, in the few or in the many, forever impracticable. Through that diversity of members and interests, general liberty had as many securities as there were separate views in the several orders, whilst, by pressing down the whole by the weight of a real monarchy, the separate parts would have been prevented from warping and starting from their allotted places.

You had all these advantages in your ancient states, but you chose to act as if you had never been molded into civil society and had everything to begin anew. You began ill, because you began by despising everything that belonged to you. [. . .]

Nothing is a due and adequate representation of a state that does not represent its ability as well as its property. But as ability is a vigorous and active principle, and as property is sluggish, inert, and timid, it never can be safe from the invasion of ability unless it be, out of all proportion, predominant in the representation. It must be represented, too, in great masses of accumulation, or it is not rightly protected. The characteristic essence of property, formed out of the combined principles of its acquisition and conservation, is to be *unequal*. The great masses, therefore, which excite envy and tempt rapacity must be put out of the possibility of danger. Then they form a natural rampart about the lesser properties in all their gradations. The same quantity of property, which is by the natural course of things divided among many, has not the same operation. Its defensive power is weakened as it is diffused. In this diffusion each man's portion is less than what, in the eagerness of his desires, he may flatter himself to obtain by dissipating the accumulations of others. The plunder of the few would indeed give but a share inconceivably small in the distribution to the many. But the many are not capable of making this calculation; and those who lead them to rapine never intend this distribution.

The power of perpetuating our property in our families is one of the most valuable and interesting circumstances belonging to it, and that which tends the most to the perpetuation of society itself. It makes our weakness subservient to our virtue, it grafts benevolence even upon avarice. The possessors of family wealth, and of the distinction which attends hereditary possession (as most concerned in it), are the natural *securities* for this transmission. With us the House of Peers is formed upon this principle. It is wholly composed of hereditary property and hereditary distinction, and made, therefore, the third of the legislature and, in the last event, the sole judge of all property in all its subdivisions. The House of Commons, too, though not necessarily, yet in fact, is always so composed, in the far greater part. Let those large proprietors be what they will—and they have their chance of being amongst the best—they are, at the very worst, the ballast in the vessel of the commonwealth. For though hereditary wealth and the rank which goes with it are too much idolized by creeping sycophants and the blind, abject admirers of power, they are too rashly slighted in shallow speculations of the petulant, assuming, short-sighted coxcombs of philosophy. Some decent, regulated pre-eminence, some preference (not exclusive appropriation) given to birth is neither unnatural, nor unjust, nor impolitic. [. . .]

If it could have been made clear to me that the king and queen of France (those I mean who were such before the triumph) were inexorable and cruel tyrants, that they had formed a deliberate scheme for massacring the National Assembly (I think I have seen something like the latter insinuated in certain publications), I should think their captivity just. If this be true, much more ought to have been done, but done, in my opinion, in another manner. The punishment of real tyrants is a noble and awful act of justice; and it has with truth been said to be consolatory to the human mind. But if I were to punish a wicked king, I should regard the dignity in avenging the crime. Justice is grave and decorous, and in its punishments rather seems to submit to a necessity than to make a choice. Had Nero, or Agrippina, or Louis the Eleventh, or Charles the Ninth been the subject; if Charles the Twelfth of Sweden, after the murder of Patkul, or his predecessor Christina, after the murder of Monaldeschi, had fallen into your hands, Sir, or into mine, I am sure our conduct would have been different.

If the French king, or king of the French (or by whatever name he is known in the new vocabulary of your constitution), has in his own person and that of his queen really deserved these unavowed, but unavenged, murderous attempts and those frequent indignities more cruel than murder, such a person would ill deserve even that subordinate executory trust which I understand is to be placed in him, nor is he fit to be called chief in a nation which he has outraged and oppressed. A worse choice for such an office in a new commonwealth than that of a deposed tyrant could not possibly be made. But to degrade and insult a man as the worst of criminals and afterwards to trust him in your highest concerns as a faithful, honest, and zealous servant is not consistent to reasoning, nor prudent in policy, nor safe in practice. Those who could make such an appointment must be guilty of a more flagrant breach of trust than any they have yet committed against the people. As this is the only crime in which your leading politicians could have acted inconsistently, I conclude that there is no sort of ground for these horrid insinuations. I think no better of all the other calumnies. [. . .]

I almost venture to affirm that not one in a hundred amongst us participates in the "triumph" of the Revolution Society. If the king and queen of

France, and their children, were to fall into our hands by the chance of
war, in the most acrimonious of all hostilities (I deprecate such an event, I
deprecate such hostility), they would be treated with another sort of trium-
phal entry into London. We formerly have had a king of France in that
situation; you have read how he was treated by the victor in the field, and
in what manner he was afterwards received in England. Four hundred years
have gone over us, but I believe we are not materially changed since that
period. Thanks to our sullen resistance to innovation, thanks to the cold
sluggishness of our national character, we still bear the stamp of our forefathers. We have not (as I conceive) lost the generosity and dignity of thinking of the fourteenth century, nor as yet have we subtilized ourselves into
savages. We are not the converts of Rousseau; we are not the disciples of
Voltaire; Helvetius has made no progress amongst us. Atheists are not our
preachers; madmen are not our lawgivers. We know that *we* have made no
discoveries, and we think that no discoveries are to be made in morality,
nor many in the great principles of government, nor in the ideas of liberty,
which were understood long before we were born, altogether as well as they
will be after the grace has heaped its mold upon our presumption and the
silent tomb shall have imposed its law on our pert loquacity. In England we
have not yet been completely embowelled of our natural entrails; we still
feel within us, and we cherish and cultivate, those inbred sentiments which
are the faithful guardians, the active monitors of our duty, the true supporters of all liberal and manly morals. We have not been drawn and trussed,
in order that we may be filled, like stuffed birds in a museum, with chaff
and rags and paltry blurred shreds of paper about the rights of men. We
preserve the whole of our feelings still native and entire, unsophisticated
by pedantry and infidelity. We have real hearts of flesh and blood beating
in our bosoms. We fear God; we look up with awe to kings, with affection
to parliaments, with duty to magistrates, with reverence to priests, and with
respect to nobility. Why? Because when such ideas are brought before our
minds, it is *natural* to be so affected; because all other feelings are false and
spurious and tend to corrupt our minds, to vitiate our primary morals, to
render us unfit for rational liberty, and, by teaching us a servile, licentious,
and abandoned insolence, to be our low sport for a few holidays, to make
us perfectly fit for, and justly deserving of, slavery through the whole course
of our lives.

You see, Sir, that in this enlightened age I am bold enough to confess that
we are generally men of untaught feelings, that, instead of casting away all
our old prejudices, we cherish them to a very considerable degree, and, to
take more shame to ourselves, we cherish them because they are prejudices;
and the longer they have lasted and the more generally they have prevailed, the more we cherish them. We are afraid to put men to live and
trade each on his own private stock of reason, because we suspect that this

stock in each man is small, and that the individuals would do better to avail themselves of the general bank and capital of nations and of ages. Many of our men of speculation, instead of exploding general prejudices, employ their sagacity to discover the latent wisdom which prevails in them. If they find what they seek, and they seldom fail, they think it more wise to continue the prejudice, with the reason involved, than to cast away the coat of prejudice and to leave nothing but the naked reason; because prejudice, with its reason, has a motive to give action to that reason, and an affection which will give it permanence. Prejudice is of ready application in the emergency; it previously engages the mind in a steady course of wisdom and virtue and does not leave the man hesitating in the moment of decision skeptical, puzzled, and unresolved. Prejudice renders a man's virtue his habit, and not a series of unconnected acts. Through just prejudice, his duty becomes a part of his nature. [. . .]

We know, and what is better, we feel inwardly, that religion is the basis of civil society and the source of all good and of all comfort. In England we are so convinced of this, that there is no rust of superstition with which the accumulated absurdity of the human mind might have crusted it over in the course of ages, that ninety-nine in a hundred of the people of England would not prefer to impiety. We shall never be such fools as to call in an enemy to the substance of any system to remove its corruptions, to supply its defects, or to perfect its construction. If our religious tenets should ever want a further elucidation, we shall not call on atheism to explain them. We shall not light up our temple from that unhallowed fire. It will be illuminated with other lights. It will be perfumed with other incense than the infectious stuff which is imported by the smugglers of adulterated metaphysics. If our ecclesiastical establishment should want a revision, it is not avarice or rapacity, public or private, that we shall employ for the audit, or receipt, or application of its consecrated revenue. Violently condemning neither the Greek nor the Armenian nor, since heats are subsided, the Roman system of religion, we prefer the Protestant, not because we think it has less of the Christian religion in it, but because, in our judgment, it has more. We are Protestants, not from indifference, but from zeal.

We know, and it is our pride to know, that man is by his constitution a religious animal; that atheism is against, not only our reason, but our instincts; and that it cannot prevail long. But if, in the moment of riot and in a drunken delirium from the hot spirit drawn out of the alembic of hell, which in France is now so furiously boiling, we should uncover our nakedness by throwing off that Christian religion which has hitherto been our boast and comfort, and one great source of civilization amongst us and amongst many other nations, we are apprehensive (being well aware that the mind will not endure a void) that some uncouth, pernicious, and degrading superstition might take the place of it.

For that reason, before we take from our establishment the natural, human means of estimation and give it up to contempt, as you have done,
and in doing it have incurred the penalties you well deserve to suffer, we
desire that some other may be presented to us in the place of it. We shall
then form our judgment.

On these ideas, instead of quarrelling with establishments, as some do
who have made a philosophy and a religion of their hostility to such institutions, we cleave closely to them. We are resolved to keep an established
church, an established monarchy, an established aristocracy, and an established democracy, each in the degree it exists, and in no greater. I shall
show you presently how much of each of these we possess.

It has been the misfortune (not, as these gentlemen think it, the glory)
of this age that everything is to be discussed as if the constitution of our
country were to be always a subject rather of alteration than enjoyment.
For this reason, as well as for the satisfaction of those among you (if any
such you have among you) who may wish to profit of examples, I venture
to trouble you with a few thoughts upon each of these establishments. I do
not think they were unwise in ancient Rome who, when they wished to
new-model their laws, set commissioners to examine the best constituted
republics within their reach.

First, I beg leave to speak of our church establishment, which is the first
of our prejudices, not a prejudice destitute of reason, but involving in it
profound and extensive wisdom. I speak of it first. It is first and last and
midst in our minds. For, taking ground on that religious system of which
we are now in possession, we continue to act on the early received and
uniformly continued sense of mankind. That sense not only, like a wise
architect, hath built up the august fabric of states, but, like a provident
proprietor, to preserve the structure from profanation and ruin, as a sacred
temple purged from all the impurities of fraud and violence and injustice
and tyranny, hath solemnly and forever consecrated the commonwealth and
all that officiate in it. This consecration is made that all who administer
the government of men, in which they stand in the person of God himself,
should have high and worthy notions of their function and destination,
that their hope should be full of immortality, that they should not look to
the paltry pelf of the moment nor to the temporary and transient praise of
the vulgar, but to a solid, permanent existence in the permanent part of
their nature, and to a permanent fame and glory in the example they leave
as a rich inheritance to the world.

Such sublime principles ought to be infused into persons of exalted situations, and religious establishment provided that may continually revive
and enforce them. Every sort of moral, every sort of civil, every sort of
politic institution, aiding the rational and natural ties that connect the
human understanding and affections to the divine, are not more than necessary
in order to build up that wonderful structure Man, whose prerogative it is

to be in a great degree a creature of his own making, and who, when made as he ought to be made, is destined to hold no trivial place in the creation. But whenever man is put over men, as the better nature ought ever to preside, in that case more particularly, he should as nearly as possible be approximated to his perfection.

The consecration of the state by a state religious establishment is necessary, also, to operate with a wholesome awe upon free citizens, because, in order to secure their freedom, they must enjoy some determinate portion of power. To them, therefore, a religion connected with the state, and with their duty toward it, becomes even more necessary than in such societies where the people, by the terms of their subjection, are confined to private sentiments and the management of their own family concerns. All persons possessing any portion of power ought to be strongly and awfully impressed with an idea that they act in trust, and that they are to account for their conduct in that trust to the one great Master, Author, and Founder of society. [. . .]

To avoid, therefore, the evils of inconstancy and versatility, ten thousand times worse than those of obstinacy and the blindest prejudice, we have consecrated the state, that no man should approach to look into its defects or corruptions but with due caution, that he should never dream of beginning its reformation by its subversion, that he should approach to the faults of the state as to the wounds of a father, with pious awe and trembling solicitude. By this wise prejudice we are taught to look with horror on those children of their country who are prompt rashly to hack that aged parent in pieces and put him into the kettle of magicians, in hopes that by their poisonous weeds and wild incantations they may regenerate the paternal constitution and renovate their father's life.

Society is indeed a contract. Subordinate contracts for objects of mere occasional interest may be dissolved at pleasure—but the state ought not to be considered as nothing better than a partnership agreement in a trade of pepper and coffee, calico, or tobacco, or some other such low concern, to be taken up for a little temporary interest, and to be dissolved by the fancy of the parties. It is to be looked on with other reverence, because it is not a partnership in things subservient only to the gross animal existence of a temporary and perishable nature. It is a partnership in all science; a partnership in all art; a partnership in every virtue and in all perfection. As the ends of such a partnership cannot be obtained in many generations, it becomes a partnership not only between those who are living, but between those who are living, those who are dead, and those who are to be born. Each contract of each particular state is but a clause in the great primeval contract of eternal society, linking the lower with the higher natures, connecting the visible and invisible world, according to a fixed compact sanctioned by the inviolable oath which holds all physical and all moral natures, each in their appointed place. This law is not subject to the will of those who by an obligation above them, and infinitely superior, are bound to submit their will to that law. The municipal corporations of that universal kingdom are not morally at liberty at their pleasure, and on their speculations of a contingent improvement, wholly to separate and tear asunder the bands of their subordinate community and to dissolve it into an unsocial, uncivil, unconnected chaos of elementary principles. It is the first and supreme necessity only, a necessity that is not chosen but chooses, a necessity paramount to deliberation, that admits no discussion and demands no evidence, which alone can justify a resort to anarchy. This necessity is no exception to the rule, because this necessity itself is a part, too, of that moral and physical disposition of things to which man must be obedient by consent or force; but if that which is only submission to necessity should be made the object of choice, the law is broken, nature is disobeyed, and the rebellious are outlawed, cast forth, and exiled from this world of reason, and order, and peace, and virtue, and fruitful penitence, into the antagonist world of madness, discord, vice, confusion, and unavailing sorrow.

13

ERNEST RENAN

What Is a Nation?

I

Since the end of the Roman Empire, or rather since the dismemberment of the empire of Charlemagne, Western Europe appears to us as divided into nations, some of which have, at certain periods, tried to establish a hegemony over others, without ever achieving any permanent success. Where Charles V, Louis XIV, and Napoleon I failed, no man in the future will probably ever succeed. To set up a new Roman Empire or a new empire such as that of Charlemagne has become an impossibility. Europe is so much divided that any attempt at universal domination would immediately produce a coalition that would compel the ambitious nation to retire within its natural limits. A kind of durable balance has been established. Centuries may pass, but France, England, Germany, and Russia, in spite of all their adventures, will retain their distinct historical individuality, like pieces on a draught-board, the squares of which are ever varying in size and importance, but never quite blend completely.

Nations, thus conceived, are a fairly recent phenomenon in history. Such nations were unknown in ancient times. Egypt, China, and old Chaldaea were by no manner of means nations. They were flocks led by an offspring of the Sun or an offspring of Heaven. There were no Egyptian citizens, any more than there are Chinese citizens. The classical antique world had its republics and royal towns, its confederations of local republics and its empires, but it hardly had a nation in our sense of the word. Athens, Sparta, Sidon, and Tyre are small centres of patriotism, however admirable; they are cities possessing relatively small territories. Gaul, Spain, and Italy, before their absorption into the Roman Empire, were assemblies of tribes, often in league with one another, but without central institutions or dynasties. Nor could the empires of Assyria or Persia or that of Alexander point to any mother country. There were never any Assyrian patriots; nor was the empire of Persia anything but a vast feudal estate. There is not a nation that traces its origin back to Alexander's colossal enterprise, which was yet so fertile in its consequences for the general history of civilization.

The Roman Empire came much nearer to being a mother country. Roman rule, at first so hard to bear, very soon became loved in return for the immense benefit conferred by the suppression of war. It was a grand association, synonymous with order, peace, and civilization. During its closing period, men of lofty mind, enlightened clerics, and the educated classes had a real sense of "the Roman Peace," as opposed to the menacing chaos of barbarism. But an empire twelve times as great as France is today could not be termed a State in the modern sense of the word. The split between East and West was inevitable. In the third century attempts at a Gallic empire failed; and it was the Germanic invasion that ushered into the world the principle which afterwards served as a basis for the existence of nationalities.

What in fact did the Germanic peoples accomplish from the time of their great invasions in the fifth century to the last Norman conquests in the tenth? They effected little change in the essential character of races, but they imposed dynasties and a military aristocracy on more or less important areas within the former empire of the West, and these areas assumed the names of their invaders. Hence we have a France, a Burgundy, a Lombardy, and—later on—a Normandy. The rapid superiority won by the Frankish Empire renewed, for a brief period, the unity of the West. But about the middle of the ninth century this empire was shattered beyond repair. The Treaty of Verdun laid down its dividing lines, immutable in principle, and from that time France, Germany, England, Italy, and Spain march forward, by ways often tortuous and beset by countless hazards, to their full national existence such as we see spread out before us today.

What is, in fact, the distinguishing mark of these various States? It is the fusion of the populations that compose them. There is no analogy between the countries we have just mentioned and the state of affairs in Turkey, where Turk, Slav, Greek, Armenian, Arab, Syrian, and Kurd are as distinct today as at the time of the conquest. Two essential circumstances contributed to this result. First, the fact that the Germanic peoples adopted Christianity as soon as they came into more or less permanent contact with the Greek and Latin peoples. When victor and vanquished have the same religion, or rather when the victor adopts the religion of the vanquished, there can be no question of the Turkish system of complete discrimination according to a man's religion. The second circumstance was that the victors forgot their own language. The grandsons of Clovis, Alaric, Gondebaud, Alboin, and Rollo spoke the Roman tongue. This fact was itself the consequence of another important particular circumstance, viz., that the Franks, Burgundians, Goths, Lombards, and Normans were accompanied by very few women of their own race. During several generations the chiefs married none but German wives. But their concubines and their children's nurses were Latins, and the whole tribe married Latin women, with the result that, from the time of the settlement of the Franks and Goths on Roman soil, the *lingua francica* and the *lingua gothica* had but a very short career. It was not so in England, since the Anglo-Saxon invaders doubtless brought wives with them. The British population fled before them, and furthermore, Latin was no longer, or rather had never been, the dominant language in Britain. If, in the fifth century, Old French had been the general language in Gaul, Clovis and his men would not have deserted their Germanic tongue in favour of Old French.

Hence we get the following most important result, namely that, in spite of the brutality of the invaders, the pattern laid down by them became, in the course of time, the very pattern of the nation. Quite rightly, *France* became the name of a country containing but an imperceptible minority of Franks. [. . .]

To forget and—I will venture to say—to get one's history wrong, are essential factors in the making of a nation; and thus the advance of historical studies is often a danger to nationality. Historical research, in fact, casts fresh light upon those deeds of violence which have marked the origin of all political formations, even of those which have been followed by the most beneficial results. Unity is always realized by brute force. The union of North and South in France was the result of a reign of terror and extermination carried on for nearly a century. The French monarchy, which is generally regarded as typifying a steady process of crystallization and as having brought about the most perfect example of national unity known to history, when studied more closely loses its glamour. It was cursed by the nation that it was engaged in moulding, and today it is only those who can see the past in perspective who can appreciate the value of its achievement.

These great laws in the history of Western Europe become obvious by contrast. Many countries have failed in such an enterprise as that which the king of France, partly by his tyranny and partly by his justice, brought to so admirable a conclusion. Beneath the crown of St. Stephen, Magyars and Slavs have remained as distinct as they were eight hundred years ago. The House of Habsburg, far from blending the diverse elements in its dominions, has kept them apart and often in opposition to each other. In Bohemia the Czech and German elements are superposed like oil and water in a glass. The Turkish policy of separating nationalities according to religion has had very much graver consequences, since it has entailed the ruin of the East. Take a town like Salonica or Smyrna, and you will find five or six communities, each with its own memories and almost nothing in common. Now it is of the essence of a nation that all individuals should have much in common, and further that they should all have forgotten much. No French citizen knows whether he is a Burgundian, an Alan, a Taifal, or a Visigoth, while every French citizen must have forgotten the massacre of St. Bartholomew's and the massacres in the South in the thirteenth century. Not ten families in France can prove their Frankish descent, and even if they could, such a proof would be inherently unsound, owing to the innumerable unknown alliances capable of upsetting all genealogical systems. The modern nation is, therefore, the historic consequence of a series of facts converging towards the same point. Sometimes unity has been brought about by a dynasty, as in the case of France; at other times it has been brought about by the direct volition of provinces, as in the case of Holland, Switzerland, and Belgium; or again, by a general sentiment, the tardy conqueror of the freaks of feudalism, as in the case of Italy and Germany. At all times such formations have been guided by the urge of some deep-seated reason. In such cases, principles burst out with the most unexpected surprises. In our own times we have seen Italy unified by its defeats and Turkey demolished by its victories. Every defeat advanced the Italian cause, while every victory served to ruin Turkey, since Italy is a nation, and Turkey, apart from Asia Minor, is not. It is to the glory of France that, by the French Revolution, she proclaimed that a nation exists of itself. It is not for us to disapprove of imitators. The principle of nations is our principle. But what, then, is a nation? Why is Holland a nation, while Hanover and the Grand Duchy of Parma are not? How is it that France persists in being a nation, when the principle that created her has vanished? Why is Switzerland, with its three languages, its two religions, and three or four races, a nation, when Tuscany, for example, which is so homogeneous, is not? Why is Austria a state and not a nation? In what does the principle of nations differ from that of races? These are points on which thoughtful men require, for their own peace of mind, to come to some conclusion. Although the affairs of the world are rarely settled by arguments of this nature, yet studious men like to bring reason to bear, on these questions, and to unravel the skein of confusion that entangles the superficial mind.

II

We are told by certain political theorists that a nation is, above all, a dynasty representing a former conquest that has been at first accepted, and then forgotten, by the mass of the people. According to these politicians, the grouping of provinces effected by a dynasty, its wars, marriages, and treaties, ends with the dynasty that has formed it. It is quite true that most modern nations have been made by a family of feudal origin, which has married into the country and provided some sort of centralizing nucleus. The boundaries of France in 1789 were in no way natural or necessary. The large area that the House of Capet had added to the narrow strip accorded by the Treaty of Verdun was indeed the personal acquisition of that family. At the time when the annexations were made no one thought about natural limits, the right of nations, or the wishes of provinces. Similarly, the union of England, Ireland, and Scotland was a dynastic performance. The only reason why Italy took so long to become a nation was that, until the present century, none of her numerous reigning families became a centre of union. It is an odd fact that she derives the royal[1] title from the obscure island of Sardinia, a land which is scarcely Italian. Holland, self-created by an act of heroic resolution, has nonetheless entered into a close bond of marriage with the House of Orange, and would run serious risks, should this union ever be endangered.

Is, however, such a law absolute? Doubtless, it is not. Switzerland and the United States which have been formed, like conglomerates, by successive additions, are based on no dynasty. I will not discuss the question insofar as it concerns France. One would have to be able to read the future in order to do so. Let us merely observe that this great French line of kings had become so thoroughly identified with the national life that, on the morrow of its downfall, the nation was able to subsist without it. Furthermore, the eighteenth century had entirely changed the situation. After centuries of humiliation, man had recovered his ancient spirit, his self-respect, and the idea of his rights. The words "mother country" and "citizen" had regained their meaning. Thus it was possible to carry out the boldest operation ever performed in history—an operation that may be compared to what, in physiology, would be an attempt to bring back to its former life a body from which brain and heart had been removed.

It must, therefore, be admitted that a nation can exist without any dynastic principle, and even that nations formed by dynasties can be separated from them without thereby ceasing to exist. The old principle, which takes into account only the right of princes, can no longer be maintained: And, besides dynastic right, there exists also national right. On what criterion is this national right to be based? By what sign is it to be known? And from what tangible fact is it properly to be derived?

1. Many will boldly reply, from race. The artificial divisions, they say, the results of feudalism, royal marriages, and diplomatic congresses, have broken down. Race is what remains stable and fixed; and this it is that constitutes a right and a lawful title. The Germanic race, for example, according to this theory, has the right to retake the scattered members of the Germanic family, even when these members do not ask for reunion. The right of the Germanic family over such-and-such a province is better than the right of its inhabitants over themselves. A sort of primordial right is thus created analogous to the divine right of kings; and the principle of ethnography is substituted for that of nations. This is a very grave error, and if it should prevail, it would spell the ruin of European civilization. The principle of the primordial right of race is as narrow and as fraught with danger for true progress as the principle of nations is just and legitimate.

We admit that, among the tribes and cities of the ancient world, the fact of race was of capital importance. The ancient tribe and city were but an extension of the family. In Sparta and Athens all citizens were related more or less closely to each other. It was the same among the Beni-Israel; and it is still so among the Arab tribes. But let us leave Athens, Sparta, and the Jewish tribe and turn to the Roman Empire. Here we have quite a different state of affairs. This great agglomeration of completely diverse towns and provinces, formed in the first place by violence and then held together by common interests, cuts at the very root of the racial idea. Christianity, characteristically universal and absolute, works even more effectively in the same direction. It contracts a close alliance with the Roman Empire, and, under the influence of these two incomparable unifying agents, the ethnographic argument is for centuries dismissed from the government of human affairs.

In spite of appearances, the barbarian invasions were a step further on this road. The barbarian kingdoms which were then cut out have nothing ethnographic about them; they were decided by the forces or whims of the conquerors, who were completely indifferent with regard to the race of the peoples whom they subjugated. Charlemagne reconstructed in his own way what Rome had already built, viz., a single empire composed of the most diverse races. The authors of the Treaty of Verdun, calmly drawing their two long lines from north to south, did not pay the slightest attention to the race of the peoples to right or left of them. The frontier changes which took place in the later Middle Ages were also devoid of all ethnographic tendencies. Let it be granted that the consistent policy of the Capets managed more or less to gather together, under the name of France, the territories of ancient Gaul; yet this was by no means the consequence of any tendency on the part of their inhabitants to unite themselves with their kindred. Dauphiné, Bresse, Provence, and Franche-Comté no longer remembered any common origin. The consciousness of Gallic race had been lost since the second century A.D., and it is only in modern times, and retrospectively, that the erudite have unearthed the peculiarities of the Gallic character.

Ethnographic considerations have, therefore, played no part in the formation of modern nations. France is Celtic, Iberic, and Germanic. Germany is Germanic, Celtic, and Slav. Italy is the country in which ethnography finds its greatest difficulties. Here Gauls, Etruscans, Pelasgians, and Greeks are crossed in an unintelligible medley. The British Isles, taken as a whole, exhibit a mixture of Celtic and Germanic blood, the proportions of which are particularly difficult to define.

The truth is that no race is pure, and that to base politics on ethnographic analysis is tantamount to basing it on a chimera. The noblest countries, England, France, and Italy, are those where breeds are most mixed. Is Germany an exception in this respect? Is she a purely Germanic country? What a delusion to suppose it! All the South was Gallic; and all the East, starting from the Elbe, is Slav. And as for those areas which are said to be really pure from the racial point of view, are they in fact so? Here we touch on one of those problems concerning which it is most important to have clear ideas and to prevent misunderstandings.

Discussions on race are endless, because the word "race" is taken by historians who are philologists and by anthropologists with physiological leanings in two quite different senses.[2] For the anthropologists race has the same meaning as it has in zoology: It connotes real descent—blood relationship.

Now the study of languages and history does not lead to the same divisions as physiology. The words "brachycephalic" and "dolichocephalic" find no place either in history or philology. Within the human group that created the Aryan tongues and the Aryan rules of life there were already brachycephalics and dolichocephalics; and the same must be said of the primitive group that created the languages and institutions termed Semitic. In other words, the zoological origins of the human race are vastly anterior to the origins of culture, civilization, and language. The primitive Aryan, Semitic, and Turanian groups were joined in no physiological unity. These groupings are historical facts which took place at a certain period, let us say fifteen or twenty thousand years ago; whereas the zoological origin of the human race is lost in impenetrable darkness. What the sciences of philology and history call the Germanic race is assuredly a quite distinct family among humankind. But is it a family in the anthropological sense? Certainly not. The distinctive German character appears in history only a very few centuries before Jesus Christ. Obviously the Germans did not emerge from the earth at that period. Before that time, when mingled with the Slavs in the great shadowy mass of Scythians, they possessed no distinctive character. An Englishman is certainly a type in the whole sum of humankind. Now the type of what is very incorrectly termed the Anglo-Saxon race[3] is neither the Briton of the time of Caesar, nor the Anglo-Saxon of Hengist, nor the Dane of Canute, nor the Norman of William the Conqueror: It is the sum total of all these. The Frenchman is neither a Gaul, nor a Frank, nor a Burgundian. He is that which has emerged from the great cauldron in which, under the eye of the king of France, the most diverse elements have been simmering. As regards his origin, an inhabitant of Jersey or Guernsey differs in no way from the Norman population of the neighbouring coast. In the eleventh century the most piercing gaze would not have perceived the slightest difference on either side of the strait. Trilling circumstances decided Philip Augustus not to take these islands together with the rest of Normandy. Separated from each other for nearly seven hundred years, the two peoples have become not only foreign to each other, but entirely dissimilar. Race, then, as we historians understand it, is something that is made and unmade. The study of race is of prime importance for the man of learning engaged on the history of humankind. It is not applicable to politics. The instinctive consciousness which has presided over the drawing of the map of Europe has held race to be no account, and the leading nations of Europe are those of essentially mixed breed.

The fact of race, therefore, while vitally important at the outset, tends always to become less so. There is an essential difference between human history and zoology. Here race is not everything, as it is with the rodents and the cats; and one has no right to go about feeling people's heads, and then taking them by the throat and saying, "You are related to us; you belong to us!" Apart from anthropological characteristics, there are such things as reason, justice, truth, and beauty, which are the same for all. For another thing, this ethnographic policy is not safe. Today you may exploit it against others; and then you see it turned against yourself. Is it certain that the Germans, who have so boldly hoisted the banner of ethnography, will not see the Slavs arrive and, in their turn, analyze village names in Saxony and Lusatia; or seek out the traces of the Wiltzes or the Obotrites; or say that they have come to settle accounts arising out of the massacres and wholesale enslavements inflicted upon their ancestors by the Ottos? It is an excellent thing for us all to know how to forget.

I like ethnography very much, and find it a peculiarly interesting science. But as I wish it to be free, I do not wish it to be applied to politics. In ethnography, as in all branches of learning, systems change. It is the law of progress. Should nations then also change together with the systems? The boundaries of states would follow the fluctuations of the science; and patriotism would depend on a more or less paradoxical dissertation. The patriot would be told: "You were mistaken: You shed your blood in such-and-such a cause; you thought you were a Celt; no, you are a German." And then, ten years later, they will come and tell you that you are a Slav. Lest we put too great a strain upon science, let us excuse the lady from giving an opinion on problems in which so many interests are involved. For you may be sure that, if you make her the handmaid of diplomacy, you will often catch her in the very act of granting other favours. She has better things to do: So let us ask her just to tell the truth.

2. What we have said about race, applies also to language. Language invites union, without, however, compelling it. The United States and England, as also Spanish America and Spain, speak the same language without forming a single nation. Switzerland, on the contrary, whose foundations are solid because they are based on the assent of the various parties, contains three or four languages. There exists in man a something which is above language: and that is his will. The will of Switzerland to be united, in spite of the variety of these forms of speech, is a much more important fact than a similarity of language, often attained by vexatious measures.

It is to the honour of France that she has never tried to attain unity of language by the use of coercion. Is it impossible to cherish the same feelings and thoughts and to love the same things in different languages? We were talking just now of the objections to making international politics dependent on ethnography. It would be no less objectionable to make them depend on comparative philology. Let us allow full liberty of discussion to these interesting branches of learning, and not mix them up with what would disturb their serenity. The political importance ascribed to languages comes from regarding them as tokens of race. Nothing could be more unsound. In Prussia, where nothing but German is now spoken, Russian was spoken a few centuries ago; in Wales, English is spoken; in Gaul and Spain, the original speech of Alba Longa; in Egypt, Arabic; and we could cite any number of other examples. Even in the beginning of things, similarity of language did not imply that of race. Take the proto-Aryan or proto-Semitic tribe. It contained slaves speaking the same language as their masters, whereas the slave very often differed from his master in race. We must repeat that these divisions into Indo-European, Semitic, and other languages, which have been laid down by comparative philologists with such admirable acumen, do not coincide with those laid down by anthropology. Languages are historical formations which afford little clue to the descent of those who speak them and which, in any case, cannot be permitted to fetter human liberty, when it is a question of deciding with what family one is to be linked for life and death.

This exclusive importance attributed to language has, like the exaggerated attention paid to race, its dangers and its objections. If you overdo it, you shut yourself up within a prescribed culture which you regard as the national culture. You are confined and immured, having left the open air of the great world outside to shut yourself up in a conventicle together with your compatriots. Nothing could be worse for the mind; and nothing could be more untoward for civilization. Let us not lose sight of this fundamental principle that man, apart from being penned up within the bounds of one language or another, apart from being a member of one race or another, or the follower of one culture or another, is above all a reasonable moral being. Above French, German, or Italian culture, there stands human culture. Consider the great men of the Renaissance. They were neither French, nor Italian, nor German. By their intercourse with the ancient world, they had rediscovered the secret of the true education of the human mind, and to that they devoted themselves body and soul. How well they did!

3. Nor can religion provide a satisfactory basis for a modern nationality. In its origin, religion was connected with the very existence of the social group, which itself was an extension of the family. The rites of religion were family rites. The religion of Athens was the cult of Athens itself, of its mythical founders, its laws and customs. This religion, which did not involve any dogmatic theology, was, in the full sense of the words, a state religion. Those who refused to practice it were not Athenians. At bottom it was the cult of the personified Acropolis; and to swear on the altar of Aglauros[4] amounted to an oath to die for one's country. This religion was the equivalent of our drawing lots for military service or of our cult of the national flag. To refuse to participate in such cult would have been tantamount to a refusal nowadays to serve in the army, and to a declaration that one was not an Athenian. On the other hand, it is clear that such a cult as this meant nothing for those who were not Athenians; so there was no proselytizing to compel foreigners to accept it, and the slaves of Athens did not practice it. The same was the case in certain small republics of the Middle Ages. No man was a good Venetian if he did not swear by St. Mark; nor a good citizen of Amalfi if he did not set St. Andrew above all

the other saints in Paradise. In these small societies, acts, which in later times became the grounds for persecution and tyranny, were justifiable and were as trivial as it is with us to wish the father of the family many happy returns of his birthday or a happy new year.

What was true of Sparta and Athens was no longer so in the kingdoms that emerged from the conquests of Alexander, and still less so in the Roman Empire. The persecutions carried out by Antiochus Epiphanes to induce the Eastern world to worship the Olympian Jove, like those of the Roman Empire to maintain the farce of a state religion, were mistaken, criminal, and really absurd. Nowadays the situation is perfectly clear, since the masses no longer have any uniform belief. Everyone believes and practices religion in his own way according to his capacities and wishes. State religion has ceased to exist; and a man can be a Frenchman, an Englishman, or a German, and at the same time a Catholic, a Protestant, or a Jew, or practice no form of worship at all. Religion has become a matter to be decided by the individual according to his conscience, and nations are no longer divided into Catholic and Protestant. Religion which, fifty-two years ago, was so important a factor in the formation of Belgium, is still equally so in the heart of every man; but it is now barely to be reckoned among the reasons that determine national frontiers.

4. Community of interest is certainly a powerful bond between men. But do interests suffice to make a nation? I do not believe it. Community of interest brings about commercial treaties. Nationality, which is body and soul both together, has its sentimental side: And a Customs Union is not a country.

5. Geography, and what we call natural frontiers, certainly plays a considerable part in the division of nations. Geography is one of the essential factors of history. Rivers have guided races: Mountains have impeded them. The former have favoured, while the latter have restricted, historic movements. But can one say, as some people believe, that a nation's boundaries are to be found written on the map, and that it has the right to award itself as much as is necessary to round off certain outlines, or to reach such-and-such a mountain or river, which are regarded as in some way dispensing the frontier *a priori*? I know no doctrine more arbitrary or fatal than this, which can be used to justify all kinds of violence. In the first place, is it the mountains, or is it the rivers that constitute these alleged natural frontiers? It is indisputable that mountains separate; but rivers tend rather to bring together. Then again all mountains cannot divide states. Which are those that separate and those that do not? From Biarritz to Tornea there is not one estuary which is more like a boundary than another. If History had so decreed, then the Loire, the Seine, the Meuse, the Elbe, and the Oder would have, as much as the Rhine has, this character of national frontier, which has been the cause of so many infringements of that fundamental right, which is the will of men. People talk of strategic grounds. Nothing is absolute; and it is evident that much must be conceded to necessity. But

these concessions must not go too far. Otherwise, everyone will demand what suits him from a military point of view and we shall have endless warfare. No; it is not the soil any more than the race which makes a nation. The soil provides the substratum, the field for struggle and labour: Man provides the soul. Man is everything in the formation of this sacred thing that we call a people. Nothing that is material suffices here. A nation is a spiritual principle, the result of the intricate workings of history; a spiritual family and not a group determined by the configuration of the earth.

We have now seen those things which do not suffice to create such a spiritual principle. They are race, language, interests, religious affinity, geography, and military necessity. What more then is required? In view of what I have already said, I shall not have to detain you very much longer.

III

A nation is a soul, a spiritual principle. Two things, which are really only one, go to make up this soul or spiritual principle. One of these things lies in the past, the other in the present. The one is the possession in common of a rich heritage of memories; and the other is actual agreement, the desire to live together, and the will to continue to make the most of the joint inheritance. Man, gentleman, cannot be improvised. The nation, like the individual, is the fruit of a long past spent in toil, sacrifice, and devotion. Ancestor worship is of all forms the most justifiable, since our ancestors have made us what we are. A heroic past, great men, and glory—I mean real glory—these should be the capital of our company when we come to found a national idea. To share the glories of the past, and a common will in the present; to have done great deeds together, and to desire to do more— these are the essential conditions of a people's being. Love is in proportion to the sacrifices one has made and the evils one has borne. We love the house that we have built and that we hand down to our successors. The Spartan song "We are what ye were, and we shall be what ye are," is, in its simplicity, the abridged version of every national anthem.

In the past, a heritage of glory and of grief to be shared; in the future, one common plan to be realized; to have suffered, rejoiced, and hoped together; these are things of greater value than identity of custom-houses and frontiers in accordance with strategic notions. These are things which are understood, in spite of differences in race and language. I said just now "to have suffered together," for indeed common suffering unites more strongly than common rejoicing. Among national memories, sorrows have greater value than victories; for they impose duties and demand common effort.

Thus we see that a nation is a great solid unit, formed by the realization of sacrifices in the past, as well as of those one is prepared to make in the future. A nation implies a past; while, as regards the present, it is all contained in one tangible fact, viz., the agreement and clearly expressed desire to continue a life in common. The existence of a nation is (if you will forgive me the metaphor) a daily plebiscite, just as that of the individual is a continual affirmation of life. I am quite aware that this is less metaphysical than the doctrine of divine right, and smacks less of brute force than alleged historic right. According to the notions that I am expounding, a nation has no more right than a king to say to a province: "You belong to me; so I will take you." A province means to us its inhabitants; and if anyone has a right to be consulted in the matter, it is the inhabitant. It is never to the true interest of a nation to annex or keep a country against its will. The people's wish is after all the only justifiable criterion, to which we must always come back.

We have excluded from politics the abstract principles of metaphysics and theology; and what remains? There remains man, with his desires and his needs. But you will tell me that the consequences of a system that puts these ancient fabrics at the mercy of the wishes of usually unenlightened minds, will be the secession and ultimate disintegration of nations. It is obvious that in such matters no principles should be pushed too far, and that truths of this nature are applicable only as a whole and in a very general sort of way. Human wishes change indeed: But what in this world does not? Nations are not eternal. They have had beginnings and will have ends; and will probably be replaced by a confederation of Europe. But such is not the law of the age in which we live. Nowadays it is a good, and even a necessary, thing that nations should exist. Their existence is the guarantee of liberty, which would be lost, if the world had but one law and one master.

By their various, and often contrasting, attainments, the nations serve the common task of humanity; and all play some instrument in that grand orchestral concert of mankind, which is, after all, the highest ideal reality that we attain. Taken separately, they all have their weak points; and I often tell myself that a man who should have the vices that are held to be virtues in nations, a man battening on empty glory, and so jealous, selfish, and quarrelsome as to be ready to draw his sword at the slightest provocation, would be the most intolerable creature. But such discordant details vanish when all is taken together. What sufferings poor humanity has endured and what trials await it yet! May it be guided by the spirit of wisdom and preserved from the countless dangers that beset the path!

And now, gentlemen, let me sum it all up. Man is the slave neither of his race, nor his language, nor his religion, nor of the windings of his rivers and mountain ranges. That moral consciousness which we call a nation is created by a great assemblage of men with warm hearts and healthy minds: And as long as this moral consciousness can prove its strength by the sacrifices demanded from the individual for the benefit of the community, it is justifiable and has the right to exist. If doubts arise concerning its frontiers, let the population in dispute be consulted: for surely they have a right to a say in the matter. This will bring a smile to the lips of the transcendental politicians, those infallible beings who spend their lives in self-deception and who, from the summit of their superior principles, cast a pitying eye upon our commonplaces. "Consult the population! Stuff and nonsense! This is only another of these feeble French ideas that aim at replacing diplomacy and war by methods of infantile simplicity." Well, gentlemen, let us wait a while. Let the kingdom of the transcendentalists endure for its season; and let us learn to submit to the scorn of the mighty. It may be, that after many fruitless fumblings, the world will come back to our modest empirical solutions. The art of being right in the future is, at certain times, the art of resigning oneself to being old-fashioned.

NOTES

1. The House of Savoy owes its royal title solely to the possession of Sardinia (1720).
2. This point has been further dealt with in a lecture, a summary of which can be seen in the journal of the French Scientific Association, 10 March 1878.
3. Germanic elements are not much more important in the United Kingdom than they were in France at the time when she possessed Alsace and Metz. The Germanic language prevailed in the British Isles solely because Latin had not completely ousted the Celtic forms of speech there, as was the case in the Gauls.
4. Aglauros, who gave her life to save her country, represents the Acropolis itself.

14

LEOPOLD RANKE

The Great Powers

If one could establish as a definition of a great power that it must be able to maintain itself against all others, even when they are united, then Frederick had raised Prussia to that position. For the first time since the days of the Saxon emperors and Henry the Lion a self-sufficient power was found in northern Germany, needing no alliance, dependent only upon itself. [. . .]

The national spirit, awakened with a start and benefiting from its own thoroughness and maturity, then developed a poetic literature, independently and with free experimentation. It thereby created a view of the world that was comprehensive, new, and, although caught in many contradictions, still more or less coherent. This literature had the inestimable quality of no longer being limited to only part of the nation. Instead it embraced the whole and made it really aware of its unity for the first time.

If new generations of great poets do not always succeed the old ones, one should not wonder too much. The great attempts are made and are successful. What one had to say has been well said, and sincere minds scorn to travel along frequented and easy roads. But the work of German genius was by no means completed. Its task was to penetrate into positive science. Many obstacles stood in the way, arising from its own development and from other influences as well. We can now hope that it will overcome them all, will become more harmonized within itself, and will then be capable of continuous new creation.

But I shall pause here since I wished to discuss politics, although all these things are very closely connected and a true political philosophy can only be inspired by a great national existence. This much is certain, that no other phenomenon contributed so much to the self-confidence with which this wave of enthusiasm was accompanied as did the life and renown of Frederick II. A nation must feel independent in order to develop freely, and never has a literature flourished save when a climax of history prepared the way for it. But it was strange that Frederick himself neither knew nor anticipated this. He labored for the emancipation of the nation, and German literature worked with him, yet he did not recognize his allies. They knew him well, however. It made the Germans proud and bold to have had a hero emerge from their midst.

As we have seen, it was a necessity of the seventeenth century that France be checked. This had now occurred in a manner that exceeded all expectation. It cannot really be said that an artificial, complex political system had been formed to this end. It merely appeared so, but the fact was that great powers had raised themselves by their own strength and that new independent national states in all their original power had taken over the world stage.

Austria, a Catholic and German nation, was in a stable military condition, full of fresh, inexhaustible vitality, rich, and, in short, a world by itself. The Graeco-Slavic principle appeared more strongly in Russia than ever before in world history. The European forms which it adopted were far from crushing this original element. They penetrated it instead, animated it, and for the first time drew forth its own strength. In England the Germanic maritime interests had developed into a colossal world power which ruled all the seas and before which all memories of earlier sea powers paled. And in Prussia the German Protestants found the support which they had long sought, at once their representation and their expression. "Even if one knew the secret," says a poet, "who would have the courage to tell it?" I shall not presume to put the character of these states into words. But we can see clearly that they were founded upon principles which had grown out of the various great developments of earlier centuries, that they were formed according to these original differences and with varying constitutions, and that they represented those historic demands which in the nature of things were made upon successive generations. In their rise and development, which, understandably enough, could not have occurred without a many-sided transformation of inner conditions, lies the principal event of the hundred years which preceded the outbreak of the French Revolution. [. . .]

[. . .] The national consciousness of a great people demands a fitting position in the European community. International relations depend not on convenience but on actual power, and the prestige of a state will always correspond to the strength of its internal development. Any nation will feel sensitive not to find itself in its rightful position. How much more so the French nation which had so often raised the singular claim of being preeminently *the* great nation! [. . .]

If the main event of the hundred years before the French Revolution was the rise of the great powers in defense of European independence, so the main event of the period since then is the fact that nationalities were rejuvenated, revived, and developed anew. They became a part of the state, for it was realized that without them the state could not exist.

It is almost generally held that our times tend towards and are capable only of dissolution. Their only significance lies in the fact that they are putting an end to the unifying or shackling institutions left over from the Middle Ages. They are striding towards this goal with the certainty of an innate impulse. It is the end-product of all great events and discoveries, of our entire civilization, in fact. It also explains the irresistible inclination towards democratic ideas and institutions, which of necessity produces all the great changes which we are witnessing. It is a general movement, in which France merely preceded the other countries.

All this is an opinion which can of course lead only to the gloomiest prospects for the future. We believe, however, that it cannot be supported against the truth of the facts. Far from being satisfied only with negation, our century has produced the most positive results. It has achieved a great liberation, not wholly in the sense of dissolution but rather in a creative, unifying sense. It is not enough to say that it called the great powers into being. It has also renewed the fundamental principle of all states, that is, religion and law, and given new life to the principle of each individual state. In just this fact lies the characteristic feature of our time.

In most epochs of world history it has been religious ties that have held the peoples together. Yet occasionally there have been other periods, which can be better compared with ours, when several larger kingdoms and free states existed side by side, linked by one political system. I shall only mention the period of the Hellenistic kingdoms after Alexander. It provides many similarities to our own, a highly developed common culture, military science, and action and interaction of complicated foreign relations, also the great importance of the trading interests and of finance, rivalry of industries, and a flowering of the exact sciences based on mathematics. But those states, produced by the enterprise of a conqueror and the dissension among his successors, had neither possessed nor been able to attain any individual principles of existence. They were based upon soldiers and money alone. It was for that very reason that they were so soon dissolved and at last entirely disappeared. It has often been asked how Rome could overcome them so quickly and completely. It happened because Rome, at least as long as she had enemies of importance, held to her principle of existence with admirable firmness.

With us it also appeared as if only the extent of our possessions, the power of the troops, the amount of wealth, and a certain share in the general civilization were of value to the state. If there were ever events qualified to dispel such an illusion, it is those of our own time. They have finally made the public aware how important moral strength and the sense of nationality are for the state. What would have become of our states if they had not received new life from the national principles upon which they were based? It is inconceivable that any state could exist without it.

World history does not present such a chaotic tumult, warring, and planless succession of states and peoples as appears at first sight. Nor is the often dubious advancement of civilization its only significance. There are forces and indeed spiritual, life-giving, creative forces, nay life itself, and there are moral energies, whose development we see. They cannot be defined or put in abstract terms, but one can behold them and observe them. One can develop a sympathy for their existence. They unfold, capture the world, appear in manifold expressions, dispute with and check and overpower one another. In their interaction and succession, in their life, in their decline or rejuvenation, which then encompasses an ever greater fullness, higher importance, and wider extent, lies the secret of world history.

As we are now attacked by a spiritual power, so must we oppose it with spiritual force. The dominion which another nation threatens to gain over us can only be combatted by developing our own sense of nationality. I do not mean an invented, illusionary nationality but the real, existing one which is expressed in the state.

But, so people will reply, is not the world developing at this moment into an ever closer community? Would not this tendency be impeded and limited by the contrast between different peoples with their national ways or different states with their individual principles?

Unless I delude myself, there is a close analogy with literature. No one spoke of a world literature at the time that French literature dominated Europe. Only since then has this idea been conceived, expressed, and propagated, in other words, only after most of the principal peoples of Europe had developed their own literature independently and often in sharp contrast. If I may be allowed to make a trivial comparison, I should like to remind the reader that the sort of company where one person is spokesman and leads the whole conversation affords neither pleasure nor profit, nor does the sort where all the people, being on the same level or, if you will, of the same mediocrity, only say the same thing. One only feels happy when many-sided personalities, freely developed, meet on a higher common ground or indeed produce this very meeting place by stimulating and complementing one another. There would be only a disagreeable monotony if the different literatures should let their individual characters be blended and melted together. No, the union of all must rest upon the independence of each single one. Then they can stimulate one another in lively fashion and forever, without one dominating or injuring the others.

It is the same with states and nations. Decided, positive prevalence of one would bring ruin to the others. A mixture of them all would destroy the essence of each one. Out of separation and independent development will emerge the true harmony.

15

ELIE KEDOURIE

Nationalism

Europe after 1815 then was destined to a long period of unrest. The victors did their best to ensure that the settlement they devised would be lasting, but the turmoil bequeathed from revolutionary and Napoleonic times, and the inexorable social changes, acting separately or jointly, always threatened, and in the end overthrew the 1815 settlement. Those who opposed it did so on the ground that it took no account of the wishes of the peoples, that rulers were imposed on subjects who had not been consulted, and that territories which were naturally one were artificially separated. The two grievances were entwined with each other, both of them indeed the outcome of philosophical speculations which had preceded and accompanied the French Revolution. Of course this is not to say that every nationalist and every libertarian in revolt against the arrangements of the Congress of Vienna was competent to explain on what metaphysical grounds he believed that men had the right to decide who was to govern them, and that humanity was divided, naturally, into nations. These ideas became the commonplaces of radicalism on the Continent, and young men, university students, in Italy, Germany, and Central Europe found it reasonable to believe in these things, and heroic to be enrolled in a secret society dedicated to liberty and nationality. [. . .]

The restlessness of this generation [. . .] was the work not only of the revolutionary legend; it proceeded from a breakdown in the transmission of political habits and religious beliefs from one generation to the next. In societies suddenly exposed to the new learning and the new philosophies of the Enlightenment and of Romanticism, orthodox settled ways began to seem ridiculous and useless. The attack was powerful and left the old generation bewildered and speechless; or if it attempted to speak, it merely gave voice to irritated admonition, obstinate opposition, or horror-stricken rejection, which only served to widen the rift and increase the distance between the fathers and the sons. [. . .] This violent revolt against immemorial restraints, this strident denunciation of decorum and measure, was inevitably accompanied by powerful social strains which may explain the dynamic and violent character of nationalist movements. These movements are ostensibly directed against the foreigner, the outsider, but they are also

160

the manifestation of a species of civil strife between the generations; nationalist movements are children's crusades; their very names are manifestoes against old age: Young Italy, Young Egypt, the Young Turks, the Young Arab Party. When they are stripped of their metaphysics and their slogans—and these cannot adequately account for the frenzy they conjure up in their followers—such movements are seen to satisfy a need, to fulfil a want. Put at its simplest, the need is to belong together in a coherent and stable community. Such a need is normally satisfied by the family, the neighbourhood, the religious community. In the last century and a half such institutions all over the world have had to bear the brunt of violent social and intellectual change, and it is no accident that nationalism was at its most intense where and when such institutions had little resilience and were ill-prepared to withstand the powerful attacks to which they became exposed. This seems a more satisfactory account than to say that nationalism is a middle-class movement. It is the case that the German inventors of nationalist doctrine came from a class which could be called the middle class, and that they were discontented with the old order in which the nobility was predominant. But the term middle class is closely tied to a particular area and a particular history, that of Western Europe. It presupposes and implies a distinct social order of which feudalism, municipal franchises, and rapid industrial development are some of the prominent features. Such features are not found in all societies, and it would therefore be misleading to link the existence of a nationalist movement to that of a middle class. In countries of the Middle and the Far East, for instance, where the significant division in society was between those who belonged to the state institution and those who did not, nationalism cannot be associated with the existence of a middle class. It developed, rather, among young officers and bureaucrats, whose families were sometimes obscure, sometimes eminent, who were educated in Western methods and ideas, often at the expense of the state, and who as a result came to despise their elders, and to hanker for the shining purity of a new order to sweep away the hypocrisy, the corruption, the decadence which they felt inexorably choking them and their society.

This breakdown in the transmission of political experience explains why nationalist movements run to extremes. Political wisdom is not to be gathered in the drab, arid world in which we actually live, it is to be culled from books of philosophy. [. . .] Literature and philosophy gave entrance to a nobler, truer world, a world more real and more exciting than the actual world; and gradually the boundary between the world of imagination and the world of reality became blurred, and sometimes disappeared altogether. What was possible in books ought to be possible in reality. The reading of books became a political, a revolutionary, activity. Thus, many a young man found himself advancing from the composition of poems to the manufacture of infernal machines; thus, in the intoxication of a poetic dream, Adam Mickiewicz found himself imploring God to bring about universal war in which Poland might once again secure independence. Politics could indeed be exciting, as exciting as the wonderful speculations of Schelling and Fichte. Mean provincial towns where nothing ever happens, dusty libraries, prosaic lecture rooms became the stage of an absorbing secret game, a game of hide-and-seek, in which nothing was as it seemed, and everything took on the glowing colours of romance. Such are the delights of conspiracy. Occasionally, of course, the drabness would break in, and there would be policemen, arrests, prison, or exile. The enclosed, secret universe of plot and conspiracy would begin to exercise an obsessive compulsion of its own, from which escape was hopeless; what started as a poetic dream would be enacted with inexorable logic as a living nightmare, in which pistols did really go off, and dynamite did really explode; where men were caught up in a web of suspicion and treason, and today's executioner became tomorrow's victim. Consider the case of the schoolboys of Plovdiv who, in 1896, formed a Macedonian terrorist group. They began by stealing their parents' jewelry; one of them then committed suicide because he could raise no more money; others stole three hundred pounds from a post office with a forged check, and kidnapped two fellow conspirators, who persuaded their parents to ransom them. Or again, consider the case of Mara Buneva who was happily married to a Bulgarian officer. In 1927, on the orders of the Internal Macedonian Revolutionary Organization, she went to Yugoslavia and opened a hat shop at Skolpje and made friends with a lawyer who had incurred the enmity of IMRO. "At midday on January 13, 1928, Mara closed her shop. She went to the bridge over the Vardar where she would meet Prelitch on his way to lunch. She stopped him, then pulled a revolver from her blouse and fired. Prelitch fell mortally wounded. Then Mara shot herself. 'I am sorry I had to kill Prelitch,' said the poor girl before she died, 'because he helped me several times.'" How and at what point, we wonder, did the schoolboys abandon their schoolboyish avocations, and the housewife forsake her housewifely cares, and become ready to commit crime and bloodshed? [. . .]

The musings of the young men dwelt on two grievances: that governments were not popular, and that they were not national. It could, of course, be reasonably argued that governments were not popular because they were not national, that because governments were controlled by foreigners, they could not minister to the welfare of the ruled. The converse of this could also be argued, namely, that once governments became national, they would come under the control of the citizens and become agencies for their welfare. This notion that national government meant popular government was made plausible by the settlement of 1815. The victorious powers not only restored dynasties to their thrones, ignoring "national" boundaries and "national" units, as these came to be understood by European radicals, but they also declared their enmity to the principles proclaimed by the revolution. They proscribed representative institutions and restored privileges abolished by the revolutionaries. It was thought to follow therefore that if the 1815 settlement were overthrown, then not only would nations assume their natural sovereign rights, but also that democratic ideas would triumph, and that these sovereign nations would practice Liberty, Equality, and Fraternity. War would then disappear, for all these nations would be, *ipso facto*, pacific and just. [. . .]

But of course it was not, it could not be, as simple as that, if only because of another commonplace nationalist attitude: "Avoid compromises," lays down Mazzini, "they are almost always immoral as well as dangerous." For if there is a divine plan which divides humanity into nations, which evil governments have disfigured, there must be no truck with evil. The relation between a country and its foreign ruler must always take the shape of a "desperate struggle." "Desperate struggle" is not kind to political liberties, and a hatred of compromise can easily turn into a hatred of those who may be suspected of compromise. It is a well-known feature of recent history that nationalist parties kill members of their own nationality whom they suspect of an inclination to compromise, and in some cases a greater number of these than of the foreigners against whom the struggle is waged fall to the assassin's bullet. A remarkable document may be cited here. In 1893 the Armenian nationalists who were trying to gain Armenian independence by violence posted this notice in Sivas: "Osmanlis! . . . the examples are before your eyes. How many hundreds of rascals in Constantinople, Van, Erzeroum, Alashkert, Harpout, Cesarea, Marsovan, Amassia and other towns have been killed by the Armenian revolutionists? What were these rascals? Armenians! Armenians! and again Armenians! If our aim was against the Mohammedans or Mohammedanism, as the Government tries to make you think, why should we kill the Armenians?" If only because of this, nationalism and·political liberties may be extremely difficult to reconcile. In any case national government and constitutional government do not necessarily go together. Greece and the Balkan states succeeded in wresting national independence from the Ottoman Empire. The grievances of the subject areas were national grievances; they were ruled by a government alien in language and religion. But their checkered history since independence suggests that national freedom is no guarantee against oppressive and iniquitous government. New ruling classes replaced the evicted Ottomans, and found extreme difficulty in ruling humanely and effectively. Neither did the formation of these national states conduce, as Mazzini hoped, to international peace. It may, of course, be argued, as the poet Wordsworth argued, that native oppression is preferable to foreign oppression. "The difference between inbred oppression and that which is from without is *essential*," he observed in *The Convention of Cintra* (1809), "inasmuch as the former does not exclude from the minds of the people a feeling of being self-governed; does not imply (as the latter does, when patiently submitted to) an abandonment of the first duty imposed by the faculty of reason." The argument is plainly sophistical, but it does recognize, by implication, as Mazzini's does not, the truth established by experience, namely, that the triumph of the national principle does not necessarily entail the triumph of liberty.

A variant of Mazzini's argument has found great vogue in recent decades in Asiatic and African countries. This variant depends on an economic interpretation of history. It is to the effect that European powers in search of markets and cheap raw materials have imposed their direct domination or indirect influence on these areas overseas and have thus distorted their political development, stunted their economies, and insulted the human dignity of their inhabitants. It is also widely argued that the liberation of these countries from European rule makes possible the creation of free societies which would bring fulfilment and contentment to their citizens. But the economic foundation on which this theory rests serves to make the domination of Europe overseas seem both tentacular and intangible. For the domination, it is argued, does not always rest on naked force: The sinister power of money holds in its grip countries outwardly independent, and rulers seemingly patriotic; and full independence with all its blessings will only come when indirect as well as direct domination will have disappeared. This variant exhibits with particular clarity the fallacy of associating national independence with efficient, humane, and just government. It is manifestly not European domination which created poverty, technical backwardness, overpopulation, or habits of despotism in Asia and Africa—it is these rather which made possible European rule overseas; and it is not the departure of European rulers—after so brief a dominion—which will change the nature of these territories, transform their poverty into wealth, or suddenly create probity in judges, moderation and public spirit in statesmen, or honesty in public servants. The truth is that good government depends as much on circumstances as on a desire for freedom and there are regions of the globe which may never know its blessings. But it is characteristic of doctrines such as self-determination to disregard the limits imposed by nature and history, and to believe that a good will alone can accomplish miracles.

In fact, it is these countries which most clearly show that nationalism and liberalism far from being twins are really antagonistic principles. In these countries, constitutionalism is unknown. Their political tradition is either a centralized despotism, which, as a method of government, has shown itself extraordinarily resilient and durable, or a fragmented tribalism which has withered and fossilized as it has come in contact with European rule. [. . .]

In such countries, if the official classes, or a significant number among them, are converted to nationalism, they may easily take over and mould the state in the image of their doctrine. In such a situation the doctrine operates to make despotism more perfect and more solidly anchored. Old-fashioned despots had neither the means nor the inclination to obtain the internal assent of their subjects; for them, external obedience was enough. But since the essence of nationalism is that the will of the individual should merge in the will of the nation, nationalist rulers in Oriental despotisms seek internal as well as external obedience. Such obedience they are now more than ever in a position to obtain, thanks to modern techniques of bureaucratic control and mass communications. [. . .]

Nationalist politics find scope, not only where foreigners rule a particular country, but also in regions of mixed population. One such region is Central and Eastern Europe. Here the German-speaking group is one of the most important. This group occupied not only the territory now known as Germany and Austria, but extended still further. German populations remained as residues of the conquests of the knightly Orders who advanced east in the Middle Ages; Germans had also settled later as colonists to people empty provinces and to introduce crafts and manufactures; so that in the nineteenth century scattered German settlements extended from the Gulf of Finland and the Baltic down to the Adriatic, and from the Bohemian mountains to the steppes of Russia. According to nationalist doctrine, all these Germans ought to form one nation and belong to the same state. Such an ambition could not but raise the most awkward problems, as appeared soon enough in the Revolution of 1848. This revolution occurred almost simultaneously in the early spring of 1848 in Berlin, Vienna, and some of the smaller German states, and almost immediately met with a complete, if short-lived, success. In the first flush of their triumph, the revolutionaries decided to convoke an Imperial German Parliament at Frankfurt to reform the political state of Germany, to give it a new democratic constitution, and to prepare some measure of union, so that the grievous harm which, the nationalists held, resulted from the division of German lands among so many rulers, could be undone. A thorny issue came soon to confront the Frankfurt Parliament. Poland was partitioned between Russia, Austria, and Prussia. The Poles of Prussian Poland, taking advantage of the revolution, asked for a measure of autonomy in the areas where they predominated. But among them lived a minority of Germans, and if autonomy were granted to the Poles, those Germans would have to live under a local government administered by Poles, and the Frankfurt Parliament had to indicate its view on the matter. There ought, really, to have been no doubt at all, since national freedom was one of the principles vindicated by the Revolution of 1848—and the Poles were universally recognized as a nationality. But when the matter came to be raised in the Frankfurt Parliament there was great opposition to these Polish pretensions. Jordan, a delegate from Berlin, sitting on the left, exclaimed: "Are half a million Germans to live under a German government and administration and form part of the great German Fatherland, or are they to be relegated to the inferior position of naturalized foreigners subject to another nation of lesser cultural content than themselves?" It was wrong to acquiesce in the Polish demands, for, he said, "it was necessary to awaken a healthy national egotism without which no people can grow into a nation." "Mere existence," he asserted,

"does not entitle a people to political independence: only the force to assert itself as a state among the others." [. . .]

Nationalism, then, does not make easy the relations of different groups
in mixed areas. Since it advocates a recasting of frontiers and a redistribution of political power to conform with the demands of a particular nationality, it tends to disrupt whatever equilibrium had been reached between
different groups, to reopen settled questions, and to renew strife. Because
their claims are uncompromising nationalists must always cast about for
opportunities to reopen an issue which, for the time being, they might consent to consider closed. Far from increasing political stability and political
liberty, nationalism in mixed areas makes for tension and mutual hatred.
The assertion of German nationality in 1848 was found to involve the necessity of Czechs and Poles never acquiring a comparable national status.
In later years, after Bismarck had founded the Reich, the claim to bring
into one national state all the Germans in Central Europe continued to be
expressed, and was known as Pan-Germanism; and it was, of course, with
Pan-German arguments that Hitler justified his dealings with Austria, Czechoslovakia, and Poland. The German question in Central and Eastern Europe
is, however, only one of the many questions created, in a way, by nationalist doctrine. But in what sense can one speak of political problems being
created by the spread of a doctrine? Doctrines do not create mixed areas, or
the relation of superior and inferior, or of dominant group and subject group.
These, certainly, were the realities of Central and Eastern Europe: a medley
of races, languages, and religions under imperial rule. This situation was
the result of no doctrine—but, if a doctrine such as nationalism does capture the intellectual and political leaders of one group, and they proceed to
act according to its tenets, then the same doctrine must spread to other
groups, who will feel impelled, in the face of threatening claims, to adopt it
for their own use. Historic quarrels are revived, old humiliations recalled,
and compromises disowned. It is a chain reaction, a vicious circle. It is in
this sense that one may speak of nationalism creating a problem in Central
and Eastern Europe.

It has sometimes been argued that since nationalism seeks to preserve a
particular national language and culture, nationalist demands may be satisfied and nationalists may be disarmed by an imperial government conced-
ing autonomy in cultural matters to the different nations under its rule.
Thus, the Austrian Social Democrats, Otto Bauer and Karl Renner, anx-
ious to preserve the unity of Austria-Hungary, and to transform it into a
socialist state, imagined schemes whereby national groups, whether concentrated in one particular territory or scattered throughout the whole empire,
should have their cultural affairs managed by their own national institutions, while economic and political matters would be managed by a single
supranational government. But such attempts to stem the tide of nationalist discontents are seldom successful, since nationalists consider that politi-

cal and cultural matters are inseparable, and that no culture can live if it is not endowed with a sovereign state exclusively its own. Such attempts only result in artistic, literary, and linguistic matters becoming the subject of acrimonious political disputes, and in being used as weapons in the nationalist struggle. In fact, cultural, linguistic, and religious autonomy for the different groups of a heterogeneous empire is practicable only when it does not rest upon, or is justified by, nationalist doctrine; such autonomy remained possible in the Ottoman Empire for several centuries—the arrangement being known as the *millet* system—precisely because nationalism was unknown, and broke down when the doctrine spread among the different groups of the empire. The *millet* system broke down because such limited autonomy could not satisfy nationalist ambitions, while at the same time, limited as it was, it came to seem to the ruling institution dangerously disruptive of the empire. These factors always render cultural autonomy by itself a precarious and illusory settlement of nationalist demands. [. . .]

The states which resulted from the application of the principle of self-determination are as full of anomalies and mixed areas as the heterogeneous empires they have replaced. In a nation-state, however, the issues raised by the presence of heterogeneous groups are much more acute than in an empire. If, in a mixed area, one group makes good a territorial claim and establishes a nation-state, other groups will feel threatened and resentful. For them to be ruled by one group claiming to rule in its own national territory is worse than to be governed by an empire which does not base its title to rule on national grounds. To an imperial government the groups in a mixed area are all equally entitled to some consideration, to a national government they are a foreign body in the state to be either assimilated or rejected. The national state claims to treat all citizens as equal members of the nation, but this fair-sounding principle only serves to disguise the tyranny of one group over another. The nation must be, all its citizens must be, animated with the same spirit. Differences are divisive and therefore treasonable. In the Hungarian Revolution of 1848 a Hungarian-Serb delegation asked for limited administrative autonomy for its people; the Hungarian national leader Kossuth vehemently rejected such pretensions and informed the Serbs: "The sword will decide between us." And it would seem that such is the logic of national unity in mixed areas. German nationalists asserted the claim that all Germans in Europe should belong to one German nation-state. One possible means of realizing such a scheme was by conquering all lands where Germans lived and incorporating them in the Reich. But another means was also possible, namely to expel into Germany proper all Germans from the lands where they were settled as minorities. Both ways have been attempted—with what terrible consequences—in modern times; either or both are inherent in any claim to transform a linguistic, ethnic, or religious group, inextricably mixed with other groups in one area, into a nation-state with a fixed territorial boundary. [. . .]

The attempts to refashion so much of the world on national lines has not led to greater peace and stability. On the contrary, it has created new conflicts, exacerbated tensions, and brought catastrophe to numberless people innocent of all politics. The history of Europe since 1919, in particular, has shown the disastrous possibilities inherent in nationalism. In the mixed area of Central and Eastern Europe, and the Balkans, empires disappeared, their ruling groups were humbled and made to pay, for a time, the penalty of previous arrogance. Whether these empires were doomed anyway, or whether it would have been possible to preserve them is mere speculation. What can be said with certainty is that the nation-states who inherited the position of the empires were not an improvement. They did not minister to political freedom, they did not increase prosperity, and their existence was not conducive to peace; in fact, the national question which their setting up, it was hoped, would solve, became, on the contrary, more bitter and envenomed: It was a national question, that of the German minorities in the new nation-states, which occasioned the outbreak of the Second World War. What may be said of Europe can with equal justice be said of the Middle East, or of Southeast Asia, wherever the pressure of circumstances or the improvidence of rulers or their failure of nerve made possible the triumph of nationalist programmes. [. . .] The invention has prevailed, and the best that can be said for it is that it is an attempt to establish once and for all the reign of justice in a corrupt world, and to repair, forever, the injuries of time. But this best is bad enough, since to repair such injuries other injuries must in turn be inflicted, and no balance is ever struck in the grisly account of cruelty and violence. For we do know with certainty that no government lasts forever, that one government goes and another comes to take its place, and that the workings of fate are unfathomable. To welcome a change or to regret it, because one set of rulers has gone and another has come, is something which we all do, for some rulers are more likely to look to our own welfare than others; but these are private preoccupations for which such private justification is reasonable. Public justification requires more; to welcome or deplore a change in government because some now enjoy power and others are deprived of it is not enough. The only criterion capable of public defense is whether the new rulers are less corrupt and grasping, or more just and merciful, or whether there is no change at all, but the corruption, the greed, and the tyranny merely find victims other than those of the departed rulers. And this is really the only question at issue between nationalism and the regimes to which it is opposed. It is a question which, in the nature of the case, admits of no final and conclusive answer.

16

ALEKSANDR SOLZHENITSYN

Rebuilding Russia

Human beings are so constituted that we can put up with such ruination and madness even when they last a lifetime, but God forbid that anyone should dare to offend or slight our *nationality*! Should that occur, nothing can restrain us in our state of chronic submission: With furious courage we snatch up stones, clubs, spears, and guns and fall upon our neighbours, intent on murder and arson. Such is man: Nothing has the capacity to convince us that our hunger, our poverty, our early deaths, the degeneration of our children—that any of these misfortunes can take precedence over national pride.

And that is why, in this attempt to propose some tentative steps toward our recovery and reconstruction, we are forced to begin, not with our unendurable wounds or debilitating suffering, but with a response to such questions as: How will the problem of the nationalities be approached? And within what geographical boundaries shall we heal our afflictions or die? And only thereafter shall we turn to the healing process itself.

WHAT IS RUSSIA?

The word "Russia" has become soiled and tattered through careless use; it is invoked freely in all sorts of inappropriate contexts. Thus, when the monster-like U.S.S.R. was lunging for chunks of Asia and Africa, the reaction the world over was: "Russia, the Russians . . ."

What exactly is Russia? Today, now? And—more important—tomorrow? Who, today, considers himself part of the future Russia? And where do Russians themselves see the boundaries of their land?

In the course of three-quarters of a century, to the sound of incessant proclamations trumpeting "the socialist friendship of peoples," the communist regime has managed to neglect, entangle, and sully the relationship among these peoples to such a degree that one can no longer see the way back to the peaceful coexistence of nationalities, that almost drowsy nonperception of distinctions that had virtually been achieved—with some lamentable exceptions—in the final decades of prerevolutionary Russia. For all that, it may not yet be too late to sort things out and come to an understanding—but not in the midst of the grievous misfortunes that are tearing at us with hurricane strength. From the vantage point of today, the more peaceful resolution, and the one holding much greater promise for the future, calls for a decisive parting of the ways for those who should separate. This is precisely due to the all-pervading ethnic bitterness that has obscured the rest of life: All else seems unimportant in the grip of a passion to which few of our people are immune.

Many of us know only too well, alas, that sharing a communal apartment can at times make life itself seem intolerable. And that is exactly how inflamed things have become in our national interrelationships.

In many of the republics at the periphery, centrifugal forces have built up such momentum that they could not be stopped without violence and bloodshed—*nor should they be checked at such cost.* The way things are moving in our country, the "Soviet Socialist Union" will break up *whatever* we do: We have no real choice, there is nothing to ponder, and it remains only to bestir ourselves in order to forestall greater misfortunes and to assure that the separation proceeds without needless human suffering and only in those cases where it is truly unavoidable.

As I see it, it must be declared loudly, clearly, and without delay that the three republics in the Baltic area, the three in Transcaucasia, four in central Asia, and Moldavia as well, if it feels drawn to Romania—that these eleven will be *separated off unequivocally and irreversibly.*

As for Kazakhstan, its present huge territory was stitched together by the communists in a completely haphazard fashion: Wherever migrating herds made a yearly passage would be called Kazakhstan. But then drawing boundaries was not considered important in those years, since we were supposedly but a short moment away from the time when all nationalities would merge into one. And Lenin in his perceptive way referred to boundaries as an issue "perhaps ten points down on the scale of priorities." (That is why they sliced the Nagorno-Karabakh region into Azerbaijan. What difference did it make where it went? What was important at the time was to play up to Turkey, that great friend of the Soviets.) And in any case Kazakhstan was considered an Autonomous Republic within the R.S.F.S.R. until 1936, when it was promoted to Union Republic status. It had been assembled from southern Siberia and the southern Ural region, plus the sparsely populated central areas which had since that time been transformed and built up by Russians, by inmates of forced-labor camps, and by exiled peoples. Today the Kazakhs constitute noticeably less than half the population of the entire inflated territory of Kazakhstan. They are concentrated in their long-standing ancestral domains along a large arc of lands in the south, sweeping from the extreme east westward almost to the Caspian Sea; the population here is indeed predominantly Kazakh. And if it should prove to be their wish to separate within such boundaries, I say Godspeed.

And so, after subtracting these twelve republics, there will remain nothing but an entity that might be called Rus, as it was designated in olden times (the word "Russian" had for centuries embraced Little Russians [Ukrainians], Great Russians, and Belorussians), or else "Russia," a name used since the eighteenth century, or—for an accurate reflection of the new circumstances—the "Russian [*Rossiiskii*] Union."

But even then such an entity would contain a hundred different nationalities and ethnic groups ranging in size from the tiny to the very considerable. And this is the very threshold from which we can and must manifest great wisdom and understanding. Only from that moment on must we marshal all the resources of our hearts and minds to the task of consolidating a fruitful commonwealth of nations, affirming the integrity of each culture and the preservation of each language.

A WORD TO THE GREAT RUSSIANS

At the beginning of this century the eminent political thinker Sergei Kryzhanovsky foresaw that "the Russian heartland does not possess the reserves of cultural and moral strength necessary to assimilate the peripheries. That [effort] weakens the Russian national core."

And this statement was made in a rich, flourishing country, before the extermination of millions of our people, an extermination, moreover, that was no blind mass killing, but rather involved a specific targeting of the *best* that Russia had produced.

Today Kryzhanovsky's words are a thousand times more valid: *We don't have the strength* for the peripheries either economically or morally. *We don't have the strength* for sustaining an empire—and it is just as well. Let this burden fall from our shoulders: It is crushing us, sapping our energy, and hastening our demise.

I note with alarm that the awakening Russian national self-awareness has to a large extent been unable to free itself of great-power thinking and of imperial delusions, that it has taken over from the communists the fraudulent and contrived notion of "Soviet patriotism," and that it takes pride in the "Soviet superpower" which during the reign of the dull-witted Brezhnev sucked dry what remained of our productivity for the sake of a massive and needless buildup of weapons (which, never used, are now being destroyed). Proud of the "superpower" status that brought shame upon us, presenting us to the whole world as a brutal, insatiable, and unbridled aggressor at a time when our knees were beginning to shake and weakness was bringing us to the verge of collapse. What a pernicious perversion of consciousness it is to argue that, "for all that, we are a huge country and we are taken seriously everywhere." Such an attitude now, when we are close to death, constitutes nothing less than a wholehearted support of communism. Was not Japan able to find a way to be reconciled with its situation, renouncing its sense of international mission and the pursuit of tempting political ventures— and did not that country flourish as a result?

The time has come for an uncompromising *choice* between an empire of which we ourselves are the primary victims and the spiritual and physical salvation of our own people. It is common knowledge that our mortality rate is increasing and has passed our birthrate: If this continues, we shall disappear from the face of the earth. Holding on to a great empire means to contribute to the extinction of our own people. And, anyway, what need is there of this heterogeneous amalgam? Do we want Russians to lose their unique characteristics? We must strive, not for the expansion of the state, but for a clarity of what remains of our spirit. By separating off twelve republics, by this seeming sacrifice, Russia will in fact free itself for a precious *inner* development, at long last turning diligent attention toward itself. Besides, what hope can there be of preserving and developing Russian culture amid the chaotic jumble of today? Less and less, surely, as things become ever more mashed and pounded together. [...]

FAMILY AND SCHOOL

Although everything linked to the ruin of today must be tended to without delay, it is even more urgent to lay the foundation of that which takes shape slowly: In the years when we will be trying to make up for lost time in every sphere, what kind of development will take place in our children? This concerns areas from pediatric medicine and early childhood care to education. For if this is not remedied immediately, we shall have no future to talk about.

The disastrous plight of women in our country is common knowledge and a regular topic of conversation that evokes no arguments, since everything is clear. The same is true of the falling birthrate, infant mortality and morbidity, and the terrifying state of our maternity clinics, day-care centers, and kindergartens.

Normal families have virtually ceased to exist in our country. Yet family ills are at the same time critically serious maladies for the state, and the family has a fundamental role in the salvation of our future. Women must have the opportunity to return to their families to take care of the children; the salary earned by men must make this possible. (However, given the expected high unemployment of the initial period, this goal will not be attainable right away: Some families will be glad that at least the woman will have kept her job.)

The schools are an equally urgent concern of ours. To think of the number of foolish experiments to which we subjected the schools in the course of seventy years! Yet only rarely did the schools produce knowledgeable individuals, and then only in some subjects, and only in select institutions of some large cities. A provincial Lomonosov, to say nothing of one coming from a village, would today have no chance of emerging or of fighting his way through (to begin with, he would have been stopped by the regulation on residence permits). The quality of the schools must be raised not only in the elite institutions of the capitals; by persistent effort this movement must start at the lowest levels and encompass the entire country. This task is in no sense less urgent than all our economic ones. Our schools have long provided poor training and inadequate education. It is intolerable that the general guidance of students should be viewed as an essentially unpaid extra burden placed on teachers: It must be compensated by a reduction of the individual's teaching load. And all of today's curricula and textbooks in the humanities are destined for fundamental revision if not outright rejection. And the drumming-in of atheism must be stopped immediately. [. . .]

IS THE SYSTEM OF GOVERNMENT REALLY THE CENTRAL ISSUE?

It goes without saying that we shall gradually reshape the entire state organism. This undertaking must begin somewhere in the "periphery"; it should not be tackled all at once. What is clear is that the process should start at the local level with grass-roots issues. While preserving a strong central authority, we must patiently and persistently expand the rights of local communities.

With time, we shall of course adopt some particular type of political structure, but in view of our total inexperience in such matters, our choice may not be a felicitous one at first, not something suited to the specific needs of our country. We must resolutely seek our own path here. We have lately been assuring ourselves that there is no need of any quest or reflection on our part, that it is simply a matter of adopting "the way it is done in the West" as quickly as possible.

But in the West it is done in, oh, so many different ways, with every country following its own tradition. One might think that we are the only people who need neither look back nor pay heed to the wise things said in our country before we were born.

Or we can put it this way: The structure of the state is secondary to the spirit of human relations. Given human integrity, any honest system is acceptable, but given human rancor and selfishness, even the most sweeping of democracies would become unbearable. If the people themselves lack fairness and honesty, this will come to the surface under any system.

Political activity is by no means the principal mode of human life, and politics is hardly the most sought-after enteprise for the majority of the people. The more energetic the political activity in a country, the greater is the loss to spiritual life. Politics must now swallow up all of a people's spiritual and creative energies. Beyond upholding its *rights*, mankind must defend its soul, freeing it for reflection and feeling.

TAKING OUR OWN MEASURE

The strength or weakness of a society depends more on the level of its spiritual life than on its level of industrialization. Neither a market economy nor even general abundance constitutes the crowning achievement of human life. The purity of social relations is a more fundamental value than the level of abundance. If a nation's spiritual energies have been exhausted, it will not be saved from collapse by the most perfect government structure or by any industrial development: A tree with a rotten core cannot stand. This is so because, of all the possible freedoms, the one that will inevitably come to the fore will be the freedom to be unscrupulous: That is the freedom that can be neither prevented nor anticipated by any law. It is an unfortunate fact that a pure social atmosphere cannot be legislated into being.

And that is why the destruction of our souls over three-quarters of a century is the most terrifying thing of all.

It is terrible to see that the corrupt ruling class—the multimillion-strong appointed bureaucracy [nomenklatura] which serves Party and state—is incapable of voluntarily giving up any of the privileges it has appropriated to itself. For decades this class has lived shamelessly at the expense of the people, and it would like to continue doing so.

And have any of the former killers and persecutors been so much as forced from their jobs or deprived of their undeservedly ample pensions? We doted on Molotov until the day he died, we are still pampering Kaganovich and who knows how many unnamed others. In Germany all such individuals, including far less important ones, were put on trial, but in our country it is they who are threatening us with lawsuits, while some, like the murderous Chekist Berzin, are even having monuments erected in their honor. But it seems beyond us to punish state criminals, and we won't live to hear a word of repentance from any of them. Might they at least be subjected to a public moral trial? But no, it looks as if we'll have to crawl on as is. . . .

And what about those glorious forces of glasnost and perestroika? Among these fashionable words we look in vain for the concept of *purification*. What we see is a stampede toward the new glasnost of all those tainted voices which had given decades of loyal service to totalitarianism. Of every four troubadours of today's glasnost, three are former toadies of Brezhnevism, and who among them has uttered a word of *personal* repentance instead of cursing the faceless "period of stagnation"? And the same individuals who for decades have befuddled the minds of university students continue to hold forth self-confidently from the rostrums of our humanities departments. Tens of thousands of "smatterers" [obrazovantsy] in our country are tarnished by their hypocrisy and weather-vane mentality: Should we not expect repentance from any of them, and must we really drag along these festering moral sores into our future?

SELF-LIMITATION

"Human rights" is currently the most fashionable and most eagerly repeated slogan among us. (But we all have very different things in mind. The educated class in capital cities visualizes human rights in terms of freedom of speech, of the press, of public assembly, and of emigration, but many would angrily demand curtailing the "rights" as they are seen by the ordinary people: the right to live and work in the same place where there is something to buy—which would bring millions into the capitals.)

"Human rights" are a fine thing, but how can we ourselves make sure that our rights do not expand at the expense of the rights of others? A society with unlimited rights is incapable of standing up to adversity. If we do not wish to be ruled by a coercive authority, then each of us must rein himself in. No constitutions, laws, or elections will by themselves assure equilibrium in a society, because it is human to persist in the pursuit of one's interests. Most people in a position to enhance their rights and seize more will do precisely that. (Hence the demise of all the ruling classes throughout history.) A stable society is achieved not by balancing opposing forces but by conscious self-limitation: by the principle that we are always duty-bound to defer to the sense of moral justice.

PART IV

Socialism, Nationalism, and Internationalism

17

KARL MARX AND
FRIEDRICH ENGELS

Manifesto of the Communist Party

A spectre is haunting Europe—the spectre of communism. All the powers of old Europe have entered into a holy alliance to exorcise this spectre: Pope and Tsar, Metternich and Guizot, French Radicals and German police-spies.

Where is the party in opposition that has not been decried as communistic by its opponents in power? Where is the opposition that has not hurled back the branding reproach of communism, against the more advanced opposition parties, as well as against its reactionary adversaries?

Two things result from this fact:

1. Communism is already acknowledged by all European powers to be itself a power.

2. It is high time that Communists should openly, in the face of the whole world, publish their views, their aims, their tendencies, and meet this nursery tale of the spectre of communism with a manifesto of the party itself.

To this end, Communists of various nationalities have assembled in London and sketched the following manifesto, to be published in the English, French, German, Italian, Flemish, and Danish languages.

I. BOURGEOIS AND PROLETARIANS

The history of all hitherto existing society is the history of class struggles. Freeman and slave, patrician and plebeian, lord and serf, guild-master and journeyman, in a word, oppressor and oppressed, stood in constant opposition to one another, carried on an uninterrupted, now hidden, now open fight, a fight that each time ended, either in a revolutionary reconstitution of society at large, or in the common ruin of the contending classes.

In the earlier epochs of history, we find almost everywhere a complicated arrangement of society into various orders, a manifold gradation of social rank. In ancient Rome we have patricians, knights, plebeians, slaves; in the Middle Ages, feudal lords, vassals, guild-masters, journeymen, apprentices, serfs; in almost all of these classes, again, subordinate gradations.

The modern bourgeois society that has sprouted from the ruins of feudal society has not done away with class antagonisms. It has but established new classes, new conditions of oppression, new forms of struggle in place of the old ones.

Our epoch, the epoch of the bourgeoisie, possesses, however, this distinctive feature: It has simplified the class antagonisms. Society as a whole is more and more splitting up into two great hostile camps, into two great classes directly facing each other—bourgeoisie and proletariat.

From the serfs of the Middle Ages sprang the chartered burghers of the earliest towns. From these burgesses the first elements of the bourgeoisie were developed.

The discovery of America, the rounding of the Cape, opened up fresh ground for the rising bourgeoisie. The East-Indian and Chinese markets, the colonization of America, trade with the colonies, the increase in the means of exchange and in commodities generally, gave to commerce, to navigation, to industry, an impulse never before known, and thereby, to the revolutionary element in the tottering feudal society, a rapid development.

The feudal system of industry, in which industrial production was monopolized by closed guilds, now no longer sufficed for the growing wants of the new markets. The manufacturing system took its place. The guild-masters were pushed aside by the manufacturing middle class; division of labour between the different corporate guilds vanished in the face of division of labour in each single workshop.

Meantime the markets kept ever growing, the demand ever rising. Even manufacture no longer sufficed. Thereupon, steam and machinery revolutionized industrial production. The place of manufacture was taken by the giant, modern industry, the place of the industrial middle class by industrial millionaires, the leaders of whole industrial armies, the modern bourgeois.

Modern industry has established the world market, for which the discovery of America paved the way. This market has given an immense development to commerce, to navigation, to communication by land. This development has, in its turn, reacted on the extension of industry; and in proportion as industry, commerce, navigation, railways extended, in the same proportion the bourgeoisie developed, increased its capital, and pushed into the background every class handed down from the Middle Ages.

We see, therefore, how the modern bourgeoisie is itself the product of a long course of development, of a series of revolutions in the modes of production and of exchange.

Each step in the development of the bourgeoisie was accompanied by a corresponding political advance of that class. An oppressed class under the sway of the feudal nobility, an armed and self-governing association in the medieval commune; here independent urban republic (as in Italy and Germany), there taxable "third estate" of the monarchy (as in France); afterwards, in the period of manufacture proper, serving either the semi-feudal or the absolute monarchy as a counterpoise against the nobility, and, in fact, cornerstone of the great monarchies in general—the bourgeoisie has at last, since the establishment of modern industry and of the world market, conquered for itself, in the modern representative state, exclusive political sway. The executive of the modern state is but a committee for managing the common affairs of the whole bourgeoisie.

The bourgeoisie, historically, has played a most revolutionary part.

The bourgeoisie, wherever it has got the upper hand, has put an end to all feudal, patriarchal, idyllic relations. It has pitilessly torn asunder the motley feudal ties that bound man to his "natural superiors," and has left no other nexus between man and man than naked self-interest, than callous "cash payment." It has drowned the most heavenly ecstasies of religious fervour, of chivalrous enthusiasm, of philistine sentimentalism, in the icy water of egotistical calculation. It has resolved personal worth into exchange value, and in place of the numberless indefeasible chartered freedoms, has set up that single, unconscionable freedom—Free Trade. In one word, for exploitation, veiled by religious and political illusions, it has substituted naked, shameless, direct, brutal exploitation.

The bourgeoisie has stripped of its halo every occupation hitherto honoured and looked up to with reverent awe. It has converted the physician, the lawyer, the priest, the poet, the man of science, into its paid wage labourers.

The bourgeoisie has torn away from the family its sentimental veil, and has reduced the family relation to a mere money relation.

The bourgeoisie has disclosed how it came to pass that the brutal display of vigour in the Middle Ages, which reactionaries so much admire, found its fitting complement in the most slothful indolence. It has been the first to show what man's activity can bring about. It has accomplished wonders far surpassing Egyptian pyramids, Roman aqueducts, and Gothic cathedrals; it has conducted expeditions that put in the shade all former exoduses of nations and crusades.

The bourgeoisie cannot exist without constantly revolutionizing the instruments of production, and thereby the relations of production, and with them the whole relations of society. Conservation of the old modes of production in unaltered form was, on the contrary, the first condition of existence for all earlier industrial classes. Constant revolutionizing of production, uninterrupted disturbance of all social conditions, everlasting uncertainty and agitation distinguish the bourgeois epoch from all earlier ones. All fixed, fast frozen relations, with their train of ancient and venerable prejudices and opinions, are swept away, all new-formed ones become antiquated before they can ossify. All that is solid melts into air, all that is holy is profaned, and man is at last compelled to face with sober senses his real conditions of life and his relations with his kind.

The need of a constantly expanding market for its products chases the bourgeoisie over the whole surface of the globe. It must nestle everywhere, settle everywhere, establish connections everywhere.

The bourgeoisie has through its exploitation of the world market given a cosmopolitan character to production and consumption in every country. To the great chagrin of reactionaries, it had drawn from under the feet of industry the national ground on which it stood. All old-established national industries have been destroyed or are daily being destroyed. They are dislodged by new industries, whose introduction becomes a life and death question for all civilized nations, by industries that no longer work up indigenous raw material, but raw material drawn from the remotest zones; industries whose products are consumed, not only at home, but in every quarter of the globe. In place of the old wants, satisfied by the production of the country, we find new wants, requiring for their satisfaction the products of distant lands and climes. In place of the old and national seclusion and self-sufficiency, we have intercourse in every direction, universal interdependence of nations. And as in material, so also in intellectual production. The intellectual creations of individual nations become common property. National one-sidedness and narrow-mindedness become more and more impossible, and from the numerous national and local literatures there arises a world literature.

The bourgeoisie, by the rapid improvement of all instruments of production, by the immensely facilitated means of communication, draws all, even the most barbarian, nations into civilization. The cheap prices of its commodities are the heavy artillery with which it batters down all Chinese walls, with which it forces the barbarians' intensely obstinate hatred of foreigners to capitulate. It compels all nations, on pain of extinction, to adopt the bourgeois mode of production; it compels them to introduce what it calls civilization into their midst, i.e., to become bourgeois themselves. In one word, it creates a world after its own image. [. . .]

The Communists are reproached with desiring to abolish countries and nationality.

The working men have no country. We cannot take from them what they have not got. Since the proletariat must first of all acquire political supremacy, must rise to be the leading class of the nation, must constitute itself *the* nation, it is, so far, itself national, though not in the bourgeois sense of the word.

National differences and antagonism between peoples are daily more and more vanishing, owing to the development of the bourgeoisie, to freedom of commerce, to the world market, to uniformity in the mode of production and in the conditions of life corresponding thereto.

The supremacy of the proletariat will cause them to vanish still faster. United action of the leading civilized countries at least, is one of the first conditions for the emancipation of the proletariat.

In proportion as the exploitation of one individual by another is put an end to, the exploitation of one nation by another will also be put an end to. In proportion as the antagonism between classes within the nation vanishes, the hostility of one nation to another will come to an end.

The charges against communism made from a religious, a philosophical, and, generally, from an ideological standpoint, are not deserving of serious examination.

Does it require deep intuition to comprehend that man's ideas, views, and conceptions, in one word, man's consciousness, change with every change in the conditions of his material existence, in his social relations, and in his social life?

What else does the history of ideas prove, than that intellectual production changes its character in proportion as material production is changed? The ruling ideas of each age have ever been the ideas of its ruling class.

When people speak of ideas that revolutionize society, they do but express the fact that within the old society the elements of a new one have been created, and that the dissolution of the old ideas keeps even pace with the dissolution of the old conditions of existence.

When the ancient world was in its last throes, the ancient religions were overcome by Christianity. When Christian ideas succumbed in the eighteenth century to rationalist ideas, feudal society fought its death battle with the then revolutionary bourgeoisie. The ideas of religious liberty and freedom of conscience merely gave expression to the sway of free competition within the domain of knowledge.

"Undoubtedly," it will be said, "religious, moral, philosophical, and juridical ideas have been modified in the course of historical development. But religion, morality, philosophy, political science, and law, constantly survived this change."

"There are, besides, eternal truths, such as Freedom, Justice, etc., that are common to all states of society. But communism abolishes eternal truths, it abolishes all religion, and all morality, instead of constituting them on a new basis; it therefore acts in contradiction to all past historical experience."

What does this accusation reduce itself to? The history of all past society has consisted in the development of class antagonisms, antagonisms that assumed different forms at different epochs.

But whatever form they may have taken, one fact is common to all past ages, viz., the exploitation of one part of society by the other. No wonder, then, that the social consciousness of past ages, despite all the multiplicity and variety it displays, moves within certain common forms, or general ideas, which cannot completely vanish except with the total disappearance of class antagonisms.

The communist revolution is the most radical rupture with traditional relations; no wonder that its development involves the most radical rupture with traditional ideas.

18

OTTO BAUER

The Nationalities Question and Social Democracy

Modern capitalism begins gradually to distinguish the lower classes in each nation more sharply from each other, for these classes too gain access to national education, to the cultural life of their nation, and to the national language. The tendency toward unification also affects the labouring masses. But only socialist society will bring this tendency to fruition. It will distinguish whole peoples from each other by the diversity of national education and civilization, in the same way as at present only the educated classes of the different nations are distinguished. True, there will be narrower communities of character within the socialist nation too; but there will be no autonomous cultural communities, for every local community, as a result of cultural intercourse, and the exchange of ideas, will itself be under the influence of the whole national culture.

Thus we arrive at a comprehensive definition of the nation. *The nation is the totality of men bound together through a common destiny into a community of character*. Through a *common destiny*: This characteristic distinguishes the nation from the international character groupings, such as an occupation, a class, or the members of a state, which rest upon a similarity, not a community, of destiny. The *totality* of the associated characters: This distinguishes them from the narrower communities of character within the nation, which never create a natural and cultural community that is determined by its own destiny, but only one that is closely connected with the whole nation, and consequently determined by the destiny of the latter. In the period of tribal communism the nation was sharply delimited in this way; the totality of all those descended from the original Baltic people, whose cultural being, through natural inheritance and cultural tradition, was determined by the destiny of that ancestral stock, constituted the nation. In socialist society the nation will again be sharply defined in this way; all those who share in national education and national cultural values, whose character is therefore shaped by the destiny of the nation which determines the content of these values, will constitute the nation. In a society which is based upon private ownership of the means of labour, the ruling classes, once the knights and now the educated classes, constitute the nation as the totality of those in whom a similar upbringing resulting from the history of the nation, and a common language and national education, produces an affinity of character. But the popular masses do not constitute the nation: They do so no longer, because the age-old community of descent no longer binds them closely enough together; and they do not yet do so, because they are not fully incorporated in the developing system of education. The difficulty of finding a satisfactory definition of the nation, upon which all earlier attempts came to grief, is therefore historically conditioned. People tried to discover the nation in our present class society, in which the old sharply defined community of descent has disintegrated into an immense number of local and descent groups, while the growth of a new community of education has not yet been able to unite these small groups in a national whole.

Thus our search for the essence of the nation reveals a grandiose historical picture. At the outset, in the period of primitive communism and nomadic agriculture, there is a unitary nation as a community of descent. Then, after the transition to settled agriculture and the development of private property, the old nation is divided into the common culture of the ruling classes on one side, and the peasants and small farmers on the other, the latter confined to narrow local regions produced by the disintegration of the old nation. Later, with the development of the capitalist mode of social production and the extension of the national cultural community, the working and exploited classes are still excluded, but the tendency to national unity on the basis of national education gradually becomes stronger than the particularistic tendency of the disintegration of the old nation, based upon common descent, into increasingly sharply differentiated local groups. Finally, when society divests social production of its capitalist integument, the unitary nation as a community of education, work, and culture emerges again. The development of the nation reflects the history of the mode of production and of property. Just as private ownership of the means of production and individual production develops out of the social system of primitive communism, and from this, again, there develops cooperative production on the basis of social ownership, so the unitary nation divides into members of the nation and those who are excluded and become fragmented into small local circles; but with the development of social production these circles are again drawn together and will eventually be absorbed into the unitary socialist nation of the future. The nation of the era of private property and individual production, which is divided into members and nonmembers, and into numerous circumscribed local groups, is the product of the disintegration of the communist nation of the past and the material for the socialist nation of the future. [. . .]

The national conception of history, which sees the driving force of events in the struggles of nations, strives for a mechanics of nations. According to this view, nations are regarded as elements which cannot be reduced any further, as fixed bodies which clash in space, and act upon each other by pressure and collision. But my conception dissolves the nation itself into a process. For me, history no longer reflects the struggles of nations; instead the nation itself appears as the reflection of historical struggles. For the nation is only manifested in the national character, in the nationality of the individual; and the nationality of the individual is only one aspect of his determination by the history of society, by the development of the conditions and techniques of labour.

Every new economic order creates new forms of state constitution and new rules for demarcating political structures. How will communities be separated from each other in socialist society? Will the nationality of the citizens determine the limits of the community in this case too?

In order to answer this question about the relation of socialism to the political principle of nationality, we must start from the fact that only socialism will give the whole people a share in the national culture. With the uprooting of the population through social production, and the development of the nation into a homogeneous community of education, labour, and culture, the more circumscribed local associations will lose their vigour, while the bond which unites all members of the nation will become increasingly strong. Today the Tyrolean peasant is closely linked with the fellow members of his province through the distinctive peasant culture of the province and is sharply distinguished from the Germans outside the province. This fact of national life is reflected in national consciousness. The Tyrolean peasant feels himself to be first of all a Tyrolean and only rarely remembers that he is a German. The Tyrolean worker is already quite different; he has little share in the particular way of life of the Tyrolean peasants, and he is linked with the German nation by much stronger bonds. By making every German a product of German culture, and by giving him the opportunity to share in the benefits of the progress of German culture, socialist society will, for the first time, abolish particularism within the nation. There is no doubt that this development will strengthen the principle of political nationality.

Another group of phenomena has a similar influence. The peasant masses are completely bound by tradition; the household possessions of their ancestors are dear to them, while everything new is hateful. Their love for the values of the past also has political consequences; it is the root of their attachment to the church, their local patriotism, their dynastic loyalty. We have seen the significance of this fact in our investigation of the forces which assure Austria's stability; the peasants who cannot free themselves from the chains of centuries-old tradition are one of the supports of this state. If on the one hand the socialist mode of production integrates the masses for the first time into the national cultural community and thereby strengthens their national consciousness, so on the other hand it destroys their attachment to the ideologies of past centuries which is an obstacle to the full realization of the nationality principle. It not only increases the driving force of the nationality principle, but also clears away the obstacles from its course.

Nevertheless, all this only prepares the victory of the nationality principle. It will only be achieved by that flood tide of rationalism which will submerge all traditional ideologies as soon as the dam of capitalism is broken. In the great period of transition from capitalist to socialist society, in which everything old is destroyed, all old authorities are overturned, and the old property relations are finally eliminated, what is old and traditional loses it sanctity. Only now will the masses learn to overthrow the old in order to create on its ruins new structures to serve their purposes. This revolution in the consciousness of the masses will be consolidated by the everyday praxis of socialist society, which gives the masses for the first time the power to determine their own destiny, to decide by free discussion and resolution their own future, and thus make the development of human culture a deliberate, intentional, conscious human act. It will be made possible by socialist education, which will provide every individual with the cultural objects of the whole nation and indeed a good part of those of the whole human race. Only in this way can the individual be liberated from the traditions of restricted local circles, broaden his views, and be enabled to establish his own ends and make an intelligent choice of the means to those ends. No state boundary which past ages established for their own purposes will be sacrosanct for the people living in socialist society. Only now will all peoples be ready to confront the question which, in the nineteenth century, was only a question for the educated, concerning the relation between the internal community and external power, which appears in the antagonism between nation and state. While the narrow local associations within the nation become weaker, the national cultural community embraces more closely the people as a whole, and the national community becomes for them a certain and unalterable fact; but they conceive external power as a means serving human ends, which must adapt itself to human ends. So there comes to life in them the basic idea of the nationality principle, the principle of adaptation of external power to inner community.

The content of the nationality principle is the rule that the external power should consolidate and serve the internal community. But this principle will only become causally effective as a motive when the transformation of the techniques and conditions of labour makes the traditional forms of the state which do not correspond to this principle insupportable. So it was at an earlier time, that when the traditional small state no longer corresponded with its need, the bourgeoisie inscribed the principle of nationality on its banner. It will be so again, as soon as the transformation of social production from its capitalist to its socialist form changes the human spirit, destroys old cultural values, and prepares to confront the question of the "natural" limits of the state.

But if the masses see the free national community as their goal, socialism also shows them the way to this goal; for socialism is necessarily based upon democracy. Even such a democratic community will compel minorities to bow to the will of the whole; it is unimportant whether it does this by direct compulsion or by excluding them from their share in the process and profits of labour. But such a community will never be able to incorporate whole nations which do not want to belong to it. How could nations in which the masses are in full possession of the national culture, provided with the rights of participation in legislation and self-government, and armed, be compelled to bow to the yoke of a community to which they do not wish to belong? All state power rests on the power of weapons. The present-day people's army is still, thanks to an ingenious procedure, a tool of power in the hands of an individual, a family, or a class, just like the armies of knights and mercenaries in the past. The army of the democratic community in socialist society, made up of highly cultivated men, who no longer obey the command of a foreign power in their workplaces, and are called to full participation in political life, in legislation, and administration, is no longer a separate power, but is nothing more than the armed people itself. With this vanishes all possibility of rule by a foreign nation.

At present, the situation of the nationalities in our society is not based on the fact that whole nations do not have the power to achieve the national state to which they aspire, nor only on the fact that large sections of many nations, under the influence of the ideologies of past epochs and as a result of their exclusion from the cultural community of the nation, resist the idea of national unity and freedom. The thoroughgoing implementation of the principle of nationality is also impeded by the fact that the modern state is at the same time an economic region. Should it not strive, therefore, to embrace an area which can, at least to some extent, be economically independent? Would not the productivity of labour fall, if a socialist community, in order to implement strictly the principle of national demarcation, desired only to encompass a small economic region, without regard for production?

We should remember here, in the first place, that only socialism will be able to implement successfully the international division of labour. Simple commodity production greatly increased the productivity of labour, by extending the division of labour, at first within a limited area, in a town and its surrounding trading region. Capitalism subsequently promoted the division of labour within large economic regions, and in this way again greatly increased the productivity of labour. This process already laid the basis for an international division of labour. [. . .] Nevertheless, capitalist society has not achieved and now never will achieve a free exchange of commodities and an international division of labour. For the goal of capitalist economic policy is not the greatest possible increase in the productivity of labour, but the greatest possible augmentation of profits. It seeks to attain this goal not by allocating productive capital to those individual branches of production which would make possible the greatest increase in the productivity of labour, but by accelerating the flow of unused capital into the sphere of production, and extending continually its markets and spheres of investment. Only where the requirements of the international division of labour happen to coincide with the requirements of capitalist economic policy—as was the case in England until recently—is freedom of trade realized in capitalist society.

In socialist society, on the contrary, where the means of production is no longer capital, capitalist economic policy no longer has any sense. Socialist society, therefore, will be able to achieve for the first time an international division of labour and the corresponding distribution of labour. Of course, this will not happen at a single stroke. If a state has developed an iron industry behind protective tariffs, instead of making use of the richer iron ores of other countries through a free exchange of goods, socialist society could not suddenly shut down the existing furnaces and steel works. But the number of workers, and the productive apparatus of society, grows every year; and the new workers, the new means of production, will regularly be applied to those branches of production which enjoy the most favourable conditions, and their products will be exchanged for those of other countries. In this way the socialist community will be able to accomplish, in a few decades, the division of labour between states that classical economics advocated.

Thus, for the first time, the greatest obstacle to the implementation of the nationality principle will be eliminated. For then even the smallest nation will be able to create an independently organized national economy; while the great nations produce a variety of goods, the small nation will apply its whole labour-power to the production of one or a few kinds of goods, and will acquire all other goods from other nations by exchange. In spite of its small size it will enjoy all the advantages of large-scale enterprise. Even those peoples whose territory has been most meagerly endowed with natural resources will be able to establish an independent economy; after all, Ricardo showed conclusively that even the economic region least favoured by nature has a role in the international division of labour, namely to produce those goods in the manufacture of which the superiority of all other countries is proportionately least, and to exchange these goods for the products of all other economic regions. Hence, through the international division of labour, the whole of civilized humanity becomes a great organism; and precisely by this means the political freedom and unity of all nations becomes possible. In a society in which each community is supposed to be autarchic and to supply its own needs, the full implementation of the nationality principle is impossible; national freedom is necessarily denied to the small nations, the nations whose territory provides less favourable conditions for production. As soon as the international division of labour embraces all peoples, the most important barrier preventing the reconciliation of the political division of humanity with its incorporation in historical cultural communities, falls.

Even the shifts within the organization of social labour assume an entirely new character in socialist society. The unregulated migration of individuals, dominated by the blind laws of capitalist competition, will then cease, and will be replaced by a conscious regulation of migration by the socialist communities. They will encourage immigrants where an increase in the number of workers will raise the productivity of labour; they will induce a part of the population to emigrate, where increasing numbers result in a declining yield. This deliberate regulation of immigration and emigration will give every nation, for the first time, control over its linguistic boundaries. It will no longer be possible for social migration to infringe again and again the nationality principle, against the will of the nation.

It is no accident that the realization of the nationality principle is linked with the victory of socialism. In the era of tribal communism, communities were, at least originally, nationally unified. Even where a tribe was subjugated by a foreign people, it did not initially lose its own political organization, but only became dependent as a community on the community of the victors, to whom it owed tribute. The political disruption of the nation first began with the disintegration of the old communist nation into narrow local associations. And foreign domination only became possible with class divisions, with the cleavage into members of the nation and those who are excluded. The opposition between rulers and ruled, exploiting and exploited classes, assumes the form of the domination of the historical nations over those without history. With the development of social production in the form of capitalist commodity production, political particularism is forced to retreat; the need to extend the division of labour within large economic regions creates great national states on the ruins of countless small states. But as a result of the same development foreign domination also becomes intolerable; the nations without history awaken to historical life and likewise strive to achieve national state. Finally social production sheds its capitalist shell, and only then is a national cultural community attained. Only then does all particularism within the nation vanish and all rule of one nation over other peoples become impossible, only then does the division of labour embrace the whole of humanity, and there is no longer any obstacle to the political organization of humanity into free nations. The political organization of humanity reflects its national cultural being, which is determined in turn by the development of the techniques and conditions of labour. Political particularism and foreign rule are the political forms of an epoch which is characterized from the point of view of nationality by the division of the nation into members and outcasts, and by the disintegration of the nation into narrow local associations; and economically by settled agriculture, private ownership of the means of labour, and landlordism. The principle of nationality is the constitutional principle of the unitary and autonomous nation in a particular epoch of social production. The construction of the great national states in the nineteenth century is only the precursor of an era in which the principle of nationality will be fully realized, just as the extension of the cultural community by modern capitalism is the precursor of the full attainment of the national cultural community by socialism, and as social production in its capitalist form is the precursor of cooperative production by and for society. . . .

We have seen that socialism leads necessarily to the realization of the principle of nationality. But while socialist society gradually constructs above the national community a federal state in which the communities of the individual nations are once again incorporated, the principle of nationality changes into that of national autonomy, from a rule for the formation of states into a rule of the state constitution. The socialist principle of nationality expresses a higher unity of the principle of nationality and national autonomy.

Thus the socialist principle of nationality is able to combine the advantages of both the bourgeois principle of nationality and national autonomy. By organizing the nation as a community it gives it the right to legislate and to administer itself, power to dispose over the means and the product of labour, military power. But by incorporating the nation into a community of international law, established as a corporate entity, it secures for the nation power even beyond the limits of its territory. Let us suppose, for example, that socialist society could raise the productivity of labour in Germany by reducing the number of workers on German soil, while raising the productivity of labour in south Russia by increasing the number of workers. It would then seek to transfer a part of the German population to south Russia. But Germany would not send its sons and daughters to the east without assuring their cultural independence. So the German colonists would not enter the community of the Ukraine as individuals, but as a corporate legal entity. If the national territorial bodies first unite in an international community, there now arises, as a result of planned colonization, foreign-speaking associations of people within the national communities, associations which are legally bound, in many respects, to the territorial bodies of their nation, and in other respects, to the community of the foreign nation. Socialist society will undoubtedly present a variegated picture of national associations of people and territorial bodies; it will be as different from the centralized, atomistic constitution of present-day states as from the equally varied and complex organization of medieval society. I do not intend to outline here a fantasy of the coming society. What is said about it here is the result of sober reflection upon its nature. The transformation of men by the socialist mode of production leads necessarily to the organization of humanity in national communities. The international division of labour leads necessarily to the unification of the national communities in a social structure of a higher order. All nations will be united for the common domination of nature, but the totality will be organized in national communities which will be encouraged to develop autonomously and to enjoy freely their national culture—that is the socialist principle of nationality.

19

JOSEPH STALIN

Marxism and the National-Colonial Question

A nation is a historically evolved, stable community of language, territory, economic life, and psychological make-up manifested in a community of culture.

It goes without saying that a nation, like every other historical phenomenon, is subject to the law of change, has its history, its beginning and end.

It must be emphasized that none of the above characteristics is by itself sufficient to define a nation. On the other hand, it is sufficient for a single one of these characteristics to be absent and the nation ceases to be a nation.

It is possible to conceive people possessing a common "national character," but they cannot be said to constitute a single nation if they are economically disunited, inhabit different territories, speak different languages, and so forth. Such, for instance, are the Russian, Galician, American, Georgian, and Caucasian Highland Jews, who do not, in our opinion, constitute a single nation.

It is possible to conceive people with a common territory and economic life who nevertheless would not constitute a single nation because they have no common language and no common "national character." Such, for instance, are the Germans and Letts in the Baltic region.

Finally, the Norwegians and the Danes speak one language, but they do not constitute a single nation owing to the absence of the other characteristics.

It is only when all these characteristics are present that we have a nation.

It might appear that "national character" is not one of the characteristics but the *only* essential characteristic of a nation, and that all the other characteristics are only *factors* in the development of a nation, rather than its characteristics. Such, for instance, is the view held by R. Springer, and particularly by O. Bauer, Social Democratic theoreticians on the national question well known in Austria. [. . .]

What is the national program of the Austrian Social Democrats?

It is expressed in two words: national autonomy.

That means, first, that autonomy is granted, let us say, not to Bohemia or Poland, which are inhabited mainly by Czechs and Poles, but to Czechs and Poles generally, irrespective of territory, no matter what part of Austria they inhabit.

That is why this autonomy is called *national* and not territorial.

It means, secondly, that the Czechs, Poles, Germans, and so on, scattered over the various parts of Austria, taken personally, as individuals, are to be organized into integral nations, and as such to form part of the Austrian state. In this way Austria will represent not a union of autonomous regions, but a union of autonomous nationalities, constituted irrespective of territory.

It means, thirdly, that the national institutions which are to be created for this purpose for the Poles, Czechs, and so forth, are to have jurisdiction only over "cultural," not "political" questions. Specifically political questions will be left to the Pan-Austrian parliament (the Reichsrat).

That is why this autonomy is called *cultural*, national cultural autonomy. [. . .]

It is not difficult to see that this program retains certain traces of "territorialism," but that in general it is a formulation of the idea of national autonomy. It is therefore not without cause that Springer, the first agitator on behalf of national autonomy, greets it with enthusiasm; Bauer also supports this program, calling a "theoretical victory" for national autonomy; only, in the interest of greater clarity, he proposes to replace Point 4 by a more definite formulation, which would declare the necessity of "constituting the national minority within each self-governing region into a juridical public corporation" for the management of educational and other cultural affairs.

Such is the national program of the Austrian Social Democratic Party.

Let us examine its scientific foundations.

Let us see how the Austrian Social Democratic Party justifies the national autonomy it advocates.

Let us turn to the theoreticians of national autonomy, Springer and Bauer.

National autonomy proceeds from the conception of a nation as a union of individuals without regard to definite territory.

According to Springer: "Nationality is not essentially connected with territory"; it is "an autonomous union of persons."[1]

Bauer also speaks of a nation as a "community of persons" which "does not enjoy exclusive sovereignty in any particular region."

But the persons constituting a nation do not always live in one compact mass; they are frequently divided into groups, and in that form are interspersed among foreign national organisms. It is capitalism which drives them into other regions and cities in search of a livelihood. But when they enter foreign national territories and there form minorities, these groups are made to suffer by the local national majorities in the way of limitations on their language, schools, etc. Hence national collisions. Hence the "unsuitability" of territorial autonomy. The only solution to such a situation, according to Springer and Bauer, is to organize the minorities of the given nationality dispersed over various parts of the state into a single, general, interclass national union. Such a union alone, in their opinion, can protect the cultural interests of national minorities, and it alone is capable of putting an end to national discord. [. . .]

Bauer expresses himself in the same spirit when he proposes, as "a demand of the working class," that "the minorities should be constituted into juridical public corporations based on the personal principle."[2]

But how is a nation to be organized? How is one to determine to what nation any given individual belongs? [. . .]

According to Bauer, the Austrian Social Democratic Party is striving by the creation of these interclass institutions "to make national culture . . . the possession of the whole people and thereby *fuse all the members of the nation into a national cultural community.*"[3] (Our italics.)

One might think that all this concerns Austria alone. But Bauer does not agree. He emphatically declares that national autonomy is essential for all states which, like Austria, consist of several nationalities. [. . .]

The first thing that strikes the eye is the entirely inexplicable and absolutely unjustifiable substitution of national autonomy for self-determination of nations. One or the other: Either Bauer failed to understand the meaning of self-determination, or he did understand it but for some reason or other deliberately narrowed its meaning. For there is no doubt (1) that national autonomy presupposes the integrity of the multinational state, whereas self-determination transcends this integrity and (2) that self-determination endows a nation with sovereign rights, whereas national autonomy endows it only with "cultural" rights. That, in the first place.

In the second place, a combination of internal and external conditions is fully possible at some future time by virtue of which one or another of the nationalities may decide to secede from a multinational state, say from Austria (did not the Ruthenian Social Democrats at the Brünn Party Congress announce their readiness to unite the "two parts" of their people into one whole?). What, in such a case, becomes of national autonomy, which is *"inevitable for the proletariat of all nations"*?

What sort of "solution" of the problem is it that mechanically squeezes nations into the Procrustes' bed of an integral state?

Further. National autonomy is contrary to the whole course of development of nations. It calls for the organization of nations; but can they be artificially welded if in actual reality, by virtue of economic development, whole groups are torn from them and dispersed over various regions? There is no doubt that in the early stages of capitalism nations become welded together. But there is also no doubt that in the higher stages of capitalism a process of dispersion of nations sets in, a process whereby whole groups separate off from nations in search of a livelihood, subsequently settling finally in other regions of the state; in the course of which these settlers lose their old contacts, acquire new contacts in their new domicile, from generation to generation acquire new habits and new tastes, and possibly a new language. . . .

One asks: Is it possible to unite into a single national union groups that have grown so distinct? Where are the magic hoops to unite what cannot be united? Is it conceivable that, for instance, the Germans of the Baltic provinces and the Germans of Transcaucasia can be "welded into a single nation"? But if it is not conceivable and not possible, wherein does national autonomy differ from the utopia of the old nationalists, who endeavored to turn back the wheel of history?

But the cohesion and unity of a nation diminish not only as a result of migration. They diminish also from internal causes, owing to the growing acuteness of the class struggle. In the early stages of capitalism one may still speak of a "cultural community" between the proletariat and the bourgeoisie. But as large-scale industry develops and the class struggle becomes more and more acute, this "community" begins to melt away. One cannot seriously speak of the "cultural community" of a nation when the masters and the workers of a nation have ceased to understand each other. What "common fate" can there be when the bourgeoisie thirsts for war, and the proletariat declares "war on war"? Can a single interclass national union be formed from such contradictory elements? And, after this, can one speak of the "fusion of all the members of the nation into a national cultural community"?[4] Is it not obvious that national autonomy is contrary to the whole course of the class struggle?

But let us assume for a moment that the slogan "Organize the nation" is practicable. One might understand bourgeois nationalist parliamentarians endeavoring to "organize" a nation for the purpose of securing additional votes. But since when have Social Democrats begun to occupy themselves with "organizing" nations, "constituting" nations, "creating" nations?

What sort of Social Democrats are they who in a period of extreme aggravation of the class struggle organize interclass national unions? Hitherto the Social Democratic Party of Austria, like every other Social Democratic Party, had one aim, namely, to organize the proletariat. This aim has apparently become "antiquated." Springer and Bauer are now setting a "new" aim, a more thrilling aim, namely, to "create," to "organize" a nation.

Besides, logic has its obligations: He who adopts national autonomy must also adopt this "new" aim; but to adopt the latter means to abandon the class position and to adopt the path of nationalism.

Springer's and Bauer's national autonomy is a subtle form of nationalism.

And it is by no means fortuitous that the national program of the Austrian Social Democrats enjoins a concern for the "*preservation* and *development* of the national peculiarities of the peoples." Just think: to "preserve" such "national peculiarities" of the Transcaucasian Tatars as self-flagellation at the festival of *Shakhsei-Vakhsei*; or to "develop" such "national peculiarities" of the Georgians as the vendetta!

A demand of this character is quite in place in an outright bourgeois nationalist program; and if it appears in the program of the Austrian Social Democrats it is because national autonomy tolerates rather than precludes such demands.

But if national autonomy is unsuitable now, it will be still more unsuitable in the future society, a socialist society.

Bauer's prophecy regarding the division of "humanity into nationally delimited communities" is refuted by the whole course of development of present-day humanity. National partitions are being demolished and are falling, rather than becoming firmer.

As early as the forties Marx declared that "national differences and antagonisms between peoples are daily more and more vanishing" and that "the supremacy of the proletariat will cause them to vanish still faster." The subsequent development of mankind, accompanied as it was by the colossal growth of capitalist production, the shuffling of nationalities, and the amalgamation of people within ever larger territories, emphatically corroborates Marx's thought.

Bauer's desire to represent socialist society as a "checkered picture of national unions and territorial corporations" is a timid attempt to replace Marx's conception of socialism by the reformed conception of Bakunin. The history of socialism proves that every such attempt harbors the elements of inevitable failure.

We shall not dwell on the "socialist principle of nationality" glorified by Bauer, which, in our opinion, replaces the socialist principle of the *class struggle* by the bourgeois principle of "*nationality.*" If national autonomy is based on such a dubious principle, it must be confessed that it can only cause harm to the working-class movement.

True, such nationalism is not so transparent, for it is skillfully masked by socialist phrases, but it is all the more harmful to the proletariat for that reason. We can always cope with open nationalism, for it can easily be discerned. It is much more difficult to combat a nationalism which is masked and unrecognizable beneath its mask. Protected by the armor of socialism, it is less vulnerable and more tenacious. Implanted among the workers, it poisons the atmosphere and spreads noxious ideas of mutual mistrust and aloofness among the workers of the different nationalities.

But this does not exhaust the harm caused by national autonomy. It tends not only to create aloofness, but also to break up a united working-class movement. The idea of national autonomy creates the psychological conditions that make for the division of a united workers' party into separate parties built on national lines. The breakup of the party is followed by the breakup of the trade unions, and complete isolation is the result. In this way a united class movement is broken up into separate national rivulets.

Austria, the home of "national autonomy," provides the most deplorable examples of this. Since 1897 (the Wimberg Party Congress) the one-time united Austrian Social Democratic Party has been breaking up into separate parties. The breakup became still more marked after the Brünn Congress (1899), which adopted national autonomy. Matters have finally come to such a pass that in place of a united international party we now have six national parties, of which the Czech Social Democratic Party will even have nothing to do with the German Social Democratic Party.

But with the parties are associated the trade unions. In Austria, both in the parties and in the trade unions, the main brunt of the work is borne by the same Social Democratic workers. There was therefore reason to fear that separatism in the party would lead to separatism in the trade unions and that the trade unions would also break up. That, in fact, has been the case: The trade unions have also divided according to nationality. Now things frequently go so far that the Czech workers will even break a strike of the German workers, or will unite at the municipal elections with the Czech bourgeois against the German workers.

It will be seen from this that national autonomy is no solution for the national problem. Nay more, it only serves to aggravate and confuse the problem by creating a soil which favors the destruction of the unity of the working-class movement, fosters national aloofness among the workers, and intensifies friction between them.

Such is the harvest of national autonomy.

NOTES

1. R. Springer, *Das nationale Problem* (*The National Problem*) (Leipzig and Vienna, 1902), 15.
2. O. Bauer, *Die Nationalitätenfrage und die Sozialdemokratie* (*The National Question and Social Democracy*) (Vienna, 1924), 530.
3. Bauer, *Die Nationalitätenfrage*, 531.
4. Bauer, *Die Nationalitätenfrage*, 531.

20

ROSA LUXEMBURG

The National Question and Autonomy

I. THE RIGHT OF NATIONS TO SELF-DETERMINATION

Among other problems, the 1905 revolution in Russia has brought into focus the nationality question. Until now, this problem has been urgent only in Austria-Hungary. At present, however, it has become crucial also in Russia, because the revolutionary development made all classes and all political parties acutely aware of the need to solve the nationality question as a matter of practical politics. All the newly formed or forming parties in Russia, be they radical, liberal, or reactionary, have been forced to include in their programs some sort of a position on the nationality question, which is closely connected with the entire complex of the state's internal and external policies. For a workers' party, nationality is a question both of program and of class organization. The position a workers' party assumes on the nationality question, as on every other question, must differ in method and basic approach from the positions of even the most radical bourgeois parties, and from the positions of the pseudo-socialistic, petit bourgeois parties. Social democracy, whose political program is based on the scientific method of historical materialism and the class struggle, cannot make an exception with respect to the nationality question. Moreover, it is only by approaching the problem from the standpoint of scientific socialism that the politics of social democracy will offer a solution which is *essentially uniform*, even though the program must take into account the wide variety of forms of the nationality question arising from the social, historical, and ethnic diversity of the Russian empire.

In the program of the Social Democratic Labor Party (RSDLP) of Russia, such a formula, containing a general solution of the nationality question in all its particular manifestations, is provided by the ninth point; this says that the party demands a democratic republic whose constitution would insure, among other things, "*that all nationalities forming the state have the right to self-determination.*"

This program includes two more extremely important propositions on the same matter. These are the seventh point, which demands the abolition of classes and the full legal equality of all citizens without distinction of sex, *religion, race,* or *nationality,* and the eighth point, which says that the several ethnic groups of the state should have the right to schools conducted in their respective national languages at state expense, and the right to use their languages at assemblies and on an equal level with the state language in all state and public functions. Closely connected to the nationality question is the third point of the program, which formulates the demand for wide self-government on the local and provincial level in areas which are characterized by special living conditions and by the special composition of their populations. Obviously, however, the authors of the program felt that the equality of all citizens before the law, linguistic rights, and local self-government were not enough to solve the nationality problem, since they found it necessary to add a special paragraph granting each nationality the "right to self-determination."

What is especially striking about this formula is the fact that it doesn't represent anything specifically connected with socialism nor with the politics of the working class. "The right of nations to self-determination" is at first glance a paraphrase of the old slogan of bourgeois nationalism put forth in all countries at all times: "the right of nations to freedom and independence." [. . .]

II. The general and cliché-like character of the ninth point in the program of the Social Democratic Labor Party of Russia shows that this way of solving the question is foreign to the position of Marxian socialism. A "right of nations" which is valid for all countries and all times is nothing more than a metaphysical cliché of the type of "rights of man" and "rights of the citizen." Dialectic materialism, which is the basis of scientific socialism, has broken once and for all with this type of "eternal" formula. For the historical dialectic has shown that there are no "eternal" truths and that there are no "rights." . . . In the words of Engels, "What is good in the here and now, is an evil somewhere else, and vice versa"—or, what is right and reasonable under some circumstances becomes nonsense and absurdity under others. Historical materialism has taught us that the real content of these "eternal" truths, rights, and formulae is determined only by the *material* social conditions of the environment in a given historical epoch.

On this basis, scientific socialism has revised the entire store of democratic clichés and ideological metaphysics inherited from the bourgeoisie. Present-day social democracy long since stopped regarding such phrases as "democracy," "national freedom," "equality," and other such beautiful things as eternal truths and laws transcending particular nations and times. On the contrary, Marxism regards and treats them only as expressions of certain definite historical conditions, as categories which, in terms of their material content and therefore their political value, are subject to constant change, which is the *only* "eternal" truth.

When Napoleon or any other despot of his ilk uses a plebiscite, the extreme form of political democracy, for the goals of Caesarism, taking advantage of the political ignorance and economic subjection of the masses, we do not hesitate for a moment to come out wholeheartedly against that "democracy," and are not put off for a moment by the majesty or the omnipotence of the people, which, for the metaphysicians of bourgeois democracy, is something like a sacrosanct idol.

When a German like Tassendorf or a tsarist gendarme, or a "truly Polish" National Democrat defends the "personal freedom" of strikebreakers, protecting them against the moral and material pressure of organized labor, we don't hesitate a minute to support the latter, granting them the fullest moral and historical right to *force* the unenlightened rivals into solidarity, although from the point of view of formal liberalism, those "willing to work" have on their side the right of "a free individual" to do what reason, or unreason, tells them.

When, finally, liberals of the Manchester School demand that the wage worker be left completely to his fate in the struggle with capital in the name of "the equality of citizens," we unmask that metaphysical cliché which conceals the most glaring economic inequality, and we demand, point-blank, the legal protection of the class of wage workers, thereby clearly breaking with formal "equality before the law."

The nationality question cannot be an exception among all the political, social, and moral questions examined in this way by modern socialism. It cannot be settled by the use of some vague cliché, even such a fine-sounding formula as "the right of all nations to self-determination." For such a formula expresses either absolutely nothing, so that it is an empty, noncommittal phrase, or else it expresses the unconditional duty of socialists to support all national aspirations, in which case it is simply false.

On the basis of the general assumptions of historical materialism, the position of socialists with respect to nationality problems depends primarily on the concrete circumstances of each case, which differ significantly among countries, and also change in the course of time in each country. [. . .]

A glaring example of how the change of historical conditions influences the evaluation and the position of socialists with respect to the nationality question is the so-called Eastern question. During the Crimean War in 1855, the sympathies of all democratic and socialist Europe were on the side of the Turks and against the South Slavs who were seeking their liberty. The "right" of all nations to freedom did not prevent Marx, Engels, and Liebknecht from speaking against the Balkan Slavs and from resolutely supporting the integrity of the Turks. For they judged the national movements of the Slavic peoples in the Turkish empire not from the standpoint of the "eternal" sentimental formulae of liberalism, but from the standpoint of the material conditions which determined the *content* of these national movements. [. . .]

III. What is more, in taking such a stand Marx and Engels were not at all indulging in party or class egoism, and were not sacrificing entire nations to the needs and perspectives of Western European democracy, as it might have appeared.

It is true that it sounds much more generous, and is more flattering to the overactive imagination of the young "intellectual," when the socialists announce a general and universal introduction of freedom for all existing suppressed nations. But the tendency to grant all peoples, countries, groups, and all human creatures the right to freedom, equality, and other such joys by one sweeping stroke of the pen, is characteristic only of the youthful period of the socialist movement, and most of all of the phraseological bravado of anarchism.

The socialism of the modern working class, that is, scientific socialism, takes no delight in the radical and wonderful-sounding solutions of social and national questions, but examines primarily the real issues involved in these problems. [. . .]

Actually, even if as socialists we recognized the immediate right of all nations to independence, the fates of nations would not change an iota because of this. The "right" of a nation to freedom as well as the "right" of the worker to economic independence are, under existing social conditions, only worth as much as the "right" of each man to eat off gold plates, which, as Nicolaus Chernyshevski wrote, he would be ready to sell at any moment for a ruble. In the 1840s the "right to work" was a favorite postulate of the Utopian Socialists in France, and appeared as an immediate and radical way of solving the social question. However, in the Revolution of 1848 that "right" ended, after a very short attempt to put it into effect, in a terrible fiasco, which could not have been avoided even if the famous "national workshops" had been organized differently. An analysis of the real conditions of the contemporary economy, as given by Marx in his *Capital*, must lead to the conviction that even if present-day governments were forced to declare a universal "right to work," it would remain only a fine-sounding phrase, and not one member of the rank and file of the reserve army of labor waiting on the sidewalk would be able to make a bowl of soup for his hungry children from that right.

Today, social democracy understands that the "right to work" will stop being an empty sound only when the capitalist regime is abolished, for in that regime the chronic unemployment of a certain part of the industrial proletariat is a necessary condition of production. Thus, social democracy does not demand a declaration of that imaginary "right" on the basis of the existing system, but rather strives for the abolition of the system itself by the class struggle, regarding labor organizations unemployment insurance, etc., only as temporary means of help.

In the same way, hopes of solving all nationality questions within the capitalist framework by insuring to all nations, races, and ethnic groups the possibility of "self-determination" is a complete utopia. And it is a utopia from the point of view that the objective system of political and class forces condemns many a demand in the political program of social democracy to be unfeasible in practice. For example, important voices in the ranks of the international workers' movement have expressed the conviction that a demand for the universal introduction of the eight-hour day by legal enactment has no chance of being realized in bourgeois society because of the growing social reaction of the ruling classes, the general stagnation of social reforms, the rise of powerful organizations of businessmen, etc. Nonetheless, no one would dare call the demand for the eight-hour day a utopia, because it is in complete accordance with the progressive development of bourgeois society.

However, to resume: The actual possibility of "self-determination" for all ethnic groups or otherwise defined nationalities is a utopia precisely because of the trend of historical development of contemporary societies. Without examining those distant times at the dawn of history when the nationalities of modern states were constantly moving about geographically, when they were joining, merging, fragmenting, and trampling one another, the fact is that all the ancient states without exception are, as a result of that long history of political and ethnic upheavals, extremely mixed with respect to nationalities. Today, in each state, ethnic relics bear witness to the upheavals and intermixtures which characterized the march of historical development in the past. [. . .] Historical development, especially the modern development of capitalism, does not tend to return to each nationality its independent existence, but moves rather in the opposite direction. [. . .]

The development of *world powers*, a characteristic feature of our times growing in importance along with the progress of capitalism, from the very outset condemns all small nations to political impotence. Apart from a few of the most powerful nations, the leaders in capitalist development, which possess the spiritual and material resources necessary to maintain their political and economic independence, "self-determination," the independent existence of smaller and petty nations, is an illusion, and will become even more so. The return of all, or even the majority of the nations which are today oppressed, to independence would only be possible if the existence of small states in the era of capitalism had any chances or hopes for the future. Besides, the big-power economy and politics—a condition of survival for the capitalist states—turn the politically independent, formally equal, small European states into mutes on the European stage and more often into scapegoats. Can one speak with any seriousness of the "self-determination" of peoples which are formally independent, such as Montenegrins, Bulgarians, Rumanians, the Serbs, the Greeks, and, as far as that goes, even the Swiss, whose very independence is the product of the political struggles and diplomatic game of the "Concert of Europe"? From this point of view, the idea of insuring all "nations" the possibility of self-determination is equivalent to reverting from Great-Capitalist development to the small medieval states, far earlier than the fifteenth and sixteenth centuries.

The other principal feature of modern development, which stamps such an idea as utopian, is capitalist *imperialism*. The example of England and Holland indicates that under certain conditions a capitalist country can even completely skip the transition phase of "national state" and create at once, in its manufacturing phase, a colony-holding state. The example of England and Holland, which, at the beginning of the seventeenth century, had begun to acquire colonies, was followed in the eighteenth and nineteenth centuries by all the great capitalist states. The fruit of that trend is the continuous destruction of the independence of more and more new countries and peoples, of entire continents.

The very development of international trade in the capitalist period brings with it the inevitable, though at times slow ruin of all the more primitive societies, destroys their historically existing means of "self-determination," and makes them dependent on the crushing wheel of capitalist development and world politics. [. . .]

A general attempt to divide all existing states into national units and to re-tailor them on the model of national states and statelets is a completely hopeless, and historically speaking, reactionary undertaking.

IV. [. . .] In a class society, "the nation" as a homogeneous sociopolitical entity does not exist. Rather, there exist within each nation, classes with antagonistic interests and "rights." There literally is not one social area, from the coarsest material relationships to the most subtle moral ones, in which the possessing class and the class-conscious proletariat hold the same attitude, and in which they appear as a consolidated "national" entity. In the sphere of economic relations, the bourgeois classes represent the interests of exploitation—the proletariat the interests of work. In the sphere of legal relations, the cornerstone of bourgeois society is private property; the interest of the proletariat demands the emancipation of the propertyless man from the domination of property. In the area of the judiciary, bourgeois society represents class "justice," the justice of the well-fed and the rulers; the proletariat defends the principle of taking into account social influences on the individual, of humaneness. In international relations, the bourgeoisie represents the politics of war and partition, and at the present stage, a system of trade war; the proletariat demands a politics of universal peace and free trade. In the sphere of the social sciences and philosophy, bourgeois schools of thought and the school representing the proletariat stand in diametric opposition to each other. The possessing classes have their worldview; it is represented by idealism, metaphysics, mysticism, eclecticism; the modern proletariat has its theory—dialectic materialism. Even in the sphere of so-called universal conditions—in ethics, views on art, on behavior— the interests, worldview, and ideals of the bourgeoisie and those of the enlightened proletariat represent two camps, separated from each other by an abyss. And whenever the formal strivings and the interests of the proletariat and those of the bourgeoisie (as a whole or in its most progressive

part) seem identical—for example, in the field of democratic aspirations—
there, under the identity of forms and slogans, is hidden the most complete
divergence of contents and essential politics.

There can be no talk of a collective and uniform will, of the self-determination of the "nation" in a society formed in such a manner. If we find
in the history of modern societies "national" movements, and struggles for
"national interests," these are usually class movements of the ruling strata
of the bourgeoisie, which can in any given case represent the interest of
the other strata of the population only insofar as under the form of "national interests" it defends progressive forms of historical development, and
insofar as the working class has not yet distinguished itself from the mass of
the "nation" (led by the bourgeoisie) into an independent, enlightened political
class. [. . .]

For social democracy, the nationality question is, like all other social and
political questions, primarily *a question of class interests*. [. . .]

Society will win the ability to freely determine its national existence
when it has the ability to determine its political being and the conditions
of its creation. "Nations" will control their historical existence when human society controls its social processes.

Therefore, the analogy which is drawn by partisans of the "right of nations to self-determination" between that "right" and all democratic demands, like the right of free speech, free press, freedom of association and
of assembly, is completely incongruous. These people point out that we
support the freedom of association because we are the party of political
freedom; but we still fight against hostile bourgeois parties. Similarly, they
say, we have the democratic duty to support the self-determination of nations, but this fact does not commit us to support every individual tactic of
those who fight for self-determination.

The above view completely overlooks the fact that these "rights," which
have a certain superficial similarity, lie on completely different historical
levels. The rights of association and assembly, free speech, the free press,
etc., are the legal forms of existence of a mature bourgeois society. But "the
right of nations to self-determination" is only a metaphysical formulation
of an idea which in bourgeois society is completely nonexistent and can be
realized only on the basis of a socialist regime. [. . .]

V. Let us take a concrete example in an attempt to apply the principle
that the "nation" should "determine itself."

With respect to Poland at the present stage of the revolution, one of the
Russian Social Democrats belonging to the editorial committee of the now
defunct paper, *Iskra*, in 1906 explained the concept of the indispensable
Warsaw constituent assembly in the following way:

> If we start from the assumption that the political organization of Russia
> is the decisive factor determining the current oppression of the nation-

alities, then we must conclude that the proletariat of the oppressed nationalities and the annexed countries should be extremely active in the organization of an all-Russian constituent assembly.

This assembly could, if it wished, carry out its revolutionary mission, and break the fetters of force with which tsardom binds to itself the oppressed nationalities.

And there is no other satisfactory, that is, revolutionary way of solving that question than by implementing the rights of the nationalities to determine their own fate.[1] The task of a united proletarian party of all nationalities in the assembly will be to bring about such a solution of the nationality question, and this task can be realized by the Party only insofar as it is based on the movement of the masses, on the pressure they put on the constituent assembly. [. . .]

The presentation by the proletariat of the demand for a constituent assembly for Poland should not be taken to mean that the Polish nation would be represented in the all-Russian assembly by any delegation of the Warsaw sejm.

I think that such representation in the all-Russian assembly would not correspond to the interests of revolutionary development. It would join the proletariat and bourgeois elements of the Polish sejm by bonds of mutual solidarity and responsibility, in contradiction to the real mutual relations of their interests.

In the all-Russian assembly, the proletariat and bourgeoisie of Poland should not be represented by one delegation. But this would occur even if a delegation were sent from the sejm to an assembly which included representatives of all the parties of the sejm proportionally to their numbers. In this case, the direct and independent representation of the Polish proletariat in the assembly would disappear, and the very creation of real political parties in Poland would be made difficult. Then the elections to the Polish sejm, whose main task is to define the political relations between Poland and Russia, would not show the political and social faces of the leading parties, as elections to an all-Russian assembly could do; for the latter type of elections would advance, besides the local, partial, historically temporary and specifically national questions, *the general questions of politics and socialism, which really divide contemporary societies.*[2]

[. . .] The Russian Social Democratic Labor Party leaves the solution of the Polish question up to the Polish "nation." The Polish Socialists should not pick it up but try, as hard as they can, to solve this question according to the interests and will of the proletariat. However, the party of the Polish proletariat is organizationally tied to the all-state party, for instance, the Social Democracy of the Kingdom of Poland and Lithuania is a part of the Russian Social Democratic Labor Party. [. . .]

Let us suppose for the sake of argument, that in the federal constituent assembly, two contradictory programs are put forth from Poland: the autonomous program of national democracy and the autonomous program of Polish social democracy, which are quite at odds with respect to internal tendency as well as to political formulation. What will the position of Russian social democracy be with regard to them? Which of the programs will it recognize as an expression of the will and "self-determination" of the Polish "nation"? Polish social democracy never had any pretensions to be speaking in the name of the "nation." National democracy comes forth as the expresser of the "national" will. Let us also assume for a moment that this party wins a majority at the elections to the constituent assembly by taking advantage of the ignorance of the petit bourgeois elements as well as certain sections of the proletariat. In this case, will the representatives of the all-Russian proletariat, complying with the requirements of the formula of their program, come out in favor of the proposals of national democracy and go against their own comrades from Poland? Or will they associate themselves with the program of the Polish proletariat, leaving the "right of nations" to one side as a phrase which binds them to nothing? Or will the Polish Social Democrats be forced, in order to reconcile these contradictions in their program, to come out in the Warsaw constituent assembly, as well as in their own agitation in Poland, in favor of their own autonomous program, but in the federal constituent assembly, as members well aware of the discipline of the Social Democratic Party of Russia, for the program of national democracy, that is, against their own program?

Let us take yet another example. Examining the question in a purely abstract form, since the author has put the problem on that basis, let us suppose, to illustrate the principle, that in the national assembly of the Jewish population of Russia—for why should the right to create separate constituent assemblies be limited to Poland, as the author wants?—the Zionist Party somehow wins a majority and demands that the all-Russian constituent assembly vote funds for the emigration of the entire Jewish community. On the other hand, the class representatives of the Jewish proletariat firmly resist the position of the Zionists as a harmful and reactionary utopia. What position will Russian social democracy take in this conflict?

It will have two choices. The "right of nations to self-determination" might be essentially identical with the determination of the national question by the proletariat in question—that is, with the nationality program of the concerned Social Democratic parties. In such a case, however, the formula of the "right of nations" in the program of the Russian party is only a mystifying paraphrase of the class position. Or, alternatively, the Russian proletariat as such could recognize and honor only the will of the national *majorities* of the nationalities under Russian subjugation, even though the proletariat of the respective "nations" should come out against this majority with their own class program. And in this case, it is a political dualism of a special type; it gives dramatic expression to the discord between the "national" and class positions; it points up the conflict between the position of the federal workers' party and that of the parties of the particular nationalities which make it up.

NOTES

1. Emphasis in the entire citation is ours [Luxemburg's].
2. Here as everywhere I speak of a definite manner of solving the nationality question for Poland, not touching those changes which may prove themselves indispensable while resolving this question for other nations—*Note of the author of the cited article.*

21

VLADIMIR ILYICH LENIN

The Right of Nations to Self-Determination

WHAT IS SELF-DETERMINATION OF NATIONS?

Naturally, this is the first question to arise when any attempt is made to consider what self-determination is, from a Marxist viewpoint. What is meant by that term? Should we seek for an answer in legal definitions deduced from all sorts of "general concepts" of law? Or should we seek an answer in the historical and economic study of the national movements? [. . .]

Rosa Luxemburg, who declaims a great deal about the alleged abstract and metaphysical nature of the point in question [. . .] succumb[s] to the sin of abstraction and metaphysics. It is Rosa Luxemburg herself who is continually straying into generalities about self-determination (including the very amusing speculation on the question of how the will of the nation is to be ascertained), without anywhere clearly and precisely asking herself whether the issue is determined by juridical definitions or by the experience of the national movements throughout the world.

A precise formulation of this question, which a Marxist cannot avoid, would at once have shaken nine-tenths of Rosa Luxemburg's arguments. This is not the first time national movements have arisen in Russia, nor are they peculiar to Russia alone. Throughout the world, the period of the final victory of capitalism over feudalism has been linked with national movements. The economic basis of those movements is the fact that in order to achieve complete victory for commodity production the bourgeoisie must capture the home market, must have politically united territories with a population speaking the same language, and all obstacles to the development of this language and to its consolidation in literature must be removed. Language is the most important means of human intercourse. Unity of language and its unimpeded development are most important conditions for genuinely free and extensive commercial intercourse on a scale commensurate with modern capitalism, for a free and broad grouping of the population in all its separate classes and, lastly, for the establishment of close connection between the market and each and every proprietor, big or little, seller and buyer.

Therefore, the tendency of every national movement is towards the formation of *national states*, under which these requirements of modern capitalism are best satisfied. The profoundest economic factors drive towards this goal, and therefore, for the whole of Western Europe, nay, for the entire civilized world, the *typical*, normal state for the capitalist period is the national state.

Consequently, if we want to learn the meaning of self-determination of nations not by juggling with legal definitions, or "inventing" abstract definitions, but by examining the historical and economic conditions of the national movements, we shall inevitably reach the conclusion that self-determination of nations means the political separation of these nations from alien national bodies, the formation of an independent national state.

Later on we shall see still other reasons why it would be incorrect to understand the right to self-determination to mean anything but the right to separate state existence. At present, we must deal with Rosa Luxemburg's efforts to "dismiss" the unavoidable conclusion that the striving to form a national state rests on deep economic foundations. [. . .]

For the question of the political self-determination of nations in bourgeois society, and of their independence as states, Rosa Luxemburg has substituted the question of their economic independence. This is as intelligent as if someone, in discussing the demand in the program for the supremacy of parliament, i.e., the assembly of people's representatives, in a bourgeois state, were to expound the perfectly correct conviction that big capital is supreme under any regime in a bourgeois country.

There is no doubt that the greater part of Asia, the most populous part of the world, consists either of colonies of the "Great Powers" or of states which are extremely dependent and oppressed as nations. But does this commonly known circumstance in any way shake the undoubted fact that in Asia itself the conditions for the most complete development of commodity production, for the freest, widest, and speediest growth of capitalism, have been created only in Japan, i.e., only in an independent national state? This state is a bourgeois state, therefore, it, itself, has begun to oppress other nations and to enslave colonies. We cannot say whether Asia will have time before the downfall of capitalism to become crystallized into a system of independent national states, like Europe; but it remains an undisputed fact that capitalism, having awakened Asia, has called forth national movements everywhere in that continent, too; that the tendency of these movements is towards the creation of national states there; that the best conditions for the development of capitalism are ensured precisely by such states. The example of Asia speaks in *favor* of Kautsky and *against* Rosa Luxemburg.

The example of the Balkan states also speaks against her, for everyone can see now that the best conditions for the development of capitalism in

the Balkans are created precisely in proportion to the creation of independent national states in that peninsula.

Therefore, Rosa Luxemburg notwithstanding, the example of the whole
of progressive, civilized mankind, the example of the Balkans, and the example
of Asia prove that Kautsky's proposition is absolutely correct: The national
state is the rule and the "norm" of capitalism; the heterogeneous nation
state represents backwardness, or is an exception. From the standpoint of
national relations, the best conditions for the development of capitalism
are undoubtedly provided by the national state. This does not mean, of
course, that such a state, based on bourgeois relations, could eliminate the
exploitation and oppression of nations. It only means that Marxists cannot
ignore the powerful *economic* factors that give rise to the aspiration to
create national states. It means that "self-determination of nations" in the
program of the Marxists *cannot*, from a historical-economic point of view,
have any other meaning than political self-determination, political independence, the formation of a national state. [. . .]

While recognizing equality and an equal right to a national state, [the
proletariat] attaches supreme value to the alliance of the proletarians of all
nations, and evaluates every national demand, every national separation,
from the angle of the class struggle of the workers. This call for practicalness
is merely a call for the uncritical acceptance of bourgeois aspirations.

We are told: By supporting the right to secession you are supporting the
bourgeois nationalism of the oppressed nations. [. . .]

Our reply to this is: No, a "practical" solution of this question is important for the bourgeoisie. The important thing for the workers is to distinguish
the *principles* of two trends. If the bourgeoisie of the oppressed nation fights
against the oppressing one, we are always, in every case, and more resolutely than anyone else, *in favor*; for we are the staunchest and the most
consistent enemies of oppression. But if the bourgeoisie of the oppressed
nation stands for *its own* bourgeois nationalism we are opposed. We fight
against the privileges and violence of the oppressing nation, but we do not
condone the strivings for privileges on the part of the oppressed nation.

If we do not raise and advocate the slogan of the *right* to secession we
shall play into the hands, not only of the bourgeoisie, but also of the feudal
landlords and the despotism of the *oppressing* nation. Kautsky long ago advanced this argument against Rosa Luxemburg, and the argument is indisputable. When Rosa Luxemburg, in her anxiety not to "assist" the nationalistic
bourgeoisie of Poland, rejects the *right* to secession in the program of the
Russian Marxists, she is *in fact* assisting the Great-Russian Black-Hundreds.
She is in fact assisting opportunist resignation to the privileges (and worse
than privileges) of the Great Russians.

Carried away by the struggle against nationalism in Poland, Rosa Luxemburg
has forgotten the nationalism of the Great Russians, although *this* nationalism is the most formidable at the present time, it is the nationalism that is

less bourgeois and more feudal, and it is the principal obstacle to democracy and to the proletarian struggle. The bourgeois nationalism of *every* oppressed nation has a general democratic content which is directed *against* oppression, and it is this content that we support *unconditionally*, while strictly distinguishing it from the tendency towards national exceptionalism, while fighting against the tendency of the Polish bourgeoisie to oppress the Jews, etc., etc.

This is "impractical" from the standpoint of a bourgeois and a philistine; but it is the only policy in the national question that is practical, that is based on principles, and that really furthers democracy, liberty, and proletarian unity.

The recognition of the right to secession for all; the appraisal of each concrete question of secession from the point of view of removing all inequality, all privileges, all exceptionalism.

Let us examine the position of an oppressing nation. Can a nation be free if it oppresses other nations? It cannot. The interests of the freedom of the Great-Russian population demand a struggle against such oppression. The long, age-long history of the suppression of the movements of the oppressed nations, the systematic propaganda in favor of such suppression on the part of the "upper" classes, have created enormous obstacles to the cause of freedom of the Great-Russian people itself, in the form of prejudices, etc.

The Great-Russian Black-Hundreds deliberately foster and fan these prejudices. The Great-Russian bourgeoisie tolerates them or panders to them. The Great-Russian proletariat cannot achieve *its own* aims, cannot clear the road to freedom for itself unless it systematically combats these prejudices.

In Russia, the creation of an independent national state so far remains the privilege of one nation, the Great-Russian nation. We, the Great-Russian proletarians, defend no privileges, and we do not defend this privilege. In our fight we take the given state as our basis; we unite the workers of all nations in the given state; we cannot vouch for any particular path of national development, we are marching to our class goal by *all* possible paths.

But we cannot advance to that goal unless we combat all nationalism, unless we fight for the equality of the workers of all nations. Whether the Ukraine, for example, is destined to form an independent state is a matter that will be determined by a thousand factors, which cannot be foreseen. Without attempting idle "*guesses*," we firmly uphold what is beyond doubt: the right of the Ukraine to form such a state. We respect this right; we do not uphold the privileges of the Great Russians over the Ukrainians; we *teach* the masses to recognize that right, and to reject the *state* privileges of any nation.

In the leaps which all nations take in the period of bourgeois revolutions, clashes and struggle over the right to a national state are possible and probable. We proletarians declare in advance that we are *opposed* to Great-Russian privileges, and this is what guides our entire propaganda and agitation.

In her quest for "practicalness" Rosa Luxemburg has overlooked the *principal* practical task both of the Great-Russian proletariat and of the proletariat of other nationalities: the task of daily agitation and propaganda against all state and national privileges and for the right, the equal right of all nations to their national state. This task is (at present) our principal task in the national question, for only in this way can we defend the interests of democracy and the alliance of all proletarians of all nations on an equal footing.

This propaganda may be "impractical" from the point of view of the Great-Russian oppressors as well as from the point of view of the bourgeoisie of the oppressed nations (both demand a *definite* "yes" or "no," and accuse the Social Democrats of being "vague"). In reality it is this propaganda, and only this propaganda, that ensures the really democratic, the really socialist education of the masses. Only such propaganda ensures the greatest chances of national peace in Russia, should she remain a heterogeneous national state, and the most peaceful (and for the proletarian class struggle, harmless) division into separate national states, should the question of such a division arise. [. . .]

To accuse the supporters of freedom of self-determination, i.e., freedom to secede, of encouraging separatism, is as foolish and as hypocritical as accusing the advocates of freedom of divorce of wishing to destroy family ties. Just as in bourgeois society the defenders of privilege and corruption, on which bourgeois marriage rests, oppose freedom of divorce, so, in the capitalist state, repudiation of the right to self-determination, i.e., the right of nations to secede, is tantamount to defending the privileges of the dominating nation and police methods of administration as against democratic methods.

No doubt, the political corruption engendered by the relations prevailing in capitalist society sometimes leads members of parliament and journalists to indulge in frivolous and even in just nonsensical twaddle about a particular nation seceding. But only reactionaries can allow themselves to be frightened (or pretend to be frightened) by such twaddle. Those who stand by democratic principles, i.e., who insist that questions of state must be decided by the people, know very well that there is a very big difference between what the politicians prate about and what the people decide. The people know from daily experience the value of geographical and economic ties and the advantages of a big market and of a big state. They will, therefore, resort to secession only when national oppression and national friction make joint life absolutely intolerable and hinder all economic intercourse. In that case, the interests of capitalist development and of the freedom of the class struggle will be best served by secession. [. . .]

The interests of the working class and of its struggle against capitalism demand complete solidarity and the closest unity of the workers of all nations; they demand strong opposition to the nationalistic policy of the bourgeoisie of every nationality. Hence, Social Democrats would be equally running counter to proletarian policy and subordinating the workers to the policy of the bourgeoisie if they were to repudiate the right of nations to self-determination, i.e., the right of an oppressed nation to secede, or if they were to support all the national demands of the bourgeoisie of the oppressed nations. It makes no difference to the wage worker whether he is exploited chiefly by the Great-Russian bourgeoisie rather than by the non-Russian bourgeoisie, or by the Polish bourgeoisie rather than the Jewish bourgeoisie, etc. The wage worker who understands his class interests is equally indifferent to the state privileges of the Great-Russian capitalists and to the promises of the Polish or Ukrainian capitalists to set up an earthly paradise when they obtain state privileges. Capitalism is developing and will continue to develop, in one way or another, both in united heterogeneous states and in separate national states.

In any case the wage workers will be exploited. And in order to be able to fight successfully against exploitation, the proletariat must be free of nationalism, must be absolutely neutral, so to speak, in the struggle for supremacy that is going on among the bourgeoisie of the various nations. If the proletariat of any one nation gives the slightest support to the privileges of "its" national bourgeoisie, this will inevitably rouse distrust among the proletariat of the other nation; it will weaken the international class solidarity of the workers and divide them, to the delight of the bourgeoisie. And repudiation of the right to self-determination, or secession, inevitably means, in practice, supporting the privileges of the dominating nation. [. . .]

To sum up: From the point of view of the theory of Marxism in general the question of the right of self-determination presents no difficulties. No one can seriously dispute the London resolution of 1896, or the fact that self-determination implies only the right to secession, or the fact that the formation of independent national states is the tendency of all bourgeois-democratic revolutions. [. . .]

It is easy to understand that the recognition by the Marxists of the *whole of Russia*, and first and foremost by the Great Russians, of the *right* of nations to secede in no way precludes *agitation* against secession by Marxists of a particular *oppressed* nation, just as the recognition of the right to divorce does not preclude agitation against divorce in a particular case. [. . .]

Such a state of affairs sets the proletariat of Russia a twofold, or, rather, a two-sided task: first, to fight against all nationalism and, above all, against Great-Russian nationalism; to recognize not only complete equality of rights for all nations in general, but also equality of rights as regards forming an independent state, i.e., the right of nations to self-determination, to secession. And second, precisely in the interests of the successful struggle against the nationalism of all nations in *any* form, it sets the task of preserving the unity of the proletarian struggle and of the proletarian organizations, of amalgamating these organizations into an international association, in spite of the bourgeois strivings for national segregation.

Complete equality of rights for all nations; the right of nations to self-determination; the amalgamation of the workers of all nations—this is the national program that Marxism, the experience of the whole world, and the experience of Russia, teaches the workers.

PART V

Integral Nationalism, Fascism, and Nazism

22

CHARLES MAURRAS

The Future of French Nationalism

> Nothing is done today, all
> will be done tomorrow.

All that remains for the thinking Frenchman to do is to see that his will
and not that of another be done: not the will of the oligarchy, not the will
of the foreigner.

There remains, that is to say, the imperative of rugged effort in the field
of real and practical action, the effort that has tried to hold our country
together, to preserve its heritage, to save it from itself, to resolve its crises
along the way; this loyal effort is too old and proud a servant of France to
interrupt or slow down the work it has begun. Those whose age has brought
them near to death know that this work depends on friends who are worthy
of our trust, because, for more than forty years, their slogan, and ours, has
been: "Use every means, even legal." Having worked "for 1950," they will
work for the year 2000, for they have never lost sight of their vision: "For
France to have long life, long live the king!"

We could not have sustained our hope if our sense of national pride had
not been steadfastly in the forefront of our minds. On that score, my mind
is easy.

There is much talk of giving up in whole or in part our national sovereignty. Mere words. Let us leave them to the professors of law. These gentlemen have made their quibbles so well respected, *intus et in cute*, these
last years that we can count on them to find something new to add to all
the most glorious dung-heaps of the intelligence. The treasures of reality
and fact are stronger than they. What they consider to be outdated and
ready to be thrown overboard has only to suffer the tiniest scratch, the
shadow of a threat, and you will see the outraged reaction that will follow!
Proof that there is nothing in the world today to equal the sense of national pride. Those who would like to give up a portion of it, will bring no
benefit to the cosmopolis they dream of: With our heritage they will merely
fatten other already overblown nationalities. The outstanding facts of our
time are national facts: the astonishing persistence of England in the English soul during the years 1940 to 1945, the Pan-Slav or rather Pan-Rus-
sian evolution of the Soviets, the resistance that Russia encounters in the

nations she thought to annex under the dual inspiration of race and creed, the awakening of the mighty conscience of America, the rebirth of German Nazism, all these are cases of acute nationalism. Not all are creditable. We would be mad to imitate or wish for them all. We would be even more insane not to take note of this evidence of a worldwide trend. In France, patriotism saw all this in many different colors after the victory of Foch: such enmity, such disgrace! Great parties characterized by their "appeal to the masses" were sick or tired of the French language and had no time for anything but Marxist gibberish. The Germans had only to set up camp in France for all their offers to rebuild Europe to be rejected and Frenchmen, whether bourgeois, peasants, workers, or noblemen, with very few exceptions saw only the hated "Boche" [French slang for German—EDS.]. In a twinkling the national spirit was reestablished. The country had to stomach the humiliation of many an expedient hypocrisy. The universal use of this noble disguise is one more proof of its value and glaring necessity: We shall see.

The nationalism of my friends and myself bears witness to a passion and a doctrine. A holy passion, a doctrine motivated by ever-increasing human needs. The majority of our fellow citizens see in this a virtue whose promptings are sometimes painful but always honorable. But, certain other Frenchmen, especially those in the legal world, to be found in all parties, find themselves, and will go on finding themselves, driven back upon nationalism as upon some necessary compromise. The more their divisions based on vested interest multiply and widen, the more they need an occasion to sound the note of the supreme duty, invoking the only means they have of prolonging their own power. These means are called France.

How can they escape it, divided as they are by everything else? Upon what argument, what honest common denominator can they reason together but that? There is no longer any yardstick common to both bourgeois economics and working-class economics. Working class and bourgeois are names of sects. The name of the country is France, so it is to that name that reference must be made. What is to the advantage of the country? If the criterion of the country first is accepted which presupposes the renunciation to a certain extent of partisan errors, it is found to contain the essence of our philosophy which consists of presenting, approaching, and resolving all current political problems from the point of view of the national interest: We must select and reject what that openly acknowledged arbiter would select and reject.

Of course this imperative is strictly limited. The struggling parties will always do their utmost to grab as much as they decently can. But their alliances crumble if they cannot pretend at least to act in the name of motives which dare to go further than their own vested interests. Will they refuse to make this gesture? A refusal could sound the alarm for the body and the spirit of the real nation to arise, and even the electoral situation itself could be endangered. If, on the other hand, these specialists in disunity pretend to believe in the unifying power of the nationalist consensus, all onlookers of good will and reasonable intelligence will be satisfied.

So gently, violently, slowly or hastily the carnivorous parties, all equally ruinous, will either perish from their own excessive appetites or, as parties, will have to give way to some extent to the imperative of nationalism—or at the very least to a recognition of its existence. Practice will strengthen it. Exercise may not create new limbs but it loosens up and fortifies the ones already there. The various party doctrines will gradually be stripped down to their basic elements of empty promises and threats upon which their failures will inflict ever-increasing ridicule. Their faith will soon be no more than a memory without the redeeming virtue of relevance, the physical trace of which has long since been lost and men will jeer more and more contemptuously at these quaint relics, these false principles which sought the allegiance of empire and nation and who now pronounce their own obsequies.

Then a task of real significance can be restarted: the realization of the nation's great hope of setting aside a class and merging its parties.

French nationalism as a movement will not satisfy its aspirations without the return of the king. While we wait for this day to come, the dominance of the parties will have slackened, and, because of abuses perpetrated by them, mortality will once again belong to the French people, and French instincts and interests will have been restored to their former state.

We must not throw up our hands in horror at this word "interest." However uncouth it may sound, it has the merit of being appropriate. This word is full of the strength to preserve us from a grave error which could ruin everything.

If, instead of placating opposing factions and bringing them together on the basis of common interest, we are shamefaced and hesitant, if we try to find nobler criteria in the sphere of moral and sacred principles appropriate to the realms of morality and religion, this is what will happen: Since, in social and political life, the genuine antagonisms of the modern conscience are deep and numerous, since the false dogma of individualism on the essentials of family, marriage, and association is in direct contradiction with the rich customs and traditions of prosperous peoples which are also those that conform to the moral teachings of Catholicism, it will be particularly difficult if not impossible to achieve unity or even union in the sphere of moral principles. If we were to undertake such a venture, we would merely encounter the same contradiction in terms which we have so often experienced in the past.

These conflicting principles can submit to compromise but cannot produce one or create one, nor transform their divided and divisive natures into principles of compromise or agreement.

The bases for conciliation are few in number. I know only one.

When, in an argument over divorce or the family or association, you have exhausted all the fundamental pros and cons, drawn from reason and morality, without having achieved a shred of agreement, there is left to you only one neutral avenue to explore—that of examining the value of divorce or marriage or whatever from the point of view of the practical public interest. I do not assert that this examination is an easy one to make, or that it is clear or that it leaves no room for doubt. It can contribute some elements of light and harmony. But if, when you reach this point, you slander the notion of the public interest, if you disavow, humiliate, reject this vulgar compromise of the public good, you lose the precious and positive element of union which could result from it, and, having deprived yourself of this benefit, you find yourself once again in the presence of all the bitterness which will stem from the return to those violent disputes that should have been allayed by the common interest in social harmony.

It is all very well to accuse national and civic interest of artfully tending to eliminate what is called, not without a certain hypocrisy, the spiritual: It is simply not true. The truth is quite different. We have named and honored as the highest inspiration of our guardian laws and ideas all the different forms of the spiritual, especially the Catholic. We have opened the gates of the city to them. We have begged them to enter it, purify it, pacify it, exalt it, and bless it. By asking of each its prayers, by honoring and acknowledging their benefits, we have thereby given thanks for all the blessings of social and international emulation that these spirits could by their acts encourage. If, in addition, we have not asked them to give us the harmony we desire, it is because they do not possess it, being opposed to one another: The spiritual, unless it be reduced to a mere form of words, is an element of controversy. The God of Robespierre and Rousseau is not the God of Clotilde and of St. Remy. The social and moral principles of Rome are not those of London or Moscow. To aspire to their fusion, by covering up what contradictions they contain, is to begin by mutilating them and to end by suppressing them all. From the moment unity of conscience disappears, as it has done in France, the only way left of respecting the spiritual is to welcome every worthy manifestation of it, under its proper names, in its purest and most divergent form, without altering the meaning of words, without using words to improvise empty agreement. The spiritual that was neither Catholic, Protestant, nor Jewish would have neither vigor nor virtue. It must be one or the other, if the fruitfulness of the fruitful and the good deeds of the good are to be safeguarded; of such is the grandeur of humanity and of the superhuman. There exists a natural religion and a natural morality. This is a fact. But it is also a fact that their cardinal principles, as defined by Catholicism, are not acknowledged by other faiths. Nothing I can do will alter this. I cannot make Reformation morality reject individualism or the Calvinists accept the correct notion of religious worship. We can refuse to see reality, but reality, in the social order, confronts us nevertheless with clearly differentiated choices which we cannot avoid.

We can hope for all things from the abundance, the variety, the contrast of the moral ideas presented to us, except the creation of their opposite—uniformity. Therefore it will be impossible for anyone, be he Catholic, Jew, Huguenot, or Freemason, to impose his own individual concepts as standard for the whole community. His concepts apply to him, whereas the standard must be the same for all. And so the members of the community will be obliged to find something else to serve as a common standard, something which applies equally to all and is capable of creating unity between them all. What can they find? We still see only one answer: that imperative whose commands, needs, and simple conventions oblige them to share one common lot.

In other words, we must once again break off the discussion of the true and the beautiful to turn our attention to the humble and positive good. Good will not be an absolute, but the good of the French people at that level of politics where we find what Plato called the royal art, where we find set aside all schools of thought, all churches, all sects, where divorce, for example, would be considered no longer in relationship to this or that right or obligation, to this or that divine authorization or prohibition, but solely in terms of the common interest of the family and the good of the city. So much the better for those, such as the Catholics, who are already in agreement with this concept of the public good. They will do well not to speak disdainfully of it. For in the final analysis we do not present for thought and action too unworthy or inferior an object. Let us remember that peace is a noble state: The social well-being of a nation, the material and moral interest each citizen has in its preservation, these are things which lift man up and sustain him in the highest spheres of his finest and proudest actions. St. Augustine's "tranquillity of order" is a majestic aim. He who pursues and contemplates it will never wander from the ascending path of positive human progress. To leave the plane of ethics is not to disregard it provided one follows the true path of politics. No young conscript to the patriotic virtues is diminished by drawing his inspiration from "the eternal France"; no veteran of the law, in a kingdom that even in the sixth century the Pope had placed above all other kingdoms, can be attacked for asserting that "the King of France never dies." All this is a part of our heritage which we find in its rightful place as the supreme inspiration of our human nature.

The generation of the young may possibly feel these lofty sentiments to be somewhat remote. That is because this generation has seen so many shifts and somersaults. They have some difficulty in distinguishing what is firm and immutable: They have never been shown it thanks to an apparently never-ending cycle of instability and ruin. This cycle must not be regarded as more fundamental than it really is. It is an accident which stems almost entirely from the classical debilitating effect of a cancer which has been well-known since men first reasoned about the state of society, since the golden days of Athens and then from age to age for more than two thousand years, ever since the Visigoth kingdoms of Spain were handed over to the Saracens, or the Italian republics to their convulsions, all by the common effect of anarchy. The experience of Poland gave us bitter proof of this truth only shortly before our own cruel ordeal began, and our last one hundred and fifty years are an instructive lesson in themselves.

The cancer is a serious one but it can be cured—and quickly. We will find it much easier to tackle if we take care not to embellish it with names other than its own. If we say "the prevailing idea" instead of "the revolutionary idea," we are saying nothing for we are defining nothing. If we say "demagogy" instead of "democracy," our shaft is misaimed. What we risk regarding as abuse or excess, is, in fact, fundamental and inherent. That is why I have devoted so much attention to exactness of terminology. Only a sane policy framed in clear and precise language can emerge unscathed from the Tower of Babel. That is how I emerged unscathed. That is how France will do likewise, and how French nationalism will by force of circumstance be reaffirmed. Nothing is finished; if nothing lasts forever, nothing is lost forever.

Above and beyond hope there exists a certain faith and trust which, though unrelated to religious faith, are not unlike it at the humble level of our earthbound certainties. I will never cease to repeat that Frenchmen have two natural obligations: One is to count upon the patriotism of their country, the other is to have faith in its genius; they will be redeemed by both for the second is ever more profoundly imbued with the first. It will be infinitely more difficult to destroy these two great French qualities than for them to endure and reawaken. Such qualities would find their own extinction a more arduous task than the most dogged effort to survive or the most painful pangs of rebirth.

23

BENITO MUSSOLINI

Fascism

FUNDAMENTAL IDEAS

Like all sound political conceptions, fascism is action and it is thought; action in which doctrine is immanent, and doctrine arising from a given system of historical forces in which it is inserted, and working on them from within. It has therefore a form correlated to contingencies of time and space; but it has also an ideal content which makes it an expression of truth in the higher region of the history of thought. There is no way of exercising a spiritual influence in the world as a human will dominating the will of others, unless one has a conception both of the transient and the specific reality on which that action is to be exercised, and of the permanent and universal reality in which the transient dwells and has its being. To know men one must know man; and to know man one must be acquainted with reality and its laws. There can be no conception of the state which is not fundamentally a conception of life: philosophy or intuition, system of ideas evolving within the framework of logic or concentrated in a vision or a faith, but always, at least potentially, an organic conception of the world.

Thus many of the practical expressions of fascism—such as party organization, system of education, discipline—can only be understood when considered in relation to its general attitude toward life. A spiritual attitude. Fascism sees in the world not only those superficial, material aspects in which man appears as an individual, standing by himself, self-centered, subject to natural law which instinctively urges him toward a life of selfish momentary pleasure; it sees not only the individual but the nation and the country; individuals and generations bound together by a moral law, with common traditions and a mission which suppressing the instinct for life closed in a brief circle of pleasure, builds up a higher life, founded on duty, a life free from the limitations of time and space, in which the individual, by self-sacrifice, the renunciation of self-interest, by death itself, can achieve that purely spiritual existence in which his value as a man consists.

The conception is therefore a spiritual one, arising from the general reaction of the century against the flaccid materialistic positivism of the nineteenth century. Anti-positivistic but positive; neither skeptical nor agnostic;

neither pessimistic nor supinely optimistic as are, generally speaking, the doctrines (all negative) which place the center of life outside man; whereas, by the exercise of his free will, man can and must create his own world.

Fascism wants man to be active and to engage in action with all his energies; it wants him to be manfully aware of the difficulties besetting him and ready to face them. It conceives of life as a struggle in which it behooves a man to win for himself a really worthy place, first of all by fitting himself (physically, morally, intellectually) to become the implement required for winning it. As for the individual, so for the nation, and so for mankind. Hence the high value of culture in all its forms (artistic, religious, scientific), and the outstanding importance of education. Hence also the essential value of work, by which man subjugates nature and creates the human world (economic, political, ethical, intellectual).

The positive conception of life is obviously an ethical one. It invests the whole field of reality as well as the human activities which master it. No action is exempt from moral judgment; no activity can be despoiled of the value which a moral purpose confers on all things. Therefore life, as conceived of by the Fascist, is serious, austere, religious; all its manifestations are poised in a world sustained by moral forces and subject to spiritual responsibilities. The Fascist disdains an "easy" life.

The fascist conception of life is a religious one, in which man is viewed in his immanent relation to a higher law, endowed with an objective will transcending the individual and raising him to conscious membership of a spiritual society. Those who perceive nothing beyond opportunistic considerations in the religious policy of the fascist regime fail to realize that fascism is not only a system of government but also and above all a system of thought.

In the fascist conception of history, man is man only by virtue of the spiritual process to which he contributes as a member of the family, the social group, the nation, and in function of history to which all nations bring their contribution. Hence the great value of tradition in records, in language, in customs, in the rules of social life. Outside history man is a nonentity. Fascism is therefore opposed to all individualistic abstractions based on eighteenth-century materialism; and it is opposed to all Jacobinistic utopias and innovations. It does not believe in the possibility of "happiness" on earth as conceived by the economistic literature of the eighteenth century, and it therefore rejects the teleological notion that at some future time the human family will secure a final settlement of all its difficulties. This notion runs counter to experience which teaches that life is in continual flux and in process of evolution. In politics fascism aims at realism; in practice it desires to deal only with those problems which are the spontaneous product of historic conditions and which find or suggest their own solutions. Only by entering into the process of reality and taking possession of the forces at work within it, can man act on man and on nature.

Anti-individualistic, the fascist conception of life stresses the importance of the state and accepts the individual only insofar as his interests coincide with those of the state, which stands for the conscience and the universal will of man as a historic entity. It is opposed to classical liberalism which arose as a reaction to absolutism and exhausted its historical function when the state became the expression of the conscience and will of the people. Liberalism denied the state in the name of the individual; fascism reasserts the rights of the state as expressing the real essence of the individual. And if liberty is to be the attribute of living men and not of abstract dummies invented by individualistic liberalism, then fascism stands for liberty, and for the only liberty worth having, the liberty of the state and of the individual within the state. The fascist conception of the state is all-embracing; outside of it no human or spiritual values can exist, much less have value. Thus understood, fascism, is totalitarian, and the fascist state—a synthesis and a unit inclusive of all values—interprets, develops, and potentiates the whole life of a people.

No individuals or groups (political parties, cultural associations, economic unions, social classes) [are] outside the state. Fascism is therefore opposed to socialism to which unity within the state (which amalgamates classes into a single economic and ethical reality) is unknown, and which sees in history nothing but the class struggle. Fascism is likewise opposed to trade unionism as a class weapon. But when brought within the orbit of the state, fascism recognizes the real needs which gave rise to socialism and trade unionism, giving them due weight in the guild or corporative system in which divergent interests are coordinated and harmonized in the unity of the state.

Grouped according to their several interests, individuals form classes; they form trade unions when organized according to their several economic activities; but first and foremost they form the state, which is no mere matter of numbers, the sum of the individuals forming the majority. Fascism is therefore opposed to that form of democracy which equates a nation to the majority, lowering it to the level of the largest number; but it is the purest form of democracy if the nation be considered—as it should be—from the point of view of quality rather than quantity, as an idea, the mightiest because the most ethical, the most coherent, the truest, expressing itself in a people as the conscience and will of the few, if not, indeed, of one, and ending to express itself in the conscience and the will of the mass, of the whole group ethnically molded by natural and historical conditions into a nation, advancing, as one conscience and one will, along the self-same line of development and spiritual formation. Not a race, nor a geographically defined region, but a people, historically perpetuating itself; a multitude unified by an idea and imbued with the will to live, the will to power, self-consciousness, personality.

Insofar as it is embodied in a state, this higher personality becomes a nation. It is not the nation which generates the state; that is an antiquated naturalistic concept which afforded a basis for nineteenth-century publicity in favor of national governments. Rather is it the state which creates the nation, conferring volition and therefore real life on a people made aware of their moral unity.

The right to national independence does not arise from any merely literary and idealistic form of self-consciousness; still less from a more or less passive and unconscious de facto situation, but from an active, self-conscious, political will expressing itself in action and ready to prove its rights. It arises, in short, from the existence, at least in *fieri*, of a state. Indeed, it is the state which, as the expression of a universal ethical will, creates the right to national independence.

A nation, as expressed in the state, is a living, ethical entity only insofar as it is progressive. Inactivity is death. Therefore the state is not only authority which governs and confers legal form and spiritual value on individual wills, but it is also power which makes its will felt and respected beyond its own frontiers, thus affording practical proof of the universal character of the decisions necessary to ensure its development. This implies organization and expansion, potential if not actual. Thus the state equates itself to the will of man, whose development cannot be checked by obstacles and which, by achieving self-expression, demonstrates its own infinity.

The fascist state, as a higher and more powerful expression of personality, is a force, but a spiritual one. It sums up all the manifestations of the moral and intellectual life of man. Its functions cannot therefore be limited to those of enforcing order and keeping the peace, as the liberal doctrine had it. It is no mere mechanical device for defining the sphere within which the individual may duly exercise his supposed rights. The fascist state is an inwardly accepted standard and rule of conduct, a discipline of the whole person; it permeates the will no less than the intellect. It stands for a principle which becomes the central motive of man as a member of civilized society, sinking deep down into his personality; it dwells in the heart of the man of action and of the thinker, of the artist and of the man of science: soul of the soul.

Fascism, in short, is not only a lawgiver and a founder of institutions, but an educator and a promoter of spiritual life. It aims at refashioning not only the forms of life but their content—man, his character, and his faith. To achieve this purpose it enforces discipline and uses authority, entering into the soul and ruling with undisputed sway. Therefore it has chosen as its emblem the lictor's rods, the symbol of unity, strength, and justice.

POLITICAL AND SOCIAL DOCTRINE

[. . .] Fascism is now clearly defined not only as a regime but as a doctrine. This means that fascism, exercising its critical faculties on itself and on others, has studied from its own special standpoint and judged by its own standards all the problems affecting the material and intellectual interests now causing such grave anxiety to the nations of the world, and is ready to deal with them by its own policies.

First of all, as regards the future development of mankind—and quite apart from all present political considerations—fascism does not, generally speaking, believe in the possibility or utility of perpetual peace. It therefore discards pacifism as a cloak for cowardly supine renunciation in contradistinction to self-sacrifice. War alone keys up all human energies to their maximum tension and sets the seal of nobility on those peoples who have the courage to face it. All other tests are substitutes which never place a man face to face with himself before the alternative of life or death. Therefore all doctrines which postulate peace at all costs are incompatible with fascism. Equally foreign to the spirit of fascism, even if accepted as useful in meeting special political situations—are all internationalistic or league superstructures which, as history shows, crumble to the ground whenever the heart of nations is deeply stirred by sentimental, idealistic, or practical considerations. Fascism carries this anti-pacifistic attitude into the life of the individual. "I don't care a damn" (me ne frego)—the proud motto of the fighting squads scrawled by a wounded man on his bandages, is not only an act of philosophic stoicism, it sums up a doctrine which is not merely political: It is evidence of a fighting spirit which accepts all risks. It signifies a new style of Italian life. The Fascist accepts and loves life; he rejects and despises suicide as cowardly. Life as he understands it means duty, elevation, conquest; life must be lofty and full, it must be lived for oneself but above all for others, both nearby and far off, present and future.

The population policy of the regime is the consequence of these premises. The Fascist loves his neighbor, but the word "neighbor" does not stand for some vague and unseizable conception. Love of one's neighbor does not exclude necessary educational severity; still less does it exclude differentiation and rank. Fascism will have nothing to do with universal embraces; as a member of the community of nations it looks other peoples straight in the eyes; it is vigilant and on its guard; it follows others in all their manifestations and notes any changes in their interests; and it does not allow itself to be deceived by mutable and fallacious appearances.

Such a conception of life makes fascism the resolute negation of the doctrine underlying so-called scientific and Marxian socialism, the doctrine of historic materialism which would explain the history of mankind in terms of the class struggle and by changes in the processes and instruments of production, to the exclusion of all else.

That the vicissitudes of economic life—discoveries of raw materials, new technical processes, scientific inventions—have their importance, no one denies; but that they suffice to explain human history to the exclusion of other factors is absurd. Fascism believes now and always in sanctity and heroism, that is to say in acts in which no economic motive—remote or immediate—is at work. Having denied historic materialism, which sees in men mere puppets on the surface of history, appearing and disappearing on the crest of the waves while in the depths the real directing forces move and work, fascism also denies the immutable and irreparable character of the class struggle which is the natural outcome of this economic conception of history; above all it denies that the class struggle is the preponderating agent in social transformations. Having thus struck a blow at socialism in the two main points of its doctrine, all that remains of it is the sentimental aspiration—old as humanity itself—toward social relations in which the sufferings and sorrows of the humbler folk will be alleviated. But here again fascism rejects the economic interpretation of felicity as something to be secured socialistically, almost automatically, at a given stage of economic evolution when all will be assured a maximum of material comfort. Fascism denies the materialistic conception of happiness as a possibility, and abandons it to the economists of the mid-eighteenth century. This means that fascism denies the equation: well-being = happiness, which sees in men mere animals, content when they can feed and fatten, thus reducing them to a vegetative existence pure and simple.

After socialism, fascism trains its guns on the whole block of democratic ideologies, and rejects both their premises and their practical applications and implements. Fascism denies that numbers, as such, can be the determining factor in human society; it denies the right of numbers to govern by means of periodical consultations; it asserts the irremediable and fertile and beneficent inequality of men who cannot be leveled by any such mechanical and extrinsic device as universal suffrage. Democratic regimes may be described as those under which the people are, from time to time, deluded into the belief that they exercise sovereignty, while all the time real sovereignty resides in and is exercised by other and sometimes irresponsible and secret forces. Democracy is a kingless regime infested by many kings who are sometimes more exclusive, tyrannical, and destructive than one, even if he be a tyrant. This explains why fascism—although, for contingent reasons, it was republican in tendency prior to 1922—abandoned that stand before the march on Rome, convinced that the form of government is no longer a matter of pre-eminent importance, and because the study of past and present monarchies and past and present republics shows that neither monarchy nor republic can be judged *sub specie aeternitatis*, but that each stands for a form of government expressing the political evolution, the history, the traditions, and the psychology of a given country.

Fascism has outgrown the dilemma: monarchy v. republic, over which democratic regimes too long dallied, attributing all insufficiencies to the former and proning the latter as a regime of perfection, whereas experience teaches that some republics are inherently reactionary and absolutist while some monarchies accept the most daring political and social experiments.

In one of his philosophic Meditations Renan—who had pre-fascist intuitions—remarks:

> Reason and science are the products of mankind, but it is chimerical to seek reason directly for the people and through the people. It is not essential to the existence of reason that all should be familiar with it; and even if all had to be initiated, this could not be achieved through democracy which seems fated to lead to the extinction of all arduous forms of culture and all highest forms of learning. The maxim that society exists only for the well-being and freedom of the individuals composing it does not seem to be in conformity with nature's plans, which care only for the species and seem ready to sacrifice the individual. It is much to be feared that the last word of democracy thus understood (and let me hasten to add that it is susceptible of a different interpretation) would be a form of society in which a degenerate mass would have no thought beyond that of enjoying the ignoble pleasures of the vulgar.

So far Renan. In rejecting democracy fascism rejects the absurd conventional lie of political equalitarianism, the habit of collective irresponsibility, the myth of felicity and indefinite progress. But if democracy be understood as meaning a regime in which the masses are not driven back to the margin of the state, then the writer of these pages has already defined fascism as an organized, centralized, authoritarian democracy.

Fascism is definitely and absolutely opposed to the doctrines of liberalism, both in the political and the economic sphere. The importance of liberalism in the nineteenth century should not be exaggerated for present-day polemical purposes, nor should we make of one of the many doctrines which flourished in that century a religion for mankind for the present and for all time to come. Liberalism really flourished for fifteen years only. It arose in 1830 as a reaction to the Holy Alliance which tried to force Europe to recede further back than 1789; it touched its zenith in 1848 when even Pius IX was a liberal. Its decline began immediately after that year. If 1848 was a year of light and poetry, 1849 was a year of darkness and tragedy. The Roman Republic was killed by a sister republic, that of France. In that same year Marx, in his famous Communist Manifesto, launched the gospel of socialism. In 1851 Napoleon III made his illiberal coup d'état and ruled France until 1870 when he was turned out by a popular rising following one of the severest military defeats known to history. The victor was Bismarck who never even knew the whereabouts of liberalism and its prophets. It is symptomatic that throughout the nineteenth century the religion of liberalism was completely unknown to so highly civilized a people as the Germans but for one parenthesis which has been described as the "ridiculous parliament of Frankfort" which lasted just one season. Germany attained her national unity outside liberalism and in opposition to liberalism, a doctrine which seems foreign to the German temperament, essentially monarchical, whereas liberalism is the historic and logical anteroom to anarchy.

The three stages in the making of German unity were the three wars of 1864, 1866, and 1870, led by such "liberals" as Moltke and Bismarck. And in the upbuilding of Italian unity liberalism played a very minor part when compared to the contribution made by Mazzini and Garibaldi who were not liberals. But for the intervention of the illiberal Napoleon III we should not have had Lombardy, and without that of the illiberal Bismarck at Sadowa and at Sedan very probably we should not have had Venetia in 1866 and in 1870 we should not have entered Rome. The years going from 1870 to 1915 cover a period which marked, even in the opinion of the high priests of the new creed, the twilight of their religion, attacked by decadentism in literature and by activism in practice. Activism: that is to say nationalism, futurism, fascism.

The liberal century, after piling up innumerable Gordian knots, tried to cut them with the sword of the world war. Never has any religion claimed so cruel a sacrifice. Were the gods of liberalism thirsting for blood?

Now liberalism is preparing to close the doors of its temples, deserted by the peoples who feel that the agnosticism it professed in the sphere of economics and the indifferentism of which it has given proof in the sphere of politics and morals, would lead the world to ruin in the future as they have done in the past.

This explains why all the political experiments of our day are antiliberal, and it is supremely ridiculous to endeavor on this account to put them outside the pale of history, as though history were a preserve set aside for liberalism and its adepts; as though liberalism were the last word in civilization beyond which no one can go.

The fascist negation of socialism, democracy, liberalism, should not, however, be interpreted as implying a desire to drive the world backwards to positions occupied prior to 1789, a year commonly referred to as that which opened the demo-liberal century. History does not travel backwards. The fascist doctrine has not taken De Maistre as its prophet. Monarchical absolutism is of the past, and so is ecclesiolatry. Dead and done for are feudal privileges and the division of society into closed, uncommunicating casts. Neither has the fascist conception of authority anything in common with that of a police-ridden state.

A party governing a nation "totalitarianly" is a new departure in history. There are no points of reference nor of comparison. From beneath the ruins of liberal, socialist, and democratic doctrines, fascism extracts those elements which are still vital.

24

ADOLF HITLER

Mein Kampf

NATION AND RACE

There are numberless examples in history showing with terrible clarity how each time Aryan blood has become mixed with that of inferior peoples the result has been an end of the culture-sustaining race. North America, the population of which consists for the most part of Germanic elements, which mixed very little with inferior colored nations, displays humanity and culture very different from that of Central and South America, in which the settlers, mainly Latin in origin, mingled their blood very freely with that of the aborigines. Taking the above as an example, we clearly recognize the effects of racial intermixture. The man of Germanic race on the continent of America having kept himself pure and unmixed, has risen to be its master; and he will remain master so long as he does not fall into the shame of mixing the blood.

Perhaps the pacifist-humane idea is quite a good one in cases where the man at the top has first thoroughly conquered and subdued the world to the extent of making himself sole master of it. Then the principle when applied in practice, will not affect the mass of the people injuriously. Thus first the struggle and then pacifism. Otherwise, it means that humanity has passed the highest point in its development, and the end is not domination by any ethical idea, but barbarism, and chaos to follow. Some will naturally laugh at this, but this planet traveled through the ether for millions of years devoid of humanity, and it can only do so again if men forget that they owe their higher existence, not to the ideas of a mad ideologue, but to understanding and ruthless application of age-old natural laws.

All that we admire on this earth—science, art, technical skill and invention—is the creative product of only a small number of nations, and originally, perhaps, of one single race. All this culture depends on them for its very existence. If they are ruined, they carry with them all the beauty of this earth into the grave.

If we divide the human race into three categories—founders, maintainers, and destroyers of culture—the Aryan stock alone can be considered as representing the first category.

The Aryan races—often in absurdly small numbers—overthrow alien nations, and, favored by the numbers of people of lower grade who are at their disposal to aid them, they proceed to develop, according to the special conditions for life in the acquired territories—fertility, climate, etc.— the qualities of intellect and organization which are dormant in them. In the course of a few centuries they create cultures, originally stamped with their own characteristics alone, and develop them to suit the special character of the land and the people which they have conquered. As time goes on, however, the conquerors sin against the principle of keeping the blood pure (a principle which they adhered to at first), and begin to blend with the original inhabitants whom they have subjugated, and end their own existence as a peculiar people; for the sin committed in Paradise was inevitably followed by expulsion.

From all time creative nations have been creative through and through, whether superficial observers do or do not realize it. Nothing but completed accomplishment is recognized by such people, for most men in this world are incapable of perceiving genius in itself, and see only the outward signs of it in the form of inventions, discoveries, buildings, paintings, etc. Even then it takes a long time before they arrive at comprehending it. Just as individual genius strives, under the spur of special inducements, to work out expression of itself in practical ways, so, in the life of nations, actual application of the creative forces which are in them is not produced except at the call of certain definite circumstances. We see this most clearly in the race which was and is the carrier of human cultural development—the Aryan.

For the development of the higher culture it was necessary that men of lower civilization should have existed, for none but they could be a substitute for the technical instruments, without which higher development was inconceivable. In its beginnings human culture certainly depended less on the tamed beast and more on employment of inferior human material.

It was not until the conquered races had been enslaved that a like fate fell on the animal world; the contrary was not the case, as many would like to believe. For it was the slave who first drew the plough, and after him the horse. None but pacifist fools can look on this as yet another token of human depravity; others must see clearly that this development was bound to happen in order to arrive at a state of things in which those apostles are able to loose their foolish talk on the world.

Human progress is like ascending an endless ladder; a man cannot climb higher unless he has first mounted the lowest rung. Thus the Aryan had to follow the road leading him to realization, and not the one which exists in the dreams of a modern pacifist.

But the road which the Aryan had to tread was clearly marked out. As a conqueror he overthrew inferior men, and their work was done under his control, according to his will and for his purposes. But while extracting useful, if hard, work out of his subjects, he not only protected their lives, but also perhaps gave them an existence better than their former so-called freedom. So long as he continued to look on himself as the overlord, he not only maintained his mastery, but he was also the upholder and fosterer of culture. But as soon as the subjects began to raise themselves and—probably—to assimilate their language with that of the conqueror, the sharp barrier between lord and servant fell. The Aryan renounced purity of his own blood, and with it his right to stay in the Eden which he had created for himself. He sank, overwhelmed in the mixing of races, and by degrees lost forever his capacity for civilization until he began to resemble the subjected aboriginal race more than his fathers, both in mind and body. For a time he could still enjoy the blessings of civilization, but first indifference set in, and finally oblivion. This is how civilizations and empires break up, to make room for new creations.

Blood mixture, with the lowering of the racial level which accompanies it, is the one and only reason that old civilizations disappear. It is not lost wars which ruin mankind, but loss of the powers of resistance, which belong to pure blood alone.

There is in our German language a word which is finely descriptive—readiness to obey the call of duty (*Pflichterfüllung*)—service in the general interest. The idea underlying such an attitude we call "idealism," in contradistinction to "egoism"; and by it we understand the capacity for self-sacrifice in the individual for the community, for his fellow men.

It is at times when ideals are threatening to disappear that we are able to observe an immediate diminution of that strength which is the essence of the community and a necessary condition of culture. Then selfishness becomes the governing force in a nation, and in the hunt after happiness the ties of order are loosened and men fall out of heaven straight into hell.

The exact opposite of the Aryan is the Jew. In hardly any nation in the world is the instinct of self-preservation more strongly developed than in the "chosen people." The best proof of this is the fact that the race still continues to exist. Where is there a people which for the last two thousand years has shown so little change in internal characteristics as the Jewish race? What race, in fact, has been involved in greater revolutionary changes than that one, and yet has survived intact after the most terrific catastrophes? How their determined will to live and to maintain the type is expressed by these facts!

The Jew's intellectual qualities were developed in the course of centuries. Today we think him "cunning," and in a certain sense it was the same at every epoch. But his intellectual capacity is not the result of personal development, but of education by foreigners.

Thus, since the Jew never possessed a culture of his own, the bases of his intellectual activity have always been supplied by others. His intellect has in all periods been developed by contact with surrounding civilizations. Never the opposite.

It is utterly incorrect to point to the fact that the Jews hold together in struggling with their fellow men—or rather in plundering them—and conclude from it that they have a certain ideal of self-sacrifice.

Even in this the Jew is guided by nothing more nor less than pure self-seeking; and that is why the Jewish State—which is supposed to be the living organism for maintaining and increasing a race—is entirely without frontiers. For the conception of a state with definite boundaries always implies the idealistic sentiment of a race within the state, also a proper conception of the meaning of work as an idea. For want of this conception, ambition is lacking to form or even maintain a state with definite boundaries. There is thus no basis on which a culture may be built up.

Thus the Jewish nation, with all its obvious intellectual qualities, has no real culture—certainly none peculiar to itself. For whatever culture the Jew appears to possess today is in the main the property of other peoples, which has become corrupted under his manipulation.

Originally the Aryan was probably a nomad and then, as time went on, he became settled; this, if nothing else, proves that he was never a Jew! No, the Jew is not a nomad, for even the nomad had already a definite attitude towards the conception "work," destined to serve as a basis for further development, so far as he possessed the necessary intellectual qualifications. But he did possess the power of forming ideals, if in a very rarefied form, so that his conception of life may have been alien, but not unsympathetic, to the Aryan races. In the Jew, however, that conception has no place; he was never a nomad, but was ever a parasite in the bodies of other nations. His having on occasion deserted his former sphere of life was not on all fours with his intentions, but was the consequence of his being at various periods ejected by the nations whose hospitality he had abused. His propagation of himself throughout the world is a typical phenomenon with all parasites; he is always looking for fresh feeding ground for his race.

His life within other nations can be kept up in perpetuity only if he succeeds in convincing the world that with him it is not a question of a race, but of a "religious bond," one however peculiar to himself. This is the first great lie!

In order to continue existing as a parasite within the nation, the Jew must set to work to deny his real inner nature. The more intelligent the individual Jew is, the better will he succeed in his deception—to the extent of making large sections of the population seriously believe that the Jew genuinely is a Frenchman or an Englishman, a German or an Italian, though of a different religion.

The present vast economic development is leading to a change in the social stratification of the nation. The small industries are gradually dying out, making it rarer for the worker to be able to secure a decent existence and visibly driving him to become one of the proletarian class. The outcome of all this is the "factory worker," whose essential distinguishing mark is that he is practically unable in later life to maintain his dignity and individuality. In the truest sense of the word he is possessionless; old age means suffering to him and can hardly be called life at all.

There was once at an earlier period a similar situation which was urgently in need of solution; a solution was discovered. Beside farmers and artisans was appearing a new state, whose officials were servants of the state and possessionless in the truest sense of the word. The state found a way out of that unhealthy condition of things; it assumed responsibility for the welfare of its servant who was unable himself to provide for his old age, and instituted the pension on retirement. Thus a whole class, left without possessions, was skillfully delivered from social misery and incorporated in the body of the nation.

Of late years the state has had to face the same question on a far larger scale. Fresh masses of people, amounting to millions, have been constantly removing from the villages to the large towns, to earn a living as factory workers in the new industries.

Thus a new class has actually come into being to which but little attention has been paid, and a day will come when one will have to ask whether the nation has the strength by its own efforts once more to incorporate the new class in the general community or whether the distinction of class and class is to broaden into a rift.

While the bourgeoisie has been ignoring this most difficult question and letting things happen as they please, the Jew has been considering the boundless possibilities which present themselves as regards the future. On the one hand he is making use of his capitalistic methods for exploiting humanity to the very full, and on the other he is getting ready to sacrifice his sway and very soon will come out as their leader in the fight against himself. "Against himself" is, of course, only a figurative expression, for the great master of lies knows very well how to emerge with apparently clean hands and burden others with the blame. Since he has the impudence to lead the masses in person, it never occurs to the latter that it is the most infamous betrayal of all time.

The Jew's procedure is as follows: He addresses himself to the workers, pretends to have pity for their lot or indignation at their misery and poverty in order to gain their confidence. He takes trouble to study the real or imaginary hardness of their lives and to arouse a longing for a change of existence. With untold cleverness he intensifies the demand for social justice dormant in all men of Aryan stock and so stamps the struggle for removal of social evils with a quite definite character of universal world importance. He founds the doctrine of Marxism.

By mingling it inextricably with a whole mass of demands which are socially justifiable, he ensures the popularity of the doctrine, while on the other hand he causes decent people to be unwilling to support demands which, being presented in such a form, appear wrong from the start, nay, impossible of realization. For under the cloak of purely social ideas there lie hidden truly devilish intentions, and these are brought into the open with impudent downrightness and frankness. By categorically denying the importance of personality, and so of the nation and its racial significance, they destroy the elementary principles of all human culture.

The Jew divides the organization of his world-teaching into two categories, which, though apparently separate, really form an inseparable whole; the political and the labor movements.

The trade union movement is the more wooing one. It offers the workman help and protection in his hard fight for existence, for which he has to thank the greed or short-sightedness of many an employer, and also the possibility of wresting better living conditions. If the worker shrinks from entrusting the blind caprice of men, often heartless and with but little sense of responsibility, with the defense of his right to live as a man, at a time when the state—i.e., the organized community—is paying practically no attention to him, he will have to protect his interests himself. Now that the so-called national bourgeoisie, blinded by money interest, is setting every obstacle in the way of this struggle for a living, and is not only opposing, but universally and actively working against all attempts to shorten the inhumanly long hours of work, put an end to child labor, protect the women, and produce healthy conditions in factories and dwellings—the cleverer Jew is identifying himself with the underdog. He is gradually assuming leadership of the trade union movement—all the easier because what matters to him is not so much genuine removal of social evils as the formation of a blindly obedient fighting force in industry for the purpose of destroying national economic independence.

The Jew forcibly drives all competitors off the field. Helped by his innate greedy brutality, he sets the trade union movement on a footing of brute force. Anyone with intelligence enough to resist the Jewish lure is broken by intimidation, however determined and intelligent he may be. These methods are vastly successful.

By means of the trade union, which might have been the saving of the nation, the Jew actually destroys the bases of the nation's economics.

The political organization proceeds on parallel lines with the foregoing. It works in with the trade union movement, since the latter prepares the masses for the political organization, and in fact drives them forcibly into it. It is, moreover, the constant money source out of which the political organization feeds its vast machine. It is the organ of control for the political work and acts as whipper-in for all great demonstrations, political in character. Finally it loses its economic character altogether, serving the political idea with its chief weapon, the general strike.

By creating a press, which is on the intellectual level of the least educated, the political and labor organization obtains means of compulsion, enabling it to make the lowest strata of the nation ready for the most hazardous enterprises.

It is the Jewish press which, in an absolutely fanatical campaign of calumny, tears down all which may be regarded as the prop of a nation's independence, its civilization, and its economic autonomy. It roars especially against those who have strength of character enough not to bow to Jewish domination or whose intellectual capacity appears to the Jew in the light of a menace to himself.

The ignorance displayed by the mass of the people as to the true nature of the Jews and the lack of instinctive perception of our upper class make the people easy dupes of this Jewish campaign of lies. While the natural timidity of the upper class makes it turn away from a man who is being thus attacked by the Jews with lies and calumny, the stupidity or simple-mindedness of the masses causes them to believe all they hear. The state authorities either cower in silence or—more frequently still—in order to put an end to the Jews' press campaign, they persecute those who are being unjustly attacked, and this, in the eyes of such Jacks-in-office, stands for vindication of state authority and maintenance of peace and order.

Thus, if we review all the causes of the German collapse, the final and decisive one is seen to be the failure to realize the racial problem and, more especially, the Jewish menace.

The defeats on the field of battle of August 1918 might have been borne with the utmost ease. It was not they which overthrew us; what overthrew us was the force which prepared for those defeats by robbing the nation of all political and moral instinct and strength, by schemes which had been under way for many decades. In ignoring the question of maintaining the racial basis of our nationality, the old empire disregarded the one and only law which makes life possible on this earth.

The loss of racial purity ruins the fortunes of a race forever; it continues to sink lower and lower and its consequences can never be expelled again from body and mind.

Thus all attempts at reform, and all social work, all political efforts, every increase of economic prosperity, and every apparent addition to scientific knowledge went for nothing. The nation and the organism which made life possible for it on this earth—i.e., the state—did not grow sounder, but waned visibly more and more. The brilliance of the old empire failed to conceal the inner weakness, and all attempts to add strength to the Reich came to nothing each time, because they persisted in ignoring the most essential questions of all.

That is why in August 1914, a nation did not rush full of determination into the battle; it was merely the last flicker of a national instinct of self-preservation face to face with the advancing forces of Marxism and pacifism, crippling the body of our nation. But since in those fateful days no one realized the domestic foe, resistance was all in vain, and Providence chose not to reward the victorious sword, but followed the law of eternal retribution.

PART VI

Anticolonialism and National Liberation Movements

25

SUN YAT-SEN

Three Principles of the People

The population of the world today is approximately a billion and a half. One-fourth of this number live in China, which means that one out of every four persons in the world is a Chinese. The total population of the white races of Europe also amounts to four hundred million. The white division of mankind, which is now the most flourishing, includes four races: in central and northern Europe, the Teutons, who have founded many states, the largest of which is Germany, others being Austria, Sweden, Norway, Holland, and Denmark; in Eastern Europe, the Slavs, who also have founded a number of states, the largest being Russia, and, after the European war, the new countries of Czechoslovakia and Yugoslavia; in Western Europe, the Saxons or Anglo-Saxons, who have founded two large states—England and the United States of America; in southern Europe, the Latins, who have founded several states, the largest being France, Italy, Spain, and Portugal, and who have migrated to South America forming states there just as the Anglo-Saxons migrated to North America and built up Canada and the United States. The white peoples of Europe, now numbering only four hundred million persons, are divided into four great stocks which have established many states. Because the national spirit of the white race was highly developed, when they had filled up the European continent they expanded to North and South America in the Western Hemisphere and to Africa and Australia in the southern and eastern parts of the Eastern Hemisphere.

The Anglo-Saxons at present occupy more space on the globe than any other race. Although this race originated in Europe, the only European soil it holds are the British Isles—England, Scotland, and Ireland—which occupy about the same position in the Atlantic that Japan occupies in the Pacific. The Anglo-Saxons have extended their territory westward to North America, eastward to Australia and New Zealand, and southward to Africa until they possess more land and are wealthier and stronger than any other race. Before the European war the Teutons and the Slavs were the strongest races; moreover, by reason of the sagacity and ability of the Teutonic peoples, Germany was able to unite more than twenty small states into a great German confederation. At the beginning an agricultural nation, it developed into an industrial nation and through industrial prosperity its army and navy became exceedingly powerful.

Before the European war all the European nations had been poisoned by imperialism. What is imperialism? It is the policy of aggression upon other countries by means of political force, or, in the Chinese phrase, "long-range aggression." As all the peoples of Europe were imbued with this policy, wars were continually breaking out; almost every decade had at least one small war and each century one big war. The greatest of all was the recent European war, which may be called the World War because it finally involved the whole world and pulled every nation and people into its vortex. The causes of the European war were, first, the rivalry between the Saxon and Teutonic races for control of the sea. Germany in her rise to greatness had developed her navy until she was the second sea power in the world; Great Britain wanted her own navy to rule the seas so she tried to destroy Germany, whose sea power was next to hers. From this struggle for first place on the sea came the war.

A second cause was each nation's struggle for more territory. In Eastern Europe there is a weak state called Turkey. For the past hundred years the people of the world have called it the "sick man of Europe." Because the government was unenlightened and the sultan was despotic, it became extremely helpless and the European nations wanted to partition it. Because the Turkish question had not been solved for a century and every nation of Europe was trying to solve it, war resulted. The first cause of the European war, then, was the struggle between white races for supremacy; the second cause was the effort to solve critical world problems. If Germany had won the war, she would have held the supreme power on the sea after the war and Great Britain would have lost all her territory, breaking into pieces like the old Roman Empire. But the result of the war was defeat for Germany and the failure of her imperialistic designs.

The recent European war was the most dreadful war in the history of the world. Forty to fifty million men were under arms for a period of four years, and near the end of the war they still could not be divided into conquerors and vanquished. One side in the war was called the Entente; the other side, the Allied Powers. The Allied Powers (Central Powers) at first included Germany and Austria; Turkey and Bulgaria later joined them. The Entente Powers (the Allies) at first were Serbia, France, Russia, England, and Japan; Italy and the United States joined afterwards. The United States' entry into the war was due entirely to racial considerations. During the first two years of the war Germany and Austria were in the ascendancy. Paris and the English Channel were almost captured by the German and Austrian armies. The Teutons thought that Great Britain was certainly done for, and the British themselves were thoroughly alarmed. Seeing that the American people are of the same race as they, the British used the plea of race relationship to stir up the people of the United States. When America realized that England, of her own race, was in danger of being destroyed by Germany, of an alien race, inevitably "the creature sorrowed for its kind" and America threw in her lot with England to defend the existence of the Anglo-Saxons. Moreover, fearing that her own strength would be insufficient, America tried with all her might to arouse all the neutral countries of the world to join in the war to defeat Germany.

During the war there was a great phrase, used by President Wilson and warmly received everywhere—"self-determination of peoples." Because Germany was striving by military force to crush the peoples of the European Entente, Wilson proposed destroying Germany's power and giving autonomy henceforth to the weaker and smaller peoples. His idea met a world welcome, and although the common people of India still opposed Great Britain, their destroyer, yet many small peoples, when they heard Wilson say that the war was for the freedom of the weak and small peoples, gladly gave aid to Great Britain. Although Annam had been subjugated by France and the common people hated the French tyranny, yet during the war they still helped France to fight, also because they had heard of Wilson's just proposition. And the reason why other small peoples of Europe, such as Poland, Czechoslovakia, and Romania, all enlisted on the side of the Entente against the Allied Powers was because of the self-determination principle enunciated by President Wilson. China, too, under the inspiration of the United States, entered the war; although she sent no armies, yet she did contribute hundreds of thousands of laborers to dig trenches and to work behind the lines. As a result of the noble theme propounded by the Entente all the oppressed peoples of Europe and of Asia finally joined together to help them in their struggle against the Allied Powers. At the same time, Wilson proposed, to guard the future peace of the world, fourteen points, of which the most important was that each people should have the right of self-determination. When victory and defeat still hung in the balance, England and France heartily endorsed these points, but when victory was won and the Peace Conference was opened, England, France, and Italy realized that Wilson's proposal of freedom for nations conflicted too seriously with the interests of imperialism; and so, during the conference, they used all kinds of methods to explain away Wilson's principles. The result was a peace treaty with most unjust terms; the weaker, smaller nations not only did not secure self-determination and freedom but found themselves under an oppression more terrible than before. This shows that the strong states and the powerful races have already forced possession of the globe and that the rights and privileges of other states and nations are monopolized by them. Hoping to make themselves forever secure in their exclusive position and to prevent the smaller and weaker peoples from again reviving, they sing praises to cosmopolitanism, saying that nationalism is too narrow; really their espousal of internationalism is but imperialism and aggression in another guise.

But Wilson's proposals, once set forth, could not be recalled; each one of the weaker, smaller nations who had helped the Entente to defeat the Allied

Powers and had hoped to attain freedom as a fruit of the victory was doomed to bitter disappointment by the results of the Peace Conference. Then Annam, Burma, Java, India, the Malay Archipelago, Turkey, Persia, Afghanistan, Egypt, and the scores of weak nations in Europe were stirred with a great, new consciousness; they saw how completely they had been deceived by the Great Powers' advocacy of self-determination and began independently and separately to carry out the principle of the "self-determination of peoples."

Many years of fierce warfare had not been able to destroy imperialism because this was a conflict of imperialisms between states, not a struggle between savagery and civilization or between might and right. So the effect of the war was merely the overthrow of one imperialism by another imperialism; what survived was still imperialism. But from the war there was unconsciously born in the heart of mankind a great hope—the Russian Revolution. The Russian Revolution had begun much earlier, as far back as 1905, but had not accomplished its purpose. Now during the European war the efforts of the revolutionists were crowned with success. The reason for the outbreak of revolution again at this time was the great awakening of the people as a result of their war experience. Russia sent over ten million soldiers into the field—not a puny force. Without Russia's part in the war, the Entente's line on the western front would long before have been smashed by Germany; because Russia was embarrassing the Germans on the eastern front, the Entente Powers were able to break even with Germany for two or three years and finally turn defeat into victory. Just halfway through the war, Russia began to reflect, and she realized that in helping the Entente to fight Germany she was merely helping several brute forces to fight one brute force and that no good results would come of it in the end. A group of soldiers and citizens awoke, broke away from the Entente, and concluded a separate peace with Germany.

As far as their legitimate national interests were concerned, the German and the Russian people had absolutely no cause for quarrel; but when it came to imperialistic designs, they vied with each other in aggressions until conflict was inevitable. Moreover, Germany went so far beyond bounds that Russia, in self-protection, could not but move in accord with England, France, and the others. Later, when the Russian people awoke and saw that imperialism was wrong, they started a revolution within their own country, first overthrowing their own imperialism; at the same time, to avoid foreign embarrassments, they made peace with Germany. Before long, the Entente also signed a peace with Germany and then all sent soldiers to fight Russia. Why? Because the Russian people had awakened to the fact that their daily sufferings were due to imperialism and that to get rid of their sufferings they must eliminate imperialism and embrace self-determination. Every other nation opposed this policy and so mobilized to fight Russia, yet Russia's proposal and Wilson's were undesignedly similar; both declared that the weaker, smaller nations had the right of self-determination and freedom.

When Russia proclaimed this principle, the weaker, smaller peoples of the world gave their eager support to it and all together began to seek self-determination. The calamitous war through which Europe had passed brought, of course, no great imperialistic gain, but, because of the Russian Revolution, a great hope was born in the heart of mankind.

Of the billion and a half people in the world, the most powerful are the four hundred million whites on the European and American continents; from this base the white races have started out to swallow up other races. The American red aborigines are gone, the African blacks will soon be exterminated, the brown race of India is in the process of dissolution, the yellow races of Asia are now being subjected to the white man's oppression and may, before long, be wiped out.

But the one hundred fifty million Russians, when their revolution succeeded, broke with the other white races and condemned the white man's imperialistic behavior; now they are thinking of throwing in their lot with the weaker, smaller peoples of Asia in a struggle against the tyrannical races. So only two hundred fifty million of tyrannical races are left, but they are still trying by inhuman methods and military force to subjugate the other twelve hundred fifty million. So hereafter mankind will be divided into two camps: On one side will be the twelve hundred fifty million; on the other side, the two hundred fifty million. Although the latter group is in the minority, yet they hold the most powerful positions on the globe and their political and economic strength is immense. With these two forces they are out to exploit the weaker and smaller races. If the political arm of navies and armies is not strong enough, they bear down with economic pressure. If their economic arm is at times weak, they intervene with political force of navies and armies. The way their political power cooperates with their economic power is like the way in which the left arm helps the right arm; with their two arms they have crushed most terribly the twelve hundred fifty million. But "Heaven does not always follow man's desires." The Slavic race of one hundred fifty million suddenly rose up and struck a blow at imperialism and capitalism, warring for mankind against inequality. In my last lecture I told of the Russian who said, "The reason why the Powers have so defamed Lenin is because he dared to assert that the twelve hundred fifty million majority in the world were being oppressed by the two hundred fifty million minority." Lenin not only said this, but also advocated self-determination for the oppressed peoples and launched a campaign for them against injustice. The powers attacked Lenin because they wanted to destroy a prophet and a seer of mankind and obtain security for themselves. But the people of the world now have their eyes opened and know that the rumors created by the powers are false; they will not let themselves be deceived again. The political thinking of the peoples of the world has been enlightened to this extent.

Now we want to revive China's lost nationalism and use the strength of our four hundred million to fight for mankind against injustice; this is our divine mission. The powers are afraid that we will have such thoughts and are setting forth a specious doctrine. They are now advocating cosmopolitanism to inflame us, declaring that, as the civilization of the world advances and as mankind's vision enlarges, nationalism becomes too narrow, unsuited to the present age, and hence that we should espouse cosmopolitanism. In recent years some of China's youths, devotees of the new culture, have been opposing nationalism, led astray by this doctrine. But it is not a doctrine which wronged races should talk about. We, the wronged races, must first recover our position of national freedom and equality before we are fit to discuss cosmopolitanism. The illustration I used in my last lecture of the coolie who won first prize in the lottery has already made this very clear. The lottery ticket represents cosmopolitanism; the bamboo pole, nationalism. The coolie, on winning first prize, immediately threw away his pole in which he had hidden, for safety, his lottery ticket—thus losing both his pole and his prize—just as we, fooled by the promises of cosmopolitanism, have discarded our nationalism. We must understand that cosmopolitanism grows out of nationalism; if we want to extend cosmopolitanism we must first establish strongly our own nationalism. If nationalism cannot become strong, cosmopolitanism certainly cannot prosper. Thus we see that cosmopolitanism is hidden inside the bamboo pole; if we discard nationalism and go and talk cosmopolitanism we are just like the coolie who threw his bamboo pole into the sea. We put the cart before the horse. I said before that our position is not equal to that of the Annamese or the Koreans; they are subject peoples and slaves while we cannot even be called slaves. Yet we discourse about cosmopolitanism and say that we do not need nationalism. Gentlemen, is this reasonable?

According to history, our four hundred million Chinese have also come down the road of imperialism. Our forefathers constantly employed political force to encroach upon weaker and smaller nations; but economic force in those days was not a serious thing, so we were not guilty of economic oppression of other peoples. Then compare China's culture with Europe's ancient culture. The Golden Age of European culture was in the time of Greece and Rome, yet Rome at the height of its power was contemporaneous with as late a dynasty in China as the Han. At that time China's political thinking was very profound; many orators were earnestly opposing imperialism and much anti-imperialistic literature was produced, the most famous being "Discussions on Abandoning the Pearl Cliffs." Such writings opposed China's efforts to expand her territory and her struggle over land with the southern barbarians, which shows that as early as the Han dynasty China already discouraged war against outsiders and had developed the peace idea to broad proportions.

In the Sung dynasty, China was not only ceasing to encroach upon other peoples, but she was even being herself invaded by foreigners. The Sung

dynasty was overthrown by the Mongols and the nation did not again revive until the Ming dynasty. After this restoration, China became much
less aggressive. However, many small states in the South China Sea wanted
to bring tribute and to adopt Chinese culture, giving voluntary adherence
because of their admiration for our culture and not because of military pressure
from China. The small countries in the Malay Archipelago and the South
China Sea considered it a great honor for China to annex them and receive their tribute; China's refusal would have brought them disgrace. [. . .]

Our four hundred million are not only a most peaceful but also a most
civilized race. The new cultures which have flourished of late in Europe
and which are called anarchism and communism are old things in China.
For instance, Hwang-Lao's political philosophy is really anarchism and what
is Lieh-tze's dream of the land of the Hua-hsü people who lived in a natural state without ruler or laws but another theory of anarchism? Modern
youths in China, who have not studied carefully into these old Chinese
theories, think that their ideas are the newest things in existence, unaware
that, though they may be new in Europe, they are thousands of years old
here. What Russia has been putting into practice is not pure communism
but Marxism; Marxism is not real communism. What Proudhon and Bakunin
advocated is the only real communism. Communism in other countries is
still in the stage of discussion; it has not been fully tried out anywhere. But
it was applied in China in the time of Hung Hsiu-ch'uan; his economic
system was the real thing in communism and not mere theory.

European superiority to China is not in political philosophy but altogether
in the field of material civilization, all the daily provisions for clothing,
food, housing, and communication have become extremely convenient and
time-saving, and the weapons of war—poison gas and such—have become
extraordinarily perfected and deadly. All these new inventions and weapons
have come since the development of science. It was after the seventeenth
and eighteenth centuries, when Bacon, Newton, and other great scholars
advocated the use of observation, experiment, and investigation of all things,
that science came into being. So when we speak of Europe's scientific progress
and of the advance of European material civilization, we are talking about
something which has only two hundred years' history. A few hundred years
ago, Europe could not compare with China, so now if we want to learn
from Europe we should learn what we ourselves lack—science—but not
political philosophy. Europeans are still looking to China for the fundamentals of political philosophy. You all know that the best scholarship today
is found in Germany. Yet German scholars are studying Chinese philosophy
and even Indian Buddhist principles to supplement their partial conceptions of science. Cosmopolitanism has just flowered out in Europe during
this generation, but it was talked of two thousand years ago in China. Europeans cannot yet discern our ancient civilization, yet many of our race have
thought of a political world civilization; and as for international morality,

our four hundred million have been devoted to the principle of world peace. But because of the loss of our nationalism, our ancient morality and civilization have not been able to manifest themselves and are now even declining.

The cosmopolitanism which Europeans are talking about today is really a principle supported by force without justice. The English expression "might is right" means that fighting for acquisition is just. The Chinese mind has never regarded acquisition by war as right; it considers aggressive warfare barbarous. This pacifist morality is the true spirit of cosmopolitanism. Upon what foundation can we defend and build up this spirit?—Upon nationalism. Russia's one hundred fifty million are the foundation of Europe's cosmopolitanism and China's four hundred million are the foundation of Asia's cosmopolitanism. As a foundation is essential to expansion, so we must talk nationalism first if we want to talk cosmopolitanism. "Those desiring to pacify the world must first govern their own state." Let us revive our lost nationalism and make it shine with greater splendor, then we will have some ground for discussing internationalism.

26

JAWAHARLAL NEHRU

The Discovery of India

II. INDIA'S GROWTH ARRESTED

[. . .] In India from the earliest days there was a search for those basic principles, for the unchanging, the universal, the absolute. Yet the dynamic outlook was also present and an appreciation of life and the changing world. On these two foundations a stable and progressive society was built up, though the stress was always more on stability and security and the survival of the race. In later years the dynamic aspect began to fade away, and in the name of eternal principles the social structure was made rigid and unchanging. It was, as a matter of fact, not wholly rigid, and it did change gradually and continuously. But the ideology behind it and the general framework continued unchanged. The group idea as represented by more or less autonomous castes, the joint family, and the communal self-governing life of the village were the main pillars of this system, and all these survived for so long because, in spite of their failings, they fulfilled some essential needs of human nature and society. They gave security and stability to each group and a sense of group freedom. Caste survived because it continued to represent the general power relationships of society, and class privileges were maintained, not only because of the prevailing ideology, but also because they were supported by vigor, intelligence, and ability, as well as a capacity for self-sacrifice. That ideology was not based on a conflict of rights but on the individual's obligations to others and a satisfactory performance of his duties, on cooperation within the group and between different groups, and essentially on the idea of promoting peace rather than war. While the social system was rigid, no limit was placed on the freedom of the mind.

Indian civilization achieved much that it was aiming at, but in that very achievement life began to fade away, for it is too dynamic to exist for long in a rigid, unchanging environment. Even those basic principles, which are said to be unchanging, lose their freshness and reality when they are taken for granted and the search for them ceases. Ideas of truth, beauty, and freedom decay, and we become prisoners following a deadening routine.

The very thing India lacked, the modern West possessed and possessed to excess. It had the dynamic outlook. It was engrossed in the changing world, caring little for ultimate principles, the unchanging, the universal. It paid little attention to duties and obligations, and emphasized rights. It was active, aggressive, acquisitive, seeking power and domination, living in the present and ignoring the future consequences of its actions. Because it was dynamic, it was progressive and full of life, but that life was a fevered one and the temperature kept on rising progressively.

If Indian civilization went to seed because it became static, self-absorbed, and inclined to narcissism, the civilization of the modern West, with all its great and manifold achievements, does not appear to have been a conspicuous success or to have thus far solved the basic problems of life. Conflict is inherent in it, and periodically it indulges in self-destruction on a colossal scale. It seems to lack something to give it stability, some basic principles to give meaning to life, though what these are I cannot say. Yet because it is dynamic and full of life and curiosity, there is hope for it.

India, as well as China, must learn from the West, for the modern West has much to teach, and the spirit of the age is represented by the West. But the West is also obviously in need of learning much, and its advances in technology will bring it little comfort if it does not learn some of the deeper lessons of life, which have absorbed the minds of thinkers in all ages and in all countries.

India had become static, and yet it would be utterly wrong to imagine that she was unchanging. No change at all means death. Her very survival as a highly evolved nation shows that there was some process of continuous adaptation going on. When the British came to India, though technologically somewhat backward she was still among the advanced commercial nations of the world. Technical changes would undoubtedly have come and changed India as they had changed some Western countries. But her normal development was arrested by the British power. Industrial growth was checked, and as a consequence social growth was also arrested. The normal power relationships of society could not adjust themselves and find an equilibrium, as all power was concentrated in the alien authority, which based itself on force and encouraged groups and classes which had ceased to have any real significance. Indian life thus progressively became more artificial, for many of the individuals and groups who seemed to play an important role in it had no vital functions left and were there only because of the importance given to them by the alien power. They had long ago finished their role in history and would have been pushed aside by new forces if they had not been given foreign protection. They became straw-stuffed symbols or protégés of foreign authority, thereby cutting themselves further away from the living currents of the nation. Normally they would have been weeded out or diverted to some more appropriate function by revolution or democratic process. But so long as foreign authoritarian rule continued, no such development could take place. And so India was cluttered up with these emblems of the past and the real changes that were taking place were hidden behind an artificial facade. No true social balances or power relationships within society could develop or become evident, and unreal problems assumed an undue importance. [...]

IV. THE IMPORTANCE OF THE NATIONAL IDEA CHANGES NECESSARY IN INDIA

A blind reverence for the past is bad and so also is a contempt for it, for no future can be founded on either of these. The present and the future inevitably grow out of the past and bear its stamp, and to forget this is to build without foundations and to cut off the roots of national growth. It is to ignore one of the most powerful forces that influence people. Nationalism is essentially a group memory of past achievements, traditions, and experiences, and nationalism is stronger today than it has ever been. Many people thought that nationalism had had its day and must inevitably give place to the ever-growing international tendencies of the modern world. Socialism with its proletarian background derided national culture as something tied up with a decaying middle class. Capitalism itself became progressively international with its cartels and combines and overflowed national boundaries. Trade and commerce, easy communications and rapid transport, the radio and cinema all helped to create an international atmosphere and to produce the delusion that nationalism was doomed.

Yet whenever a crisis has arisen, nationalism has emerged again and dominated the scene, and people have sought comfort and strength in their old traditions. One of the remarkable developments of the present age has been the rediscovery of the past and of the nation. [...]

For countries like India we have too much of the past about us and have ignored the present. We have to get rid of that narrowing religious outlook, that obsession with the supernatural and metaphysical speculations, that loosening of the mind's discipline in religious ceremonial and mystical emotionalism, which come in the way of our understanding ourselves and the world. We have to come to grips with the present, this life, this world, this nature which surrounds us in its infinite variety. Some Hindus talk of going back to the Vedas; some Muslims dream of an Islamic theocracy. Idle fancies, for there is no going back to the past; there is no turning back even if this was thought desirable. There is only one-way traffic in Time.

India must therefore lessen her religiosity and turn to science. She must get rid of the exclusiveness in thought and social habit which has become like a prison to her, stunting her spirit and preventing growth. The idea of ceremonial purity has erected barriers against social intercourse and narrowed the sphere of social action. The day-to-day religion of the orthodox Hindu is more concerned with what to eat and what not to eat, whom to eat with and from whom to keep away, than with spiritual values. The rules and regulations of the kitchen dominate his social life. The Muslim is fortunately free from these inhibitions, but he has his own narrow codes and ceremonials, a routine which he rigorously follows, forgetting the lesson of brotherhood which his religion taught him. His view of life is perhaps even more limited and sterile than the Hindu view, though the average Hindu today is a poor representative of the latter view, for he has lost that traditional freedom of thought and the background that enriches life in many ways.

Caste is the symbol and embodiment of this exclusiveness among the Hindus. It is sometimes said that the basic idea of caste might remain but its subsequent harmful development and ramifications should go; that it should not depend on birth but on merit. This approach is irrelevant and merely confuses the issue. In a historical context a study of the growth of caste has some value, but obviously we cannot go back to the period when caste began; in the social organization of today it has no place left. If merit is the only criterion and opportunity is thrown open to everybody, then caste loses all its present-day distinguishing features and, in fact, ends. Caste has in the past not only led to the suppression of certain groups but to a separation of theoretical and scholastic learning from craftsmanship and a divorce of philosophy from actual life and its problems. It was an aristocratic approach based on traditionalism. This outlook has to change completely, for it is wholly opposed to modern conditions and the democratic ideal. The functional organization of social groups in India may continue, but even that will undergo a vast change as the nature of modern industry creates new functions and puts an end to many old ones. The tendency today everywhere is toward a functional organization of society, and the concept of abstract rights is giving place to that of functions. This is in harmony with the old Indian ideal.

The spirit of the age is in favor of equality, though practice denies it almost everywhere. We have gotten rid of slavery in the narrow sense of the word, that a man can be the property of another. But a new slavery, in some ways worse than the old, has taken its place all over the world. In the name of individual freedom, political and economic systems exploit human beings and treat them as commodities. And again, though an individual cannot be the property of another, a country and a nation can still be the property of another nation, and thus group slavery is tolerated. Racialism also is a distinguishing feature of our times, and we have not only master nations but also master races.

Yet the spirit of the age will triumph. In India, at any rate, we must aim at equality. That does not and cannot mean that everybody is physically or intellectually or spiritually equal or can be made so. But it does mean equal opportunities for all and no political, economic, or social barrier in the way of any individual or group. It means a faith in humanity and a belief that there is no race or group that cannot advance and make good in its own way, given the chance to do so. It means a realization of the fact that the backwardness or degradation of any group is not due to inherent failings in it but principally to lack of opportunities and long suppression by other groups. It should mean an understanding of the modern world wherein real progress and advance, whether national or international, have become very much a joint affair and a backward group pulls back others. Therefore not only must equal opportunities be given to all, but special opportunities for educational, economic, and cultural growth must be given to backward groups so as to enable them to catch up to those who are ahead of them. Any such attempt to open the doors of opportunity to all in India will release enormous energy and ability and transform the country with amazing speed. [. . .]

In India, as elsewhere, we are too much under the bondage of slogans and set phrases deriving from past events and ideologies which have little relevance today, and their chief function is to prevent reasoned thought and a dispassionate consideration of the situation as it exists. There is also the tendency toward abstractions and vague ideals, which arouse emotional responses and are often good in their way, but which also lead to a wooliness of the mind and unreality. In recent years a great deal has been written and said on the future of India and especially on the partition or unity of India. And yet the astonishing fact remains that those who propose "Pakistan" or partition have consistently refused to define what they mean or to consider the implications of such a division. They move on the emotional plane only, as also many of those who oppose them, a plane of imagination and vague desire, behind which lie imagined interests. Inevitably, between these two emotional and imaginative approaches there is no meeting ground. And so Pakistan and Akhand Hindustan (undivided India) are bandied about and hurled at each other. It is clear that group emotions and conscious or subconscious urges count and must be attended to. It is at least equally clear that facts and realities do not vanish by our ignoring them or covering them up by a film of emotion; they have a way of emerging at awkward moments and in unexpected ways. Any decisions taken primarily on the basis of emotions, or when emotions are the dominating consideration, are likely to be wrong and to lead to dangerous developments.

It is obvious that whatever may be the future of India, and even if there is a regular partition, the different parts of India will have to cooperate with each other in a hundred ways. Even independent nations have to cooperate with each other; much more must Indian provinces or such parts as emerge from a partition, for these stand in an intimate relationship to each other and must hang together or deteriorate, disintegrate, and lose their freedom. [. . .]

Thus we arrive at the inevitable and ineluctable conclusion that, whether Pakistan comes or not, a number of important and basic functions of the state must be exercised on an all-India basis if India is to survive as a free state and progress. The alternative is stagnation, decay, and disintegration, leading to loss of political and economic freedom, both for India as a whole and its various separated parts. As has been said by an eminent authority:

"The inexorable logic of the age presents the country with radically different alternatives: union plus independence or disunion plus dependence." What form the union is to take, and whether it is called union or by some other name, is not so important, though names have their own significance and psychological value. The essential fact is that a number of varied activities can only be conducted effectively on a joint all-India basis. Probably many of these activities will soon be under the control of international bodies. The world shrinks and its problems overlap. It takes less than three days now to go right across the world by air, from any one place to another, and tomorrow, with the development of stratosphere navigation, it may take even less time. India must become a great world center of air travel. India will also be linked by rail to western Asia and Europe on the one side, and to Burma and China on the other. Not far from India, across the Himalayas in the north, lies in Soviet Asia one of the highly developed industrial areas, with an enormous future potential. India will be affected by this and will react in many ways.

The way of approach, therefore, to the problem of unity or Pakistan is not in the abstract and on the emotional level, but practically and with our eyes on the present-day world. That approach leads us to certain obvious conclusions: that a binding cement in regard to certain important functions and matters is essential for the whole of India. Apart from them there may be and should be the fullest freedom for constituent units, and an intermediate sphere where there is both joint and separate functioning. There may be differences of opinion as to where our sphere ends and the other begins, but such differences, when considered on a practical basis, are generally fairly easy of adjustment.

But all this must necessarily be based on a spirit of willing cooperation, on an absence of a feeling of compulsion, and on the sensation of freedom in each unit and individual. Old vested interests have to go; it is equally important that no new ones are created. Certain proposals, based on metaphysical conceptions of groups and forgetting the individuals who comprise them, make one individual politically equal to two or three others and thus create new vested interests. Any such arrangement can only lead to grave dissatisfaction and instability.

The right of any well-constituted area to secede from the Indian federation or union has often been put forward, and the argument of the U.S.S.R. advanced in support of it. That argument has little application, for conditions there are wholly different and the right has little practical value. In the emotional atmosphere in India today it may be desirable to agree to this for the future in order to give that sense of freedom from compulsion which is so necessary. The Congress has in effect agreed to it. But even the exercise of that right involves a pre-consideration of all those common problems to which reference has been made. Also there is grave danger in a possibility of partition and division to begin with, for such an attempt might well scotch the very beginnings of freedom and the formation of a free national state. Insuperable problems will rise and confuse all the real issues. Disintegration will be in the air, and all manner of groups who are otherwise agreeable to a joint and unified existence will claim separate states for themselves, or special privileges which are encroachments on others. The problem of the Indian states will become far more difficult of solution, and the states system, as it is today, will get a new lease on life. The social and economic problems will be far harder to tackle. Indeed, it is difficult to conceive of any free state emerging from such a turmoil, and if something does emerge, it will be a pitiful caricature full of contradictions and insoluble problems.

Before any such right of secession is exercised there must be a properly constituted, functioning, free India. It may be possible then, when external influences have been removed and real problems face the country, to consider such questions objectively and in a spirit of relative detachment, far removed from the emotionalism of today, which can only lead to unfortunate consequences which we may all have to regret later. Thus it may be desirable to fix a period, say ten years after the establishment of the free Indian state, at the end of which the right to secede may be exercised through proper constitutional process and in accordance with the clearly expressed will of the inhabitants of the area concerned.

27

SATI AL-HUSRI

Muslim Unity and Arab Unity

I have read and heard many opinions and observations concerning Muslim unity and Arab unity, and which is to be preferred. I have been receiving for some time now various questions concerning this matter: Why, it is asked, are you interested in Arab unity, and why do you neglect Muslim unity? Do you not see that the goal of Muslim unity is higher than the goal of Arab unity, and that the power generated by Muslim union would be greater than that generated by Arab union? Do you not agree that religious feeling in the East is much stronger than national feeling? Why, then, do you want us to neglect the exploitation of this powerful feeling and to spend our energies in order to strengthen a weak feeling? Do you believe that the variety of languages will prevent the union of the Muslims? Do you not notice that the principles of communism, socialism, Freemasonry, and other systems unite people of different languages, races, countries, and climates; that none of these differences have prevented them from coming to understanding, from drawing nearer to one another, and from agreeing on one plan and one creed? Do you not know that every Muslim in Syria, Egypt, or Iraq believes that the Indian Muslim, the Japanese Muslim, or the European Muslim is as much his brother as the Muslim with whom he lives side by side? Whence, then, the impossibility of realizing Muslim union? Some say that Muslim unity is more powerful than any other and that its realization is easier than the realization of any other. What do you say to this? Some pretend, mistakenly, that the idea of Arab union is a plot the aim of which is to prevent the spread of the idea of Muslim union, in order to isolate some of the countries of the Muslim world and facilitate their continued subjugation. What is your opinion of this allegation?

I have heard and read, and I still hear and read, many similar questions which occur in conversations, in private letters, or in open letters. I have therefore thought to devote this essay to the full discussion of these problems and to the frank explanation of my view concerning them.

I think that the essential point which has to be studied and solved when deciding which to prefer, Muslim unity or Arab unity, may be summarized as follows: Is Muslim unity a reasonable hope capable of realization? Or is it a utopian dream incapable of realization? And assuming the first alternative,

is its realization easier or more difficult than the realization of Arab unity?
Does one of these two schemes exclude the other? And is there a way of
realizing Muslim unity without realizing Arab unity? When we think about
such questions and analyze them, we have, in the first place, to define
clearly what we mean by Muslim unity and by Arab unity and to delimit
without any ambiguity the use of the two expressions.

It goes without saying that Arab unity requires the creation of a political
union of the different Arab countries the inhabitants of which speak Arabic. As for Muslim unity, that naturally requires the creation of a political
union of the different Muslim countries, the inhabitants of which profess
the Muslim religion, regardless of the variety of their languages and races.
It is also well known that the Muslim world includes the Arab countries,
Turkey, Iran, Afghanistan, Turkestan, parts of India, the East Indies, the
Caucasus, North Africa, as well as parts of central Africa, without considering a few scattered units in Europe and Asia, as in Albania, Yugoslavia,
Poland, China, and Japan. Further, there is no need to show that the Arab
countries occupy the central portion of this far-flung world.

Whoever will examine these evident facts and picture the map of the
Muslim world, noticing the position of the Arab world within it, will have
to concede that Arab unity is much easier to bring about than Muslim
unity, and that this latter is not capable of realization, assuming that it can
be realized, except through Arab unity. It is not possible for any sane person to imagine union among Cairo, Baghdad, Tehran, Kabul, Haiderabad,
and Bukhara, or Kashgar, Persia, and Timbuctoo, without there being a
union among Cairo, Baghdad, Damascus, Mecca, and Tunis. It is not possible for any sane person to conceive the possibility of union among Turks,
Arabs, Persians, Malayans, and Negroes, while denying unity to the Arabs
themselves. If, contrary to fact, the Arab world were more extensive and
wider than the Muslim world, it would have been possible to imagine a
Muslim union without Arab union, and it would have been permissible to
say that Muslim union is easier to realize than Arab union. But as the
position is the exact opposite, there is no logical scope whatever for such
statements and speculations. We must not forget this truth when we think
and speak concerning Muslim unity and Arab unity. The idea of Muslim
unity is, it is true, wider and more inclusive than the concept of Arab
unity, but it is not possible to advocate Muslim unity without advocating
Arab unity. We have, therefore, the right to assert that whoever opposes
Arab unity also opposes Muslim unity. As for him who opposes Arab unity,
in the name of Muslim unity or for the sake of Muslim unity, he contradicts the simplest necessities of reason and logic.

Having established this truth, to disagree with which is not logically possible, we ought to notice another truth which is no less important. We
must not forget that the expression "unity," in this context, means political
unity; and we must constantly remember that the concept of Islamic unity

greatly differs from that of Muslim brotherhood. Unity is one thing and affection another, political unity is one thing and agreement on a certain principle another. To advocate Muslim unity, therefore, is different from advocating the improvement of conditions in Islam and different also from advocating an increase in understanding, in affection, and in cooperation among Muslims. We can therefore say that he who talks about the principle of Muslim brotherhood, and discusses the benefits of understanding among the Muslims, does not prove that Muslim unity is possible. Contrariwise, he who denies the possibility of realizing Muslim unity does not deny the principle of Muslim brotherhood or oppose the efforts toward the awakening of the Muslims and understanding among them. What may be said concerning the ideal of brotherhood is not sufficient proof of the possibility of realizing Muslim unity. Further, it is not intelligent or logical to prove the possibility of realizing Muslim unity by quoting the example of Freemasonry or socialism or communism, because the Freemasons do not constitute a political unity and the socialist parties in the different European countries have not combined to form a new state. Even communism itself has not formed a new state, but has taken the place of the tsarist Russian state. We have, therefore, to distinguish quite clearly between the question of Muslim brotherhood and that of Muslim unity, and we must consider directly whether or not it is possible to realize Muslim unity in the political sense.

If we cast a general glance at history and review the influence of religions over the formation of political units, we find that the world religions have not been able to unify peoples speaking different languages, except in the Middle Ages, and that only in limited areas and for a short time. The political unity which the Christian church sought to bring about did not at any time merge the Orthodox world with the Catholic. Neither did the political unity which the papacy tried to bring about in the Catholic world last for any length of time. So it was also in the Muslim world; the political unity which existed at the beginning of its life was not able to withstand the changes of circumstance for any length of time. Even the Abbasid caliphate, at the height of its power and glory, could not unite all the Muslims under its political banner. Similarly, the lands ruled by this caliphate did not effectively preserve their political unity for very long. Nor was it long after the founding of the caliphate that its control over some of the provinces became symbolic rather than real; it could not prevent the secession of these provinces and their transformation into independent political units. It deserves to be mentioned in this connection that the spread of the Muslim religion in some areas took place after the Muslim caliphate lost effective unity and real power, so much so that in some countries Islam spread in a manner independent of the political authority, at the hands of missionary tradesmen, holy men, and dervishes. In short, the Muslim world, within its present extensive limits, never at any time formed a political unity. If, then, political unity could not be realized in past centuries, when social life was simple and political relations were primitive, when religious customs controlled every aspect of behavior and thought, it will not be possible to realize it in this century, when social life has become complicated, political problems have become intractable, and science and technology have liberated themselves from the control of tradition and religious beliefs.

I know that what I have stated here will displease many doctors of Islam; I know that the indications of history which I have set out above will have no influence over the beliefs of a great many of the men of religion, because they have been accustomed to discuss these matters without paying heed to historical facts or to the geographical picture; nor are they used to distinguishing between the meaning of religious brotherhood and the meaning of political ties. They have been accustomed to confuse the principles of Islamic brotherhood, in its moral sense, and the idea of Islamic unity, in its political sense. I think it useless to try to persuade these people of the falsity of their beliefs, but I think it necessary to ask them to remember what reason and logic require in this respect. Let them maintain their belief in the possibility of realizing Islamic unity, but let them at the same time agree to the necessity of furthering Arab unity, at least as one stage toward the realization of the Islamic unity in which they believe. In any event, let them not oppose the efforts which are being made to bring about Arab unity, on the pretext of serving the Islamic unity which they desire. I repeat here what I have written above: Whoever opposes Arab unity, on the pretext of Muslim unity, contradicts the simplest requirements of reason and logic, and I unhesitatingly say that to contradict logic to this extent can be the result only of deceit or of deception. The deceit is that of some separatists who dislike the awakening of the Arab nation and try to arouse religious feeling against the idea of Arab unity, and the deception is that of the simple-minded, who incline to believe whatever is said to them in the name of religion, without realizing what hidden purposes might lurk behind the speeches. I therefore regard it as my duty to draw the attention of all the Muslim Arabs to this important matter and I ask them not to be deceived by the myths of the separatists on this chapter.

Perhaps the strangest and most misleading views that have been expressed regarding Arab unity and Islamic unity are the views of those who say that the idea of Arab unity was created to combat Islamic unity in order to isolate some Islamic countries, the better to exercise continuous power over them. I cannot imagine a view further removed from the realities of history and politics or more contradictory to the laws of reason and logic. The details I have mentioned above concerning the relation of Muslim unity to Arab unity are sufficient, basically, to refute such allegations. Yet I think it advisable to add to these details some observations for further proof and clarity. It cannot be denied that the British, more than any other state, have humored and indulged the Arab movement. This is only because they are more practiced in politics and quicker to understand the psychology of nations and the realities of social life. Before anybody else they realized the hidden powers lying in the Arab idea, and thought it wise, therefore, to humor it somewhat, instead of directly opposing it. This was in order to preserve themselves against the harm they might sustain through it and to make it more advantageous to their interests.

We must understand that British policy is a practical policy, changing with circumstances and always making use of opportunities. We must not forget that it was Great Britain who, many times, saved the Ottoman state, then the depository of the Islamic caliphate, from Russian domination. She it was who halted Egyptian armies in the heart of Anatolia to save the seat of the Muslim caliphate from these victorious troops, and she it was who opposed the union of Egypt with Syria at the time of Muhammad Ali. Whoever, then, charges that the idea of Arab unity is a foreign plot utters a greater falsehood than any that has ever been uttered, and he is the victim of the greatest of deceptions. We must know full well that the idea of Arab unity is a natural idea. It has not been artificially started. It is a natural consequence of the existence of the Arab nation itself. It is a social force drawing its vitality from the life of the Arabic language, from the history of the Arab nation, and from the connectedness of the Arab countries. No one can logically pretend that it is the British who created the idea of Arab unity, unless he can prove that it is the British who have created the Arabic language, originating the history of the Arab nation and putting together the geography of the Arab countries. The idea of Arab unity is a natural concept springing from the depths of social nature and not from the artificial views which can be invented by individuals or by states. It remained latent, like many natural and social forces, for many centuries, as a result of many historical factors which cannot be analyzed here. But everything indicates that this period is now at an end, that the movement has come into the open and will manifest itself with ever-increasing power. It will, without any doubt, spread all over the Arab countries, to whom it will bring back their ancient glory and primeval youth; it will indeed bring back what is most fertile, most powerful, and highest in these countries. This ought to be the faith of the enlightened among the speakers of the *dad*.

28

AYATOLLAH KHOMEINI

Islamic Government

A. THE NATURE OF ISLAM, MONARCHY, AND COLONIALISM

Islam is the religion of the strugglers who want right and justice, the religion of those demanding freedom and independence and those who do not want to allow the infidels to dominate the believers.

But the enemies have portrayed Islam in a different light. They have drawn from the minds of the ordinary people a distorted picture of Islam and implanted this picture even in the religious academies. The enemies' aim behind this was to extinguish the flame of Islam and to cause its vital revolutionary character to be lost, so that the Muslims would not think of seeking to liberate themselves and to implement all the rules of their religion through the creation of a government that guarantees their happiness under the canopy of an honorable human life.

They have said that Islam has no relationship whatsoever with organizing life and society or with creating a government of any kind and that it only concerns itself with the rules of menstruation and childbirth. It may contain some ethics. But beyond this, it has no bearing on issues of life and of organizing society. It is regrettable that all this has had its bad effect not only on the ordinary people but also among college people and the students of theology. They misunderstand Islam and are ignorant of it. Islam has become as strange to them as alien people. It has become difficult for the missionary to familiarize people with Islam. On the other hand, there stands a line of the agents of colonialism to drown Islam with clamor and noise. [. . .]

You, the youths who are the soldiers of Islam, must examine more thoroughly the brief statements I am making to you and must familiarize people throughout your life with the laws and rules of Islam, and must do so with every possible means: in writing, in speeches, and in actions. Teach the people about the catastrophes, tragedies, and enemies that have engulfed Islam since its inception. Do not hide what you know from the people and do not let people imagine that Islam is like present-day Christianity, that there is no difference between the mosque and the church and that Islam can do no more than regulate man's relationship with his God.

At a time when darkness prevailed over the Western countries, when American Indians were inhabiting America, when absolute regimes exercising domination and racial discrimination and resorting to the excessive use of force with total disregard for the public opinion and for the laws were in existence in the Roman and Persian empires—at that time, God made laws which he revealed to the greatest prophet, Muhammad, may God's peace and prayers be upon him, so that man may be born under their canopy. Everything has its ethics and its laws. Before man's birth and until the time he is lowered into his grave, laws have been drawn up to govern him. Social relationships have been drawn up and government has been organized, in addition to determining the duties of worship. Rights in Islam are high-level, complete, and comprehensive rights. Jurists have often quoted the Islamic rules, laws, and regulations on dealings, permissibles, punishment, jurisdiction; on regulating relations between states and peoples, on war and peace, and on human rights. [. . .]

At times, the foreigners whisper to the people: "Islam is deficient. Its judiciary laws are not what they should be." To further deceive and mislead the people, the agents of the British tried, on the instructions of their masters, to import foreign positional laws in the wake of the well-known revolution and of the establishment of a constitutional regime in Iran. When they wanted to draw up the country's basic law—meaning the constitution—those agents resorted to Belgian laws which they borrowed from the Belgian embassy. A number of those agents, whom I do not wish to name, copied those laws and corrected their defects from the group of French and British laws, adding to them some Islamic laws for the purpose of camouflage and deception. The provisions in the constitution that define the system of government and that set up the monarchy and the hereditary rule as a system of government for the country are imported from England and Belgium and copied from the constitutions of the European countries. These provisions are alien to Islam and are in conflict with it.

Is there monarchy, hereditary rule, or succession to the throne in Islam? How can this happen in Islam when we know that the monarchic rule is in conflict with the Islamic rule and with the Islamic political system? Islam abolished monarchy and succession to the throne. When it first appeared, Islam considered the sultanic systems of rule in Iran. . . . God's prophet, may God's prayers be upon him, sent messages to the king of the Romans (Hercules) and the king of Persia urging them to set the people free to worship God alone because only God is the sultan. Monarchy and succession to the throne are the ominous and null system of government against which al-Husayn, the master of martyrs, rose and fought. Rejecting injustice and refusing to submit to Yazid's succession and rule, al-Husayn staged his historic revolution and urged all the Muslims to follow suit. There is no hereditary monarchic system in Islam. If they consider this a defect in Islam, then let them say: Islam is defective. . . .

What we are suffering from currently is the consequence of that misleading propaganda whose perpetrators got what they wanted and which has required us to exert a large effort to prove that Islam contains principles and rules for the formation of government.

This is our situation. The enemies have implanted these falsehoods in the minds of people in cooperation with their agents, have ousted Islam's judiciary and political laws from the sphere of application, and have replaced them by European laws in contempt of Islam for the purpose of driving it away from society. They have exploited every available opportunity for this end.

These are the destructive plans of colonialism. If we add to them the internal elements of weakness among some of our people, we find that the result is that people begin to grow smaller and to despise themselves in the face of the material progress of the enemies. When some states advance industrially and scientifically, some of us grow smaller and begin to think that our failure to do the same is due to our religion and that the only means to achieve such progress is to abandon religion and its laws and to violate the Islamic teachings and beliefs. When the enemies went to the moon, these people imagined that religion was the obstacle preventing them from doing the same! I would like to tell these people: The laws of the Eastern or the Western camps are not what led them to this magnificent advance in invading outer space. The laws of these two camps are totally different. Let them go to Mars or anywhere they wish; they are still backward in the sphere of securing happiness to man, backward in spreading moral virtues, and backward in creating a psychological and spiritual progress similar to the material progress. They are still unable to solve their social problems because solving these problems and eliminating hardship requires an ideological and moral spirit. The material gains in the sphere of overcoming nature and invading space cannot accomplish this task. Wealth, capabilities, and resources require the Islamic faith, creed, and ethics to become complete and balanced, to serve man and to avert from him injustice and poverty. We alone possess such morals and laws. Therefore, we should not cast aside our religion and our laws, which are directly connected with man's life and which harbor the nucleus of reforming people and securing their happiness in this world and in the hereafter, as soon as we see somebody go to the moon or make something.

The ideas disseminated by the colonialists among us include their statement: "There is no government in the Islamic legislation and there are no government organizations in Islam. Assuming that here are important Shari'a laws, these laws lack the elements to guarantee their implementation. Consequently, Islam is a legislator and nothing more." It is evident that such statements are an indivisible part of the colonialist plans that seek to divert the Muslims away from thinking of politics, government, and administration. These statements are in conflict with our primary beliefs. We believe in government and we believe in the need for the prophet to appoint a caliph (successor) after him and he did. . . .

You must show Islam as it should be shown. Define governance to the people as it is. Tell them: We believe in governance; that the prophet, God's prayers be upon him, appointed a successor on the orders of God; we believe in the need for forming government; and we seek to implement God's order and rule to manage people, run their affairs, and care for them. The struggle for forming government is a twin to the faith in governance. Write and disseminate the laws of Islam and do not conceal them. Pledge to apply an Islamic rule, rely on yourselves, and be confident of victory.

The colonialists prepared themselves more than three centuries ago and started from the zero point. They have gotten what they wanted. Let us now start from scratch. Do not allow the Westerners and their followers to dominate you. Familiarize the people with the truth of Islam so that the young generation may not think that the men of religion in the mosques of Qum and al-Najaf believe in the separation of church from state, that they study nothing other than menstruation and childbirth, and that they have nothing to do with politics. The colonialists have spread in school curricula the need to separate church from the state and have deluded people into believing that the ulema of Islam are not qualified to interfere in the political and social affairs. The lackeys and followers of the colonialists have reiterated these words. In the prophet's time, was the church separated from the state? Were there at the time theologians and politicians? At the time of the caliphs and the time of 'Ali, the emir of the faithful, was the state separated from the church? Was there an agency for the church and another for the state?

The colonialists and their lackeys have made these statements to isolate religion from the affairs of life and society and to tacitly keep the ulema of Islam away from the people and drive people away from the ulema because the ulema struggle for the liberation and independence of the Muslims. . . .

B. Proof of Need for Forming Government and Revolution

NEED FOR EXECUTIVE AGENCIES

A collection of laws is not enough to reform society. For a law to be an element for reforming and making people happy, it requires an executive authority. This is why God, may He be praised, created on earth, in addition to the laws, a government and an executive and administrative agency. The great prophet, may God's prayers be upon him, headed all the executive agencies running the Muslim society. In addition to the tasks of conveying, explaining, and detailing the laws and the regulations, he took care of implementing them until he brought the state of Islam into existence. In his time, the prophet was not content with legislating the penal code, for example, but also sought to implement it. He cut off hands, whipped and stoned. After the prophet, the tasks of the caliph were no less than those of the prophet. The appointment of a caliph was not the sole purpose of explaining the laws but also for implementing them. This is the goal that endowed the caliphate with importance and significance. The prophet, had he not appointed a caliph to succeed him, would have been considered to have failed to convey his message. . . .

NEED FOR CONTINUED IMPLEMENTATION OF LAWS

It is obvious that the need for implementing the laws was not exclusive to the prophet's age and that this need continues because Islam is not limited by time or place. Because Islam is immortal, it must be implemented and observed forever. If what was permissible by Muhammad is permissible until the day of resurrection and what was forbidden by Muhammed is forbidden to the day of resurrection, then Muhammad's restrictions must not be suspended, his teachings must not be neglected, punishment must not be abandoned, tax collection must not be stopped, and defense of the nation of the Muslims and of their lands must not be abandoned. The belief that Islam came for a limited period and for a certain place violates the essentials of the Islamic beliefs. Considering that the implementation forever of laws after the venerable prophet, may God's prayers be upon him, is one of the essentials of life, then it is necessary for government to exist and for this government to have the qualities of an executive and administrative authority. Without this, social chaos, corruption, and ideological and moral deviation would prevail. This can be prevented only through the creation of a just government that runs all aspects of life.

"Horses you can muster so that you may scare away the enemies of God and your enemies." Had the Muslims adhered to the meaning of this Koranic phrase and had they been ready to fight under all circumstances, it would not have been possible for a handful of Jews to occupy our land and to damage and burn our al-Aqsa Mosque without being faced with any resistance. All this came about as an inevitable result of the failure to form an upright and faithful government. Had the current Muslim rulers tried to implement the laws of Islam, abandoning all their differences, putting aside their disputes and their division, and uniting in one hand in the face of the others, the bands of Jews and the puppets of America and Britain would not have been able to reach what they have reached, regardless of how much America and Britain help them. The reason for this is, of course, the fact that the Muslim rulers are unfit and unqualified.

The phrase "prepare for them all the force you can muster . . ." orders that we be fully prepared and alert so that the enemies may not subject us to the worst forms of torture. But we did not unite, we split into factions, our hearts were disunited and we did not get ready and so the unjust went beyond all limits in tyrannizing us and inflicting injustice upon us. . . .

NEED FOR POLITICAL REVOLUTION

At the early stage of Islam, the Ommiads and those supporting them tried to obstruct the stability of the government of Imam 'Ali ibn Abu Talib, even though it was a government that pleased God and the prophet. With their hateful efforts, the method and system of government changed and deviated from Islam because the programs of the Ommiads were in complete conflict with the teachings of Islam. The Abbasides came after the Ommiads and followed the same path. The caliphate changed and turned into a sultanate and a hereditary monarchy. The rule became similar to that of the emperors of Persia and Rome and the pharaohs of Egypt. This situation has continued until our present day.

The Shari'a and reason require us not to let governments have a free hand. The proof of this is evident. The persistence of these governments in their transgressions means obstructing the system and laws of Islam whereas there are numerous provisions that describe every non-Islamic system as a form of idolatry and a ruler or an authority in such a system as a false god. We are responsible for eliminating the traces of idolatry from our Muslim society and for keeping it away from our life. At the same time, we are responsible for preparing the right atmosphere for bringing up a faithful generation that destroys the thrones of false gods and destroys their illegal powers because corruption and deviation grow on their hands. This corruption must be wiped out and erased and the severest punishment must be inflicted upon those who cause it. In His venerable book, God describes Pharaoh as "a corrupter." Under the canopy of a pharaonic rule that dominates and corrupts society rather than reforms it, no faithful and pious person can live abiding by and preserving his faith and piety. Such a person has before him two paths, and no third to them: either be forced to commit sinful acts or rebel against and fight the rule of false gods, try to wipe out or at least reduce the impact of such a rule. We only have the second path open to us. We have no alternative but to work for destroying the corrupt and corrupting systems and to destroy the symbol of treason and the unjust among the rulers of peoples.

This is a duty that all Muslims wherever they may be are entrusted—a duty to create a victorious and triumphant Islamic political revolution.

NEED FOR ISLAMIC UNITY

On the other hand, colonialism has partitioned our homeland and has turned the Muslims into peoples. When the Ottoman state appeared as a united state, the colonialists sought to fragment it. The Russians, the British, and their allies united and fought the Ottomans and then shared the loot, as you all know. We do not deny that most rulers of the Ottoman state lacked ability, competence, and qualifications and many of them ruled the people in a despotic monarchic manner. However, the colonialists were afraid that some pious and qualified person would, with the help of the people, assume leadership of the Ottoman state and (would safeguard) its unity, ability, strength, and resources, thus dispersing the hopes and aspirations of the colonialists. This is why as soon as World War I ended, the colonialists partitioned the country into mini-states and made each of these mini-states their agent. Despite this, a number of these mini-states later escaped the grip of colonialism and its agents.

The only means that we possess to unite the Muslim nation, to liberate its lands from the grip of the colonialists, and to topple the agent governments of colonialism, is to seek to establish our Islamic government. The efforts of this government will be crowned with success when we become able to destroy the heads of treason, the idols, the human images, and the false gods who disseminate injustice and corruption on earth.

The formation of a government is then for the purpose of preserving the unity of the Muslims after it is achieved. This was mentioned in the speech of Fatimah al-Zahra', may peace be upon her, when she said: " . . . In obeying us lies the nation's order, and our imamhood is a guarantee against division." [. . .]

ISLAMIC SYSTEM OF GOVERNMENT:
DISTINCTION FROM OTHER POLITICAL SYSTEMS

The Islamic government is not similar to the well-known systems of government. It is not a despotic government in which the head of state dictates his opinion and tampers with the lives and property of the people. The prophet, may God's prayers be upon him, and 'Ali, the emir of the faithful, and the other imams had no power to tamper with people's property or with their lives. The Islamic government is not despotic but constitutional. However, it is not constitutional in the well-known sense of the word, which is represented in the parliamentary system or in the people's councils. It is constitutional in the sense that those in charge of affairs observe a number of conditions and rules underlined in the Koran and in the Sunna and represented in the necessity of observing the system and of applying the dictates and laws of Islam. This is why the Islamic government is the government of the divine law. The difference between the Islamic government and the constitutional governments, both monarchic and republican, lies in the fact that the people's representatives or the king's representatives are the ones who codify and legislate, whereas the power of legislation is confined to God, may He be praised, and nobody else has the right to legislate and nobody may rule by that which has not been given power by God. This is why Islam replaces the legislative council by a planning council that works to run the affairs and work of the ministries so that they may offer their services in all spheres.

All that is mentioned in the book (Koran) and in the Sunna is acceptable and obeyed in the view of the Muslims. This obedience facilitates the state's responsibilities, however, when the majorities in the constitutional monarchic or republican governments legislate something, the government has to later exert efforts to compel people to obey, even if such obedience requires the use of force.

29

LÉOPOLD SÉDAR SENGHOR

On African Socialism

From our ancestors, we have inherited our own method of knowledge. Why should we change it when Europeans now tell us it is the very method of the twentieth century—and the most fruitful method?

Let us then consider the Negro African as he faces the object to be known, as he faces the Other: God, man, animal, tree or pebble, natural or social phenomenon. In contrast to the classic European, the Negro African does not draw a line between himself and the object; he does not hold it at a distance, nor does he merely look at it and analyze it. After holding it at a distance, after scanning it without analyzing it, he takes it vibrant in his hands, careful not to kill or fix it. He touches it, feels it, *smells* it. The Negro African is like one of those Third Day Worms [an allusion to the Age of Reptiles], a pure field of sensations. Subjectively, at the tips of his sensory organs, his insect antennas, he discovered the Other. Immediately he is moved, going centrifugally from subject to object on the waves of the Other. This is more than a simple metaphor; contemporary physics has discovered universal energy under matter: waves and radiations. Thus the Negro African *sympathizes*, abandons his personality to become identified with the Other, dies to be reborn in the Other. He does not assimilate; he is assimilated. He lives a common life with the Other; he lives in a symbiosis. To use Paul Claudel's expression, he "knows the Other." Subject and object are dialectically face to face in the very act of knowledge. It is a long caress in the night, an embrace of joined bodies, the act of love. "I want you to feel me," says a voter who wants you to know him well. "I think, therefore I am," Descartes writes. The observation has already been made that one always thinks something, and the logician's conjunction "therefore" is unnecessary. The Negro African could say, "I feel, I dance the Other; I am." To dance is to discover and to re-create, especially when it is a dance of love. In any event, it is the best way to know. Just as knowledge is at once discovery and creation—I mean, re-creation and recreation, after the model of God.

Young people have criticized me for reducing Negro-African knowledge to pure emotion, for denying that there is an African "reason" or African techniques. This is the hub of the problem; I should like to explain my thought

268

once again. Obviously, there is a European civilization and a Negro-African civilization. Anyone who has not explained their differences and the reasons for them has explained nothing and has left the problem untouched.

Thus, I explain myself. However paradoxical it may seem, the vital force of the Negro African, his surrender to the object, is animated by reason. Let us understand each other clearly; it is not the *reasoning eye* of Europe, it is the *reason of the touch*, better still, the *reasoning embrace*, the sympathetic reason, more closely related to the Greek *logos* than to the Latin *ratio*. For *logos*, before Aristotle, meant both reason and the word. At any rate, Negro-African speech does not mold the object into rigid categories and concepts without touching it; it polishes things and restores their original color, with their texture, sound, and perfume; it perforates them with its luminous rays to reach the essential surreality in its innate humidity—it would be more accurate to speak of subreality. European reasoning is analytical, discursive by utilization; Negro-African reasoning is intuitive by participation. [. . .]

Does this mean, as certain young people would like to interpret my remarks, that the Negro African lacks discursive reason, that he has never used any? I have never said so. In truth, every ethnic group possesses different aspects of reason and all the virtues of man, but each has stressed only one aspect of reason, only certain virtues. No civilization can be built without using discursive reason and without techniques. Negro-African civilization is no exception to this rule: Witness the astonishment of the earliest European navigators disembarking in Africa to discover well-organized states, with government, administration, justice, and army, with techniques (remarkable for that date) for working in wood, ivory, bronze, iron, basketry, weaving, and terra cotta, with medical and agricultural techniques worthy of Europe.

From all that, I will conclude that we must maintain the Negro-African method of knowledge, but integrate into it the methods Europe has used throughout her history—classical logic, Marxian dialectics, and that of the twentieth century. Negro-African reason is traditionally dialectical, transcending the principles of identity, noncontradiction, and the "excluded middle." Let us merely be careful not to be led astray by the narrow determinism of Marxism, by abstraction. Let us hold firmly to the *concrete*, and we shall find, underlying the *concrete*, beyond the *discontinuous* and the *undetermined*, the liberty that legitimates not only our faith but the *African road to socialism*. [. . .]

[. . .] The alienation of the Negro Berber does not stem from Negro-Berber capitalism, nor even from European capitalism. Nor does it stem from the class struggle. Rather, it results from the domination of one country over another—or rather, of one ethnic group over another. Here, political and cultural domination, colored by racism, is fused with economic domination.

Hence, for us, man is not without a country, nor is he without a color or a history, a fatherland or a civilization. It is West African man, our neighbor, exactly defined in time and space. He is Malian, Mauritanian, Eburnian, Wolof, Targui, Songhai, Hausa, Fon, or Mossi. He is a man of flesh and blood, nourished on milk, millet, rice, and yams. He is a man humiliated for centuries, less perhaps in his nudity and hunger than in his skin and civilization, in his dignity.

Without this analysis, it is vain to define the program of the PFA or any African party. Unless one bears in mind the two realities of our present situation—the colonial fact and our cultural heritage. I know only too well that history, in its inexorable march, has reached the foot of the colonialist Bastille, that it is beginning to undermine the crumbling outer wall. Every republic in Black Africa can take its independence whenever it deems the moment opportune. Nevertheless, the sequels of colonialism remain and we must absorb and transcend them. As for our West African civilization, however charred it may be by the fire of conquest, it is now becoming verdant once again in the springtime of a new era, even before the first shower of independence.

Our task is clear, with regard to the present and to the past—colonization and traditional civilization, the history that we have lived. We must emerge from our alienation to build a new state. Political, economic, and social disalienation, once again, are all prerequisites of cultural disalienation. Contrary to the notion of numerous African politicians, culture is not an appendage that can be lopped off without damage. It is not even a simple political means. Culture is the precondition and the goal of any policy worthy of the name.

What would be the use of raising the living standard of our masses without a rise in the standard of culture? What good would it do to increase purchasing power only for the comfort of belly and backside: to buy parasols and sunglasses, even automobiles, refrigerators, washing machines, and the like? What would be the advantage, unless we occupy our leisure by creating works of art to provide spiritual nourishment for our people? In my opinion, sport can be a work of art, like the cinema, radio, television, the theatre, the novel, and poetry, sculpture, and painting, the dance and music. . . . I remind you that, in northern Sudanese countries with a single rainy season, people worked only during the four months of that rainy season. The other eight months, they were busy with social activities—I mean cultural activities—living in communion, by and within the community with other men, their brothers, more precisely, with the solidary forces of the entire universe: the living and the dead, men and animals, plants and pebbles. I am not saying that in the twentieth century it is unnecessary to reduce artistic activities for the benefit of political and economic interests. In the final analysis, all these activities are social, therefore cultural. Culture is inside and outside, above and beneath all human activities: It is the spirit that animates them, that gives a civilization its unique style.

In our return to our cultural roots, and particularly to the Negro-African method of knowledge and comprehension of the world, we cannot reject

European methods, but we also cannot forget Europe's lessons in building a
nation, the socialist state. For the reasons discussed in my *Report* and, first
and foremost, for historical reasons. We are now living the final stage of
world unification through interdependence. Thus, though our humanism
must have West African man as its major objective, it cannot, without
peril, end with West Africa, not even with all of Africa. An effective humanism must be *open*; it obviously excludes not only *Malianism*—since we
are not only Malians here assembled—but also nationalism and Pan-Negroism
(I do not say *Négritude*), Pan-Africanism and, with greater reason, Pan-
Arabism. The one "pan-ism" that meets twentieth-century requirements is,
I dare say, pan-humanism—a humanism that includes all men on the dual
basis of their contribution and their comprehension.

We shall make this salutary effort of reflection and construction if, in re-
studying colonialism, we succeed in placing it in the historical process of
world and African unification. Let us stop denouncing colonialism and Europe
and attributing all our ills to them. Besides being not entirely fair, this is a
negative approach, revealing our inferiority complex, the very complex the
colonizer inoculated in us and whose accomplices we thereby are secretly
becoming. It is too easy an alibi for our own laziness, for our selfishness as
intellectuals, for our failures. It would be more positive for us and our people
to analyze the colonial fact objectively, while psychoanalyzing our resentment.

Examined in historical perspective, the only fair perspective, colonization
will appear to us at first glance as a general fact of history. Races, peoples,
nations, and civilizations have always been in contact, and therefore in
conflict. To be sure, conquerors sow ruin in their wake, but they also sow
ideas and techniques that germinate and blossom into new harvests. Europe
did not lose from the Roman conquest, nor did India from the Aryan conquest, nor the Middle East and North Africa from the Arab conquest.

The latest colonization, that of Europe over the world, was the work of
the Renaissance. It stemmed from a social surge; it was stimulated and achieved
by the confrontation of revolutionary ideas and techniques. It sprang from
the humbling of the feudal landed gentry by monarchical centralization,
and especially from the emergence in cities and communes of an intellectual and commercial bourgeoisie. Under the urging of this rising class that
would later wage the French Revolution, the mind was freed and invented
new techniques. It pushed God back toward heaven, *de-sacralized* the world
and opened it fully to the European's feverish quest. The Renaissance was
bourgeois and atheistic, mercantile and materialistic; it bore the seal of one
essential aspect of the European mind. Thus it was iconoclastic, destructive
of civilized values. But when examined more profoundly, on the level of
universal history, the sanguinary event rises to the plane of an Advent; it
is *revolution*. Any revolution worthy of the name is, however, an upsurge
of consciousness, consciousness of oneself and of others. I would say
consciousness of the world, like the earlier great revolutions of Christianity,

Islam, and Buddhism; and, like the subsequent French Revolution and capitalism, which were mingled within it, the Renaissance was a conqueror. But
it exported not only merchants and soldiers; with professors, physicians,
engineers, administrators, and missionaries, it also exported ideas and techniques. It not only destroyed, it built; it not only killed, it cured and educated; it gave birth to a new world, an entire world of our brothers, men of
other races and continents!

When placed again in context, colonization will appear to us as a necessary evil, a historical necessity whence good will emerge, but on the sole
condition that we, the colonized of yesterday, become conscious and that
we will it. Slavery, feudalism, capitalism, and colonialism are the successive
parturitions of history, painful like all parturitions. With the difference that
here the child suffers more than the mother. That does not matter. If we
are fully conscious of the scope of the *Advent*, we shall cease to inveigh
against it; we shall be more attentive to contributions than to defects, to
possibilities of rebirth rather than to death and destruction. Without the
deaths, without the Arab and European depredations, no doubt the Negro
Africans and Berbers would by now have created more ripe and more suc-
culent fruits. I doubt that they would have caught up so soon with the
advances caused in Europe by the Renaissance. The evil of colonization is
less these ruptures than that we were deprived of the freedom to choose
those European contributions most appropriate to our spirit.

As Arabia had before, Europe brought us virtues to fill the void she had
provoked, seeds to be sown in the ashes of the devastated lands. With the
development of the sciences, she brought us more efficient techniques than
those at our disposal; these enabled us to build new cities on the ruins of
the conquest. Like Arabia, by ruining the old Negro-African *animism*, which
was not without value, it proposed to us a religion more attuned to contemporary values. Indeed, like the marabouts, even more so than the marabouts,
the missionaries were iconoclasts, destroyers of values. With this difference:
that Islam, with its horror of imagery, has done more damage to cultural
values, and Christianity, with occidental materialism, did more harm to
moral values. (To speak only of Christianity, the best of the Christians—a
Georges Gusdorf or a François Mauriac—have deplored certain methods of
evangelization and the fact that the missionaries followed and sometimes
preceded the merchants and soldiers. There is a seamy side to every human
enterprise.) Nevertheless, Islam and Christianity gave us spiritual values as
substitutes: more elaborate religions, more rational or, to repeat, more attuned to the present age. Once we have chosen them, it is our task to
adapt these religions to our historical and sociological conditions: It is our
task to *Negrofy* them.

To summarize on this point, *independence* and *nation-building* require, first,
along with *self-determination*, freedom of *choice*. We acquired this freedom
with the Constitution of 4 October 1958. They also require the proper

choice: in terms of West African, of our own, and of world realities. It is a question of placing our nation not only in the Africa of today, but also in the *civilization of the universal* yet to be built. The latter, as I like to repeat, will be a symbiosis of the most fecundating elements of all civilizations. In this perspective, we shall begin by returning to our West African sources—Negro African and Berber—to imbibe there deeply. This presupposes a prior inventory of our virtues and *defects*. With this as a starting point, we shall make our own choices.

In truth, we have already made them. We have chosen the reconstruction of the former West African Federation and we have chosen independence in the multinational confederation with France. Furthermore, we have chosen as a means of realizing this the *African road to socialism*. Finally—and this is the purpose of this lecture—we have a choice to make in our final option. Everything in "scientific socialism" is not to be accepted, especially its *atheistic* materialism—I do not say its dialectical materialism. For the major contradiction of Marxism is that it presents itself as a *science*, whereas, despite its denials, it is based on an ethic. I have said that if historical development inevitably leads to socialism and communism, why worry about it? In the name of what is our participation in this movement required? And how can one pass from *being* to *duty* except in the name of a transcendence of religious origin? For us, socialism is a *method* to be tested in contact with African realities. It is basically a question, after choosing lucidly, of assimilating our choices. To assimilate is to transform foods that are foreign to us, to make of them our flesh and blood—in a word, to *Negrofy* and *Berberize* them. This brings us back to Negro-Berber humanism; we must integrate the Negro Berber in his material determinations by transcending them in the name of certain spiritual values. For it is the spirit, in the final analysis, that judges and transcends the material determinants that have formed it. *Priority* of matter, if you will, but *primacy* of spirit.

30

FRANTZ FANON

The Wretched of the Earth

National liberation, national renaissance, the restoration of nationhood to the people, commonwealth: Whatever may be the headings used or the new formulas introduced, decolonization is always a violent phenomenon. At whatever level we study it—relationships between individuals, new names for sports clubs, the human admixture at cocktail parties, in the police, on the directing boards of national or private banks—decolonization is quite simply the replacing of a certain "species" of men by another "species" of men. Without any period of transition, there is a total, complete, and absolute substitution. It is true that we could equally well stress the rise of a new nation, the setting up of a new state, its diplomatic relations, and its economic and political trends. But we have precisely chosen to speak of that kind of tabula rasa which characterizes at the outset all decolonization. Its unusual importance is that it constitutes, from the very first day, the minimum demands of the colonized. To tell the truth, the proof of success lies in a whole social structure being changed from the bottom up. The extraordinary importance of this change is that it is willed, called for, demanded. The need for this change exists in its crude state, impetuous and compelling, in the consciousness and in the lives of the men and women who are colonized. But the possibility of this change is equally experienced in the form of a terrifying future in the consciousness of another "species" of men and women: the colonizers.

Decolonization, which sets out to change the order of the world, is, obviously, a program of complete disorder. But it cannot come as a result of magical practices, nor of a natural shock, nor of a friendly understanding. Decolonization, as we know, is a historical process: that is to say that it cannot be understood, it cannot become intelligible nor clear to itself except in the exact measure that we can discern the movements which give it historical form and content. Decolonization is the meeting of two forces, opposed to each other by their very nature which results from and is nourished by the situation in the colonies. Their first encounter was marked by violence and their existence together—that is to say the exploitation of the native by the settler—was carried on by dint of a great array of bayonets and cannon. The settler and the native are old acquaintances. In fact,

274

the settler is right when he speaks of knowing "them" well. For it is the settler who has brought the native into existence and who perpetuates his existence. The settler owes the fact of his very existence, that is to say his property, to the colonial system.

Decolonization never takes place unnoticed, for it influences individuals and modifies them fundamentally. It transforms spectators crushed with their inessentiality into privileged actors, with the grandiose glare of history's floodlights upon them. It brings a natural rhythm into existence, introduced by new men, and with it a new language and a new humanity. Decolonization is the veritable creation of new men. But this creation owes nothing of its legitimacy to any supernatural power; the "thing" which has been colonized becomes man during the same process by which it frees itself.

In decolonization, there is therefore the need of a complete calling in question of the colonial situation. If we wish to describe it precisely, we might find it in the well-known words: "The last shall be first and the first last." Decolonization is the putting into practice of this sentence. That is why, if we try to describe it, all decolonization is successful.

The naked truth of decolonization evokes for us the searing bullets and bloodstained knives which emanate from it. For if the last shall be first, this will only come to pass after a murderous and decisive struggle between the two protagonists. That affirmed intention to place the last at the head of things, and to make them climb at a pace (too quickly, some say) the well-known steps which characterize an organized society, can only triumph if we use all means to turn the scale, including, of course, that of violence.

You do not turn any society, however primitive it may be, upside down with such a program if you are not decided from the very beginning, that is to say from the actual formulation of that program, to overcome all the obstacles that you will come across in so doing. The native who decides to put the program into practice, and to become its moving force, is ready for violence at all times. From birth it is clear to him that this narrow world, strewn with prohibitions, can only be called in question by absolute violence.

The colonial world is a world divided into compartments. It is probably unnecessary to recall the existence of native quarters and European quarters, of schools for natives and schools for Europeans; in the same way we need not recall apartheid in South Africa. Yet, if we examine closely this system of compartments, we will at least be able to reveal the lines of force it implies. This approach to the colonial world, its ordering and its geographical layout, will allow us to mark out the lines on which a decolonized society will be reorganized.

The colonial world is a world cut in two. The dividing line, the frontiers are shown by barracks and police stations. In the colonies it is the policeman and the soldier who are the official, instituted go-betweens, the spokesmen of the settler and his rule of oppression. In capitalist societies the educational system, whether lay or clerical, the structure of moral reflexes handed down from father to son, the exemplary honesty of workers who are given a medal after fifty years of good and loyal service, and the affection which springs from harmonious relations and good behavior—all these aesthetic expressions of respect for the established order serve to create around the exploited person an atmosphere of submission and of inhibition which lightens the task of policing considerably. In the capitalist countries a multitude of moral teachers, counselors, and "bewilderers" separate the exploited from those in power. In the colonial countries, on the contrary, the policeman and the soldier, by their immediate presence and their frequent and direct action maintain contact with the native and advise him by means of rifle butts and napalm not to budge. It is obvious here that the agents of government speak the language of pure force. The intermediary does not lighten the oppression, nor seek to hide the domination; he shows them up and puts them into practice with the clear conscience of an upholder of the peace; yet he is the bringer of violence into the home and into the mind of the native.

The zone where the natives live is not complementary to the zone inhabited by the settlers. The two zones are opposed, but not in the service of higher unity. Obedient to the rules of pure Aristotelian logic, they both follow the principle of reciprocal exclusivity. No conciliation is possible, for of the two terms, one is superfluous. The settler's town is a strongly built town, all made of stone and steel. It is a brightly lit town; the streets are covered with asphalt, and the garbage cans swallow all the leavings, unseen, unknown, and hardly thought about. The settler's feet are never visible, except perhaps in the sea; but there you're never close enough to see them. His feet are protected by strong shoes although the streets of his town are clean and even, with no holes or stones. The settler's town is a well-fed town, an easygoing town; its belly is always full of good things. The settler's town is a town of white people, of foreigners.

The town belonging to the colonized people, or at least the native town, the Negro village, the medina, the reservation, is a place of ill fame, peopled by men of evil repute. They are born there, it matters little where or how; they die there, it matters not where, nor how. It is a world without spaciousness; men live there on top of each other, and their huts are built one on top of the other. The native town is a hungry town, starved of bread, of meat, of shoes, of coal, of light. The native town is a crouching village, a town on its knees, a town wallowing in the mire. It is a town of niggers and dirty Arabs. The look that the native turns on the settler's town is a look of lust, a look of envy; it expresses his dreams of possession—all manner of possession: to sit at the settler's table, to sleep in the settler's bed, with his wife if possible. The colonized man is an envious man. And this the settler knows very well; when their glances meet he ascertains bitterly, always on the defensive, "They want to take our place." It is true, for there is no native who does not dream at least once a day of setting himself up in the settler's place.

This world divided into compartments, this world cut in two is inhabited by two different species. The originality of the colonial context is that economic reality, inequality, and the immense difference of ways of life never come to mask the human realities. When you examine at close quarters the colonial context, it is evident that what parcels out the world is to begin with the fact of belonging to or not belonging to a given race, a given species. In the colonies the economic substructure is also a superstructure. The cause is the consequence; you are rich because you are white, you are white because you are rich. This is why Marxist analysis should always be slightly stretched every time we have to do with the colonial problem.

Everything up to and including the very nature of precapitalist society, so well explained by Marx, must here be thought out again. The serf is in essence different from the knight, but a reference to divine right is necessary to legitimize this statutory difference. In the colonies, the foreigner coming from another country imposed his rule by means of guns and machines. In defiance of his successful transplantation, in spite of his appropriation, the settler still remains a foreigner. It is neither the act of owning factories, nor estates, nor a bank balance which distinguishes the governing classes. The governing race is first and foremost those who come from elsewhere, those who are unlike the original inhabitants, "the others."

The violence which has ruled over the ordering of the colonial world, which has ceaselessly drummed the rhythm for the destruction of native social forms and broken up without reserve the systems of reference of the economy, the customs of dress and external life, that same violence will be claimed and taken over by the native at the moment when, deciding to embody history in his own person, he surges into the forbidden quarters. To wreck the colonial world is henceforward a mental picture of action which is very clear, very easy to understand, and which may be assumed by each one of the individuals which constitute the colonized people. To break up the colonial world does not mean that after the frontiers have been abolished lines of communication will be set up between the two zones. The destruction of the colonial world is no more and no less than the abolition of one zone, its burial in the depths of the earth or its expulsion from the country.

The natives' challenge to the colonial world is not a rational confrontation of points of view. It is not a treatise on the universal, but the untidy affirmation of an original idea propounded as an absolute. The colonial world is a Manichaean world. It is not enough for the settler to delimit physically, that is to say with the help of the army and the police force, the place of the native. As if to show the totalitarian character of colonial exploitation the settler paints the native as a sort of quintessence of evil. Native society is not simply described as a society lacking in values. It is not enough for the colonist to affirm that those values have disappeared from, or still better never existed in, the colonial world. The native is declared

insensible to ethics; he represents not only the absence of values, but also
the negation of values. He is, let us dare to admit, the enemy of values,
and in this sense he is the absolute evil. He is the corrosive element, destroying all that comes near him; he is the deforming element, disfiguring
all that has to do with beauty or morality; he is the depository of maleficent
powers, the unconscious and irretrievable instrument of blind forces. Monsieur Meyer could thus state seriously in the French National Assembly
that the Republic must not be prostituted by allowing the Algerian people
to become part of it. All values, in fact are irrevocably poisoned and dis-
eased as soon as they are allowed in contact with the colonized race. The
customs of the colonized people, their traditions, their myths—above all,
their myths—are the very sign of that poverty of spirit and of their constitutional depravity. That is why we must put the DDT which destroys parasites, the bearers of disease, on the same level as the Christian religion
which wages war on embryonic heresies and instincts, and on evil as yet
unborn. The recession of yellow fever and the advance of evangelization
form part of the same balance sheet. But the triumphant communiqués from
the missions are in fact a source of information concerning the implanta-
tion of foreign influences in the core of the colonized people. I speak of
the Christian religion, and no one need be astonished. The church in the
colonies is the white people's church, the foreigner's church. She does not
call the native to God's ways but to the ways of the white man, of the
master, of the oppressor. And as we know, in this matter many are called
but few chosen.

At times this Manichaeism goes to its logical conclusion and dehuman-
izes the native, or to speak plainly it turns him into an animal. In fact, the
terms the settler uses when he mentions the native are zoological terms.
He speaks of the yellow man's reptilian motions, of the stink of the native
quarter, of breeding swarms, of foulness, of spawn, of gesticulations. When
the settler seeks to describe the native fully in exact terms he constantly
refers to the bestiary. The European rarely hits on a picturesque style; but
the native, who knows what is in the mind of the settler, guesses at once
what he is thinking of. Those hordes of vital statistics, those hysterical
masses, those faces bereft of all humanity, those distended bodies which are
like nothing on earth, that mob without beginning or end, those children
who seem to belong to nobody, that laziness stretched out in the sun, that
vegetative rhythm of life—all this forms part of the colonial vocabulary.
General de Gaulle speaks of "the yellow multitudes" and François Mauriac
of the black, brown, and yellow masses which soon will be unleashed. The
native knows all this, and laughs to himself every time he spots an allusion
to the animal world in the other's words. For he knows that he is not an
animal; and it is precisely at the moment he realizes his humanity that he
begins to sharpen the weapons with which he will secure its victory.

As soon as the native begins to pull on his moorings, and to cause anxiety to the settler, he is handed over to well-meaning souls who in cultural congresses point out to him the specificity and wealth of Western values. But every time Western values are mentioned they produce in the native a sort of stiffening or muscular lockjaw. During the period of decolonization, the native's reason is appealed to. He is offered definite values, he is told frequently that decolonization need not mean regression, and that he must put his trust in qualities which are well-tried, solid, and highly esteemed. But it so happens that when the native hears a speech about Western culture he pulls out his knife—or at least he makes sure it is within reach. The violence with which the supremacy of white values is affirmed and the aggressiveness which has permeated the victory of these values over the ways of life and of thought of the native mean that, in revenge, the native laughs in mockery when Western values are mentioned in front of him. In the colonial context the settler only ends his work of breaking in the native when the latter admits loudly and intelligibly the supremacy of the white man's values. In the period of decolonization, the colonized masses mock at these very values, insult them, and vomit them up. [. . .]

The native discovers that his life, his breath, his beating heart are the same as those of the settler. He finds out that the settler's skin is not of any more value than a native's skin; and it must be said that this discovery shakes the world in a very necessary manner. All the new, revolutionary assurance of the native stems from it. For if, in fact, my life is worth as much as the settler's, his glance no longer shrivels me up nor freezes me, and his voice no longer turns me into stone. I am no longer on tenterhooks in his presence; in fact, I don't give a damn for him. Not only does his presence no longer trouble me, but I am already preparing such efficient ambushes for him that soon there will be no way out but that of flight.

We have said that the colonial context is characterized by the dichotomy which it imposes upon the whole people. Decolonization unifies that people by the radical decision to remove from it its heterogeneity, and by unifying it on a national, sometimes a racial, basis. We know the fierce words of the Senegalese patriots, referring to the maneuvers of their president, Senghor: "We have demanded that the higher posts should be given to Africans; and now Senghor is Africanizing the Europeans." That is to say that the native can see clearly and immediately if decolonization has come to pass or no, for his minimum demands are simply that the last shall be first. [. . .]

We have seen that this same violence, though kept very much on the surface all through the colonial period, yet turns in the void. We have also seen that it is canalized by the emotional outlets of dance and possession by spirits; we have seen how it is exhausted in fratricidal combats. Now the problem is to lay hold of this violence which is changing direction. When formerly it was appeased by myths and exercised its talents in finding fresh ways of committing mass suicide, now new conditions will make possible a completely new line of action.

Nowadays a theoretical problem of prime importance is being set, on the historical plane as well as on the level of political tactics, by the liberation of the colonies: When can one affirm that the situation is ripe for a move-ment of national liberation? In what form should it first be manifested? Because the various means whereby decolonization has been carried out have appeared in many different aspects, reason hesitates and refuses to say which is a true decolonization, and which a false. We shall see that for a man who is in the thick of the fight it is an urgent matter to decide on the means and the tactics to employ: that is to say, how to conduct and orga-nize the movement. If this coherence is not present there is only a blind will toward freedom, with the terribly reactionary risks which it entails.

What are the forces which in the colonial period open up new outlets and engender new aims to the violence of colonized peoples? In the first place there are the political parties and the intellectual or commercial elites. Now, the characteristic feature of certain political structures is that they proclaim abstract principles but refrain from issuing definite commands. The entire action of these nationalist political parties during the colonial period is action of the electoral type: a string of philosophico-political dis-sertations on the themes of the rights of peoples to self-determination, the rights of man to freedom from hunger and human dignity, and the unceas-ing affirmation of the principle: "One man, one vote." The national politi-cal parties never lay stress upon the necessity of a trial of armed strength, for the good reason that their objective is not the radical overthrowing of the system. Pacifists and legalists, they are in fact partisans of order, the new order—but to the colonialist bourgeoisie they put bluntly enough the demand which to them is the main one: "Give us more power." On the specific question of violence, the elite are ambiguous. They are violent in their words and reformist in their attitudes. When the nationalist political leaders say something, they make quite clear that they do not really think it.

This characteristic on the part of the nationalist political parties should be interpreted in the light both of the makeup of their leaders and the nature of their followings. The rank and file of a nationalist party is urban. The workers, primary schoolteachers, artisans, and small shopkeepers who have begun to profit—at a discount, to be sure—from the colonial setup, have special interests at heart. What this sort of following demands is the betterment of their particular lot: increased salaries, for example. The dia-logue between these political parties and colonialism is never broken off. Improvements are discussed, such as full electoral representation, the lib-erty of the press, and liberty of association. Reforms are debated. Thus it need not astonish anyone to notice that a large number of natives are mili-tant members of the branches of political parties which stem from the mother country. These natives fight under an abstract watchword: "Government by the workers," and they forget that in their country it should be *nationalist* watchwords which are first in the field. The native intellectual has clothed his aggressiveness in his barely veiled desire to assimilate himself to the colonial world. He has used his aggressiveness to serve his own individual interests.

Thus there is very easily brought into being a kind of class of affranchised slaves, or slaves who are individually free. What the intellectual demands is the right to multiply the emancipated, and the opportunity to organize a genuine class of emancipated citizens. On the other hand, the mass of the people have no intention of standing by and watching individuals increase their chances of success. What they demand is not the settler's act of parliament, but the settler's place. The immense majority of natives want the settler's farm. For them, there is no question of entering into competition with the settler. They want to take his place.

The peasantry is systematically disregarded for the most part by the propaganda put out by the nationalist parties. And it is clear that in the colonial countries the peasants alone are revolutionary, for they have nothing to lose and everything to gain. The starving peasant, outside the class system, is the first among the exploited to discover that only violence pays. For him there is no compromise, no possible coming to terms; colonization and decolonization are simply a question of relative strength. The exploited man sees that his liberation implies the use of all means, and that of force first and foremost. When in 1956, after the capitulation of Monsieur Guy Mollet to the settlers in Algeria, the Front de Libération Nationale, in a famous leaflet, stated that colonialism only loosens its hold when the knife is at its throat, no Algerian really found these terms too violent. The leaflet only expressed what every Algerian felt at heart: Colonialism is not a thinking machine, nor a body endowed with reasoning faculties. It is violence in its natural state, and it will only yield when confronted with greater violence.

At the decisive moment, the colonialist bourgeoisie, which up till then has remained inactive, comes into the field. It introduces that new idea which is in proper parlance a creation of the colonial situation: nonviolence. In its simplest form this nonviolence signifies to the intellectual and economic elite of the colonized country that the bourgeoisie has the same interests as them and that it is therefore urgent and indispensable to come to terms for the public good. Nonviolence is an attempt to settle the colonial problem around a green baize table, before any regrettable act has been performed or irreparable gesture made, before any blood has been shed. But if the masses, without waiting for the chairs to be arranged around the baize table, listen to their own voice and begin committing outrages and setting fire to buildings, the elites and the nationalist bourgeois parties will be seen rushing to the colonialists to exclaim, "This is very serious! We do not know how it will end; we must find a solution—some sort of compromise."

This idea of compromise is very important in the phenomenon of decolonization, for it is very far from being a simple one. Compromise involves the colonial system and the young nationalist bourgeoisie at one and the same time. The partisans of the colonial system discover that the masses may destroy everything. Blown-up bridges, ravaged farms, repressions, and fighting harshly disrupt the economy. Compromise is equally attractive to the nationalist bourgeoisie, who, since they are not clearly aware of the possible consequences of the rising storm, are genuinely afraid of being swept away by this huge hurricane and never stop saying to the settlers: "We are still capable of stopping the slaughter; the masses still have confidence in us; act quickly if you do not want to put everything in jeopardy." One step more, and the leader of the nationalist party keeps his distance with regard to that violence. He loudly proclaims that he has nothing to do with these Mau-Mau, these terrorists, these throat-slitters. At best, he shuts himself off in a no-man's-land between the terrorists and the settlers and willingly offers his services as go-between; that is to say, that as the settlers cannot discuss terms with these Mau-Mau, he himself will be quite willing to begin negotiations. Thus it is that the rearguard of the national struggle, that very party of people who have never ceased to be on the other side in the fight, find themselves somersaulted into the van of negotiations and compromise—precisely because that party has taken very good care never to break contact with colonialism. [. . .]

The settler's work is to make even dreams of liberty impossible for the native. The native's work is to imagine all possible methods for destroying the settler. On the logical plane, the Manichaeism of the settler produces a Manichaeism of the native. To the theory of the "absolute evil of the native" the theory of the "absolute evil of the settler" replies.

The appearance of the settler has meant in the terms of syncretism the death of the aboriginal society, cultural lethargy, and the petrification of individuals. For the native, life can only spring up again out of the rotting corpse of the settler. This, then, is the correspondence, term by term, between the two trains of reasoning.

But it so happens that for the colonized people this violence, because it constitutes their only work, invests their characters with positive and creative qualities. The practice of violence binds them together as a whole, since each individual forms a violent link in the great chain, a part of the great organism of violence which has surged upwards in reaction to the settler's violence in the beginning. The groups recognize each other and the future nation is already indivisible. The armed struggle mobilizes the people; that is to say, it throws them in one way and in one direction.

The mobilization of the masses, when it arises out of the war of liberation, introduces into each man's consciousness the ideas of a common cause, of a national destiny, and of a collective history. In the same way the second phase, that of the building-up of the nation, is helped on by the existence of this cement which has been mixed with blood and anger. Thus we come to a fuller appreciation of the originality of the words used in these underdeveloped countries. During the colonial period the people are called upon to fight against oppression; after national liberation, they are called upon to fight against poverty, illiteracy, and underdevelopment. The struggle, they say, goes on. The people realize that life is an unending contest.

We have said that the native's violence unifies the people. By its very structure, colonialism is separatist and regionalist. Colonialism does not simply state the existence of tribes; it also reinforces it and separates them. The colonial system encourages chieftaincies and keeps alive the old marabout confraternities. Violence is in action all-inclusive and national. It follows that it is closely involved in the liquidation of regionalism and of tribalism. Thus the national parties show no pity at all toward the caids and the customary chiefs. Their destruction is the preliminary to the unification of the people.

At the level of individuals, violence is a cleansing force. It frees the native from his inferiority complex and from his despair and inaction; it makes him fearless and restores his self-respect. Even if the armed struggle has been symbolic and the nation is demolished through a rapid movement of decolonization, the people have the time to see that the liberation has been the business of each and all and that the leader has no special merit. From thence comes that type of aggressive reticence with regard to the machinery of protocol which young governments quickly show. When the people have taken violent part in the national liberation they will allow no one to set themselves up as "liberators." They show themselves to be jealous of the results of their action and take good care not to place their future, their destiny, or the fate of their country in the hands of a living god. Yesterday they were completely irresponsible; today they mean to understand everything and make all decisions. Illuminated by violence, the consciousness of the people rebels against any pacification. From now on the demagogues, the opportunists, and the magicians have a difficult task. The action which has thrown them into a hand-to-hand struggle confers upon the masses a voracious taste for the concrete. The attempt at mystification becomes, in the long run, practically impossible.

PART VII

American Perspectives on
Nationalism

31

ABRAHAM LINCOLN

First Inaugural Address, March 1861

Apprehension seems to exist among the people of the southern states, that by the accession of a Republican administration, their property, and their peace, and personal security, are to be endangered. There has never been any reasonable cause for such apprehension. Indeed, the most ample evidence to the contrary has all the while existed, and been open to their inspection. It is found in nearly all the published speeches of him who now addresses you. I do but quote from one of those speeches when I declare that "I have no purpose, directly or indirectly, to interfere with the institution of slavery in the states where it exists. I believe I have no lawful right to do so, and I have no inclination to do so." Those who nominated and elected me did so with full knowledge that I had made this, and many similar declarations, and had never recanted them. [...]

It is seventy-two years since the first inauguration of a president under our national Constitution. During that period fifteen different and greatly distinguished citizens, have, in succession, administered the executive branch of the government. They have conducted it through many perils; and, generally, with great success. Yet, with all this scope for precedent, I now enter upon the same task for the brief constitutional term of four years, under great and peculiar difficulty. A disruption of the federal Union heretofore only menaced, is now formidably attempted.

I hold, that in contemplation of universal law, and of the Constitution, the Union of these states is perpetual. Perpetuity is implied, if not expressed, in the fundamental law of all national governments. It is safe to assert that no government proper, ever had a provision in its organic law for its own termination. Continue to execute all the express provisions of our national Constitution, and the Union will endure forever—it being impossible to destroy it, except by some action not provided for in the instrument itself.

Again, if the United States be not a government proper, but an association of states in the nature of contract merely, can it, as a contract, be peaceably unmade, by less than all the parties who made it? One party to a contract may violate it—break it, so to speak; but does it not require all to lawfully rescind it?

Descending from these general principles, we find the proposition that, in legal contemplation, the Union is perpetual, confirmed by the history of the Union itself. The Union is much older than the Constitution. It was formed in fact, by the Articles of Association in 1774. It was matured and continued by the Declaration of Independence in 1776. It was further matured and the faith of all the then thirteen states expressly plighted and engaged that it should be perpetual, by the Articles of Confederation in 1778. And finally, in 1787, one of the declared objects for ordaining and establishing the Constitution, was "*to form a more perfect union.*"

But if destruction of the Union, by one, or by a part only, of the states, be lawfully possible, the Union is *less* perfect than before the Constitution, having lost the vital element of perpetuity.

It follows from these views that no state, upon its own mere motion, can lawfully get out of the Union,—that *resolves* and *ordinances* to that effect are legally void, and that acts of violence, within any state or states, against the authority of the United States, are insurrectionary or revolutionary, according to circumstances.

I therefore consider that, in view of the Constitution and the laws, the Union is unbroken; and, to the extent of my ability, I shall take care, as the Constitution itself expressly enjoins upon me, that the laws of the Union be faithfully executed in all the states. Doing this I deem to be only a simple duty on my part; and I shall perform it, so far as practicable, unless my rightful masters, the American people, shall withhold the requisite means, or, in some authoritative manner, direct the contrary. I trust this will not be regarded as a menace, but only as the declared purpose of the Union that it *will* constitutionally defend, and maintain itself.

In doing this there needs to be no bloodshed or violence; and there shall be none, unless it be forced upon the national authority. The power confided to me, will be used to hold, occupy, and possess the property, and places belonging to the government, and to collect the duties and imposts; but beyond what may be necessary for these objects, there will be no invasion—no using of force against, or among the people anywhere. Where hostility to the United States, in any interior locality, shall be so great and so universal, as to prevent competent resident citizens from holding the federal offices, there will be no attempt to force obnoxious strangers among the people for that object. While the strict legal right may exist in the government to enforce the exercise of these offices, the attempt to do so would be so irritating, and so nearly impracticable with all, that I deem it better to forgo, for the time, the uses of such offices.

The mails, unless repelled, will continue to be furnished in all parts of the Union. So far as possible, the people everywhere shall have that sense of perfect security which is most favorable to calm thought and reflection. The course here indicated will be followed, unless current events, and experience, shall show a modification, or change, to be proper; and in every case and exigency, my best discretion will be exercised, according to circumstances actually existing, and with a view and a hope of a peaceful solution of the national troubles, and the restoration of fraternal sympathies and affections.

That there are persons in one section, or another who seek to destroy the Union at all events, and are glad of any pretext to do it, I will neither affirm or deny; but if there be such, I need address no word to them. To those, however, who really love the Union, may I not speak?

Before entering upon so grave a matter as the destruction of our national fabric, with all its benefits, its memories, and its hopes, would it not be wise to ascertain precisely why we do it? Will you hazard so desperate a step, while there is any possibility that any portion of the ills you fly from, have no real existence? Will you, while the certain ills you fly to, are greater than all the real ones you fly from? Will you risk the commission of so fearful a mistake?

All profess to be content in the Union, if all constitutional rights can be maintained. Is it true, then, that any right, plainly written in the Constitution, has been denied? I think not. Happily the human mind is so constituted, that no party can reach to the audacity of doing this. Think, if you can, of a single instance in which a plainly written provision of the Constitution has ever been denied. If, by the mere force of numbers, a majority should deprive a minority of any clearly written constitutional right, it might, in a moral point of view, justify revolution—certainly would, if such right were a vital one. But such is not our case. All the vital rights of minorities, and of individuals, are so plainly assured to them, by affirmations and negations, guaranties and prohibitions, in the Constitution, that controversies never arise concerning them. But no organic law can ever be framed with a provision specifically applicable to every question which may occur in practical administration. No foresight can anticipate, nor any document of reasonable length contain express provisions for all possible questions. Shall fugitives from labor be surrendered by national or by state authority? The Constitution does not expressly say. May Congress prohibit slavery in the territories? The Constitution does not expressly say. Must Congress protect slavery in the territories? The Constitution does not expressly say.

From questions of this class spring all our constitutional controversies, and we divide upon them into majorities and minorities. If the minority will not acquiesce, the majority must, or the government must cease. There is no other alternative; for continuing the government, is acquiescence on one side or the other. If a minority, in such case, will secede rather than acquiesce, they make a precedent which, in turn, will divide and ruin them; for a minority of their own will secede from them, whenever a majority refuses to be controlled by such minority. For instance, why may not any portion of a new confederacy, a year or two hence, arbitrarily secede again, precisely as portions of the present Union now claim to secede from it. All who cherish disunion sentiments, are now being educated to the exact temper of doing this. Is there such perfect identity of interests among the states to compose a new Union, as to produce harmony only, and prevent renewed secession?

Plainly, the central idea of secession, is the essence of anarchy. A majority, held in restraint by constitutional checks, and limitations, and always changing easily, with deliberate changes of popular opinions and sentiments, is the only true sovereign of a free people. Whoever rejects it, does, of necessity, fly to anarchy or to despotism. Unanimity is impossible; the rule of a minority, as a permanent arrangement, is wholly inadmissible; so that, rejecting the majority principle, anarchy, or despotism in some form, is all that is left.

I do not forget the position assumed by some, that constitutional questions are to be decided by the Supreme Court; nor do I deny that such decisions must be binding in any case, upon the parties to a suit, as to the object of that suit, while they are also entitled to very high respect and consideration, in all parallel cases, by all other departments of the government. And while it is obviously possible that such decision may be erroneous in any given case, still the evil effect following it, being limited to that particular case, with the chance that it may be overruled, and never become a precedent for other cases, can better be borne than could the evils of a different practice. At the same time the candid citizen must confess that if the policy of the government, upon vital questions, affecting the whole people, is to be irrevocably fixed by decisions of the Supreme Court, the instant they are made, in ordinary litigation between parties, in personal actions, the people will have ceased to be their own rulers, having, to that extent, practically resigned their government, into the hands of that eminent tribunal. Nor is there, in this view, any assault upon the Court, or the judges. It is a duty, from which they may not shrink, to decide cases properly brought before them; and it is no fault of theirs, if others seek to turn their decisions to political purposes.

One section of our country believes slavery is *right*, and ought to be extended, while the other believes it is *wrong*, and ought not to be extended. This is the only substantial dispute. The fugitive slave clause of the Constitution, and the law for the suppression of the foreign slave trade, are each as well enforced, perhaps, as any law can ever be in a community where the moral sense of the people imperfectly supports the law itself. The great body of the people abide by the dry legal obligation in both cases, and a few break over in each. This, I think, cannot be perfectly cured; and it would be worse in both cases *after* the separation of the sections, than before. The foreign slave trade, now imperfectly suppressed, would be ultimately revived without restriction, in one section; while fugitive slaves, now only partially surrendered, would not be surrendered at all, by the other.

Physically speaking, we cannot separate. We cannot remove our respective sections from each other, nor build an impassable wall between them.

A husband and wife may be divorced, and go out of the presence, and beyond the reach of each other; but the different parts of our country cannot do this. They cannot but remain face to face; and intercourse, either amicable or hostile, must continue between them. Is it possible then to make that intercourse more advantageous, or more satisfactory, *after* separation than *before*? Can aliens make treaties easier than friends can make laws? Can treaties be more faithfully enforced between aliens, than laws can among friends? Suppose you go to war, you cannot fight always; and when, after much loss on both sides, and no gain on either, you cease fighting, the identical old questions, as to terms of intercourse, are again upon you.

This country, with its institutions, belongs to the people who inhabit it. Whenever they shall grow weary of the existing government, they can exercise their *constitutional* right of amending it, or their *revolutionary* right to dismember, or overthrow it. I cannot be ignorant of the fact that many worthy, and patriotic citizens are desirous of having the national Constitution amended. While I make no recommendation of amendments, I fully recognize the rightful authority of the people over the whole subject, to be exercised in either of the modes prescribed in the instrument itself; and I should, under existing circumstances, favor, rather than oppose, a fair opportunity being afforded the people to act upon it.

I will venture to add that, to me, the convention mode seems preferable, in that it allows amendments to originate with the people themselves, instead of only permitting them to take, or reject, propositions, originated by others, not especially chosen for the purpose, and which might not be precisely such, as they would wish to either accept or refuse. I understand a proposed amendment to the Constitution—which amendment, however, I have not seen, has passed Congress, to the effect that the federal government, shall never interfere with the domestic institutions of the states, including that of persons held to service. To avoid misconstruction of what I have said, I depart from my purpose not to speak of particular amendments, so far as to say that, holding such a provision to now be implied constitutional law, I have no objection to its being made express, and irrevocable.

The chief magistrate derives all his authority from the people, and they have conferred none upon him to fix terms for the separation of the states. The people themselves can do this also if they choose; but the executive, as such, has nothing to do with it. His duty is to administer the present government, as it came to his hands, and to transmit it, unimpaired by him, to his successor.

Why should there not be a patient confidence in the ultimate justice of the people? Is there any better, or equal hope, in the world? In our present differences, is either party without faith of being in the right? If the Almighty Ruler of nations, with his eternal truth and justice, be on your side of the North, or on yours of the South, that truth, and that justice, will surely prevail, by the judgment of this great tribunal, the American people.

By the frame of the government under which we live, these same people have wisely given their public servants but little power for mischief; and have, with equal wisdom, provided for the return of that little to their own hands at very short intervals.

While the people retain their virtue, and vigilance, no administration, by any extreme of wickedness or folly, can very seriously injure the government, in the short space of four years.

My countrymen, one and all, think calmly and *well*, upon this whole subject. Nothing valuable can be lost by taking time. If there be an object to *hurry* any of you, in hot haste, to a step which you would never take *deliberately*, that object will be frustrated by taking time; but no good object can be frustrated by it. Such of you as are now dissatisfied, still have the old Constitution unimpaired, and, on the sensitive point, the laws of your own framing under it; while the new administration will have no immediate power, if it would, to change either. If it were admitted that you who are dissatisfied, hold the right side in the dispute, there still is no single good reason for precipitate action. Intelligence, patriotism, Christianity, and a firm reliance on Him, who has never yet forsaken this favored land, are still competent to adjust, in the best way, all our present difficulty.

In *your* hands, my dissatisfied fellow countrymen, and not in *mine*, is the momentous issue of civil war. The government will not assail *you*. You can have no conflict, without being yourselves the aggressors. *You* have no oath registered in heaven to destroy the government, while *I* shall have the most solemn one to "preserve, protect, and defend" it.

I am loath to close. We are not enemies, but friends. We must not be enemies. Though passion may have strained, it must not break our bonds of affection. The mystic chords of memory, stre[t]ching from every battlefield, and patriot grave, to every living heart and hearthstone, all over this broad land, will yet swell the chorus of the Union, when again touched, as surely they will be, by the better angels of our nature.

32

RANDOLPH BOURNE

Trans-National America

No reverberatory effect of the Great War has caused American public opinion more solicitude than the failure of the "melting pot." The discovery of diverse nationalistic feelings among our great alien population has come to most people as an intense shock. It has brought out the unpleasant inconsistencies of our traditional beliefs. We have had to watch hard-hearted old Brahmins virtuously indignant at the spectacle of the immigrant refusing to be melted, while they jeer at patriots like Mary Antin who write about "our forefathers." We have had to listen to publicists who express themselves as stunned by the evidence of vigorous nationalistic and cultural movements in this country among Germans, Scandinavians, Bohemians, and Poles, while in the same breath they insist that the alien shall be forcibly assimilated to the Anglo-Saxon tradition which they unquestioningly label "American."

As the unpleasant truth has come upon us that assimilation in this country was proceeding on lines very different from those we had marked out for it, we found ourselves inclined to blame those who were thwarting our prophecies. The truth became culpable. We blamed the war, we blamed the Germans. And then we discovered with a moral shock that these movements had been making great headway before the war even began. We found that the tendency, reprehensible and paradoxical as it might be, has been for the national clusters of immigrants, as they became more and more firmly established and more and more prosperous, to cultivate more and more assiduously the literatures and cultural traditions of their homelands. Assimilation, in other words, instead of washing out the memories of Europe, made them more and more intensely real. Just as these clusters became more and more objectively American, did they become more and more German or Scandinavian or Bohemian or Polish.

To face the fact that our aliens are already strong enough to take a share in the direction of their own destiny, and that the strong cultural movements represented by the foreign press, schools, and colonies are a challenge to our facile attempts, is not, however, to admit the failure of Americanization. It is not to fear the failure of democracy. It is rather to urge us to an investigation of what Americanism may rightly mean. It is to ask ourselves whether our ideal has been broad or narrow—whether perhaps the time has not come to assert a higher ideal than the "melting pot." Surely we cannot be certain of our spiritual democracy when, claiming to melt the nations within us to a comprehension of our free and democratic institutions, we fly into panic at the first sign of their own will and tendency. We act as if we wanted Americanization to take place only on our own terms, and not by the consent of the governed. All our elaborate machinery of settlement and school and union, of social and political naturalization, however, will move with friction just insofar as it neglects to take into account this strong and virile insistence that America shall be what the immigrant will have a hand in making it, and not what a ruling class, descendant of those British stocks which were the first permanent immigrants, decides that America shall be made. This is the condition which confronts us, and which demands a clear and general readjustment of our attitude and our ideal.

I

Mary Antin is right when she looks upon our foreign-born as the people who missed the *Mayflower* and came over on the first boat they could find. But she forgets that when they did come it was not upon other *Mayflowers*, but upon a *Maiblume*, a *Fleur de Mai*, a *Fior di Maggio*, a *Majblomst*. These people were not mere arrivals from the same family, to be welcomed as understood and long-loved, but strangers to the neighborhood, with whom a long process of settling down had to take place. For they brought with them their national and racial characters, and each new national quota had to wear slowly away the contempt with which its mere alienness got itself greeted. Each had to make its way slowly from the lowest strata of unskilled labor up to a level where it satisfied the accredited norms of social success.

We are all foreign-born or the descendants of foreign-born, and if distinctions are to be made between us they should rightly be on some other ground than indigenousness. The early colonists came over with motives no less colonial than the later. They did not come to be assimilated in an American melting pot. They did not come to adopt the culture of the American Indian. They had not the smallest intention of "giving themselves without reservation" to the new country. They came to get freedom to live as they wanted to. They came to escape from the stifling air and chaos of the old world; they came to make their fortune in a new land. They invented no new social framework. Rather they brought over bodily the old ways to which they had been accustomed. Tightly concentrated on a hostile frontier, they were conservative beyond belief. Their pioneer daring was reserved for the objective conquest of material resources. In their folkways, in their social and political institutions, they were, like every colonial people, slavishly imitative of the mother country. So that, in spite of the "Revolution," our whole legal and political system remained more English than the English, petrified and unchanging, while in England itself law developed to meet the needs of the changing times.

It is just this English-American conservatism that has been our chief obstacle to social advance. We have needed the new peoples—the order of the German and Scandinavian, the turbulence of the Slav and Hun—to save us from our own stagnation. I do not mean that the illiterate Slav is now the equal of the New Englander of pure descent. He is raw material to be educated, not into a New Englander, but into a socialized American along such lines as those thirty nationalities are being educated in the amazing schools of Gary. I do not believe that this process is to be one of decades of evolution. The spectacle of Japan's sudden jump from medievalism to post-modernism should have destroyed that superstition. We are not dealing with individuals who are to "evolve." We are dealing with their children, who, with that education we are about to have, will start level with all of us. Let us cease to think of ideals like democracy as magical qualities inherent in certain peoples. Let us speak, not of inferior races, but of inferior civilizations. We are all to educate and to be educated. These peoples in America are in a common enterprise. It is not what we are now that concerns us, but what this plastic next generation may become in the light of a new cosmopolitan ideal.

We are not dealing with static factors, but with fluid and dynamic generations. To contrast the older and the newer immigrants and see the one class as democratically motivated by love of liberty, and the other by mere money-getting, is not to illuminate the future. To think of earlier nationalities as culturally assimilated to America, while we picture the later as a sodden and resistive mass, makes only for bitterness and misunderstanding. There may be a difference between these earlier and these later stocks, but it lies neither in motive for coming nor in strength of cultural allegiance to the homeland. The truth is that no more tenacious cultural allegiance to the mother country has been shown by any alien nation than by the ruling class of Anglo-Saxon descendants in these American states. English snobberies, English religion, English literary styles, English literary reverences and canons, English ethics, English superiorities, have been the cultural food that we have drunk in from our mothers' breasts. The distinctively American spirit—pioneer, as distinguished from the reminiscently English— that appears in Whitman and Emerson and James, has had to exist on sufferance alongside of this other cult, unconsciously belittled by our cultural makers of opinion. No country has perhaps had so great indigenous genius which had so little influence on the country's traditions and expressions. The unpopular and dreaded German-American of the present day is a beginning amateur in comparison with those foolish Anglophiles of Boston and New York and Philadelphia whose reversion to cultural type sees uncritically in England's cause the cause of civilization, and, under the guise of ethical independence of thought, carries along European traditions which are no more "American" than the German categories themselves. [. . .]

The non-English American can scarcely be blamed if he sometimes thinks of the Anglo-Saxon predominance in America as little more than a predominance of priority. The Anglo-Saxon was merely the first immigrant, the first to found a colony. He has never really ceased to be the descendant of immigrants, nor has he ever succeeded in transforming that colony into a real nation, with a tenacious, richly woven fabric of native culture. Colonials from the other nations have come and settled down beside him. They found no definite native culture which should startle them out of their colonialism, and consequently they looked back to their mother country, as the earlier Anglo-Saxon immigrant was looking back to his. What has been offered the newcomer has been the chance to learn English, to become a citizen, to salute the flag. And those elements of our ruling classes who are responsible for the public schools, the settlements, all the organizations for amelioration in the cities, have every reason to be proud of the care and labor which they have devoted to absorbing the immigrant. His opportunities the immigrant has taken to gladly, with almost a pathetic eagerness to make his way in the new land without friction or disturbance. The common language has made not only for the necessary communication, but for all the amenities of life.

If freedom means the right to do pretty much as one pleases, so long as one does not interfere with others, the immigrant has found freedom, and the ruling element has been singularly liberal in its treatment of the invading hordes. But if freedom means a democratic cooperation in determining the ideals and purposes and industrial and social institutions of a country, then the immigrant has not been free, and the Anglo-Saxon element is guilty of just what every dominant race is guilty of in every European country: the imposition of its own culture upon the minority peoples. The fact that this imposition has been so mild and, indeed, semiconscious does not alter its quality. And the war has brought out just the degree to which that purpose of "Americanizing," that is to say, "Anglo-Saxonizing," the immigrant has failed. [. . .]

Let the Anglo-Saxon ask himself where he would have been if these races had not come? Let those who feel the inferiority of the non-Anglo-Saxon immigrant contemplate that region of the States which has remained the most distinctively "American," the South. Let him ask himself whether he would really like to see the foreign hordes Americanized into such an Americanization. Let him ask himself how superior this native civilization is to the great "alien" states of Wisconsin and Minnesota, where Scandinavians, Poles, and Germans have self-consciously labored to preserve their traditional culture, while being outwardly and satisfactorily American. Let him ask himself how much more wisdom, intelligence, industry, and social leadership has come out of these alien states than out of all the truly American ones. The South, in fact, while this vast northern development has gone on, still remains an English colony, stagnant and complacent, having progressed culturally scarcely beyond the early Victorian era. It is culturally sterile because it has had no advantage of cross-fertilization like the northern states. What has happened in states such as Wisconsin and Minnesota is that strong foreign cultures have struck root in a new and fertile soil. America has meant liberation, and German and Scandinavian political ideas and social energies have expanded to a new potency. The process has not been at all the fancied "assimilation" of the Scandinavian or Teuton. Rather has it been a process of their assimilation of us—I speak as an Anglo-Saxon. The foreign cultures have not been melted down or run together, made into some homogeneous Americanism, but have remained distinct but cooperating to the greater glory and benefit, not only of themselves but of all the native "Americanism" around them.

What we emphatically do not want is that these distinctive qualities should be washed out into a tasteless, colorless fluid of uniformity. Already we have far too much of this insipidity—masses of people who are cultural half-breeds, neither assimilated Anglo-Saxons nor nationals of another culture. Each national colony in this country seems to retain in its foreign press, its vernacular literature, its schools, its intellectual and patriotic leaders, a central cultural nucleus. From this nucleus the colony extends out by imperceptible gradations to a fringe where national characteristics are all but lost. Our cities are filled with these half-breeds who retain their foreign names but have lost the foreign savor. This does not mean that they have actually been changed into New Englanders or Middle Westerners. It does not mean that they have been really Americanized. It means that, letting slip from them whatever native culture they had, they have substituted for it only the most rudimentary American—the American culture of the cheap newspaper, the "movies," the popular song, the ubiquitous automobile. The unthinking who survey this class call them assimilated, Americanized. The great American public school has done its work. With these people our institutions are safe. We may thrill with dread at the aggressive hyphenate, but this tame flabbiness is accepted as Americanization. The same molders of opinion whose ideal is to melt the different races into Anglo-Saxon gold hail this poor product as the satisfying result of their alchemy.

Yet a truer cultural sense would have told us that it is not the self-conscious cultural nuclei that sap at our American life, but these fringes. It is not the Jew who sticks proudly to the faith of his fathers and boasts of that venerable culture of his who is dangerous to America, but the Jew who has lost the Jewish fire and become a mere elementary, grasping animal. It is not the Bohemian who supports the Bohemian schools in Chicago whose influence is sinister, but the Bohemian who has made money and has got into ward politics. Just so surely as we tend to disintegrate these nuclei of nationalistic culture do we tend to create hordes of men and women with-

out a spiritual country, cultural outlaws, without taste, without standards
but those of the mob. We sentence them to live on the most rudimentary
planes of American life. The influences at the center of the nuclei are
centripetal. They make for the intelligence and the social values which
mean an enhancement of life. And just because the foreign-born retains
this expressiveness is he likely to be a better citizen of the American community. The influences at the fringe, however, are centrifugal, anarchical.
They make for detached fragments of peoples. Those who came to find
liberty achieve only license. They become the flotsam and jetsam of American
life, the downward undertow of our civilization with its leering cheapness
and falseness of taste and spiritual outlook, the absence of mind and sincere feeling which we see in our slovenly towns, our vapid moving pictures,
our popular novels, and in the vacuous faces of the crowds on the city
street. This is the cultural wreckage of our time, and it is from the fringes
of the Anglo-Saxon as well as the other stocks that it falls. America has as
yet no impelling integrating force. It makes too easily for this detritus of
cultures. In our loose, free country, no constraining national purpose, no
tenacious folk tradition and folk style hold the people to a line.

The war has shown us that not in any magical formula will this purpose
be found. No intense nationalism of the European plan can be ours. But do
we not begin to see a new and more adventurous ideal? Do we not see how
the national colonies in America, deriving power from the deep cultural
heart of Europe and yet living here in mutual toleration, freed from the
agelong tangles of races, creeds, and dynasties, may work out a federated
ideal? America is transplanted Europe, but a Europe that has not been disintegrated and scattered in the transplanting as in some dispersion. Its colonies
live here inextricably mingled, yet not homogeneous. They merge but they
do not fuse.

America is a unique sociological fabric, and it bespeaks poverty of imagination not to be thrilled at the incalculable potentialities of so novel a
union of men. To seek no other goal than the weary old nationalism—belligerent,
exclusive, inbreeding, the poison of which we are witnessing now in Europe—
is to make patriotism a hollow sham, and to declare that, in spite of our
boastings, America must ever be a follower and not a leader of nations.

II

If we come to find this point of view plausible, we shall have to give up
the search for our native "American" culture. With the exception of the
South and that New England which, like the Red Indian, seems to be passing into solemn oblivion, there is no distinctively American culture. It is
apparently our lot rather to be a federation of cultures. This we have been
for half a century, and the war has made it ever more evident that this is
what we are destined to remain. This will not mean, however, that there

are not expressions of indigenous genius that could not have sprung from any other soil. [. . .]

Just insofar as our American genius has expressed the pioneer spirit, the adventurous, forward-looking drive of a colonial empire, is it representative of that whole America of the many races and peoples, and not of any partial or traditional enthusiasm. And only as that pioneer note is sounded can we really speak of the American culture. As long as we thought of Americanism in terms of the "melting pot," our American cultural tradition lay in the past. It was something to which the new Americans were to be molded. In the light of our changing ideal of Americanism, we must perpetrate the paradox that our American cultural tradition lies in the future. It will be what we all together make out of this incomparable opportunity of attacking the future with a new key. [. . .]

III

The failure of the melting pot, far from closing the great American democratic experiment, means that it has only just begun. Whatever American nationalism turns out to be, we see already that it will have a color richer and more exciting than our ideal has hitherto encompassed. In a world which has dreamed of internationalism, we find that we have all unawares been building up the first international nation. The voices which have cried for a tight and jealous nationalism of the European pattern are failing. From that ideal, however valiantly and disinterestedly it has been set for us, time and tendency have moved us further and further away. What we have achieved has been rather a cosmopolitan federation of national colonies, of foreign cultures, from which the sting of devastating competition has been removed. America is already the world federation in miniature, the continent where for the first time in history has been achieved that miracle of hope, the peaceful living side by side, with character substantially preserved, of the most heterogeneous peoples under the sun. Nowhere else has such contiguity been anything but the breeder of misery. Here, notwithstanding our tragic failures of adjustment, the outlines are already too clear not to give us a new vision and a new orientation of the American mind in the world.

It is for the American of the younger generation to accept this cosmopolitanism, and carry it along with self-conscious and fruitful purpose. In his colleges, he is already getting, with the study of modern history and politics, the modern literatures, economic geography, the privilege of a cosmopolitan outlook such as the people of no other nation of today in Europe can possibly secure. If he is still a colonial, he is no longer the colonial of one partial culture, but of many. He is a colonial of the world. Colonialism has grown into cosmopolitanism, and his motherhood is not one nation, but all who have anything life-enhancing to offer to the spirit. [. . .]

[. . .] The contribution of America will be an intellectual internationalism which goes far beyond the mere exchange of scientific ideas and discoveries and the cold recording of facts. It will be an intellectual sympathy
which is not satisfied until it has got at the heart of the different cultural
expressions, and felt as they feel. It may have immense preferences, but it
will make understanding and not indignation its end. Such a sympathy will
unite and not divide.

Against the thinly disguised panic which calls itself "patriotism" and the
thinly disguised militarism which calls itself "preparedness" the cosmopolitan ideal is set. This does not mean that those who hold it are for a policy
of drift. They, too, long passionately for an integrated and disciplined America.
But they do not want one which is integrated only for domestic economic
exploitation of the workers or for predatory economic imperialism among
the weaker peoples. They do not want one that is integrated by coercion or
militarism, or for the truculent assertion of a medieval code of honor and
of doubtful rights. They believe that the most effective integration will be
one which coordinates the diverse elements and turns them consciously
toward working out together the place of America in the world situation.
They demand for integration a genuine integrity, a wholeness and sound-
ness of enthusiasm and purpose which can only come when no national
colony within our America feels that it is being discriminated against or
that its cultural case is being prejudged. This strength of cooperation, this
feeling that all who are here may have a hand in the destiny of America,
will make for a finer spirit of integration than any narrow "Americanism"
or forced chauvinism.

In this effort we may have to accept some form of that dual citizenship
which meets with so much articulate horror among us. Dual citizenship we
may have to recognize as the rudimentary form of that international citizenship to which, if our words mean anything, we aspire. We have assumed
unquestioningly that mere participation in the political life of the United
States must cut the new citizen off from all sympathy with his old allegiance. Anything but a bodily transfer of devotion from one sovereignty to
another has been viewed as a sort of moral treason against the Republic.
We have insisted that the immigrant whom we welcomed escaping from
the very exclusive nationalism of his European home shall forthwith adopt
a nationalism just as exclusive, just as narrow, and even less legitimate because it is founded on no warm traditions of his own. [. . .]

Along with dual citizenship we shall have to accept, I think, that free and
mobile passage of the immigrant between America and his native land again
which now arouses so much prejudice among us. We shall have to accept the
immigrant's return for the same reason that we consider justified our own
flitting about the earth. To stigmatize the alien who works in America for
a few years and returns to his own land, only perhaps to seek American
fortune again, is to think in narrow nationalistic terms. It is to ignore the

cosmopolitan significance of this migration. It is to ignore the fact that the returning immigrant is often a missionary to an inferior civilization.

This migratory habit has been especially common with the unskilled laborers who have been pouring into the United States in the last dozen years from every country in southeastern Europe. Many of them return to spend their earnings in their own country or to serve their country in war. But they return with an entirely new critical outlook, and a sense of the superiority of American organization to the primitive living around them. This continued passage to and fro has already raised the material standard of living in many regions of these backward countries. For these regions are thus endowed with exactly what they need, the capital for the exploitation of their natural resources, and the spirit of enterprise. America is thus educating these laggard peoples from the very bottom of society up, awaking vast masses to a newborn hope for the future. In the migratory Greek, therefore, we have not the parasitic alien, the doubtful American asset, but a symbol of that cosmopolitan interchange which is coming, in spite of all war and national exclusiveness.

Only America, by reason of the unique liberty of opportunity and traditional isolation for which she seems to stand, can lead in this cosmopolitan enterprise. Only the American—and in this category I include the migratory alien who has lived with us and caught the pioneer spirit and a sense of new social vistas—has the chance to become that citizen of the world. America is coming to be, not a nationality but a trans-nationality, a weaving back and forth, with the other lands, of many threads of all sizes and colors. Any movement which attempts to thwart this weaving, or to dye the fabric any one color, or disentangle the threads of the strands, is false to this cosmopolitan vision. I do not mean that we shall necessarily glut ourselves with the raw product of humanity. It would be folly to absorb the nations faster than we could weave them. We have no duty either to admit or reject. It is purely a question of expediency. What concerns us is the fact that the strands are here. We must have a policy and an ideal for an actual situation. Our question is, What shall we do with our America? How are we likely to get the more creative America—by confining our imaginations to the ideal of the melting pot, or broadening them to some such cosmopolitan conception as I have been vaguely sketching? [. . .]

The war has shown America to be unable, though isolated geographically and politically from a European world situation, to remain aloof and irresponsible. She is a wandering star in a sky dominated by two colossal constellations of states. Can she not work out some position of her own, some life of being in, yet not quite of, this seething and embroiled European world? This is her only hope and promise. A trans-nationality of all the nations, it is spiritually impossible for her to pass into the orbit of any one. It will be folly to hurry herself into a premature and sentimental nationalism, or to emulate Europe and play fast and loose with the forces that drag into war. No Americanization will fulfill this vision which does not recognize the uniqueness of this trans-nationalism of ours. The Anglo-Saxon attempt to fuse will only create enmity and distrust. The crusade against "hyphenates" will only inflame the partial patriotism of trans-nationals, and cause them to assert their European traditions in strident and unwholesome ways. But the attempt to weave a wholly novel international nation out of our chaotic America will liberate and harmonize the creative power of all these peoples and give them the new spiritual citizenship, as so many individuals have already been given, of a world.

33

MARCUS GARVEY

The Resurrection of the Negro

WHAT WE BELIEVE

The Universal Negro Improvement Association advocates the uniting and blending of all Negroes into one strong, healthy race. It is against miscegenation and race suicide.

It believes that the Negro race is as good as any other, and therefore should be as proud of itself as others are.

It believes in the purity of the Negro race and the purity of the white race.

It is against rich blacks marrying poor whites.

It is against rich or poor whites taking advantage of Negro women.

It believes in the spiritual Fatherhood of God and the Brotherhood of Man.

It believes in the social and political physical separation of all peoples to the extent that they promote their own ideals and civilization, the privilege of trading and doing business with each other. It believes in the promotion of a strong and powerful Negro nation in Africa.

It believes in the rights of all men.

SPEECH TO THE SECOND INTERNATIONAL CONVENTION
OF NEGROES, AUGUST 1921

Four years ago, realizing the oppression and the hardships from which we suffered, we organized ourselves into an organization for the purpose of bettering our condition, and founding a government of our own. The four years of organization have brought good results, in that from an obscure, despised race we have grown into a mighty power, a mighty force whose influence is being felt throughout the length and breadth of the world. The Universal Negro Improvement Association existed but in name four years ago, today it is known as the greatest moving force among Negroes. We have accomplished this through unity of effort and unity of purpose, it is a fair demonstration of what we will be able to accomplish in the very near future, when the millions who are outside the pale of the Universal Negro Improvement Association will have linked themselves up with us.

By our success of the last four years we will be able to estimate the grander success of a free and redeemed Africa. In climbing the heights to where we are today, we have had to surmount difficulties, we have had to climb over obstacles, but the obstacles were stepping-stones to the future greatness of this cause we represent. Day by day we are writing a new history, recording new deeds of valor performed by this race of ours. It is true that the world has not yet valued us at our true worth, but we are climbing up so fast and with such force that every day the world is changing its attitude toward us. Wheresoever you turn your eyes today you will find the moving influence of the Universal Negro Improvement Association among Negroes from all corners of the globe. We hear among Negroes the cry of "Africa for the Africans." This cry has become a positive, determined one. It is a cry that is raised simultaneously the world over because of the universal oppression that affects the Negro. You who are congregated here tonight as delegates representing the hundreds of branches of the Universal Negro Improvement Association in different parts of the world will realize that we in New York are positive in this great desire of a free and redeemed Africa. We have established this Liberty Hall as the center from which we send out the sparks of liberty to the four corners of the globe, and if you have caught the spark in your section, we want you to keep it a burning for the great cause we represent.

There is a mad rush among races everywhere toward national independence. Everywhere we hear the cry of liberty, of freedom, and a demand for democracy. In our corner of the world we are raising the cry for liberty, freedom, and democracy. Men who have raised the cry for freedom and liberty in ages past have always made up their minds to die for the realization of the dream. We who are assembled in this convention as delegates representing the Negroes of the world give out the same spirit that the fathers of liberty in this country gave out over one hundred years ago. We give out a spirit that knows no compromise, a spirit that refuses to turn back, a spirit that says "Liberty or Death," and in prosecution of this great ideal—the ideal of a free and redeemed Africa, men may scorn, men may spurn us, and may say that we are on the wrong side of life, but let me tell you that way in which you are traveling is just the way all peoples who are free have traveled in the past. If you want liberty you yourselves must strike the blow. If you must be free you must become so through your own effort, through your own initiative. Those who have discouraged you in the past are those who have enslaved you for centuries and it is not expected that they will admit that you have a right to strike out at this late hour for freedom, liberty, and democracy.

At no time in the history of the world, for the last five hundred years, was there ever a serious attempt made to free Negroes. We have been camouflaged into believing that we were made free by Abraham Lincoln. That we were made free by Victoria of England, but up to now we are still slaves, we are industrial slaves, we are social slaves, we are political slaves, and the new Negro desires a freedom that has no boundary, no limit. We desire a freedom that will lift us to the common standard of all men, whether they be white men of Europe or yellow men of Asia, therefore, in our desire to lift ourselves to that standard we shall stop at nothing until there is a free and redeemed Africa.

I understand that just at this time while we are endeavoring to create public opinion and public sentiment in favor of a free Africa, that others of our race are being subsidized to turn the attention of the world toward a different desire on the part of Negroes, but let me tell you that Africa must be free. The enemy may argue with you to show you the impossibility of a free and redeemed Africa, but I want you to take as your argument the thirteen colonies of America, that once owed their sovereignty to Great Britain, that sovereignty has been destroyed to make a United States of America. George Washington was not God Almighty. He was a man like any Negro in this building, and if he and his associates were able to make a free America, we too can make a free Africa. Hampden, Gladstone, Pitt, and Disraeli were not the representatives of God in the person of Jesus Christ. They were but men, but in their time they worked for the expansion of the British Empire, and today they boast of a British Empire upon which "the sun never sets." As Pitt and Gladstone were able to work for the expansion of the British Empire, so you and I can work for the expansion of a great African Empire. Voltaire and Mirabeau were not Jesus Christs, they were but men like ourselves. They worked and overturned the French monarchy. They worked for the democracy which France now enjoys, and if they were able to do that, we are able to work for a democracy in Africa. Lenin and Trotsky were not Jesus Christs, but they were able to overthrow the despotism of Russia, and today they have given to the world a social republic, the first of its kind. If Lenin and Trotsky were able to do that for Russia, you and I can do that for Africa. Therefore, let no man, let no power on earth, turn you from this sacred cause of liberty. I prefer to die at this moment rather than not to work for the freedom of Africa. If liberty is good for certain sets of humanity it is good for all. Black men, colored men, Negroes have as much right to be free as any other race that God Almighty ever created, and we desire freedom that is unfettered, freedom that is unlimited, freedom that will give us a chance and opportunity to rise to the fullest of our ambition and that we cannot get in countries where other men rule and dominate.

We have reached the time when every minute, every second must count for something done, something achieved in the cause of Africa. We need the freedom of Africa now, therefore, we desire the kind of leadership that will give it to us as quickly as possible. You will realize that not only individuals, but governments are using their influence against us. But what do we care about the unrighteous influence of any government? Our cause is based upon righteousness. And everything that is not righteous we have no respect for, because God Almighty is our leader and Jesus Christ our standard-bearer. We rely on them for that kind of leadership that will make us free, for it is the same God who inspired the Psalmist to write "Princes shall come out of Egypt and Ethiopia shall stretch out her hands unto God." At this moment methinks I see Ethiopia stretching forth her hands unto God and methinks I see the Angel of God taking up the standard of the Red, the Black, and the Green, and saying "Men of the Negro Race, Men of Ethiopia, follow me." Tonight we are following. We are following 400,000,000 strong. We are following with a determination that we must be free before the wreck of matter, before the crash of worlds.

It falls to our lot to tear off the shackles that bind Mother Africa. Can you do it? You did it in the Revolutionary War. You did it in the Civil War; you did it at the Battles of the Marne and Verdun; you did it in Mesopotamia. You can do it marching up the battle heights of Africa. Let the world know that 400,000,000 Negroes are prepared to die or live as free men. Despise us as much as you care. Ignore us as much as you care. We are coming 400,000,000 strong. We are coming with our woes behind us, with the memory of suffering behind us—woes and suffering of three hundred years—they shall be our inspiration. My bulwark of strength in the conflict for freedom in Africa, will be the three hundred years of persecution and hardship left behind in this Western Hemisphere. The more I remember the suffering of my forefathers, the more I remember the lynchings and burnings in the southern states of America, the more I will fight on even though the battle seems doubtful. Tell me that I must turn back, and I laugh you to scorn. Go on! Go on! Climb ye the heights of liberty and cease not in well doing until you have planted the banner of the Red, the Black, and the Green on the hilltops of Africa.

34

WOODROW WILSON

Address to a Joint Session of Congress, January 1918

Gentlemen of the Congress: Once more, as repeatedly before, the spokesmen of the Central Empires have indicated their desire to discuss the objects of the war and the possible bases of a general peace. Parleys have
been in progress at Brest-Litovsk between representatives of the Central
Powers, to which the attention of all the belligerents has been invited for
the purpose of ascertaining whether it may be possible to extend these parleys into a general conference with regard to terms of peace and settlement. The Russian representatives presented not only a perfectly definite
statement of the principles upon which they would be willing to conclude
peace, but also an equally definite program of the concrete application of
those principles. The representatives of the Central Powers, on their part,
presented an outline of settlement which, if much less definite, seemed
susceptible of liberal interpretation until their specific program of practical
terms was added. That program proposed no concessions at all either to the
sovereignty of Russia or to the preferences of the populations with whose
fortunes it dealt, but meant, in a word, that the Central Empires were to
keep every foot of territory their armed forces had occupied—every province, every city, every point of vantage—as a permanent addition to their
territories and their power. It is a reasonable conjecture that the general
principles of settlement which they at first suggested originated with the
more liberal statesmen of Germany and Austria, the men who have begun
to feel the force of their own peoples' thought and purpose, while the concrete terms of actual settlement came from the military leaders who have
no thought but to keep what they have got. The negotiations have been
broken off. The Russian representatives were sincere and in earnest. They
cannot entertain such proposals of conquest and domination.

The whole incident is full of significance. It is also full of perplexity.
With whom are the Russian representatives dealing? For whom are the representatives of the Central Empires speaking? Are they speaking for the
majorities of their respective parliaments or for the minority parties, that
military and imperialistic minority which has so far dominated their whole

policy and controlled the affairs of Turkey and of the Balkan states which have felt obliged to become their associates in this war? The Russian representatives have insisted, very justly, very wisely, and in the true spirit of modern democracy, that the conferences they have been holding with the Teutonic and Turkish statesmen should be held within open, not closed doors, and all the world has been audience, as was desired. To whom have we been listening, then? To those who speak the spirit and intention of the Resolutions of the German Reichstag of the ninth of July last, the spirit and intention of the liberal leaders and parties of Germany, or to those who resist and defy that spirit and intention and insist upon conquest and subjugation? Or are we listening, in fact, to both, unreconciled and in open and hopeless contradiction? These are very serious and pregnant questions. Upon the answer to them depends the peace of the world.

But, whatever the results of the parleys at Brest-Litovsk, whatever the confusions of counsel and of purpose in the utterances of the spokesmen of the Central Empires, they have again attempted to acquaint the world with their objects in the war and have again challenged their adversaries to say what their objects are and what sort of settlement they would deem just and satisfactory. There is no good reason why that challenge should not be responded to, and responded to with the utmost candor. We did not wait for it. Not once, but again and again, we have laid our whole thought and purpose before the world, not in general terms only, but each time with sufficient definition to make it clear what sort of definitive terms of settlement must necessarily spring out of them. Within the last week Mr. Lloyd George has spoken with admirable candor and in admirable spirit for the people and government of Great Britain. There is no confusion of counsel among the adversaries of the Central Powers, no uncertainty of principle, no vagueness of detail. The only secrecy of counsel, the only lack of fearless frankness, the only failure to make definite statement of the objects of the war, lies with Germany and her Allies. The issues of life and death hang upon these definitions. No statesman who has the least conception of his responsibility ought for a moment to permit himself to continue this tragical and appalling outpouring of blood and treasure unless he is sure beyond a peradventure that the objects of the vital sacrifice are part and parcel of the very life of society and that the people for whom he speaks think them right and imperative as he does.

There is, moreover, a voice calling for these definitions of principle and of purpose which is, it seems to me, more thrilling and more compelling than any of the many moving voices with which the troubled air of the world is filled. It is the voice of the Russian people. They are prostrate and all but helpless, it would seem, before the grim power of Germany, which has hitherto known no relenting and no pity. Their power, apparently, is shattered. And yet their soul is not subservient. They will not yield either in principle or in action. Their conception of what is right, of what is

humane and honorable for them to accept, has been stated with a frankness, a largeness of view, a generosity of spirit, and a universal human sympathy which must challenge the admiration of every friend of mankind;
and they have refused to compound their ideals or desert others that they
themselves may be safe. They call to us to say what it is that we desire, in
what, if in anything, our purpose and our spirit differ from theirs; and I
believe that the people of the United States would wish me to respond,
with utter simplicity and frankness. Whether their present leaders believe
it or not, it is our heartfelt desire and hope that some way may be opened
whereby we may be privileged to assist the people of Russia to attain their
utmost hope of liberty and ordered peace.

It will be our wish and purpose that the processes of peace, when they
are begun, shall be absolutely open and that they shall involve and permit
henceforth no secret understandings of any kind. The day of conquest and
aggrandizement is gone by; so is also the day of secret covenants entered
into in the interest of particular governments and likely at some unlooked
for moment to upset the peace of the world. It is this happy fact, now clear
to the view of every public man whose thoughts do not still linger in an
age that is dead and gone, which makes it possible for every nation whose
purposes are consistent with justice and the peace of the world to avow
now or at any other time the objects it has in view.

We entered this war because violations of right had occurred which touched
us to the quick and made the life of our own people impossible unless they
were corrected and the world secured once and for all against their recurrence. What we demand in this war, therefore, is nothing peculiar to ourselves. It is that the world be made fit and safe to live in; and particularly
that it be made safe for every peace-loving nation which, like our own,
wishes to live its own life, determine its own institutions, be assured of
justice and fair dealing by the other peoples of the world as against force
and selfish aggression. All the peoples of the world are in effect partners in
this interest, and for our own part we see very clearly that unless justice be
done to others it will not be done to us. The program of the world's peace,
therefore, is our program; and that program, the only possible program, as
we see it, is this:

1. Open covenants of peace, openly arrived at, after which there shall be
no private international understandings of any kind but diplomacy shall
proceed always frankly and in the public view.

2. Absolute freedom of navigation upon the seas, outside territorial waters,
alike in peace and in war, except as the seas may be closed in whole or in
part by international action for the enforcement of international covenants.

3. The removal, so far as possible, of all economic barriers and the establishment of an equality of trade conditions among all the nations consent-
ing to the peace and associating themselves for its maintenance.

4. Adequate guarantees given and taken that national armaments will be

reduced to the lowest point consistent with domestic safety.

5. A free, open-minded, and absolutely impartial adjustment of all colonial claims, based upon a strict observance of the principle that in determining all such questions of sovereignty the interests of the populations concerned must have equal weight with the equitable claims of the government whose title is to be determined.

6. The evacuation of all Russian territory and such a settlement of all questions affecting Russia as will secure the best and freest cooperation of the other nations of the world in obtaining for her an unhampered and unembarrassed opportunity for the independent determination of her own political development and national policy and assure her of a sincere welcome into the society of free nations under institutions of her own choosing; and, more than a welcome, assistance also of every kind that she may need and may herself desire. The treatment accorded Russia by her sister nations in the months to come will be the acid test of their good will, of their comprehension of her needs as distinguished from their own interests, and of their intelligent and unselfish sympathy.

7. Belgium, the whole world will agree, must be evacuated and restored, without any attempt to limit the sovereignty which she enjoys in common with all other free nations. No other single act will serve as this will serve to restore confidence among the nations in the laws which they have themselves set and determined for the government of their relations with one another. Without this healing act the whole structure and validity of international law is forever impaired.

8. All French territory should be freed and the invaded portions restored, and the wrong done to France by Prussia in 1871 in the matter of Alsace-Lorraine, which has unsettled the peace of the world for nearly fifty years, should be righted, in order that peace may once more be made secure in the interests of all.

9. A readjustment of the frontiers of Italy should be effected along clearly recognizable lines of nationality.

10. The peoples of Austria-Hungary, whose place among the nations we wish to see safeguarded and assured, should be accorded the freest opportunity of autonomous development.

11. Rumania, Serbia, and Montenegro should be evacuated; occupied territories restored; Serbia accorded free and secure access to the sea; and the relations of the several Balkan states to one another determined by friendly counsel along historically established lines of allegiance and nationality; and international guarantees of the political and economic independence and territorial integrity of the several Balkan states should be entered into.

12. The Turkish portions of the present Ottoman Empire should be assured a secure sovereignty, but the other nationalities which are now under Turkish rule should be assured an undoubted security of life and an absolutely

unmolested opportunity of autonomous development, and the Dardanelles should be permanently opened as a free passage to the ships and commerce of all nations under international guarantees.

13. An independent Polish state should be erected which should include the territories inhabited by indisputably Polish populations, which should be assured a free and secure access to the sea, and whose political and economic independence and territorial integrity should be guaranteed by international covenant.

14. A general association of nations must be formed under specific covenants for the purpose of affording mutual guarantees of political independence and territorial integrity to great and small states alike.

In regard to these essential rectifications of wrong and assertions of right we feel ourselves to be intimate partners of all the governments and peoples associated together against the Imperialists. We cannot be separated in interest or divided in purpose. We stand together until the end.

For such arrangements and covenants we are willing to fight and to continue to fight until they are achieved; but only because we wish the right to prevail and desire a just and stable peace such as can be secured only by removing the chief provocations to war, which this program does remove. We have no jealousy of German greatness, and there is nothing in this program that impairs it. We grudge her no achievement or distinction of learning or of pacific enterprise such as have made her record very bright and very enviable. We do not wish to injure her or to block in any way her legitimate influence or power. We do not wish to fight her either with arms or with hostile arrangements of trade if she is willing to associate herself with us and the other peace-loving nations of the world in covenants of justice and law and fair dealing. We wish her only to accept a place of equality among the peoples of the world—the new world in which we now live—instead of a place of mastery.

Neither do we presume to suggest to her any alteration or modification of her institutions. But it is necessary, we must frankly say, and necessary as a preliminary to any intelligent dealings with her on our part, that we should know whom her spokesmen speak for when they speak to us, whether for the Reichstag majority or for the military party and the men whose creed is imperial domination.

We have spoken now, surely, in terms too concrete to admit of any further doubt or question. An evident principle runs through the whole program I have outlined. It is the principle of justice to all peoples and nationalities, and their right to live on equal terms of liberty and safety with one another, whether they be strong or weak. Unless this principle be made its foundation no part of the structure of international justice can stand. The people of the United States could act upon no other principle; and to the vindication of this principle they are ready to devote their lives, their honor, and everything that they possess. The moral climax of this the culminating and final war for human liberty has come, and they are ready to put their own strength, their own highest purpose, their own integrity and devotion to the test.

35

REINHOLD NIEBUHR

Moral Man and Immoral Society

THE MORALITY OF NATIONS

The difference between the attitudes of individuals and those of groups has been frequently alluded to, the thesis being that group relations can never be as ethical as those which characterize individual relations. In dealing with the problem of social justice, it may be found that the relation of economic classes within a state is more important than international relations. But from the standpoint of analyzing the ethics of group behavior, it is feasible to study the ethical attitudes of nations first; because the modern nation is the human group of strongest social cohesion, of most undisputed central authority, and of most clearly defined membership. The church may have challenged its pre-eminence in the Middle Ages, and the economic class may compete with it for the loyalty of men in our own day; yet it remains, as it has been since the seventeenth century, the most absolute of all human associations.

Nations are territorial societies, the cohesive power of which is supplied by the sentiment of nationality and the authority of the state. The fact that state and nation are not synonymous and that states frequently incorporate several nationalities, indicates that the authority of government is the ultimate force of national cohesion. The fact that state and nation are roughly synonymous proves that, without the sentiment of nationality with its common language and traditions, the authority of government is usually unable to maintain national unity. The unity of Scotland and England within a single British state and the failure to maintain the same unity between England and Ireland, suggest both the possibilities and the limitations of transcending nationality in the formation of states. For our purposes we may think of state and nation as interchangeable terms, since our interest is in the moral attitudes of nations which have the apparatus of a state at their disposal, and through it are able to consolidate their social power and define their political attitudes and policies.

The selfishness of nations is proverbial. It was a dictum of George Washington that nations were not to be trusted beyond their own interest. "No state," declares the German author Johannes Haller, "has ever entered a treaty for any other reason than self interest," and adds: "A statesman who has any other motive would deserve to be hung." "In every part of the world," said Professor Edward Dicey, "where British interests are at stake, I am in favor of advancing these interests even at the cost of war. The only qualification I admit is that the country we desire to annex or take under our protection should be calculated to confer a tangible advantage upon the British Empire." National ambitions are not always avowed as honestly as this, as we shall see later, but that is a fair statement of the actual facts, which need hardly to be elaborated for any student of history.

What is the basis and reason for the selfishness of nations? If we begin with what is least important or least distinctive of national attitudes, it must be noted that nations do not have direct contact with other national communities, with which they must form some kind of international community. They know the problems of other peoples only indirectly and at second hand. Since both sympathy and justice depend to a large degree upon perception of need, which makes sympathy flow, and upon the understanding of competing interests, which must be resolved, it is obvious that human communities have greater difficulty than individuals in achieving ethical relationships. While rapid means of communication have increased the breadth of knowledge about world affairs among citizens of various nations, and the general advance of education has ostensibly promoted the capacity to think rationally and justly upon the inevitable conflicts of interest between nations, there is nevertheless little hope of arriving at a perceptible increase of international morality through the growth of intelligence and the perfection of means of communication. The development of international commerce, the increased economic interdependence among the nations, and the whole apparatus of a technological civilization, increase the problems and issues between nations much more rapidly than the intelligence to solve them can be created. The silk trade between America and Japan did not give American citizens an appreciation of the real feelings of the Japanese toward the American Exclusion Act. Cooperation between America and the Allies during the war did not help American citizens to recognize, and deal sympathetically with, the issues of inter-allied debts and reparations; nor were the Allies able to do justice to either themselves or their fallen foe in settling the problem of reparations. Such is the social ignorance of peoples, that, far from doing justice to a foe or neighbor, they are as yet unable to conserve their own interests wisely. Since their ultimate interests are always protected best, by at least a measure of fairness toward their neighbors, the desire to gain an immediate selfish advantage always imperils their ultimate interests. If they recognize this fact, they usually recognize it too late. Thus France, after years of intransigence, has finally accepted a sensible reparations settlement. Significantly and tragically, the settlement is almost synchronous with the victory of an extreme nationalism in Germany, which her unrelenting policies begot. America pursued a selfish and foolhardy tariff policy until it, together with other imbecilities in international life, contributed to the ruin of prosperity in the whole world. Britain, though her people are politically more intelligent than those of any modern nation, did not yield in Ireland in time to prevent the formation of a virus which is still poisoning Anglo-Irish relations. And while the American Civil War taught her a lesson, which she applied in preserving her colonial empire, there is as yet no proof that she will be wise enough to admit India into partnership, before the vehemence of Indian reaction to British imperialism will make partnership upon even a minimum basis impossible. So runs the sad story of the social ignorance of nations. [. . .]

It is of course possible that the rational interest in international justice may become, on occasion, so widespread and influential that it will affect the diplomacy of states. But this is not usual. In other words the mind, which places a restraint upon impulses in individual life, exists only in a very inchoate form in the nation. It is moreover, much more remote from the will of the nation than in private individuals; for the government expresses the national will, and that will is moved by the emotions of the populace and the prudential self-interest of dominant economic classes. Theoretically it is possible to have a national electorate so intelligent, that the popular impulses and the ulterior interests of special groups are brought under the control of a national mind. But practically the rational understanding of political issues remains such a minimum force that national unity of action can be achieved only upon such projects as are either initiated by the self-interest of the dominant groups, in control of the government, or supported by the popular emotions and hysterias which from time to time run through a nation. In other words the nation is a corporate unity, held together much more by force and emotion, than by mind. Since there can be no ethical action without self-criticism, and no self-criticism without the rational capacity of self-transcendence, it is natural that national attitudes can hardly approximate the ethical. Even those tendencies toward self-criticism in a nation which do express themselves are usually thwarted by the governing classes and by a certain instinct for unity in society itself. For self-criticism is a kind of inner disunity, which the feeble mind of a nation finds difficulty in distinguishing from dangerous forms of inner conflict. So nations crucify their moral rebels with their criminals upon the same Golgotha, not being able to distinguish between the moral idealism which surpasses, and the antisocial conduct which falls below that moral mediocrity, on the level of which every society unifies its life. While critical loyalty toward a community is not impossible, it is not easily achieved. It is therefore probably inevitable that every society should regard criticism as a proof of a want of loyalty. This lack of criticism, as Tyrrell the Catholic modernist observed, makes the social will more egotistic than the individual will. "So far as society has a self," he wrote, "it must be self-assertive, proud, self-complacent and egotistical."

The necessity of using force in the establishment of unity in a national community, and the inevitable selfish exploitation of the instruments of coercion by the groups who wield them, adds to the selfishness of nations. This factor in national life has been previously discussed and may need no further elaboration. It may be well to add that it ought not to be impossible to reduce this source of national selfishness. When governing groups are deprived of their special economic privileges, their interests will be more nearly in harmony with the interests of the total national society. At present the economic overlords of a nation have special interests in the profits of international trade, in the exploitation of weaker peoples, and in the acquisition of raw materials and markets, all of which are only remotely relevant to the welfare of the whole people. They are relevant at all only because, under the present organization of society, the economic life of a whole nation is bound up with the private enterprises of individuals. Furthermore the unequal distribution of wealth under the present economic system concentrates wealth which cannot be invested, and produces goods which cannot be absorbed, in the nation itself. The whole nation is therefore called upon to protect the investments and the markets which the economic overlords are forced to seek in other nations. If a socialist commonwealth should succeed in divorcing privilege from power, it would thereby materially reduce the selfishness of nations, though it is probably romantic to hope, as most socialists do, that all causes of international friction would be abolished. Wars were waged before the modern capitalistic social order existed, and they may continue after it is abolished. The greed of the capitalistic classes has sharpened, but not created, the imperialism of nations. [. . .]

The social ignorance of the private citizen of the nation has thus far been assumed. It may be reasonable to hope that the general level of intelligence will greatly increase in the next decades and centuries and that growing social intelligence will modify national attitudes. It is doubtful whether it will ever increase sufficiently to eliminate all the moral hazards of international relations. There is an ethical paradox in patriotism which defies every but the most astute and sophisticated analysis. The paradox is that patriotism transmutes individual unselfishness into national egoism. Loyalty to the nation is a high form of altruism when compared with lesser loyalties and more parochial interests. It therefore becomes the vehicle of all the altruistic impulses and expresses itself, on occasion, with such fervor that the critical attitude of the individual toward the nation and its enterprises is almost completely destroyed. The unqualified character of this devotion is the very basis of the nation's power and of the freedom to use the power without moral restraint. Thus the unselfishness of individuals makes for the selfishness of nations. That is why the hope of solving the larger social problems of mankind, merely by extending the social sympathies of individuals, is so vain. Altruistic passion is sluiced into the reservoirs of nationalism with great ease, and is made to flow beyond them with great difficulty. What lies beyond the nation, the community of mankind, is too vague to inspire devotion. The lesser communities within the nation, religious, economic, racial, and cultural, have equal difficulty in competing with the nation for the loyalty of its citizens. The church was able to do so when it had the prestige of a universality it no longer possesses. Future developments may make the class rather than the nation the community of primary loyalty. But for the present the nation is still supreme. It not only possesses a police power, which other communities lack, but it is able to avail itself of the most potent and vivid symbols to impress its claims upon the consciousness of the individual. Since it is impossible to become conscious of a large social group without adequate symbolism this factor is extremely important. The nation possesses in its organs of government, in the panoply and ritual of the state, in the impressive display of its fighting services, and, very frequently, in the splendors of a royal house, the symbols of unity and greatness, which inspire awe and reverence in the citizen. Furthermore the love and pious attachment of a man to his countryside, to familiar scenes, sights, and experiences, around which the memories of youth have cast a halo of sanctity, all this flows into the sentiment of patriotism; for a simple imagination transmutes the universal beneficences of nature into symbols of the peculiar blessings which a benevolent nation bestows upon its citizens. Thus the sentiment of patriotism achieves a potency in the modern soul, so unqualified, that the nation is given carte blanche to use the power, compounded of the devotion of individuals, for any purpose it desires. Thus, to choose an example among hundreds, Mr. Lloyd George during the famous Agadir Crisis in 1911 in which a European war became imminent, because marauding nations would not allow a new robber to touch their spoils in Africa, could declare in his Mansion House speech: "If a situation were to be forced upon us in which peace could only be preserved by the surrender of the great and beneficent position Britain has won by centuries of heroism and achievement, by allowing Britain to be treated, when her interests were vitally affected, as if she were of no account in the cabinet of nations, then I say emphatically that peace at that price would be a humiliation intolerable for a great country like ours to endure." The very sensitive "honor" of nations can always be appeased by the blood of its citizens and no national ambition seems too base or petty to claim and to receive the support of a majority of its patriots. [. . .]

A combination of unselfishness and vicarious selfishness in the individual thus gives a tremendous force to national egoism, which neither religious nor rational idealism can ever completely check. The idealists, whose patriotism has been qualified by more universal loyalties, must always remain a minority group. In the past they have not been strong enough to affect the actions of nations and have had to content themselves with a policy of disassociation from the nation in times of crisis, when national ambitions were in sharpest conflict with their moral ideals. Whether conscientious pacifism on the part of two percent of a national population could actually prevent future wars, as Professor Einstein maintains, is a question which cannot be answered affirmatively with any great degree of certainty. It is much more likely that the power of modern nationalism will remain essentially unchecked, until class loyalty offers it effective competition.

Perhaps the most significant moral characteristic of a nation is its hypocrisy. We have noted that self-deception and hypocrisy is an unvarying element in the moral life of all human beings. It is the tribute which morality pays to immorality; or rather the device by which the lesser self gains the consent of the larger self to indulge in impulses and ventures which the rational self can approve only when they are disguised. One can never be quite certain whether the disguise is meant only for the eye of the external observer or whether, as may be usually the case, it deceives the self. Naturally this defect in individuals becomes more apparent in the less moral life of nations. Yet it might be supposed that nations, of whom so much less is expected, would not be under the necessity of making moral pretensions for their actions. There was probably a time when they were under no such necessity. Their hypocrisy is both a tribute to the growing rationality of man and a proof of the case with which rational demands may be circumvented.

The dishonesty of nations is a necessity of political policy if the nation is to gain the full benefit of its double claim upon the loyalty and devotion of the individual, as his own special and unique community and as a community which embodies universal values and ideals. The two claims, the one touching the individual's emotions and the other appealing to his mind, are incompatible with each other, and can be resolved only through dishonesty. This is particularly evident in wartime. Nations do not really arrive at full self-consciousness until they stand in vivid, usually bellicose, juxtaposition to other nations. The social reality, comprehended in the existence of a nation, is too large to make a vivid impression upon the imagination of the citizen. He vaguely identifies it with his own little community and fireside and usually accepts the mythos which attributes personality to his national group. But the impression is not so vivid as to arouse him to any particular fervor of devotion. This fervor is the unique product of the times of crisis, when his nation is in conflict with other nations. It springs from the new vividness with which the reality and the unity of his nation's discreet existence is comprehended. In other words, it is just in the moments when the nation is engaged in aggression or defense (and it is always able to interpret the former in terms of the latter) that the reality of the nation's existence becomes so sharply outlined as to arouse the citizen to the most passionate and uncritical devotion toward it. But at such a time the nation's claim to uniqueness also comes in sharpest conflict with the generally accepted impression that the nation is the incarnation of universal values. This conflict can be resolved only by deception. In the imagination of the simple patriot the nation is not a society but Society. Though

its values are relative they appear, from his naïve perspective, to be absolute. The religious instinct for the absolute is no less potent in patriotic
religion than in any other. The nation is always endowed with an aura of
the sacred, which is one reason why religions, which claim universality, are
so easily captured and tamed by national sentiment, religion and patriotism
merging in the process. [. . .]

If it is true that the nations are too selfish and morally too obtuse and
self-righteous to make the attainment of international justice without the
use of force possible, the question arises whether there is a possibility of
escape from the endless round of force avenging ancient wrongs and creating new ones, of victorious Germany creating a vindictive France and victorious France poisoning Germany with a sense of outraged justice. The
morality of nations is such that, if there be a way out, it is not as easy as
the moralists of both the prewar and postwar period have assumed.

Obviously one method of making force morally redemptive is to place it
in the hands of a community, which transcends the conflicts of interest
between individual nations and has an impartial perspective upon them.
That method resolves many conflicts within national communities, and the
organization of the League of Nations is ostensibly the extension of that
principle to international life. But if powerful classes in national societies
corrupt the impartiality of national courts, it may be taken for granted that
a community of nations, in which very powerful and very weak nations are
bound together, has even less hope of achieving impartiality. Furthermore
the prestige of the international community is not great enough, and it
does not sufficiently qualify the will-to-power of individual nations, to achieve
a communal spirit sufficiently unified, to discipline recalcitrant nations.
Thus Japan was able to violate her covenants in her conquest of Manchu-
ria, because she shrewdly assumed that the seeming solidarity of the League
of Nations was not real, and that it only thinly veiled without restraining
the peculiar policies of various great powers, which she would be able to
tempt and exploit. Her assumption proved correct, and she was able to win
the quasi-support of France and to weaken the British support of League
policies. Her success in breaking her covenants with impunity has thrown
the weakness of our inchoate society of nations into vivid light. This weakness, also revealed in the failure of the recent Disarmament Conference
and the abortive character of all efforts to resolve the anarchy of national
tariffs, justifies the pessimistic conclusion that there is not yet a political
force capable of bringing effective social restraint upon the self-will of nations, at least not upon the powerful nations. Even if it should be possible
to maintain peace on the basis of the international status quo, there is no
evidence that an unjust peace can be adjusted by pacific means. A society
of nations has not really proved itself until it is able to grant justice to
those who have been worsted in battle without requiring them to engage in
new wars to redress their wrongs.

Since the class character of national governments is a primary, though not the only cause of their greed, present international anarchy may continue until the fear of catastrophe amends, or catastrophe itself destroys, the present social system and builds more cooperative national societies. There may not be enough intelligence in modern society to prevent catastrophe. There is certainly not enough intelligence to prompt our generation to a voluntary reorganization of society, unless the fear of imminent catastrophe quickens the tempo of social change.

PART VIII

The Contemporary Debate on Nationalism

36

MICHAEL WALZER

The New Tribalism: Notes on a Difficult Problem

All over the world today, but most interestingly and frighteningly in Eastern Europe and the Soviet Union, men and women are reasserting their local and particularist, their ethnic, religious, and national identities. The tribes have returned, and the drama of their return is greatest where their repression was most severe. It is now apparent that the popular energies mobilized against totalitarian rule, and also the more passive stubbornness and evasiveness that eroded the Stalinist regimes from within, were fueled in good part by "tribal" loyalties and passions. How these were sustained and reproduced over time is a tale that waits to be told. The tribes—most of them, at least, and all the minorities and the subject nations—were for several generations denied access to the official organs of social reproduction: the public schools and the mass media. I imagine tens of thousands of old men and women whispering to their grandchildren, singing folk songs and lullabies, repeating ancient stories. This is in many ways a heartening picture, for it suggests the inevitability of totalitarian failure. But what are we to make of the songs and stories, often as full of hatred for neighboring nations as of hope for national liberation?

The left has never understood the tribes. Faced with their contemporary resurgence, the first response is to argue for their containment within established multinational states—democratically transformed, of course, but not divided. This looks very much like a systematic repetition of the response of early twentieth-century Social Democrats to the nationalist movements that challenged the old empires. The "internationalism" of the left owes a great deal to Hapsburg and Romanov imperialism, even if leftists always intended to dispense with the dynasties. So many nations lived together in peace under imperial rule: Why couldn't they continue to live together under the aegis of social democracy? So many nations lived together in peace under communist rule: Why...? When Western Europe is forging a new unity, how can anyone defend separation in the East?

But unity in the West is itself the product of, or at least the historical successor to separation. The independence of Sweden from Denmark and, centuries later, of Norway from Sweden (and of Finland from Sweden and Russia) opened the way for Scandinavian cooperation. The division of Belgium and Holland, and the failures of French imperialism, made possible the Benelux experiment. Centuries of sovereignty for the great states of Western Europe preceded the achievement of European community. It is important to note that what was achieved first, before community, was not only sovereign statehood but also democratic government. The Swedes could have held Norway indefinitely under one or another form of authoritarian rule. But the practice of democracy, even in its earliest stages, made it clear that there was more than one *demos*, and then separation became necessary if democracy was to be sustained. The case is the same in the East. Multinationalism as it has existed there is a function of predemocratic or antidemocratic politics. But bring the "people" into political life and they will arrive, marching in tribal ranks and orders, carrying with them their own languages, historic memories, customs, beliefs, and commitments. And once they have been summoned, once they have arrived, it isn't possible to do them justice within the old political order.

Maybe it's not possible to do them justice at all. In Eastern Europe to-day, and in Caucasia, and in much of the Middle East, the prospects don't seem bright, given the sheer number of suddenly raucous tribes and the radical entanglement of their members on the same bits and pieces of land. Good fences make good neighbors only when there is some minimal agreement on where the fences should go. In the West, powerful states were created before the appearance of nationalist ideology, and they managed to repress and incorporate many of the smaller nations (Welsh, Scots, Normans, Bretons, and so on). The separations I have already noted took place alongside constructive processes that created large nation-states with more or less iden·tifiable boundaries and more or less committed members. Similar efforts in Eastern Europe seem to have failed: There aren't many committed Yugoslav or Soviet citizens. The abandonment of these identities is startling in its scope and speed, and it leaves many people who had traveled under their protection suddenly vulnerable: Serbs in Croatia, Albanians in Serbia, Armenians in Azerbaijan, Russians in the Baltic states, Jews in Russia, and so on, endlessly.

There doesn't seem to be any humane or decent way to disentangle the tribes, and at the same time the entanglements are felt to be dangerous— not only to individual life, which is reasonable enough, but also to communal well-being. Demagogues exploit the hopes for national revival, linguistic autonomy, the free development of schools and media—all supposedly threatened by cosmopolitan or antinational minorities. And other demagogues exploit the fears of the minorities, defending ancient irredentisms and looking (like the Serbs in Croatia) for outside help. In such circumstances, it is hard to say what justice means, let alone what policies it might require.

Hence the impulse of the left, uncomfortable in any case with particularist passions, to cling to whatever unities exist and make them work. The argument is very much like that of a Puritan minister in the 1640s, defending the union of husband and wife against the new doctrine of divorce: "If they might be separated for discord, some would make a commodity of strife; but now they are not best to be contentious, for the law will hold their noses together 'til weariness make them leave off struggling."

The problem, then as now, is that justice, whatever it requires, doesn't seem to permit the kinds of coercion that would be necessary to "hold their noses together." So we have to think about divorce, despite its difficulties. It is some help that divorce among nations needn't have the singular legal form of divorce in families. Self-determination for husbands and wives is relatively simple, even when important constraints are imposed upon the separated individuals. Self-determination for the many different kinds of tribes (nations, ethnic groups, religious communities) is bound to be more complicated, and the constraints that follow upon separation more various. There is room for maneuver.

I doubt that we can find a single rule or set of rules that will determine the form of the separation and the necessary constraints. But there is a general principle, which we can think of as the expression of democracy in international politics. What is at stake is the value of a historical or cultural or religious community and the political liberty of its members. This liberty is not compromised, it seems to me, by the postmodern discovery that communities are social constructions: imagined, invented, put together. Constructed communities are the only communities there are; they can't be less real or less authentic than some other sort. Their members, then, have the rights that go with membership. *They ought to be allowed to govern themselves*—insofar as they can do that, given their local entanglements.

Democracy has, of course, no natural units. Self-determination has no absolute subject. Cities, nations, federations, immigrant societies—all these can be and have been governed democratically. The contemporary tribes most certain of their singular identity and culture (the Poles or Armenians, say) are in fact historical composites. If we go back far enough in their history, we will find people's noses being held together (that's one of the methods of social construction). But if the descendants of these people, forgetting ancient indignities, regard themselves now as *fellow* members of a "community of character," within which they find identity, self-respect, and sentimental connections, why should we deny them democratic self-government?

Except... unless... were it not for the fact that the self-government of tribe A, happily divorced, makes tribe B a vulnerable and unhappy minority in its own homeland. Locked into an independent Croatia, Serbs believe (not implausibly) that they will live in insecurity. And then, surely,

the political unit has to be territorial, not cultural: All the tribes and fragments of tribes that live *here*—noses held together 'til they leave off struggling—must come under the authority of a neutral state and share a
characterless citizenship. But these can't be our only options: the dominance of one tribe or a common detribalization. For the second of the two,
if it isn't a mere cover for the first, would require coercion of a sort that,
as I have already suggested, is neither morally permissible nor politically
effective. We would not be worrying about Croatia and its Serbs, after all,
if Yugoslavia had succeeded in imposing itself upon its constituent nations;
it was, in theory at least, the very model of a neutral state.

Neutrality is likely to work well only in immigrant societies where everyone has been similarly and in most cases voluntarily transplanted, cut off
from homeland and history. In such cases—America is the prime example—tribal feelings are relatively weak. But how can one create a neutral
state in France, say, where the anciently established French rule democratically over the new immigrants from North Africa (even though the immigrants, many of them, hold "French" citizenship)? What imperial, bureaucratic,
or international authority could detribalize the French? Or the Poles in
Poland? Or the Georgians in an independent Georgia? Or the Croats in
Croatia? And then the only way to avoid domination is to multiply political units and jurisdictions, permitting a series of separations. But the series
will be endless—so we are told—each divorce justifying the next one, smaller
and smaller groups claiming the rights of self-determination; and the politics that results will be noisy, incoherent, unstable, and deadly.

I want to argue that this is a slippery slope down which we need not slide.
In fact, there are many conceivable arrangements between dominance and
detribalization and between dominance and separation—and there are moral
and political reasons for choosing different arrangements in different circumstances. The principle of self-determination is subject to interpretation
and amendment. What has been called "the national question" doesn't have
a single correct answer, as if there were only one way of "being" a nation,
one version of national history, one model of relationships among nations.
History reveals many ways, versions, and models, and so it suggests the
existence of many (more or less secure) stopping points along the slippery
slope. Consider now some of the more likely possibilities.

The easiest case is that of the "captive," that is, recently and coercively
incorporated, nation—the Baltic states are nice examples, since these were
genuine nation-states, the nationality ancient even if statehood was only
recently achieved and briefly held. The captivity was wrong for the same
reasons that the capture was wrong. The principle involved is the familiar
one that makes aggression a criminal act. What it requires now is the restoration of independence and sovereignty—which is to say: What principle

requires is what practice in this case has achieved. And by a kind of imaginative extension, we can grant the same rights to nations that *ought to have been* independent, where the solidarity of the group is plain to see and the crime of the ruling power is national oppression rather than conquest. I see no reason to deny the justice of separation in all such cases.

Except... unless... conquest and oppression are not merely abstract crimes; they have consequences in the real world: the mixing up of peoples, the creation of new and heterogeneous populations. Suppose that Russian immigrants now made up a majority of the people living in Latvia: Would any right remain of Latvian self-determination? Suppose that French colonists had come (by 1950, say) to outnumber the Arabs and Berbers of Algeria: Would the right of "Algerian" self-determination reside with the French majority? These are doubly hard questions; they are painful and they are difficult. The world changes, not necessarily in morally justifiable ways; and rights can be lost or, at least, diminished through no fault of the losers. We might want to argue for partition in cases like the ones I've just described, leaving the "natives" with less than they originally claimed; or we might want to design a regime of cultural autonomy instead of the political sovereignty that once seemed morally necessary. We look for the nearest possible arrangement to whatever was *ex ante* just, taking into account now what justice requires for the immigrants and colonists, or their children, who are not themselves the authors of the conquest or the oppression.

The case is the same with anciently incorporated nations—aboriginal peoples like the Native Americans or the Maori in New Zealand. Their rights too are eroded with time, not because the wrong done to them is wiped out (it may well grow greater, with increasingly deleterious effects on their communal life), but because the possibility no longer exists for the restoration of anything remotely resembling their former independence. They stand somewhere between a captive nation and a national, ethnic, or religious minority. Something more than equal citizenship is due them, some degree of collective self-rule, but exactly what this might mean in practice will depend on the residual strength of their own institutions and on the character of their engagement in the common life of the larger society. They cannot claim any absolute protection against the pressures and attractions of the common life—as if they were an endangered species. Confronted with modernity, all the human tribes are endangered species. All of them, whether or not they possess sovereign power, have been significantly transformed. We can recognize what might be called a right to resist transformation, to build walls against modern culture, and we can give this right more or less scope depending on constitutional structures and local circumstances; we cannot guarantee the success of the resistance.

The just treatment of national minorities depends on two sets of distinctions: first, between territorially concentrated and dispersed minorities; and second, between minorities radically different from and those that are only marginally different from the majority population. In practice, of course, both distinctions are really unmarked continuums, but it is best to begin with the clear cases. Consider, for example, a minority community with a highly distinctive history and culture and a strong territorial base—like the Albanians in Kosovo, for example. Their fellow nationals hold the adjoining state; they are trapped on the wrong side of the border as a result of some dynastic marriage or military victory long ago. The humane solution to their difficulty is to move the border; the brutal solution is to "transfer" the people; and the best practical possibility is some strong version of local autonomy, focused on cultural and educational institutions and the revenues that support them.

The opposite case is that of a marginally differentiated and territorially dispersed community, something like the ethnic and religious groups of North America (though there are exceptions in both categories: the ethnic French in Quebec, say, and the religious Amish in Pennsylvania). By and large, the experience of marginal difference and territorial dispersion gives rise to very limited claims on the state—a good reason for doubting the dangers of the slippery slope. A genuinely equal citizenship and the freedom to express their differences in the voluntary associations of civil society: This is what the members of such minorities commonly, and rightly, ask for. They may also seek some kind of subsidy from state funds for their schools, day-care centers, old-age homes, and so on. But that is a request that hangs more on political judgments than on moral principles. We will have to form an opinion about the inner strengths and weaknesses of the existing civil society. (A group that has been severely discriminated against, however, and whose access to resources is limited, does have a moral claim on the state.)

Once again, majorities have no obligation to guarantee the survival of minority cultures. They may well be struggling to survive themselves, caught up in a common competition against commercialism and international fashion. Borders provide only minimal protection in the modern world, and minorities within borders, driven by their situation to a preternatural closeness, may do better in sustaining a way of life than the more relaxed majority population. And if they do worse, that is no reason to come to their rescue; they have a claim, indeed, to physical but not to cultural security.

The adjustment of claims to circumstances is often a long and brutal business, but it does happen. We see it today, for example, in the geographically concentrated but only marginally different nations of Western Europe—Welsh, Scots, Normans, Bretons, and so on—whose members have consistently declined to support radical nationalist parties demanding independence and sovereign power. In cases like these, some sort of minimalist regionalism seems both to suit the people involved (small numbers of them—political, not ethnic or religious, minorities—always excepted) and to be politically and morally suitable. The case is the same with small or dispersed but significantly different populations, like the Amish or like Orthodox Jews in the United States, who commonly aim at a highly localized and apolitical separatism: segregated neighborhoods and parochial schools. This too seems to suit the people involved, and it is politically and morally suitable. But no theory of justice can specify the precise form of these arrangements. In fact, the forms are historically negotiated, and they depend upon shared understandings of what such negotiations mean and how they work. The Welsh and Scots have had a hand in the development of British political culture, even if this is not quite the hand they think they ought to have had. Hence their ready adjustment to parliamentary politics. Both the Amish and the Jews have learned, and added to, the repertoire of American pluralism.

Arrangements of these sorts should always be allowed, but they can't be imposed. What has made *Great* Britain possible is probably the common Protestantism of its component nations. The effort to include the Irish failed miserably. Today, the inclusion of the Slovenes in greater Yugoslavia seems to have failed for similar reasons. The case is the same for the failure of communist internationalism in Poland and Pan-Arabism in Lebanon. But I don't mean to argue that the religious differences crucial in all these cases necessarily make for separation. Sometimes they do and sometimes they don't. The differences are different in each case. They have more to do with memory and feeling than with any objective measure of dissimilarity. That's why models like my own, based on such factors as territorial concentration and cultural difference, can never be anything more than rough guides. We have to work slowly and experimentally toward arrangements that satisfy the members (not the militants) of this or that minority. There is no single correct outcome.

This experimental work is certain to be complicated by the unequal economic resources of the different tribes. It is obviously an incentive to divorce if one of the partners—a nation, say, industrially advanced or in control of mineral resources—can improve its position by walking away from the existing union. The other partners are left worse off, though some of them, at least, were never involved in any sort of national oppression. They will contest the divorce, but what they are probably entitled to, it seems to me, is the international equivalent of alimony and child support. Long-established patterns of cooperation cannot be abruptly terminated to the advantage of the most advantaged partners. On the other hand, the partners are not bound to stay together forever—not if they are, in fact, different tribes, who meet the democratic standards for autonomy or independence.

Often enough, separatist movements in the economically advantaged provinces or regions of some established union do not meet those standards. The best example is the Katangan secession of 1961, inspired, it appears, by Belgian entrepreneurs and corporate interests, without locally rooted support or, at least, without any visible signs of national mobilization. In such cases, it is entirely justifiable for unionist forces to resist the secession and to seek (and receive) international support. Obviously, there is such a thing as inauthentic tribalism: here, the manipulation of potential but not yet politically realized differences for economic gain. It doesn't follow, however, that every wealthy or resourceful tribe is inauthentic. And so there are also cases in which resistance to secession is not justified and should not be internationally supported—so long as some agreement can be negotiated that meets the interests of the people left behind. Their fear of impoverishment must be weighed against the fear of oppression or exploitation on the part of the seceding group or against its desire for cultural expression and political freedom.

The dominant feeling that makes for national antagonism, the most important cause (not the only cause) of all the tribal wars, is fear. Here I mean to follow an old argument first made in Thomas Hobbes's *Leviathan*, where it forms part of the explanation for the "war of all against all." Hobbes was thinking of the internal wars of late medieval "bastard feudalism" but also—more pertinently for our purposes—of the religious wars of his own time. There are always a few people, he writes, who "take pleasure in contemplating their own power in acts of conquest." But the greater number by far are differently motivated: They "would be glad to be at ease within modest bounds." These ordinary men and women are driven to fight not by their lust for power or enrichment, not by their bigotry or fanaticism, but by their fear of conquest and oppression. Hobbes argues that only an absolute sovereign can free them from this fearfulness and break the cycle of threats and "anticipations" (that is, preemptive violence). In fact, however, what broke the cycle, in the case of the religious wars, was not so much political absolutism as religious toleration.

The two crucial seventeenth-century arguments against toleration sound very familiar today, for they closely parallel the arguments against national separation and autonomy. The first of the two is the claim of the dominant religious establishments to represent some high value—universal truth or the divine will—that is certain to be overwhelmed in the cacophony of religious dissidence. And the second is the slippery slope argument: that the dissidence will prove endless and the new sectarianism endlessly divisive, split following split until the social order crumbles into incoherence and chaos. Certainly, toleration opened the way for a large number of new sects, though these have mostly flourished on the margins of more or less stable religious communities. But it also, and far more importantly, lowered the stakes of religious conflict: Toleration made divisiveness more tolerable. It solved the problem of fear by creating protected spaces for a great diversity of religious practices.

It seems to me that we should aim at something very much like this today: protected spaces of many different sorts matched to the needs of the different tribes. Rather than supporting the existing unions, I would be inclined to support separation whenever separation is demanded by a political movement that, so far as we can tell, represents the popular will. Let the people go who want to go. Many of them won't go all that far. And if there turn out to be political or economic disadvantages in their departure, they will find a way to reestablish connections. Indeed, if some sort of union—federation or confederation—is our goal, the best way to reach it is to abandon coercion and allow the tribes first to separate and then to negotiate their own voluntary and gradual, even if only partial, adherence to some new community of interest. Today's European Community is a powerful example, which other nations will approach at their own pace.

But—again—one nation's independence may be the beginning of another nation's oppression. It often seems as if the chief motive for national liberation is not to free oneself from minority status in someone else's country but to acquire (and then mistreat) minorities of one's own. The standard rule of intertribal relations is: Do unto others what has been done to you. Arguing for liberation, I have largely ignored the consistent failure of new nation-states to meet the moral test of the nation that comes next, to recognize in others the rights vindicated by their own independence. I don't mean to underestimate the nastiness of tribal zealots. But weren't the zealots of the religious wars equally nasty? And their latter-day descendants seem harmless enough—not particularly attractive, most of them, but also not very dangerous. Why shouldn't the same sequence, harmlessness following upon nastiness, hold for contemporary nationalists? Put them in a world where they are not threatened, and for how long will they think it in their interests to threaten others?

That at least is the Hobbesian argument. No doubt there are men and women in every tribe—Serbs and Croats; Latvians, Georgians, and Russians; Greeks and Turks; Israeli Jews and Palestinian Arabs—who take pleasure in acts of conquest, who aim above all to triumph over their neighbors and enemies. But these people will not rule in their own tribes if we can make it possible for their compatriots to live "at ease within modest bounds." Every tribe within its own modest bounds: This is the political equivalent of toleration for every church and sect. What makes it possible—though still politically difficult and uncertain—is that the bounds need not enclose, in every case, the same sort of space.

Religious toleration, however, was enforced by the state, and the godly zealots were disarmed and disempowered by the political authorities. Tribal zealots, by contrast, aim precisely at empowerment; they hope to become political authorities themselves, replacing the imperial bureaucrats who once forced them to live peacefully with their internal minorities. Who will restrain them after independence? Who will protect the Serbs in an independent Croatia or the Albanians in an independent Serbia? I have no easy answer to these questions. In a liberal democracy, national minorities can seek constitutional protection. But not many of the new nations are likely to be liberal, even if they achieve some version of democracy. The best hope for restraint lies, I think, in federal or confederal checks and balances and in international pressure. The nationality treaties of the interwar period were notable failures, but some measure of success in protecting minorities ought to be possible if nation-states are sufficiently entangled with and dependent on one another. Suppose that the leaders of the European Community of the World Bank or even the United Nations were to say to every nation seeking statehood: We will recognize your independence, trade with you or provide economic assistance—but only if you find some way to accommodate the national minorities that fear your sovereign power. The price of recognition and aid is accommodation.

What form this accommodation might take is not a matter to be determined in any a priori way (I have to keep saying this because so many people are looking for a quick theoretical fix). It will depend on the character of the new states and on a process of negotiation. Secession, border revision, federation, regional or functional autonomy, cultural pluralism: There are many possibilities and no reason to think that the choice of one of these in this or that case makes a similar choice necessary in all the other cases. As the examples I have cited from Western Europe suggest, choices are more likely to be determined by circumstances than by abstract principles. What is required is an international consensus that validates a variety of choices, supporting any political arrangement that satisfies the tribes at risk.

But there is no guarantee of satisfaction, and, sometimes, watching the tribal wars, some of us may yearn for the uniform repressiveness of imperial or even totalitarian rule. For wasn't this repression undertaken in the name, at least, of universalism? And mightn't it have produced, had it only been sustained long enough, a genuine detribalization? And then we would look back and say that just as the absolutism of early modern monarchs was necessary to defeat the aristocracy and eliminate feudalism, so the absolutism of imperial and communist bureaucrats was necessary to overcome tribalism. Perhaps the bureaucracies collapsed too soon, before they could complete their "historical task." But this line of argument repeats again the left's misunderstanding of the tribes. It is no doubt true that particular tribes can be destroyed by repression, if it is cruel enough and if it lasts long enough. The destruction of tribalism itself, however, lies beyond the reach of any repressive power. It is no one's "historical task." Feudalism is the name of a regime, and regimes can be replaced. Tribalism names the commitment of individuals and groups to their own history, culture, and identity, and this commitment (though not any particular version of it) is a permanent feature of human social life. The parochialism that it breeds is similarly permanent. It can't be overcome; it has to be accommodated, and therefore the crucial universal principle is that it must always be accommodated: not only my parochialism but yours as well, and his and hers in their turn.

When my parochialism is threatened, then I am wholly, radically parochial: a Serb, a Pole, a Jew, and nothing else. But this is an artificial situation in the modern world (and perhaps in the past too). The self is more naturally divided; at least, it is capable of division and even thrives on it. Under conditions of security, I will acquire a more complex identity than the idea of tribalism suggests. I will identify myself with more than one tribe; I will be an American, a Jew, an Easterner, an intellectual, a professor. Imagine a similar multiplication of identities around the world, and the world begins to look like a less dangerous place. When identities are multiplied, passions are divided.

We need to think about the political structures best suited to this multiplication and division. These won't be unitary structures; nor will they be identical. Some states will be rigorously neutral, with a plurality of cultures and a common citizenship; some will be federations; some will be nation-states, with minority autonomy. Sometimes cultural pluralism will be expressed only in private life; sometimes it will be expressed publicly. Sometimes different tribes will be mixed on the ground; sometimes they will be territorially grouped. Since the nature and the number of our identities will be different, even characteristically different for whole populations, a great variety of arrangements ought to be expected and welcomed. Each of them will have its usefulness and its irritations; none of them will be permanent; the negotiation of difference will never produce a final settlement. What this also means is that our common humanity will never make us members of a single universal tribe. The crucial commonality of the human race is particularism. With the end of imperial and totalitarian rule, we can at last recognize this commonality and begin the difficult negotiations it requires.

37

JÜRGEN HABERMAS

Citizenship and National Identity: Some Reflections on the Future of Europe

Three historical currents of our contemporary period, once again in flux, touch upon the relation between citizenship and national identity. First, the issue of the future of the nation-state has unexpectedly become topical in the wake of German unification, the liberation of the east central European states, and the nationality conflicts that are breaking out throughout Eastern Europe. Second, the fact that the states of the European Community are gradually growing together, especially with the impending caesura which will be created by the introduction of a common market in 1993, sheds some light on the relation between nation-state and democracy, for the democratic processes that have gone hand in hand with the nation-state lag hopelessly behind the supranational form taken by economic integration. Third, the tremendous influx of immigration from the poor regions of the East and South with which Europe will be increasingly confronted in the coming years lends the problem of asylum seekers a new significance and urgency. This process exacerbates the conflict between the universalistic principles of constitutional democracies on the one hand and the particularistic claims of communities to preserve the integrity of their *habitual* ways of life on the other. [. . .]

I. THE PAST AND FUTURE OF THE NATION-STATE

Recent events in Germany and the Eastern European countries have given a new twist to the discussion in the former Federal Republic on the gradual development of postnational society. Many German intellectuals have complained about the democratic deficit incurred by a process of unification that has been effected more at an administrative and economic level than by enlisting the participation of the citizens; they now find themselves accused of "postnational arrogance." The controversy as to the form and speed of unification has not only been fueled by contradictory feelings, but also by confusing thoughts and concepts. One side conceived of the five new states' joining the Federal Republic as restoring the unity of a nation-state torn apart four decades ago. From this viewpoint, the nation constitutes the prepolitical unity of a community with a shared common historical destiny. The other side conceived of the political unification as restoring democracy and a constitutional state in a territory where civil rights had been suspended in one form or another since 1933. From this viewpoint, what used to be West Germany was no less a nation of citizens than is the new Federal Republic. With this republican usage, the term "nation-state" is stripped of precisely those prepolitical connotations with which the expression was laden in modern Europe. Loosening the semantic connections between national citizenship and national identity takes into account that the classic form of the nation-state is at present disintegrating. [. . .]

Nationalism is the term for a specifically modern phenomenon of cultural integration. This type of national consciousness is formed in social movements and emerges from modernization processes at a time when people are at once both mobilized and isolated as individuals. Nationalism is a form of collective consciousness which both presupposes a reflexive appropriation of cultural traditions that have been filtered through historiography and which spreads only via the channels of modern mass communication. Both elements lend to nationalism the artificial traits of something that is to a certain extent a construct, thus rendering it by definition susceptible to manipulative misuse by political elites. [. . .]

The meaning of the term "nation" [has] changed from designating a prepolitical entity to something that was supposed to play a constitutive role in defining the political identity of the citizen within a democratic polity. In the final instance, the manner in which national identity determines citizenship can in fact be reversed. Thus the gist of Ernest Renan's famous saying, "the existence of a nation is . . . a daily plebiscite," is already directed *against* nationalism. After 1871, Renan was only able to counter the German Empire's claims to the Alsace by referring to the inhabitants' French nationality because he could conceive of the "nation" as a nation of citizens. The nation of citizens does not derive its identity from some common ethnic and cultural properties, but rather from the *praxis* of citizens who actively exercise their civil rights. At this juncture, the republican strand of "citizenship" completely parts company with the idea of belonging to a prepolitical community integrated on the basis of descent, a shared tradition, and a common language. Viewed from this end, the initial fusion of republicanism with nationalism only functioned as a catalyst.

The nationalism which was inspired by the works of historians and romantic writers founded a collective identity that played a *functional* role for the implementation of the citizenship that arose in the French Revolution. In the melting pot of national consciousness, the ascriptive features of one's origin were now transformed into just so many achieved properties, result-

ing from a reflexive appropriation of tradition. Hereditary nationality gave
way to an acquired nationalism, that is, to a product of one's own conscious striving. This nationalism was able to foster people's identification
with a role which demanded a high degree of personal commitment, even
to the point of self-sacrifice; in this respect, general conscription was only
the other side of the civil rights coin. Nationalism and republicanism combine in the willingness to fight and, if necessary, die for one's country.
This explains the complementary relation of mutual reinforcement that originally obtains between nationalism and republicanism, the one becoming
the vehicle for the emergence of the other.

However, this socio-psychological connection does not mean that the
two are linked in conceptual terms. Compare "freedom" in the sense of
national independence, i.e., collective self-assertion vis-à-vis other nations,
with "freedom" in the sense of those political liberties the individual citizen enjoys within a country; the two notions are so different in meaning
that, at a later point, the modern understanding of republican freedom can
cut its umbilical links to the womb of the national consciousness which
had originally given birth to it. Only briefly did the democratic nation-
state forge a close link between "ethnos" and "demos." Citizenship was never
conceptually tied to national identity. [. . .]

This concept of popular sovereignty does not refer to some substantive
collective will which would owe its identity to a prior homogeneity of descent or form of life. The consensus achieved in the course of argument in
an association of free and equal citizens stems in the final instance from an
identically applied *procedure* recognized by all. This procedure for political
will formation assumes a differentiated form in the constitution of a democratic state. Thus, in a pluralistic society, the constitution lends expression
to a *formal* consensus. The citizens wish to organize their peaceful coexistence
in line with principles which meet with the justified agreement of all because they are in the equal interest of all. Such an association is structured
by relations of mutual recognition, and given these relations, everyone can
expect to be respected by everybody else as free and equal. Everyone should
be in a position to expect that all will receive equal protection and respect
in his or her violable integrity as a unique individual, as a member of an
ethnic or cultural group, and as a citizen, i.e., as a member of a polity. This
idea of a self-determining political community has taken on concrete legal
shape in a variety of constitutions, in fact, in all political systems of Western Europe and the United States.

For a long time, however, "*Staatsbürgerschaft*," "*citoyenneté*," or "citizenship" all only meant, in the language of the law, political membership. It is
only recently that the concept has been expanded to cover the status of
citizens defined in terms of civil rights. Citizenship as membership in a
state only assigns a particular person to a particular nation whose existence
is recognized in terms of international law. This definition of membership

serves, along with the territorial demarcation of the country's borders, the purpose of a social delimitation of the state. In democratic states, which understand themselves as an association of free and equal citizens, membership depends on the principle of voluntariness. Here, the usual ascriptive characteristics of domicile and birth (*jus soli* and *jus sanguinis*) by no means justify a person's being irrevocably subjected to the sovereign authority of that country. They function merely as administrative criteria for attributing to citizens an assumed, implicit concurrence, to which the right to emigrate or to renounce one's citizenship corresponds. [. . .]

Examples of multicultural societies like Switzerland and the United States demonstrate that a political culture in the seedbed of which constitutional principles are rooted by no means has to be based on all citizens sharing the same language or the same ethnic and cultural origins. Rather, the political culture must serve as the common denominator for a constitutional patriotism which simultaneously sharpens an awareness of the multiplicity and integrity of the different forms of life which coexist in a multicultural society. In a future Federal Republic of European States, the same legal principles would also have to be interpreted from the vantage point of different national traditions and histories. One's own national tradition will, in each case, have to be appropriated in such a manner that it is related to and relativized by the vantage points of the other national cultures. It must be connected with the overlapping consensus of a common, supranationally shared political culture of the European Community. Particularist anchoring *of this sort* would in no way impair the universalist meaning of popular sovereignty and human rights.

II. NATION-STATE AND DEMOCRACY IN A UNIFIED EUROPE

The political future of the European Community sheds light on the relation between national citizenship and national identity in yet another respect. The concept of national citizenship as developed from Aristotle to Rousseau was, after all, originally tailored to the size of cities and city-states. The transformation of populations into nations which formed states occurred, as we have seen, under the sign of a nationalism which apparently succeeded in reconciling republican ideas with the larger dimensions of modern territorial states. It was, moreover, in the political forms created by the nation-state that modern trade and commerce arose. And, like the bureaucratic state apparatus, the capitalist economy also developed a systemic entelechy of its own. The markets for goods, capital, and labor obey their own logic, independent of the intentions of persons involved. Alongside administrative power, money has thus become an anonymous medium of societal integration that functions beyond the minds of individual actors. Now, this *system integration* competes with another form of integration running through the consciousness of the actors involved, i.e., *social integration* through values, norms, and processes of reaching understanding. Just one such aspect of social integration is political integration via citizenship. As a consequence, although liberal theories often deny the fact, the relation between capitalism and democracy is fraught with tension.

Examples from Third-World countries confirm that there is no linear connection between the emergence of democratic regimes and capitalist modernization. Even the welfare state compromise, practiced in Western democracies since the end of the Second World War, did not come into being automatically. And, finally, the development of the European Community brings, in its own way, the tension between democracy and capitalism to the fore. Here, it is expressed in the vertical divide between the systemic integration of economy and administration at the supranational level and the political integration that thus far works only at the level of the nation-state. The technocratic shape taken by the European Community reinforces doubts as to whether the normative expectations one associates with the role of the democratic citizen have not actually always been a mere illusion. Did the temporary symbiosis of republicanism and nationalism not merely mask the fact that the exacting concept of citizenship is at best suited for the less-complex relations within an ethnically and culturally homogeneous community?

The "European Economic Community" has meanwhile become a "European Community" that proclaims the political will to create a "European Union." Leaving India aside, the United States provides the only example for such a large edifice of 320 million inhabitants. Having said that, however, let me add that the United States is a multicultural society united by the same political culture and (at least at present) the same language, whereas the European Union would be a multilingual state of different nations. This association would still have to exhibit some similarities with de Gaulle's "Europe of Fatherlands," even if—and this is to be hoped—it were to be more like a federal republic than a loose federation of semisovereign individual states. The sort of nation-states we have seen to date would continue to exert a strong structural force in such a Europe.

That nation-states constitute a problem along the thorny path to a European Union is, however, due less to their insurmountable claims to sovereignty than to another fact: Democratic processes have hitherto only functioned within national borders. So far, the political public sphere is fragmented into national units. The question thus arises whether there can ever be such a thing as European citizenship. [. . .]

Given that the role of citizen has hitherto only been institutionalized at the level of nation-states, citizens have no effective means of debating European decisions and influencing the decision-making processes. M. R. Lepsius's terse statement sums it up: "There is no European public opinion." Now, what interests me is the question whether this disparity is just a passing imbalance that can be set right by the parliamentarization of the Brussels expertocracy or whether these suprastate bureaucracies with their orientation towards sheer economic criteria of rationality merely highlight a general trend that has for a long time also been gaining momentum within the nation-states. I am thinking of the fact that economic imperatives have gradually become independent of all else, and that politics has gradually become a matter of administration, of processes that undermine the status of the citizen and deny the republican meat of such status. [. . .]

The occurrence of [the] syndrome [. . .] of citizenship reduced to the interests of a client, becomes all the more probable the more the economy and the state apparatus—which have been institutionalized in terms of the same rights—develop a systemic autonomy and push citizens into the periphery of organizational membership. As self-regulated systems, economy and administration tend to cut themselves off from their environments and obey only their internal imperatives of money and power. They no longer fit into the model of a self-determining community of citizens. The classic republican idea of the self-conscious political integration of a community of free and equal persons is evidently too concrete and simple a notion to remain applicable to modern conditions, especially if one has in mind a nation, indeed an ethnically homogeneous community which is held together by common traditions and a shared history.

Fortunately, modern law is a medium which allows for a much more abstract notion of the citizen's autonomy. Nowadays, the sovereignty of the people has constrained itself to become a procedure of more or less discursive opinion and will formation. Still on a normative level, I assume a networking of different communication flows which, however, should be organized in such a way that these can be supposed to bind the public administration to more or less rational premises and in this way enforce social and ecological discipline on the economic system without nonetheless impinging on its intrinsic logic. This provides a model of a deliberative democracy that no longer hinges on the assumption of macro-subjects like the "people" of "the" community but on anonymously interlinked discourses or flows of communication. The model shifts the brunt of fulfilling normative expectations to the infrastructure of a political public sphere that is fueled by spontaneous sources. Citizenship can today only be enacted in the paradoxical sense of compliance with the procedural rationality of a political will-formation, the more or less discursive character of which depends on the vitality of the informal circuit of public communication. An inclusive public sphere cannot be organized as a whole; it depends rather on the stabilizing context of a liberal and egalitarian political culture. [. . .]

When assessing the chances for a future European citizenship, some empirical hints can at least be gleaned from the historical example of the institutionalization of citizenship within the nation-states. Clearly, the view that sees the rights of citizenship essentially as the product of class struggle is too narrow in focus. Other types of social movements, above all migrations and wars, were the driving force behind the development of a full-fledged status for citizens. In addition, factors that prompted the juridification of new relations of inclusion also had an impact on the political mobilization of a population and thus on the active exercise of given rights of citizenship. These and other related findings allow us to extrapolate with cautious optimism the course European developments could take; thus we are at least not condemned to resignation from the outset.

The single market will set in motion even more extensive horizontal mobility and multiply the contacts between members of different nationalities. Immigration from Eastern Europe and the poverty-stricken regions of the Third World will intensify the multicultural diversity of these societies. This will give rise to social tensions. However, if those tensions are processed productively, they will enhance political mobilization in general, and might particularly encourage the new, endogenous type of new social movements— I am thinking of the peace, ecological, and women's movements. These tendencies would strengthen the relevance public issues have for the lifeworld. The increasing pressure of these problems is, furthermore, to be expected— problems for which coordinated solutions are available only at a European level. Given these conditions, communication networks of European-wide public spheres may emerge, networks that may form a favorable context both for new parliamentary bodies of regions that are now in the process of merging and for a European Parliament furnished with greater competence.

To date, the member states have not made the legitimation of EC policy an object of controversy. By and large, the national public spheres are culturally isolated from one another. They are anchored in contexts in which political issues only gain relevance against the background of national histories and national experiences. In the future, however, differentiation could occur in a European culture between a common *political* culture and the branching *national* traditions of art and literature, historiography, philosophy, etc. The cultural elites and the mass media would have an important role to play in this regard. Unlike the American variant, a European constitutional patriotism would have to grow out of different interpretations of the same universalist rights and constitutional principles which are marked by the context of different national histories. Switzerland is an example of how a common politico-cultural self-image stands out against the cultural orientations of the different nationalities. [. . .]

III. IMMIGRATION AND THE CHAUVINISM OF PROSPERITY: A DEBATE

Hannah Arendt's analysis that stateless persons, refugees, and those deprived of rights would determine the mark of this century has turned out to be frighteningly correct. The displaced persons whom the Second World War had left in the midst of a Europe in ruins have been replaced by asylum seekers and immigrants flooding into a peaceful and wealthy Europe from the South and the East. The old refugee camps cannot accommodate the flood of new immigration. In coming years statisticians anticipate twenty to thirty million immigrants from Eastern Europe. This problem can be solved only by the joint action of the European states involved. This process would repeat a dialectic that has already taken place, on a smaller scale, during the process of German unification. The trans-national immigrants' movements function as sanctions which force Western Europe to act responsibly in the aftermath of the bankruptcy of state socialism. Europe must make a great effort to quickly improve conditions in the poorer areas of middle and Eastern Europe or it will be flooded by asylum seekers and immigrants.

The experts are debating the capacity of the economic system to absorb these people, but the readiness to politically integrate the asylum seekers depends more upon how citizens *perceive* the social and economic problems posed by immigration. Throughout Europe, right-wing xenophobic reaction against the "estrangement" (*überfremdung*) caused by foreigners has increased. The relatively deprived classes, whether they feel endangered by social decline or have already slipped into segmented marginal groups, identify quite openly with the ideologized supremacy of their own collectivity and reject everything foreign. This is the underside of a chauvinism of prosperity which is increasing everywhere. Thus the asylum problem as well brings to light the latent tension between citizenship and national identity.

One example is the nationalistic and anti-Polish sentiments in the new German state. The newly acquired status of German citizenship is bound together with the hope that the Republic's frontier of prosperity will be pushed toward the Oder and Neiße. Their newly gained citizenship also gives many of them the ethnocentric satisfaction that they will no longer be treated as second-class Germans. They forget that citizenship rights guarantee liberty because they contain a core composed of universal human rights. Article Four of the Revolutionary Constitution of 1793, which defined the status of the citizen, gave to *every* adult foreigner who lived for one year in France not just the right to remain within the country but also the active rights of a citizen. [...]

These tendencies signify only that a concept of citizenship, the normative content of which has been dissociated from that of national identity, cannot allow arguments for restrictive and obstructionist asylum or immigration policies. It remains an open question whether the European Community today, in expectation of great and turbulent migrations, can and ought to adopt even such liberal foreigner and immigration policies as the Jacobins did in their time. Today the pertinent *moral-theoretical discussion* regarding the definition of "special duties" and special responsibilities is restricted to the social boundaries of a community. Thus the state too forms a concrete legal community which imposes special duties on its citizens.

Asylum seekers and immigrants generally present the European states with the problem of whether special citizenship-related duties are to be privileged above those universal, trans-national duties which transcend state boundaries. [. . .]

Special duties are those which specific persons owe to others to whom they are obligated by virtue of being "connected" to them as dependents, thus as members of a family, as friends, as neighbors, and as co-members of a political community or nation. Parents have special obligations toward their children—and vice versa. Consulates in foreign countries have special obligations to those of their citizenry who need protection—these in turn are obligated to the institutions and laws of their own land. In this context, we think above all of positive duties, which remain undetermined, insofar as they demand acts of solidarity, engagement, and care in measures which cannot be accurately determined. Help cannot always be expected by everyone. Special duties are those which result from the relationship between the concrete community and a part of its membership, and can be understood as social attributes and factual specifications of such intrinsically undetermined duties. [. . .]

A special duty toward these "others" does not result primarily from their membership in a concrete community. It results more from the abstract co-ordinating tendencies of *judicial* institutions, which specify, according to certain attributes, certain categories of persons or agents; this process, in turn, specifies and legally enforces those positive social and factual obligations which would have been undetermined otherwise. According to this interpretation, institutionally mediated responsibilities determine those specific obligations owed to certain others active in a moral division of labor. Within such a judicially regulated moral economy, the social boundaries of a legal community only have the function of regulating the distribution of responsibilities throughout the community. That does not mean that our responsibility ends at this boundary. More must be done by the national government so that the citizenry fulfills its duties toward its nonmembers—to the asylum seekers, for example. Still, with this argument the question, "What are these duties?" has not yet been answered.

The moral point of view commits us to assess this problem impartially, and thus not just from the one-sided perspective of those living in prosperous regions, but also from the perspective of the immigrants, those who search for grace. Let us say that they seek not only political asylum but a free and dignified human existence. [. . .] Legitimate restrictions of immigration rights would then be established by competing viewpoints, such as consideration to avoid the enormity of claims, social conflicts, and burdens that might seriously endanger the public order or the economic reproduction of society. The criteria of ethnic origin, language, and education—or an "acknowledgment of belonging to the cultural community" of the land of migration, in the case of those who have Germanic status—could not establish privileges in the process of immigration and naturalization. [...]

The modern state also presents a political way of life which cannot be exhausted through the abstract form of an institutionalization of legal principles. The way of life builds a political-cultural context in which basic universalistic constitutional principles must be implemented. Then and only then will a population, because it is *accustomed* to freedom, also secure and support free institutions. For that reason, Michael Walzer is of the opinion that the right of immigration is limited by the political right of a community to protect the integrity of its life form. According to him, the right of citizens to self-determination implies the right of self-assertion to each particular way of life. [...]

The requisite competence "to act as citizens of a special political community (this particular polity)" is to be understood in another sense completely—namely, the *universalistic* sense—as soon as the political community itself implements universalistic basic laws. The identity of a political community, which may not be touched by immigration, depends primarily upon the constitutional principles rooted in a political culture and not upon an ethical-cultural form of life as a whole. That is why it must be expected that the new citizens will readily engage in the political culture of their new home, without necessarily giving up the cultural life specific to their country of origin. The *political acculturation* demanded of them does not include the entirety of their socialization. With immigration, new forms of life are imported which expand and multiply the perspective of all, and on the basis of which the common political constitution is always interpreted. [...] We can draw the following normative conclusion: The European states should agree upon a liberal immigration policy. They should not draw their wagons around themselves and their chauvinism of prosperity, hoping to ignore the pressures of those hoping to immigrate or seek asylum. The democratic right of self-determination includes, of course, the right to preserve one's own *political* culture, which includes the concrete context of citizen's rights, though it does not include the self-assertion of a privileged *cultural* life form. Only within the constitutional framework of a democratic legal system can different ways of life coexist equally. These must, however, overlap within a common political culture, which again implies an impulse to open these ways of life to others.

Only democratic citizenship can prepare the way for a condition of world citizenship which does not close itself off within particularistic biases, and which accepts a worldwide form of political communication. The Vietnam War, the revolutionary changes in Eastern and middle Europe, as well as the war in the Persian Gulf are the first *world political* events in a strict sense. Through the electronic mass media, these events were made instantaneous and ubiquitous. In the context of the French Revolution, Kant speculated on the role of the participating public. He identified a world public sphere, which today will become a political reality for the first time with the new relations of global communication. Even the superpowers must recognize worldwide protests. The obsolescence of the state of nature between bellicose states has begun, implying that states have lost some sovereignty. The arrival of world citizenship is no longer merely a phantom, though we are still far from achieving it. State citizenship and world citizenship form a continuum which already shows itself, at least, in outline form.

38

JEREMY BRECHER

"The National Question" Reconsidered from an Ecological Perspective

Nineteen-eighty-six marked the hundredth anniversary of a general strike throughout the United States for the eight-hour day, best remembered today for the trial and judicial murder of the Haymarket Martyrs. That event came to be commemorated in the worldwide holiday May Day celebrating the international solidarity of labor.

One hundred years later, May Day was barely acknowledged in North America, while in Moscow's Red Square tanks paraded and jet fighters screamed overhead. Similar celebrations occurred in the Soviet-dominated countries of Eastern Europe and in the anti-Soviet and mutually hostile communist countries of Asia. The festival of international solidarity has been transformed into a celebration of national power.

Yet the insubstantiality of national boundaries was well demonstrated on last year's May Day, not by workers of all lands joining in *The Internationale*, but by a cloud of radioactive dust circling the globe, carrying the message "Chernobyl is everywhere." It is in this context that I want to reconsider what radicals once called "the national question."

The problems of nationality, nationalism, and the nation-state have proved over the past century to be the greatest stumbling blocks to the aspirations for a better world expressed in socialist, anarchist, communist, and related radical movements. Class has not so far proved to be a unifying bond which overcomes the conflicts among different peoples. Nor has the liberation of one people from oppression by another ensured pro-social behavior on the part of the formerly oppressed once in power. Radical movements today, as over the past hundred years, seem pulled between the powerful if chauvinistic sentiments of particular ethnic, racial, and national groups on the one hand and a dedication to an abstract, cosmopolitan concept of human unity that finds little resonance in most people's actual sense of identity.

In this article I would like to present a rather unconventional approach to "the national question." It is oriented neither toward cosmopolitanism

344

nor toward national liberation. Rather, it grows out of a historical analysis of how the nation-state arose—and out of an "ecological perspective" of a world composed not of sovereign entities but of many levels of open, interacting communities.

STATE AND NATION-STATE

Like the air we breathe, the nation-state is today so nearly universal and so little questioned that it is difficult to scrutinize. We know that there are armies, courts, bureaucracies, and congresses, linked together by laws and beliefs, but to grasp the organization of these as one among many possible social forms we need to examine the historical development of the state and the nation.

No equivalent of our concept of the state existed in medieval Europe.[1] Princes and kings exercised what powers they possessed as individuals leading personal retinues and supporters, not as representatives of an institutional structure which existed independently of themselves. They did not monopolize law-making power or legitimate allegiance within their realms, for such prerogatives were shared with both feudal lords and the church. Finally, they were not sovereign, for both the Holy Roman emperor and the Catholic church, though often weak, were recognized as universal authorities to which princes and kings were subordinate.

By the seventeenth century, many European rulers had managed to assert a monopoly of power against church and feudal authorities within their realms and sovereignty against emperor and pope. This reality was recognized conceptually in the formulation of Bartolus that the Italian city-states should be recognized as "independent associations not recognizing any superior"[2] and Charles Du Moulin's argument that the powers of the crown should not be envisioned as the apex of a feudal pyramid, but rather as a unified and absolute authority under which all citizens should be ranged in a legally undifferentiated fashion as subjects.[3] With the subsequent expansion of the royal bureaucracies, theorists like Jean Bodin began to speak of "the state" as an apparatus distinct from the ruler.[4]

These "early modern" states were still far different from modern nation-states, however.[5] Those ruled were defined as subjects, not citizens. And neither the monarch nor the state apparatus needed to have any connection of origin or culture in common with those they ruled; a German could be king of England, for example. Such states ruled not nations but empires—ethnically heterogeneous and often geographically scattered agglomerations of peoples and territories. Those they ruled generally identified themselves as members of various local, regional, linguistic, and religious groups who were ruled by one or another monarch, rather than as parts of a nation. As late as 1914, "dynastic states made up the majority of the membership of the world political system."[6]

Starting in the late eighteenth century, however, nationalist movements began to arise which sought to align states as power centers with nations as communities of people who asserted common linguistic, ethnic, or historical bonds. As Benedict Anderson emphasizes, the sense of nationality lies in being part of an "imagined community" with a sense of loyalty and even love among community members.[7] It arose first in the colonists' revolts of South and North America, which replaced imperial dynastic rule with national republics. These were followed by European nationalist movements which arose from Ireland to Russia against imperial dynastic rule. These at times involved dramatic popular mobilizations and upheavals which drew previously excluded classes into political life and were experienced as moments of liberation.

In response to such popular nationalism, many imperial monarchies attempted to transform themselves into nation-states. These, along with the new states established by nationalist movements, created a kind of "official nationalism" drawing on but not identical to the popular nationalism from which it grew.

In the wake of World War II, nationalist movements throughout the rest of the world put a virtual end to colonial rule. As Anderson writes, "nation-ness is the most universally legitimate value in the political life of our time," the value people are most willing not only to kill but also to die for.[8]

THE NATION-STATE AND THE LEFT

Marx's formula that the state consists of "special bodies of armed men" plus a bureaucracy fit the dynastic state well. But it missed the fundamental strength of the nation-state, namely its tie to a self-perceived community. This gap in the theory of nationalism underlies what Tom Nairn, in his *The Break-up of Britain*, called "Marxism's great historical failure."

Marx wrote after the rise of the bureaucratic state and concurrently with the flowering of modern popular nationalism. He and Engels fluent in a dozen languages at home in as many cultures, reflected the cosmopolitanism of both the intelligentsia and the working class of that era. His famous statement in *The Communist Manifesto* that "the executive of the modern state is but a committee for managing the common affairs of the whole bourgeoisie" reflected the reality of states which ruled subjects not citizens and which sought support from the most powerful groups in society, whoever they might be. His equally famous statement, also in *The Communist Manifesto*, that "the working men have no country" also reflected a period in which national loyalties and the incorporation of the masses into national states was still primarily a thing of the future.

As a progressive cosmopolitan, Marx viewed particularistic loyalties as archaic provincialisms which were being dissolved by the march of international economic progress. This and his preoccupation with economic phenomena obscured his vision of the tremendous nationalist passions developing around him, which would prove the most important political force of the subsequent century. It would be hard to find an observation less prescient than *The Communist Manifesto*'s statement that "National differences, and antagonisms between peoples, are daily more and more vanishing."

Marx's international policy initially focused on supporting "progressive" states against "reactionary" ones—the former meaning those in which the bourgeoisie, the latter the aristocracy, formed the dominant power. In general, Marx supported the formation of larger nations out of smaller ones as encouraging capitalist economic development and thereby the rise of socialism; even colonialism could be a progressive means of social and economic development. These general precepts were modified according to strategic concerns designed to strengthen potentially revolutionary countries against those which might suppress them.

As nationalist, anti-imperialist movements proliferated, Marxists tended to interpret them primarily in economic terms, as part of an international class struggle. Wars were conflicts among imperial powers for domination of foreign possessions; national liberation movements were struggles against the capitalist powers' exploitation. At the International Congress of the Second International at Basel in 1912, socialist parties from all over the world agreed that, in the event of war among the imperial powers, workers in all countries would conduct unremitting struggle to stop the slaughter.

In the meantime, the actual rise of nationalist sentiments and social structures created a very different reality for the socialist movements in each country. In many cases, especially in Eastern Europe, socialist parties became major expressions of the rising nationalist opposition to imperialist rule. On the other hand, Marxist cosmopolitans like Victor Adler and Rosa Luxemburg opposed nationalist resistance to German domination in the Austro-Hungarian Empire and to Russian rule in Poland as reactionary opposition to larger and therefore economically progressive national units.[9]

Even more important, socialist parties and their affiliated unions and other mass organizations were becoming solidly established institutions within the developing national political systems of many countries. Socialists ran in elections, sat in parliaments, negotiated with employers, and conducted cultural activities on a mass scale. Whether they maintained a rhetoric of revolutionary internationalism or explicitly accepted the reformism that came to be referred to as "socialist revisionism," the reality was that both in consciousness and in practice they addressed their efforts to a national framework.

The proof of the pudding came with the outbreak of inter-imperialist war in 1914. The working classes and the socialist parties of most of the belligerents supported their national governments; resistance was almost nil. The long-promoted idea of mass action against war found virtually no support among populations who identified overwhelmingly not with the members of their class in other countries but with the members of all classes in their own.

The tremendous devastation of the war of course gave socialist internationalism a new lease on life in the form of the Bolshevik Revolution. Lenin and Trotsky explicitly rejected the reformism which had tied the fate of socialism to a national framework and, while supporting national liberation struggles as a form of resistance to imperialism, saw the Russian Revolution primarily as an episode in a movement which would spread across Europe and much of the rest of the world to create a united socialist polity.

By 1921 it was clear to the Soviet leaders that revolution was not on the agenda for Europe. They began the work of reorienting Soviet practice to coexistence with capitalist countries, using communist parties as a means for forestalling anti-Soviet counterrevolution.[10] This approach moved from practice to doctrine with Stalin's enunciation of "socialism in one country."

The communist gains that followed World War II in many parts of the world occurred almost without exception in a nationalist, rather than an internationalist, framework. The great advances made by communist parties in France, Italy, Yugoslavia, and elsewhere in Europe were largely based on their leadership of national resistance movements against fascist imperialism. Likewise in the Third World, communism appeared primarily as radical nationalism. As Anderson writes, "Since World War II every successful revolution has defined itself in *national* terms—the People's Republic of China, the Socialist Republic of Vietnam, and so forth."[11] In Eastern Europe, communist rule was primarily an expression of Soviet military domination rather than nationalist let alone socialist revolution.

In the 1950s and 1960s, Communist China enunciated a theory of world revolution based on the encirclement of the advanced imperialist powers (including the "social imperialist" Soviet Union) by the revolutionary movements of the impoverished Third World—the "encirclement of the cities by the countryside." But Chinese national interest soon led to an abandonment of this approach in favor of a de facto alliance with the United States— including support for some of its most reactionary clients. Today, a handful of small groups around the world propagate the concept of socialist internationalism; otherwise it is no longer a historical force.

A basic concept of labor-oriented radicalism was that the rise of the working class would create a community which cut across more particularistic identities of nationality, religion, gender, and race. What has happened instead is that class has been widely recognized as a reality, expressed in class consciousness and in working-class organizations, but class identity has in the great majority of cases been seen as an addition to, rather than a replacement of, other identities. In many cases, especially that of national identity, class identity has been regarded as subordinate. For that reason, class solidarity has not provided a basis for human unity.

AN ECOLOGICAL PERSPECTIVE

The earth, its waters, and its atmosphere, do not conform to national boundaries: that is why Chernobyl poses questions that go beyond a national framework. The same applies to the catastrophic chemical spill that polluted the Rhine in five nations;[12] to acid rain, which moves northward without respect for the U.S.-Canadian border; to the defoliation of the Third World forests; and to the continuing burning of carbon products which are currently destroying the atmospheric balance of carbon and oxygen on which life depends.

Prior to the rise of environmentalism, most radicals shared with mainstream thought a conception of the world as a collection of entities, individuals, states, pieces of property, or similar units, which, whether dominating one another or living in equality, were separate and bounded. This conception leads to a perception of rigid dichotomies between individual and society, cosmopolitanism and particularism, central authority and disorganization. While this vision no longer finds authority in the biological or physical sciences, it continues to dominate reflection on politics and society. Contemporary political discourse continues in terms of sovereign individuals, sovereign states, and private or government property.

Environmentalism, influenced in part by the science of ecology, has introduced profoundly different ways of looking at the world in which boundaries are also connections and individual entities are parts of interacting, multi-leveled natural and human systems.[13] I believe the social world, too, can be far better seen with such an ecological vision, in which the boundaries of individuals and groups are only relative and in which, while retaining their own identity, they are also part of larger, many-leveled wholes and likewise contain interacting parts within themselves.

Such a shift of perspective, abstract as it may appear, can open up creative approaches to many sterile conflicts that have led to gridlock in contemporary discourse and life.[14] So far, however, it has rarely been applied to those problems that radicals traditionally referred to as "the national question."

Historically, much radical discourse on the state has swung between the poles of cosmopolitanism and nationalism. Programmatically, these poles have involved alternatively the ideal of a world state or that of a national state ruled by the working class. In practice, movements aiming for increased working-class power in the nation-state have been ubiquitous while those aiming for world government have been marginal and generally regarded as totally utopian.

A more ecological perspective would eschew both the ideal of a world state and that of a world of sovereign nation-states, however classless they might be. It would regard the whole idea of sovereign social organizations as an anti-ecological conception.

Such an approach would aim, in effect, to reverse the three processes which led to the formation of states in the first place. First, by establishing the autonomy of lower-level forms of organization. Second, by creating trans-national links, loyalties, and institutions that are binding on individuals, groups, and nations. Third, by moving what remains of the state toward a fully participatory democracy, thereby reducing its reified, institutionalized character and making it more subject to continuing human shaping.[15] In short, a program of devolving power from the state downward and upward simultaneously, while making the residual power subject to more egalitarian and popular control.

THE DEVOLUTION DOWNWARD

The animating idea of nationalism, belief in a national community, has always presumed a set of common traits, biological, cultural, or historical, among community members. But in reality, all modern nations have been formed to a greater or lesser extent by the willing or unwilling incorpora-tion of diverse human groups. The period of nationalism has, in conse-quence, been continuously marked by the domination or destruction of "national minorities"—Jews in Central and Eastern Europe, Afro-Ameri-cans in the United States, Muslims in India, Koreans in Japan, Amerasians in Vietnam, Kurds and non-Islamic religious groups in Iran, Armenians in Turkey, and, most recently, Turks in Bulgaria.[16]

Traditionally, social movements of national minorities within nation-states have taken two forms. One has been toward equality, full civil rights, and integration within the mainstream national community, the other toward separatism and the formation of an independent nation; most minority movements have swung between these poles. Over the past couple of de-cades, however, a third alternative has emerged in many countries which can perhaps best be characterized as "multiculturalism." This approach challenges the underlying nationalist ideal of a state which represents a homogeneous national community. Instead, minority movements today often push for *both* equal rights *and* ethnic pluralism within states, sometimes accompanied by demands for federalism with autonomy for different ethnic regions.

Multiculturalism, with its emphasis on the positive value of human di-versity, can represent an important step toward a more ecologically oriented reconstruction of politics. Indeed, carried to its logical conclusion, it would amount to a historical shift in the character of the nation-state, compara-ble perhaps to the rise of religious toleration and the disestablishment of official religions that followed the Protestant Reformation.

Such an approach fits well with the efforts to devolve power downward that have marked recent social movements in both communist and capital-ist societies. Polish Solidarity and the German Greens have both developed decentralist alternatives to traditional left concepts of "seizing state power," albeit each within a national framework.

Both Solidarity and the Greens speak in terms of transferring functions of the state to society. According to Adam Michnik, the essence of the Polish movement "lay in the attempt to reconstruct society, to restore social bonds outside official institutions."[17] Given the very different historical context, the theoretical similarity of the Greens' approach is striking. The Greens "do not define power as simple control of the central state apparatus but view it as a broader network of social and political relations to be transformed throughout the whole of society."[18] This theory of power leads to a strategy for change which does not fit established models of either revolution or reform. Their goal is "to assail the State, to crumble it"; one Green slogan says, "Let's make the State into cucumber salad."[19] Far from trying to "capture state power" by either electoral or revolutionary means, their demands on the state are designed to transfer wealth and power away from centralized corporate and bureaucratic structures to decentralized communities.[20]

Both multiculturalism and decentralism lead toward a society based on multiple identities: local, regional, national, global, ethnic, gender, linguistic, religious, political, and so forth. Such a vision is not the same as an abstract cosmopolitanism, for it recognizes and even cherishes the historically developed differences among groups. But it refuses to reduce human individuals and groups to such abstract definitions as "bourgeois," "worker," "Russian," "American" because it always sees them as many other things as well. And it undermines all forms of chauvinism, because it recognizes not only the relative boundaries that divide people but also the various larger commonalities that unite them. It provides a framework for abolishing today's lethal concentrations of national power while protecting social groups which want to preserve and elaborate their cultural identities.

THE DEVOLUTION UPWARD

It is widely recognized that nation-states are not able to perform the basic functions that generally legitimate them. No state in the world provides an effective medium for ordinary people to organize their common interests in ways they themselves control. No state is able to provide security to its own people against either environmental degradation or nuclear annihilation. Like the duels and rebellions of feudal lords in the early modern period, most of the actions of state authorities are antisocial and threatening to those they affect.

But this understanding has not yet been translated into a consciousness of the need to transcend the nation-state system per se. In this regard the left is generally no more radical than the right; generally leftists simply defend those nationalisms they perceive as anti-imperialist.[21] This approach leaves the *system* of nation-states unquestioned.

It is not one or another country but the nation-state system as now constituted that threatens the future of humanity.[22] In itself, a decentralist devolution of power downward will not solve the basic problems of environmental and nuclear destruction, for units smaller than the nation can still wield genocidal destructive capacity. Some sort of global regulation is required to create a secure and livable world. Yet the devolution of power upward from the nation-state raises the thorny issues of international law and/or a world state.

WORLD LAW

The concept of international law has not been a popular one with the left. For anarchists, the concept of law itself is problematic, and the image of a uniform global authority system can resemble the ultimate statist nightmare. More conventional leftists generally hold that the real power issues will be determined by a struggle among nations and classes and that concepts of world law tend to suppress this struggle by legitimating the privileges of those who are presently on top. They point to the tendency of contemporary international law to favor established regimes against insurgencies[23] and to require the payment of international debts that have been forced on debtors through imperialist domination.

Leftist suspicion also grows out of the conservatism of international law's main tradition of support. Important strands of the world federalist movement, for example, originated in a concept of Anglo-American cooperation to use international law against bolshevism. Much of the support for international law comes from lawyers, who often give it a conservative interpretation. But we need to take a fresh look at these questions in the framework of the "ecological perspective" sketched above.

The concept of law itself is subject to so much mystification that one almost wishes to use a new term. For most people, the law still has something of the sacred about it. In practice, law is usually connected to two often contradictory realities: the norms of the community on the one hand and the ability of particular social groups to use the legal apparatus to shape society to their wishes on the other. Modern legal historians have taught us to think of law as an arena of conflicting interests, rather than either an imposition by the state or a pure expression of the will of the community.[24] What laws exist and how they are interpreted and administered at a given time is a result of the historical power relations among different groups. For purposes of this essay, I will use "law" simply to mean rules which define the acceptable behavior of individuals and organizations, together with procedures intended to enforce those rules.

Within an ecological perspective, law thus conceived is entirely appropriate: It is essentially a higher-level regulation which can serve as a means for the community as a whole and its constituent parts to maintain their conditions of existence.[25] Since the human species has no biologically pre-program means for such regulation, we must provide it through conscious social regulation—or face the threat of power centers run amok which confronts us at present.

If this concept of "law in general" should be an acceptable one, it does not imply that existing law, whether national or international, should be accepted. Even if law provides for the survival of the community by putting limits on the actions of individuals, states, or other units, that does not justify its use for the strong to dominate the weak or the wealthy to exploit the poor. A commitment to rules limiting acceptable behavior does not necessarily entail accepting all existing laws as just. Indeed, there is undoubtedly a place for civil disobedience against international law just as there is against national law.[26]

Perhaps we should think in terms of a people's concept of world law, law as something to be imposed on nation-states by the cumulative pressure of individuals and social groups. I suspect that the content of such law will turn out to be largely in accord with international law as it now exists. A large proportion of the evil things nation-states do are today illegal.[27] A large part of the things one would wish to stop are already defined as war crimes and crimes against humanity. For example, it is presently illegal for one nation to use military force against another without United Nations' authorization except to repel a direct attack. The U.S. harassment of Nicaragua and the Soviet invasion of Afghanistan each violate international law in at least half a dozen different ways.

While the language of international law speaks in terms of national sovereignty, I believe that the right is correct in asserting that it actually restricts the most important aspects of national sovereignty. Strictly applied, even today's international law would limit nation-states to a sovereignty more like that of the U.S. states or the Canadian provinces than that of the lawless rampagers sovereign states are today.

In sum, we should wholeheartedly support the concept of world law as a system of limitations on the sovereignty of nation-states. Where states and other organizations violate those aspects of international law which protect peace and serve human needs, we should bring every possible internal and external pressure to bear to stop them.[28] At the same time, we should articulate a critique of those (I believe relatively minor) aspects of international law which form obstacles to the struggle for social justice.

GLOBAL ORGANIZATION

Similar doubts surround moves toward global organization or a world state. Leftists (if they think about the subject at all) generally fear that, given the present distribution of power, such a state would simply be a vehicle to enforce the interests of some alignment of the world's present ruling classes. Its primary function would be to suppress those attempting to achieve social change throughout the globe. For anarchists, a world state implies the same problems as a national state—with the added horror that it is universal and therefore inescapable. Here again, an ecological perspective seems to suggest alternative approaches that cut across some of the neat categories of established discourse.

I believe the fear of a world state is a legitimate one on both anarchist and Marxist grounds. A world state (most plausibly created by a voluntary or forced unification of the existing dominant social groups of different countries) has the potential, at least in theory, for becoming a means for greatly curtailing human freedom, indeed, even for creating universal slavery under a world ruling class monopolizing the means of violence and subsistence.

There is no reason, however, that international regulation need take the form of a world state. An agency whose function is to regulate the use of nuclear energy, for example, need not be more than loosely coordinated with one which oversees disarmament or use of ocean food resources. The devolution downward of the powers of nation-states and corporations can provide an additional protection against overcentralized authority.[29]

Some of the rudiments of the kinds of organs we need already exist in the form of the World Court, the U.N., and the agencies created by various international treaties. Others will have to be created through transnational links among individuals and organizations[30] and through new, sovereignty-limiting treaties. Certain needs—notably for peace-protection of the environment, and global redistribution of resources[31]—can be achieved only through global institutions.

It is often alleged that these institutions simply reflect the opinions of whatever superpower is able to dominate them. In the post–World War II period, leftists routinely charged, with some reason, that the United Nations and most other international agencies were dominated by the United States. During the 1960s and 1970s, the right charged, again with some reason, that these groups had become in effect pawns of Soviet foreign policy, with large majorities consistently favoring even the most blatantly improper Soviet activities.

In the past few years, however, the U.N., the World Court, and other international agencies have become increasingly independent of either superpower—as indicated by their condemnation of both U.S. policy in Nicaragua and Soviet policy in Afghanistan. If this independence can be sustained, it can be one starting point for limiting both superpower domination and the destructive features of national sovereignty.

STRATEGY

Nation-states are powerful and they try to use their power to perpetuate themselves. The most obvious criticism of a program for the devolution of power—either downward or upward—is simply that existing power centers will prevent it. But it is also apparent that given enough time the nation-state system is likely to destroy itself—taking the world along with it. Our search should be, not for an alternative whose success can be guaranteed, but for the strategy that offers us the best basis for hope.

The institutions of the modern state were not built up overnight; they are the result of a long series of partial struggles growing out of specific issues and particular alignments.[32] The devolution of state power upward and downward, by the same token, is unlikely to be either rapid or smooth.

State power depends on a coalition of supporters and a broad base of consent, both internal and external. It can therefore in principle be effectively challenged by the withdrawal or threatened withdrawal of support or consent.[33]

The overall process by which the powers of nation-states can be devolved finds no clear historical precedent. It is unlikely to look very much like a national revolution or like traditional concepts of a world revolution, although national revolutions and world crises certainly might be part of such a process.

But an ecological approach suggests myriad opportunities for actions based on internationalization, decentralization, and democratization. While these opportunities arise out of concrete historical junctures which must be taken as they come, such junctures are predictable and we can learn how to take advantage of them to move in the directions we need to go.

Radical change is possible in part because we confront not a unified ruling class but rather a collection of quarreling power centers struggling with each other and blind to most of the consequences of their own actions. A strategy for developing power can take advantage of this by playing on contradictions within and among ruling classes and state bureaucracies which make it difficult for them to consistently oppose such a development. Some examples:

• Nuclear war, environmental degradation, and national lawlessness threaten the existence of everyone, including the leaders of all the world's ruling groups.[34]

• We are witnessing a "decoupling" of the nation-state from the multinational corporation and the world economy, which is eroding the long-standing alliance between capitalist business groupings and the nation-state and creating new alignments that are as yet difficult to discern.

• Military spending is devastating the economies of all countries, including the superpowers, whose leaders know that military spending is undermining internal stability and their ability to achieve their own goals.

By combining the threat of withdrawal of external and internal consent, it is possible to take advantage of the disunity among different ruling groups and the contradictions among the interests of each. I am proposing a basic pincer strategy of "piggy in the middle" in which internal and external forces combine to pressure each nation into accepting restrictions on its sovereign right to do ill. Here are some of the elements of such a strategy.

CHANGING SOCIETY

While any strategy will eventually have to challenge states, people can start changing society without being strong enough to change government policies. Direct linking of communities via "sister city" arrangements and other person-to-person activities—used recently to link communities in the United States to communities in Nicaragua and the Soviet Union and to build grass-roots connections between local peace groups in various countries—provides one example. Actions which promote a multicultural perspective within a country can help undermine attitudes of national chauvinism and promote a valuing of or at least a live-and-let-live attitude toward the people of other countries. Such activities can transform social attitudes and help lay the basis for a withdrawal of consent from the nation-state system.

For those of us on the left, one contribution we can make to such a process is transforming our own thinking. All over the world radicals need to extend their discussions beyond determining who are the good guy and bad guy nations to a critique of the nation-state system itself and the necessity of moving beyond it.[35]

Those who share such a vision can then begin to argue for it in whatever arenas are available to them, encourage its adoption by a variety of social movements, and support its incorporation within a larger domestic bloc. The nature of this process will of course differ in different places; in some countries, nationalism is already widely regarded as an archaic and dangerous worldview, while in others national pride and strength remain primary values.[36]

If sovereignty is the right of nations to do whatever they want in the world, progressively limiting their freedom of action is the key to reducing the destructive aspects of sovereignty. Nations can be pressured both to cease particular evils, such as an illegal war, and to change broader policies, by, for example, acceding to international disarmament treaties.

The extent to which internal and external constraints already limit the supposed sovereignty of even the superpowers is not always recognized. The rise of the Solidarity union in Poland and the decision of the Soviet Union not to invade to suppress it (thereby allowing it to remain as a massive underground presence) resulted in large part from the devastating effects on Soviet relations in Eastern and Western Europe and the rest of the world that such an invasion would have had.[37] The Reagan administration, almost panting in its eagerness to destroy the Sandinista regime in Nicaragua, has nonetheless been forestalled from doing so by a combination of active resistance in the United States, more passive but widespread popular fear of involvement in "another Vietnam," diplomatic opposition from Latin America and Europe, and world public opinion, all buttressing the resistance of the Sandinistas themselves. Such pressure sometimes fails, but even in defeat it can exact a heavy price, for example the price—a split with its European allies and the revitalization of the European peace movement—

that the United States paid for its bombing of Libya and its abandonment of SALT II.[38]

Breakup of Blocs

External consent to the superpower arms race and imperialism primarily takes the form of the bloc system. The withdrawal of such consent has been the basic goal of those parts of the peace movement, such as the European Nuclear Disarmament campaign (END), which have aimed for the removal of their countries from the superpower blocs and the development of nuclear free zones. This approach represents a crucial part of a "piggy-in-the-middle" strategy for limiting the superpowers. Indeed, fear of the European peace movement and its demands for withdrawal from the U.S. bloc is perhaps the principal restraint today on U.S. foreign policy. Even though the movement is not yet strong enough to force any country to pull out of NATO, the threat to do so nonetheless exercises a significant deterrent effect on the United States.

The overall strategy proposed here requires coordinating a variety of efforts inside and outside each country to enforce rules of behavior which may conflict with national sovereignty but which are necessary for human survival. Models for such coordination—not necessarily adequate ones—can be seen in the labor and leftist internationals, Amnesty International, Greenpeace, the movement for a free South Africa, etc.

Such international movements can nurture the development of a worldwide bloc or alignment of forces to represent the withdrawal of consent from the system of national sovereignty. A sketch of the elements of such a bloc might include independent international institutions; peace movements; groupings of nonaligned countries; religious and other trans-national bodies. While such a bloc is unlikely to find a single organizational embodiment, its constituents can certainly articulate the concept of a community of those individuals and institutions everywhere who are attempting to move the world from a sovereign state system to global regulation.

Such a bloc can become the constituency for a wide range of programs which represent the clear interests of the great majority of people in all countries. The efforts of Greenpeace and other groups to create international pressure for a complete ban on nuclear testing, for example, give one indication of what pulling together such a bloc would entail. Pressure on the United States to cease its harassment of Nicaragua, and the development of the Contadora alternative for reducing superpower involvement in Central America, are others. END proposals for the denuclearization of Europe suggest a third. In the wake of Three Mile Island and Chernobyl, an international ban on nuclear power plants and the phasing out of those that exist might provide another.

Such efforts do not require new movements, but rather the stressing of

an additional dimension of environmental, peace, and human rights struggles already under way. Focusing on such issues can be a means toward
simultaneously transforming consciousness within each country and forcing
concrete limits on the unbridled destructiveness of nation-states.

The nation-state system represents a historically created concentration of
power that threatens the freedom and the existence of individuals and social
groups. The solution is neither to replace it with a world state nor to dissolve
it into isolated communes. Rather, we need to devolve some of its powers
upward to higher-level regional and global institutions, and devolve others
of its powers downward to the many kinds of groups that make up society.
   The goal would be a many-layered system in which each aspect of social
life would be regulated at the appropriate level: The abolition of nuclear
weapons and the preservation of oceans and atmosphere would be organized
globally, the plans for a particular community would be made by those directly
affected, and intermediate issues would be decided by networks of decision-
making institutions in between. Individuals would recognize themselves and
each other as members of many groups, some larger, some smaller, but no
one of which is so closed off from others as to justify their annihilation.
   Such an overall vision can be incorporated into the goals of many different movements in all parts of the world. It involves both the withdrawal of
consent from the existing state system and the construction of new identities and communities. The historical development toward such a world is
likely to occur neither through a single revolutionary upheaval nor through
a smooth process of constitutionally sanctioned reform, but rather through
confrontations which force one or another state to devolve some of its power
downward or upward. It is the cumulative effect of such actions that can
turn the state from its present menace to a delicious cucumber salad. Chernobyl
is everywhere; so, therefore, is the struggle against Chernobyl.

NOTES

1. The following discussion of the rise of the state is based on Quentin Skinner's
   The Foundations of Modern Political Thought (Cambridge: Cambridge University
   Press, 1978). It focuses on European-originated societies because they are where
   the modern state and nation initially arose.
2. Skinner, *Foundations*, 351.
3. As paraphrased in Skinner, *Foundations*, 352.
4. Skinner, *Foundations*, 356. It is hard not to be struck by the parallels of this
   concept of the state and the bourgeois concept of private property, the liberal
   concept of the private individual, and even the Newtonian concept of physical objects. Recent scholarship has indeed traced links in the development of
   these conceptions—links which were noted long ago by William Blake.
5. My discussion of nationalism is based largely on Benedict Anderson's *Imagined
   Communities: Reflections on the Origin and Spread of Nationalism* (London:
   Verso, 1983).

6. Anderson, *Imagined Communities*, 28.
7. Anderson traces a number of causes of the development of national communities, emphasizing the role of newspapers and other forms of "print capitalism." Definitions of nationality are of course multiple, ambiguous, and even contradictory: Far from being "natural" entities, they are constructed, synthetic creations, often based on historical and racial myths with little basis in fact. I think Anderson underestimates the role that racial concepts and aspirations for economic integration have played in the development of national consciousness and the extent to which national consciousness is a response to instrusion and oppression by other groups.
8. Anderson, *Imagined Communities*, 12. ·
9. See the appendix on the national question in J. P. Nettl's *Rosa Luxemburg* (London: Oxford University Press, 1966) for the subtleties and modifications of Luxemburg's position.
10. See Paul Mattick, *Anti-Bolshevik Communism* (London: Merlin Press, 1978) for a discussion of this reorientation of Soviet policy.
11. Anderson, *Imagined Communities*, 12.
12. The correspondence of the Chernobyl and Rhine disasters aptly demonstrates that neither communist nor capitalist systems can deal safely with contemporary technology.
13. Among the many efforts to formulate this idea, some of the most interesting are in Gregory Bateson's *Steps toward an Ecology of Mind* (New York: Ballantine Books, 1972). For a classic statement, see Ludwig von Bertalanffy's *General Systems Theory* (New York: George Braziller, 1968). Murray Bookchin's pioneering efforts to apply ecology to politics are presented in *Post-Scarcity Anarchism* (Berkeley: Ramparts Press, 1971) and other works. Obviously such ideas are not entirely new and have affinities with many earlier approaches. Hegelian and Marxist dialectics also stress the relativity of boundaries and the importance of the wholes of which individuals are part, but their goal of conscious human domination of nature distinguishes them from an ecological perspective. The organic philosophies of China, notably Taoism, generated similar perspectives, albeit in a prescientific context. See Joseph Needham, *Science and Civilization in China* (Cambridge: Cambridge University Press, 1956), vol. 2. Many so-called primitive people, for instance, Native Americans, incorporated similar elements in their worldviews.
14. This shift can help us reinterpret many of the basic issues in the tradition of working-class oriented radicalism. I have explored some of these in my review of two recent books by Stanley Aronowitz in *Our Generation*, Fall/Winter 1985–86, and in "Socialism Is What You Make It" in *Socialist Visions*, ed. Steve Rosskamm Shalom (Boston: South End Press, 1983).
15. I have tried to deal with some of the issues of making institutions subject to human control through reversibility of decision making and other means in "Socialism Is What You Make It" in *Socialist Visions*.
16. As part of Bulgaria's campaign against its Turkish minority, the Islamic custom of male circumcision has been denounced as "a key link in the arsenal of ideological diversion of imperialism for the isolation and separation of the workers of our country." "New Line in Bulgaria: Turks? What Turks?" *The New York Times*, 20 Apr. 1986.
17. Quoted in Jonathan Schell, "Reflections: A Better Today," *The New Yorker*, 3 Feb. 1986. Of course the dichotomy between "state" and "society" means something different in state socialist countries than in capitalist ones, since in the latter many of the most oppressive and undemocratic institutions, notably corporations, are part not of the state but of "society."

18. Carl Boggs, "The Greens, Anti-Militarism and the Global Crisis," *Radical America* 17, no. 1: 15–16.
19. Quoted in John Ely, "The Greens," *Radical America* 17, no. 1.
20. This passage draws in part on my "The Reconstruction of Radical Politics," *Workers' Democracy* 17 (Summer 1985).
21. Some leftists attempt to consistently support the right of self-determination of all nations; others define certain nations as "imperialist" and thereby define all opposition to them as "anti-imperialist" and therefore good.
22. This of course does not imply that individual nations should not be held accountable for their actions in the here and now.
23. For example, it is legal to supply weapons to a government but not to an insurgency against it. This principle does not always favor imperialism: It has been a crucial legal support of the Sandinista government in its struggle against the U.S.-backed Contra insurgency, for example.
24. See, for example, the appendix to E. P. Thompson's *Whigs and Hunters* (New York: Pantheon, 1975), and Staughton Lynd's "Communal Rights" in *Texas Law Review* (May 1984).
25. Many anarchists accept the concept of law in this very broad sense. They then ask very pertinent questions about whether it is created by free agreement or coercion and deceit; whether it is enforced by coercion; whether it perpetuates hierarchy and domination; and whether it is subject to and supportive of change and development.
26. A plausible example might be repudiation of debts run up by regimes that have been imposed by imperial powers.
27. I came to this conclusion, much to my own surprise, while exploring the application of international law to U.S. military intervention in Central America.
28. This is the logic underlying various international law–based defenses now being used in U.S. courts by those arrested for protesting U.S. intervention in Central America, the U.S. denial of political asylum to Central American refugees, and U.S. production of first-strike weapons. They demand that the U.S. government conform to international law advocated above, in which individuals and groups try to enforce law on states.
29. Keeping global institutions accountable to ordinary people and responsive to their changing needs will always remain a problem. The same is true, however, of any social institution.
30. For example, agencies have been created directly by people in different countries without recourse to the treaty-making powers of states for such purposes as preserving threatened varieties of grain and monitoring the arms race.
31. It is striking that one of the few voices recently to call for global regulation of capital allocation in the interest of poor countries has been the rather conservative Catholic Pope John Paul II.
32. For a sense of the way this process unfolded in many different historical contexts, see the essays in Charles Bright and Susan Harding, eds., *Statemaking and Social Movements* (Ann Arbor: University of Michigan Press, 1984), especially "Swordplay and Statemaking" by Robert A. Schneider.
33. This crucial argument, which underlies both Marxist and Gandhian theories of political power, is developed at length in Gene Sharp's *The Politics of Nonviolence* (Boston: Porter Sargent, 1973). Of course, the process is made more complex by the fact that those whose support is essential may not be those most likely to withdraw support.
34. This is the grain of truth in the somewhat misleading cliché that "nobody wants a nuclear war"—misleading because there are those who want the benefits of being able to threaten a nuclear war.

35. This doesn't mean abandoning judgment of bad actions by nations, but asserting the framework of supranational law to which nations must be made accountable.
36. Various polls indicate that the United States and the United Kingdom value national pride and power very highly, while most of continental Europe and Japan tend to deride them. Many analysts plausibly relate these values to experiences of victory, defeat, and devastation in past wars.
37. Adam Michnik made the devastating effects on the Soviet Union of an invasion of Poland the basis for his theory of the "self-limiting revolution," which became one of the underpinnings of Solidarity. See Jonathan Schell, "Reflections: A Better Today," *The New Yorker,* 3 Feb. 1986.
38. The bombing of Libya, highly popular within the United States, also illustrates the point that constraints upon national sovereignty are more likely to be effective when they combine internal and external pressure.

39

ERIC HOBSBAWM

Nationalism in the Late Twentieth Century

Let me conclude with some reflections on nationalism in the last part of the twentieth century. At first sight there has been a triumphant world-wide advance of "the principle of nationality." All states of the globe are today officially "nations," all liberation movements tend to be "national" liberation movements, "national" agitations disrupt the oldest nation-states in Europe—Spain, France, the United Kingdom, even, in a modest way, Switzerland—the socialist regimes of the East, the new Third-World states liberated from colonialism, even the federations of the New World, where Canada remains torn and in the United States pressure is growing to make English the only language for public official purposes, in response to the mass immigration of Spanish Americans, the first wave of immigrants not to feel the attractions of linguistic assimilation. Above all, where ideologies are in conflict, the appeal to the imagined community of the nation appears to have defeated all challengers. [. . .]

Yet while nobody can possibly deny the growing and sometimes dramatic, impact of nationalist, or ethnic politics, there is one major respect in which the phenomenon today is functionally different from the "nationalism" and the "nations" of nineteenth- and earlier twentieth-century history. It is no longer a major vector of historical development. In the "developed" world of the nineteenth century, the building of a number of "nations" which combined nation-state and national economy was plainly a central fact of historical transformation and seen to be such. In the "dependent" world of the first half of the twentieth century, and for obvious reasons especially in the colonized part of it, movements for national liberation and independence were the main agents for the political emancipation of most of the globe, that is to say for an elimination of imperial administration and, more significantly, direct military domination by the imperial powers, a situation that would have appeared almost inconceivable even half a century ago. While, as we have seen, these national liberation movements in the Third World were in theory modeled on the nationalism of the West, in practice the states they attempted to construct were, as we have also seen, generally the opposite of the ethnically and linguistically homogeneous entities which came to be seen as the standard form of "nation-state" in the West. Nevertheless, even in this respect they were de facto more like than unlike the Western nationalism of the liberal era. Both were typically unificatory as well as emancipatory, though in the latter case the reach exceeded the grasp more frequently than in the earlier.

The characteristic nationalist movements of the late twentieth century are essentially negative, or rather divisive. Hence the insistence on "ethnicity" and linguistic differences, each or both sometimes combined with religion. In one sense they may be regarded as the successors to, sometimes the heirs of, the small-nationality movements directed against the Habsburg, tsarist, and Ottoman empires, that is to say against what were considered historically obsolete modes of political organization, in the name of a (perhaps misconceived) model of political modernity, the nation-state. In another sense most of them are quite the opposite, namely rejections of modern modes of political organization, both national and supranational. Time and again they seem to be reactions of weakness and fear, attempts to erect barricades to keep at bay the forces of the modern world, similar in this respect to the resentment of Prague Germans pressed into a corner by Czech immigration rather than to that of the advancing Czechs. This is not only the case of small linguistic communities vulnerable to quite modest demographic changes, such as the thinly populated hills and coasts of Welsh-speaking Wales, or Estonia, whose one million or so Estonian speakers would in any case place it at the very lower limit of populations capable of maintaining a modern linguistic culture at all levels. It is not surprising that the most explosive issue in both areas is the uncontrolled immigration of monoglot speakers of the English or Russian language respectively. However, similar reactions are to be found among much larger populations whose linguistic/cultural existence is not, or does not seem, in any way threatened. The most absurd example of this is the movement, which acquired political clout in some states of the United States in the late 1980s, to declare English as the only *official* language of the United States. For while Hispanophone immigration is indeed sufficiently massive in some parts of the United States to make it desirable, and sometimes necessary, to address this public in its own language, the idea that the supremacy of English in the United States is, or is likely to be, in jeopardy, is political paranoia.

What fuels such defensive reactions, whether against real or imaginary threats, is a combination of international population movements with the ultra-rapid, fundamental, and unprecedented socioeconomic transformations so characteristic of the third quarter of our century. French Canada may illustrate this combination of an intensified petit bourgeois linguistic nationalism with mass future shock. On paper the French language, spoken as a native tongue by a quarter of Canada's population, a community about half the size of Canada's native Anglophones, and buttressed by the official bilingualism of the federation, the international backing of French culture, and upwards of 130,000 students in Francophone universities (1988), seems safe enough. And yet the stance of Quebec nationalism is that of a people in headlong retreat before historical forces which threaten to overwhelm it. [. . .]

Massive population mobility naturally intensifies this disorientation, as do economic shifts, some of them not unconnected with the rise of local nationalism. Wherever we live in an urbanized society, we encounter strangers: uprooted men and women who remind us of the fragility, or the drying up of our own families' roots.

What, if anything, have such ethnic/nationalist reactions in common with the recent rise of "fundamentalism" in many parts of the globe, which has been described as appealing to "people who cannot tolerate random and haphazard existence and unexplained conditions (and thus) often converge on those who offer most complete, inclusive and extravagant world views."[1] It is seen as "always reactive, reactionary." "Some force, tendency, or enemy must be perceived as potentially or actually eroding, corroding, or endangering one's movement and what it holds dear." The "fundamentals" that fundamentalism stresses "always come from some earlier, presumably primal and pure . . . stage in one's own sacred history." They "are used for setting boundaries, for attracting one's kind and alienating other kinds, for demarcating." [. . .]

The similarities with a number of recent ethnic/nationalist phenomena are evident, especially where these are themselves linked with, or seek to reestablish links with, a group-specific religious faith—as among (Christian) Armenians opposing (Muslim) Azeri Turks, or in the recent and markedly Old Testament phase of Likud Zionism in Israel, so different from the aggresively secularist, and even antireligious ideology of the movement's founders. It seems probable that the visiting extraterrestrial would see ethnic exclusiveness and conflict, xenophobia and fundamentalism as aspects of the same general phenomenon. Nevertheless there is one important distinction. Fundamentalism, whatever its religious version, provides a detailed and concrete program for both individuals and society, even if it is one selected from texts or traditions whose suitability for the late twentieth century is not obvious. What the alternative to the present, degenerate and evil, society is, presents no immediate problem: Women are once again hidden from sight, or married ones have their hair shorn; thieves are once again punished by having hands or legs cut off; alcohol, or whatever else is ritually prohibited, is banned; and Koran, or Bible, or whatever constitutes the authoritative compendium of eternal wisdom, provides complete practical and moral guidance on all subjects, as interpreted by those whose business it is to do so. The call of ethnicity or language provides no guidance to the future at all. It is merely a protest against the status quo or, more precisely, against "the others" who threaten the ethnically defined group. For, unlike fundamentalism which, however narrow and sectarian in its actual appeal, draws its strength from the claim to *universal* truth, theoretically applicable to all, nationalism by definition excludes from its purview all who do not belong to its own "nation," i.e., the vast majority of the human race. Moreover, while fundamentalism can, at least to some extent, appeal to what remains of genuine custom and tradition or past practice as embodied in religious practice, as we have seen nationalism in itself is either hostile to the real ways of the past, or arises on its ruins.

On the other hand nationalism has one advantage over fundamentalism. Its very vagueness and lack of programmatic content gives it a potentially universal support within its own community. Except in genuinely traditional societies reacting against the initial impact of modernity, fundamentalism appears to be, universally, a minority phenomenon. This may be concealed either by the power of regimes which impose it on their peoples, whether they like it or not (as in Iran), or by the capacity of fundamentalist minorities to mobilize strategically placed votes effectively in democratic systems, as in Israel and the United States. But it may be taken for granted that nowadays the "moral majority" is not a real (electoral) majority, just as a "moral victory" (the traditional euphemism for defeat) is not a real victory. Yet ethnicity *can* mobilize the vast majority of its community—provided its appeal remains sufficiently vague or irrelevant. [. . .]

The declining historical significance of nationalism is today concealed not only by the visible spread of ethnic/linguistic agitations, but also by the semantic illusion which derives from the fact that all states are today officially "nations," though many of them patently have nothing in common with what the term "nation-state" is commonly held to mean; that therefore all movements seeking to win independence think of themselves as establishing nations even when they are patently not doing so; and that all movements for regional, local, or even sectional interests against centralization and state bureaucracy will, if they possibly can, put on the fashionable national costume. Nations and nationalism therefore appear more influential and omnipresent than they are. [. . .]

In fact, the rise of separatist and ethnic agitations is partly due to the fact that, contrary to common belief, the principle of state creation since World War II, unlike that after World War I, had nothing to do with Wilsonian national self-determination. It reflected three forces: decolonization, revolution, and, of course, the intervention of outside powers. Since more than half the states at present existing are less than forty years old, this seriously limits the incidence of the traditional "principle of nationality."

Decolonization meant that, by and large, independent states were created out of existing areas of colonial administration, within their colonial frontiers. These had, obviously, been drawn without any reference to, or sometimes even without the knowledge of, their inhabitants and therefore had no national or even protonational significance for their populations; except for colonial-educated and Westernized native minorities of varying, but generally exiguous size. [. . .]

The appeal of most such "nations" and "national movements" was the opposite of the nationalism which seeks to bond together those deemed to have common ethnicity, language, culture, historical past, and the rest. In effect it was *internationalist*. The internationalism of the leaders and cadres of national liberation movements in the Third World is more obvious where such movements played a leading part in the liberation of their countries than where countries were decolonized from above, for the postindependence breakdown of what previously operated, or seemed to operate, as a united movement of "the people" is more dramatic. Sometimes, as in India, the unity of the movement has already cracked before independence.

More commonly, soon after independence tensions develop between the component parts of the independence movement (e.g., in Algeria, Arabs and Berbers), between peoples actively involved in it and those not, or between the emancipated nonsectional secularism of the leaders and the feelings of the masses. However, while the cases where multiethnic and multicommunal states have fractured, or are close to breaking, naturally attract most attention—the partition of the Indian subcontinent in 1947, the splitting of Pakistan, the demands for Tamil separatism in Sri Lanka— it should never be forgotten that these are special cases in a world where multiethnic and multicommunal states are the norm. [. . .]

As we can now see in melancholy retrospect, it was the great achievement of the communist regimes in multinational countries to limit the disastrous effects of nationalism within them. The Yugoslav revolution succeeded in preventing the nationalities within its state frontiers from massacring each other almost certainly for longer than ever before in their history, [. . .] though this achievement is now unfortunately crumbling. [. . .] Unlike the U.S.S.R., whose potential for national disruption, so long kept in check (except during World War II) can now be seen through the new transparency of glasnost. In fact, the "discrimination" or even "oppression" against which champions of various Soviet nationalities abroad protest, is far less than the expected consequences of the withdrawal of Soviet power. Official Soviet anti-Semitism, which has undoubtedly been observable since the foundation of the state of Israel in 1948, must be measured against the rise of popular anti-Semitism since political mobilization (including that of reactionaries) became permitted again, not to mention the massacre of Jews on a considerable scale *by local elements* in the Baltic states and Ukraine as the Germans marched in but *before the systematic German killing of Jews began*. Indeed, it may be argued that the current wave of ethnic or mini-ethnic agitations is a response to the overwhelmingly non-national and non-nationalist principles of state formation in the greater part of the twentieth-century world. However, this does not mean that such ethnic reactions provide in any sense an alternative principle for the political restructuring of the world in the twenty-first century.

[. . .] "The nation" today is visibly in the process of losing an important part of its old functions, namely that of constituting a territorially bounded "national economy" which formed a building block in the larger "world economy," at least in the developed regions of the globe. Since World War II, but especially since the 1960s, the role of "national economies" has been undermined or even brought into question by the major transformations in the international division of labor, whose basic units are trans-national or multinational enterprises of all sizes, and by the corresponding development of international centers and networks of economic transactions which are, for practical purposes, outside the control of state governments. The number of *intergovernmental* international organizations grew from 123 in 1951 through 280 in 1972 to 365 in 1984; the number of international *nongovernmental* organizations from 832 through 2,173 in 1972, more than doubling to 4,615 in the next twelve years. Probably the only functioning "national economy" of the late twentieth century is the Japanese.

Nor have the old (developed) "national economies" been replaced as the major building blocks of the world system only by larger associations or federations of "nation-states" such as the European Economic Community, and collectively controlled international entities like the International Monetary Fund, even though the emergence of these is also a symptom of the retreat of the world of "national economies." Important parts of the system of international transactions, such as the Eurodollar market, are outside any control whatever.

All this has, of course, been made possible both by technological revolutions in transport and communication, and by the lengthy period of free movements of the factors of production over a vast area of the globe which has developed since World War II. This has also led to the massive wave of international and intercontinental migration, the largest since the decades before 1914, which has, incidentally, both aggravated intercommunal frictions, notably in the form of racism, and made a world of national territories "belonging" exclusively to the natives who keep strangers in their place, even less of a realistic option for the twenty-first century than it was for the twentieth. At present we are living through a curious combination of the technology of the late twentieth century, the free trade of the nineteenth, and the rebirth of the sort of interstitial centers characteristic of world trade in the Middle Ages. City-states like Hong Kong and Singapore revive, extraterritorial "industrial zones" multiply inside technically sovereign nation-states like Hanseatic Steelyards, and so do offshore tax havens in otherwise valueless islands whose only function is, precisely, to remove economic transactions from the control of nation-states. The ideology of nations and nationalism is irrelevant to any of these developments.

This does not mean that the economic functions of states have been diminished or are likely to fade away. On the contrary, in both capitalist and noncapitalist states they have grown, in spite of a tendency in both camps to encourage private or other nonstate enterprise in the 1980s. Quite apart from the continued importance of state direction, planning, and management even in countries dedicated in theory to neoliberalism, the sheer weight of what public revenue and expenditure represent in the economies of states, but above all their growing role as agents of substantial redistributions of the social income by means of fiscal and welfare mechanisms, have probably made the national state a more central factor in the lives of the world's inhabitants than before. National economies, however undermined by the trans-national economy, coexist and intertwine with it. However, except for the most self-sealed at one end—and how many of these are left after even Burma appears to consider reentering the world?—and perhaps Japan at the other extreme, the old "national economy" is not what it was. Even the United States, which in the 1980s still seemed sufficiently vast and dominant to deal with its economic problems without taking any notice of anyone else, at the end of that decade became aware that it "had ceded considerable control over its economy to foreign investors . . . [who] now hold the power to help keep the U.S. economy growing, or to help plunge it into recession."[2] As for all small and practically all medium-sized states their economies had plainly ceased to be autonomous, insofar as they had once been so.

[. . .] The basic political conflicts which are likely to decide the fate of the world today have little to do with nation-states, because for half a century there has not existed an international state system of the nineteenth-century European type. [. . .]

Politically the post-1945 world has not been unified but bipolar, and organized round two superpowers which may just be describable as jumbo-sized nations, but certainly not as parts of an international state system of the nineteenth century or pre-1939 type. At most third-party states, whether aligned with a superpower or nonaligned, could act as a brake on superpower action, though there is no strong evidence that they did so to much effect in the last forty years. Moreover, as far as the United States was concerned—but vestigially this was probably also true of the U.S.S.R. before the Gorbachev era—the basic conflict was ideological, the triumph of the "right" ideology being equated with the supremacy of the appropriate superpower. Post-1945 world politics have been basically the politics of revolution and counterrevolution, with national issues intervening only to underline or disturb the main theme. Admittedly there were signs in the late 1980s that this pattern was breaking down, if only because both superpowers were becoming too weak economically to maintain their former roles, and because the model of a world divided by the October Revolution clearly had little relation to the realities of the late twentieth century. A more multilateral international system might revive in time. Nevertheless, even within such a system the role of nations was not likely to be central because the main players in such a game would be units far larger than the states that most of the characteristic, i.e., separatist, nationalist agitations of the late twentieth century were designed to form. [. . .]

Even a genuinely multilateral world system effectively dominated by an oligarchy of the important states, such as was envisaged in the Security Council as originally set up, would not be an international system in which most nations and nation-states played a significant role.

As we might expect, nationalism today reflects something like the crisis of the old Wilsonian-Leninist ideology and program, which is due to its political failure and to the sharply diminished relevance of "nation" and "nation-state" to the political and economic structure of the globe. Nationalism, however powerful the emotion of being in an "imagined community," is nothing without the creation of nation-states, and a world of such states, fitting the present ethnic-linguistic criteria of nationality, is not a feasible prospect today. [. . .]

Far more of the currently existing national movements than care to be reminded of it, have in practice given up envisaging total state independence as their final aim, at all events in Europe, the traditional home of the principle of nationality. Here most such movements appear to be reactions against the centralization—i.e., the remoteness—of state, economic, or cultural power, against bureaucratization, or else they express various other local or sectional discontents capable of being wrapped in colored banners. [. . .]

[T]he most striking thing about the new agitations of political nationalism in Western countries is their instability and impermanence, compared with the strength and stability of the sentiments of national identity they claim to express. This is evident if we follow the checkered fortunes of Scottish and Welsh nationalist parties, or of such xenophobic bodies as the French National Front. [. . .]

We may also detect a crisis of national consciousness in the old nations, and for similar reasons. That consciousness, as it emerged in nineteenth-century Europe, was situated somewhere in the quadrilateral described by the points People-State-Nation-Government. In theory these four elements coincided. In Hitler's phrase (where the word *Volk* stands for both "people" and "nation") Germany consisted of "*Ein Volk, ein Reich, ein Führer,*" i.e., one people/nation, one state, one government. In practice the ideas of the state and government tended to be determined by political criteria typical of the period since the era of great eighteenth-century revolutions, but the idea of "people" and "nation" largely by prepolitical criteria which were helpful in the creation of the imagined and imaginary community. Politics constantly tended to take over and remold such prepolitical elements for its own purposes. The organic connection between the four elements was taken for granted. But that is no longer possible in the historical or old-established large nation-states. [. . .]

The idea of "the nation," once extracted, like the mollusk, from the apparently hard shell of the "nation-state," emerges in distinctly wobbly shape. Not, of course, that Germans have ceased to think of themselves as "Germans."

What they are uncertain about, with good reason, is the political or other implications of "Germanness." One suspects that similar enquiries in other historic "nation-states" would produce similarly confused responses. What, for instance, is the relation between "Frenchness" and *francophonie* (a term which did not even exist until recently—it is first recorded in 1959). [. . .] Until the 1960s "Britishness," in terms of law and administration, was a simple matter of being born to British parents or on British soil, marrying a British citizen, or being naturalized. It is a far from simple matter today.

None of this means that nationalism is not very prominent in world politics today, or that there is less of it than there once was. What I am arguing is rather that, in spite of its evident prominence, nationalism is historically less important. It is no longer, as it were, a global political program, as it may be said to have been in the nineteenth and earlier centuries. It is at most a complicating factor, or a catalyst for other developments. It is not implausible to present the history of the Eurocentric nineteenth-century world as that of nation-building. [. . .] We still present the history of the major European states of Europe after 1870 in this manner. [. . .] Is anyone likely to write the world history of the late twentieth and early twenty-first centuries in such terms? It is most unlikely.

On the contrary, it will inevitably have to be written as the history of a world which can no longer be contained within the limits of "nations" and "nation-states" as these used to be defined, either politically, or economically, or culturally, or even linguistically. It will see "nation-states" and "nations" or ethnic/linguistic groups primarily as retreating before, resisting, adapting to, being absorbed or dislocated by, the new supranational restructuring of the globe. Nations and nationalism will be present in this history, but in subordinate, and often rather minor roles. [. . .]

"Nation" and "nationalism" are no longer adequate terms to describe, let alone to analyze, the political entities described as such, or even the sentiments once described by these words. It is not impossible that nationalism will decline with the decline of the nation-state, without which being English or Irish or Jewish, or a combination of all these, is only one way in which people describe their identity among the many others which they use for this purpose, as occasion demands. It would be absurd to claim that this day is already near. However, I hope it can at least be envisaged. After all, the very fact that historians are at least beginning to make some progress in the study and analysis of nations and nationalism suggests that, as so often, the phenomenon is past its peak. The owl of Minerva which brings wisdom, said Hegel, flies out at dusk. It is a good sign that it is now circling round nations and nationalism.

NOTES

1. Martin E. Marty, "Fundamentalism as a Social Phenomenon," *Bulletin, The American Academy of Arts and Sciences* 42, no. 2 (Nov. 1988): 15–29.
2. *The Wall Street Journal*, 5 Dec. 1988, 1.

INDEX

Aboriginal peoples, 326
Action Français, 11
Acton, John, 5, 6, 108–18
Addresses to the German Nation
(Fichte), 5, 62–70
"Address to a Joint Session of
Congress" ("Fourteen Points")
(Wilson), 15, 306–11
Adler, Victor, 346
Africa: Garvey's movement, 302–5;
socialism, 268–73. *See also*
Colonialism
African-Americans, 15
Afrocentrism, 15
al-Husayn, ibn, 261
al-Husri, Sati, 12, 13, 255–59
Alienation: as condition for slavery,
25–26
Altruism: loyalty to nation as, 315–16
al-Zahra', Fatimah, 266
Americanism: reassessment of meaning,
292–93
Anarchism, 201, 246, 352
Anderson, Benedict, 1, 346, 347
Anticolonialism, 12–14. *See also*
Colonialism; Imperialism
Antin, Mary, 293
Anti-Semitism, 7, 12, 230–37; Zionism
and, 125–31
Arabs: Islamic government, 260–67;
unity, 255–59
Arendt, Hannah, 339
Argentina: proposed Jewish state in,
128–29
Aristotle, 269
Arminius, 68
Armstrong, John, 1
Articles of Association, 287
Articles of Confederation, 287
Aryan race, 230–37
Assimilation: African, 268; dynamics in
United States of, 294–95; Jewish,
127; misdirection in United States,
292. *See also* Immigration; Migration

Asylum seekers, 340–41
Autonomy: law and abstract notions
of, 338; Stalinist critique of
national, 192–97

Bakunin, Mikhail, 196, 246
Bartolus, 345
Bauer, Otto, 10, 15, 166, 183–91,
192, 193–96
Bernardin de Saint-Pierre, Jacques
Henri (Abbe de Saint-Pierre), 3,
26–30
Berzin (Soviet Chekist), 174
Bipolar world, 368
Bismarck, Otto von, 228, 229
Bodin, Jean, 345
Body politic: components of, 23;
harm and protection, 23–24
Bourbons, 109
Bourgeoisie: ascendancy in Germany,
120–21; class antagonism and,
178–79; function in anticolonial
movements of colonialist, 281; and
growth of markets, 179; as
historically revolutionary, 179–80;
historical role of, 179–80; and
national self-determination, 199; in
oppressed nations, 210; production
revolutionized by, 180–81. *See also*
Class; Socialism; Working class
Bourne, Randolph, 14, 15, 292–301
Break-up of Britain, The (Nairn), 346
Brecher, Jeremy, 16, 17, 344–61
Brest-Litovsk treaty, 306–7
Buller, Charles, 105
Buneva, Mara, 162
Burke, Edmund, 7, 8, 16, 109, 134–42
Busching, Anton, 45

Capital (Marx), 201
Capitalism: development of world
powers under, 202; division of
labor, 187–88; national state as
norm under, 210; profit as goal of,

187–88; rights under, 201;
submission to established order
under, 276; system and social
integration, 336–37; tendency toward
unification of, 183. *See also*
Bourgeoisie; Class; Colonialism;
Imperialism; Socialism
"Captive" nations, 325–26
Caste system, 248, 251
Catholic church, 3, 219, 257, 345;
nationality and, 113–14. *See also*
Religion
Chernyshevski, Nicolaus, 201
China, 240–47
Christianity. *See* Catholic church;
Religion
Citizens: as body politic component,
23; as co-legislative members of
state, 40; nation of, 334
Citizenship: asylum and, 340–41; dual,
299; political membership and,
335–36; reduction to interest of
client, 338
"Citizenship and National Identity:
Some Reflections on the Future of
Europe" (Habermas), 333–43
Civil society: freedom and equality
demanded in, 327; religion as basis
of, 139
Civil War (United States), 14–15, 291
Class: in colonized nations, 281;
economic power and political
leadership relationship, 119; failure as
unifying bond, 344; Indian caste
system, 248, 251; international
solidarity based on, 9–10; national
economic life and, 315; nation in
class society, 203–4; particularistic
identities and, 347. *See also*
Bourgeoisie; Working class
Class struggle, 196; anti-imperialist
movements as, 347; fascism's
rejection of, 224, 227; history as,
178–79
Claudel, Paul, 268
Cold War: nationalism and end of, 1;
nationalism's use during, 9
Colonialism, 8–9; African socialism,
268–73; dehumanization as
consequence of, 278–79; Indian
development arrested by, 249; Islam
and, 262–63; national liberation

movements and (*see* National
liberation movements); natives'
challenge to, 277–78; native zones,
276–77; violence and, 277; Wilson's
"Fourteen Points" and, 309; world
division through, 275–76. *See also*
Imperialism
Colonization, 7
Colony: Kant's definition of, 42
Commodity of interest, 152
Communism, 178–82, 246. *See also*
Bourgeoisie; Socialism; Working class
*Communist Manifesto. See Manifesto of
the Communist Party*
Community: nation as, 190–91; of
reciprocal action, 44; as social
construction, 324; trade and, 44–45
"Community of character" concept, 10
Confederation: social compact and, 23
Confederation of Bar, 32
Congress of Vienna (1815), 5
Consciousness: of freedom, 81–82; and
national development, 157; nation as
moral, 153–55; revolution as upsurge
of, 272; socialist, 186; war to create
full development of national, 317–18;
world spirit revealed through, 79–80
Conservatism: nationalism and, 7–9
*Considerations on Representative
Government* (Mill), 6, 98–107
Constitution, U.S.: minority secession
and, 288–89; perpetual union under,
286–87; rights under, 288
Constitutional law: to Hegel, 71–75
Convention of Cintra, The
(Wordsworth), 163
Cooperation: Maurras's opposition to,
11–12; societal formation of, 54
Cosmopolitanism, 245, 246–47, 298
Cosmopolitan right, 44–45
Country. *See* Nation
Culture: anticolonialism and return to
roots of, 270–71; immigration and
retention of national, 296–97;
nationalism and preservation of,
166–67; nationalism as cultural
integration, 334; native "American,"
297–98; socialism and, 185

Decentralism, 351
Declaration of Independence, 287
Declaration of the Rights of Man, 87, 134

Decolonization, 365; compromise and, 282; as program of disorder, 274–75. *See also* Colonialism; National liberation movements

de Gaulle, Charles, 278

De Maistre, 229

Democracy: fascism and, 227; and nation-state in unified Europe, 336–39; natural units lacking in, 324; socialism and, 187

Dependencies: government by free state of, 103–6

Descartes, René, 268

Despotism: governmental, 105–6; ruling class nationalism and, 164–65

Dialectics: history as, 78, 83–84

Dicey, Edward, 313

Diet of Europe, 28

Discovery of India, The (Nehru), 13, 248–54

Disraeli, Benjamin, 304

Diversity: freedom and, 6

Division of labor, 187–88

Dreyfus affair, 7, 11

Du Moulin, Charles, 345

Durham, John, 105

Duties of Man, The (Mazzini), 6, 87–97

Duty: to country, 91–97; Hegel's conception of, 71–72

Dynasty: nation as, 146–47

Ecology: national question from perspective of, 344–61

"Economic Policy and the National Interest in Imperial Germany" (Weber), 6, 119–24

Education, 33–34, 88; political, 123; rights and, 89–90; in Russia, 172–73

Engels, Friedrich, 9–10, 178–82, 200, 346

Enlightenment: nationalism's roots in, 3–4

Environment: national genius and, 48–49

Environmentalism, 349

Eternal continuance: human influence on, 64–65; love and, 65; state as means to, 68–69

Ethics: as consciousness and duty, 85; ethical paradox in patriotism, 315–16; nation as source of, 12

Ethnicity: as twentieth-century factor,

362–63; xenophobia, 364–65

Europe: commonality of customs, 31–32; division into nations, 143; nation-state and democracy in unified, 336–39; Wilson's "Fourteen Points" proposal affecting, 308–10; World War I, 241–42

European Community, 16, 330, 333, 336–39, 340

Expansionism, 7

Family: in Russia, 172

Fanon, Frantz, 12, 14, 274–83

Fascism, 2, 11–12; conception of state, 224–25; democracy and, 227; fundamental ideas of, 222–25; liberalism and, 228–29; political and social doctrine, 225–29; spiritual conception, 222–23

Fascism (Mussolini), 12, 222–29

Fear: as cause of national antagonism, 329

Federation of nations, 61

Fénelon, François, 108

Feudalism, 3

Fichte, Johann Gottlieb, 2, 5, 9, 12, 13, 60–70, 162

"First Inaugural Address" (Lincoln), 286–91

Foundations of Natural Law, The (Fichte), 5

Foundations of Natural Law According to the Principles of the Theory of Science (Fichte), 60–61

"Fourteen Points" (Wilson), 15, 306–11

France, 216–21

Frederick II (Prussia), 156

Freedom: consciousness of, 81–82; differing meanings of, 335; disappearance of opposition between necessity and, 85; internal peace and limiting of, 66; national diversity and, 6; Rousseau's concept of, 22; slavery and, 25–26; state as actuality of, 71; U.S. immigration and, 295

Free state: government of dependencies by, 103–6

French Revolution, 4, 5, 7, 16, 87, 110, 134–42, 334; liberalism's roots in, 5

"Future of French Nationalism, The" (Maurras), 11–12, 216–21

Gandhi, Mahatma, 13
Garibaldi, Giuseppe, 229
Garvey, Marcus, 14, 15, 302–5
Gellner, Ernest, 1
"General Will": Rousseau's conception
   of, 4
Geneva Manuscript, The (Rousseau), 4,
   22–26
Geography, 152–53
Germans: fatherland and nation, 69–70;
   resistance to Romans, 67–68
Germany, 119–24, 228–29; imperialism,
   243; Nazism, 230–37; reunification,
   333–34
Gladstone, William, 304
Glasnost, 174, 366
Government: citizenship and political
   membership in, 335–36; of
   dependencies by free state, 103–6;
   despotic, 105–6; implementation of
   laws, 264–65; Islamic, 260–67;
   Islamic and other systems compared,
   266–67; nationality and boundaries of,
   100–101; nationality and representative,
   98–103; need for executive agencies,
   263–64; popularity of, 162–63. See
   also Nation; State
Government of Poland, The (Rousseau),
   4, 30–34
"Great Powers, The" (Ranke), 8,
   156–59
Greenfeld, Liah, 1
Green movement, 351
Grotius, Hugo, 25
Gusdorf, Georges, 272

Habermas, Jürgen, 16–17, 333–43
Habsburgs, 109
Haller, Albrecht von, 48
Haller, Johannes, 312
Hampden, John, 304
Hannibal, 28
Harmony: Enlightenment methods for
   achievement of, 4
Hayes, Carlton, 1
Hegel, Georg Wilhelm Friedrich, 5–6,
   71–86
Henry IV (France), 30
Herder, Johann Gottfried von, 3, 4, 5,
   48–57
Herzl, Theodor, 5, 7, 125–31
Historical contingency, 2

History: answerability before, 123–24;
   bourgeoisie's role in, 179–80; as class
   struggle, 178–79; colonization in,
   271–72; decolonization as process of,
   274–75; as dialectic process, 78,
   83–84; economic interpretation of,
   164; fascist conception of, 223;
   Hegel's conception, 78–79; Hegel's
   philosophy of, 79–86; national
   conception of, 184–85; nationality
   and conditions of, 200; national
   spirit as part of, 83; necessity for
   study, 145; as process of spirit's self-
   discovery, 84; as record of spirit's
   efforts to attain knowledge, 81;
   reverence for past, 250; spirit in,
   79–80; state as object of, 85
Hitler, Adolf, 11, 12, 230–37, 369
Hobbes, Thomas, 329
Hobsbawm, Eric, 1, 16, 17, 362–71
Hohenzollerns, 109
Holy Roman Empire, 3
Human beings: mind as nature of, 73
Humanity: duty to, 91–92; nations to
   serve common task of, 154
Human rights, 175
Hwang-Lao, 246
Hypocrisy: as moral characteristic of
   nations, 317–18

Idea: inner development of, 73; mind
   as, 72; nation as realization of, 78
Idealism: Nazi, 232; patriotism and,
   316–17
Ideology: nationalism and, 1–2
Immigration: chauvinism of prosperity
   and, 339–43; freedom and, 295;
   national culture and, 296–97;
   political acculturation and, 342;
   political asylum, 340–41; returned
   immigrants, 299–300; under
   socialism, 189; in United States,
   293–94. See also Assimilation;
   Migration
Imperialism, 203; Chinese, 245–46;
   definition of, 241; left
   internationalism and, 322; World
   War I and, 243. See also Colonialism
India, 248–54
Industrialization: markets and, 179;
   spiritual life vs., 174
Integral nationalism, 11–12, 216–21

Integration: system and social, 336–37
Interest: real and apparent compared, 27
Internationalism: Enlightenment background of, 3–4; imperialism and left, 322; intellectual internationalism as U.S. contribution, 299; of national liberation movements, 366; socialism and, 9–11
International justice: rational interest in, 314
International law, 352–54; Fichte's concept of, 60–61; Hegel's concept of, 76–77
International right: elements of, 38–39; as right of states in relation to one another, 38; warfare and, 38
Islam: government, 260–67; unity, 255–59
Islamic Government (Khomeini), 13, 260–67

Jewish homeland. *See* Zionism
Jewish State, A (Herzl), 7, 125–31
Judgment on Saint-Pierre's Project for Perpetual Peace (Rousseau), 26–30
Junker Estate, 119

Kaganovich, 174
Kant, Immanuel, 3, 4, 9, 17, 38–47, 76, 342
Kautsky, Karl, 209, 210
Kedourie, Elie, 1, 7, 8–9, 160–68
Khomeini, Ruhollah, 12, 13, 260–67
Knowledge: as ultimate aim of spirit, 80–81
Kohn, Hans, 1
Kossuth, Louis, 167
Kryzhanovsky, Sergei, 171

Language, 150–51, 166–67, 208; Arab unity and commonality of, 256; linguistic nationalism, 363–64; unity and religion and, 257
Lasting Peace, A (Saint-Pierre), 27
Law: through will of people, 110
League of Nations, 2, 15, 318; Wilson's proposal for, 242, 310
League of Nations (Kantian concept), 76
Left (political): international law and, 352; nation-state and, 346–48; tribalism not understood by, 322

Lenin, Vladimir Ilyich, 10, 11, 208–14, 244, 304, 347
Lepsius, M. R., 337
Leviathan (Hobbes), 329
Liberalism: fascist opposition to, 228–29; nationalism and, 5–7; nationalism as antagonistic principle to, 164–65; religion as basis of, 6
Liebknecht, Karl, 200
Lieh-txe, 246
Lincoln, Abraham, 14, 286–91, 304
Literature, 161–62
Lloyd George, David, 307, 316
Love: eternal self-conception and, 65
Luxemburg, Rosa, 10–11, 198–207, 208, 209, 210, 212, 346

Magna Carta, 134
Manifesto of the Communist Party (Marx and Engels), 9–10, 178–82, 228, 346–47
Markets: ascendancy of bourgeoisie and growth of, 179; international conflict related to, 9–10; national mobility and single European, 339
Marx, Karl, 9–10, 17, 178–82, 196, 200, 201, 228, 277; conception of state, 346–47
Marxism. *See* Class struggle; Communism; Socialism
Marxism and the National-Colonial Question (Stalin), 10, 192–97
Material improvements: nation and fulfillment of, 93–94; rights and, 90–91
Mauriac, François, 272, 278
Maurras, Charles, 11–12, 216–21
May Day, 344
Mazzini, Giuseppe, 5, 6, 12, 87–97, 163, 164, 229
Mein Kampf (Hitler), 12, 230–37
Melting pot concept, 15; failure of, 292, 298
Mercantilism, 3
Metaphysics of Morals, The (Kant), 4, 38–47
Michnik, Adam, 351
Mickiewicz, Adam, 161
Migration: national unity and, 195; under socialism, 189. *See also* Assimilation; Immigration
Mill, John Stuart, 5, 6, 98–107, 112

Millet system, 167
Mind: as idea, 72; as nature of human beings en masse, 73; objectivity of, 73; as substantiality of state, 74
Mirabeau, Victor, 304
Mollet, Guy, 281
Molotov, Vyacheslav, 174
Moltke, Helmuth, 229
Monarchy: Islam and, 261; political unity consolidated by, 3; social regulation in interest of, 108
Moral consciousness: nation as, 153–55
Moral Man and Immoral Society (Niebuhr), 15–16, 312–19
Moral relationships: force as redemptive, 318; hypocrisy as characteristic of nations, 317–18; state of nature to social state passage and, 24
Moral truth: communism to abolish eternal, 182; utility, 26–27
Muhammad (prophet), 261, 264
Multiculturalism, 15, 350, 351
"Muslim Unity and Arab Unity" (al-Husri), 13, 255–59
Mussolini, Benito, 11, 12, 222–29

Nairn, Tom, 346
Napoleon, 2, 111
Napoleon III, 228, 229
Nation: as association, 95–96; Bauer's definition of, 10, 183–84; "captive," 325–26; chain of cultivation, 55; changed meaning of term, 334; of citizens, 334; in class society, 203–4; common agreement lacking without, 93; as community, 190–91; consciousness and development of, 157; and democracy in unified Europe, 336–39; development of principle as spirit of, 82–83; development of world powers, 202; duty to, 91–97; as dynasty, 146–47; fascist conception of, 224–25; force in establishment of unity of, 315; as fundamental political unit, 6; fusion of populations, 144–45; historical development of, 184–85; as historic consequence, 145–46; hypocrisy as moral characteristic of, 317–18; left and nation-state, 346–48; loss of old functions, 366–67; loyalty as altruism,

315–16; and material improvements, 93–94; migration and unity of, 195; minority secession and, 288–89; as moral consciousness, 153–55; morality of, 312–19; national autonomy and development of, 194–95; national institutions, 31; natural existence of, 82; necessity for private activities and public services, 35–36; past and future of nation-state, 333–36; patriotism to serve, 316; realization of Idea in form of, 78; as recent phenomenon, 143; Renan's notion of, 8; right to self-determination of, 198–207; selfishness of, 312–14; settlement rights of, 45; socialist conception of, 183–84, 185; socialist organization of economy, 188–89; as soul or spiritual principle, 153–55; as source of ethics, 12; spirit in history of, 79–80; spiritual and family values necessary to, 9; as spiritual individual, 84–85; Stalinist definition of, 192; state and nation-state, 345–46; state not synonymous with, 312; state vs. federation of, 61; as territorial society, 312; territory as foundation of, 96; theory as auxiliary of revolution, 110; Third Estate as, 36; unified government and, 95; war and consciousness of, 317–18; world mind development and, 78. See also Government; State
National genius: environment and, 48–49
Nationalism: American perspectives on, 14–16; bourgeois, 210–11; as civil strife between generations, 160–61; communist regimes' limiting of, 366; conservatism and, 7–9; contemporary debate on, 16–18; as cultural integration, 334; culture and, 166–67; declining significance of, 365; despotism and, 164–65; Enlightenment background of, 3–4; eruption at end of Cold War, 1; French, 216–21; fundamentalism and, 365; ideology and, 1–2; integral, 11–12, 216–21; in late twentieth century, 362–71; liberalism and, 5–7; liberalism as antagonistic principle to, 164–65; linguistic, 363–64; national liberation movements and (see

National liberation movements); of oppressed and oppressors, 11; in regions of mixed population, 165–66; republicanism and, 334–35; socialism and, 9–11, 346–48

Nationalism (Kedourie), 8–9, 160–68

"Nationalism in the Late Twentieth Century" (Hobsbawm), 362–71

Nationalities Question and Social Democracy, The (Bauer), 10, 183–91

Nationalities question debate, 10

Nationality: as basis of state's political capacity, 116; church and, 113–14; difference between state and, 114–16; external power to serve internal community, 186–87; government borders and, 100–101; historical conditions influencing, 200; merging and absorption, 101–3; position of worker's party on, 198; Ranke's sense of, 8; representative government and, 98–103; and state forms, 112–13; theory of nationality as adversary of rights of, 117; working class and, 181

"Nationality" (Acton), 6, 108–18

National liberation movements, 8–9, 12–14; conditions for development of, 280; internationalism of, 366; nationalist parties in, 280–81. *See also* Colonialism; Imperialism

National minorities: just treatment of, 326–27; social movement forms taken by, 350

National Question and Autonomy, The (Luxemburg), 10–11, 198–207

"'National Question' Reconsidered from an Ecological Perspective, The" (Brecher), 17, 344–61

Nations and Nationalism (Hobsbawm), 17

Natural law: Herder on, 52–53; religion to fulfill, 63–64

Natural products: as artifacts of state, 39

Nature: cooperation and, 54; and degrees of civilization, 52–57; human naturalization, 50–52; of human species, 48–49; human welfare and, 56; institutions and conformity to, 135; state of nature to social state passage, 24; state rooted in, 60

Nazism, 11–12, 230–37

"Negritude" concept, 14

Nehru, Jawaharlal, 12, 13, 248–54

Neutrality, 325

"New Tribalism, The: Notes on a Difficult Problem" (Walzer), 16, 322–32

"New World Order", 1

Niebuhr, Reinhold, 14, 15–16, 312–19

Nobility: social functions and exemptions, 36–37

On African Socialism (Senghor), 14, 268–73

On the Social Contract (Rousseau), 4

Ottoman Empire: *millet* system in, 167

Pacifism, 230; fascist rejection of, 226

Pakistan, 252

Palestine: proposed Jewish state in, 128–29

Pan-Europeanism, 6

Patriotism, 299; as assured conviction, 73–74; ethical paradox in, 315–16; idealism and, 316–17; state and content of, 74

Peace: and limiting of freedom, 66; and right of state, 41–42; rights of, 42; Rousseau's judgment on Saint-Pierre's project for, 26–30; as ultimate purpose of rights, 46–47; Wilson's Fourteen Points for, 308–10

Peasantry: anticolonial nationalist parties and, 281; bound by tradition, 185

People: as body politic component, 23

Perestroika, 174

Perfection: natural law and, 52–53

Philosophy, 161–62

Philosophy of Right, The (Hegel), 5–6, 71–79

Philosophy of World History, The (Hegel), 6, 79–86

Pitt, William, 304

Pius IX (pope), 228

Poland, 30–34, 109, 204–6

Political antecedents: nationality and identity of, 98

Political asylum, 340–41

Political compromise, 163; decolonization and, 282

Political dominance: class and, 119

Population: fascist policy on, 226

Power: as body politic component, 23; breakup of blocs, 357–58; downward

devolution of, 350–51; and nation-
state self-perpetuation, 354–55;
sovereigns' expansion of, 27–28;
sovereigns' losses and gains and, 29;
upward devolution of, 351–52
Prejudice, 138–39
Private activities; classes of, 35
Privilege: public service and, 36–37
Production: bourgeois revolution in,
180–81; division of labor, 187–88;
intellectual-material relationship, 182
Proletariat. See Working class
Property, 136–37; as right, 39
Prosperity: immigration and chauvinism
of, 339–43
Protestantism, 3
Proudhon, Pierre Joseph, 246
Prussia, 119–20; as great power, 156
Public services: four categories, 35–36

Quebec, 363–64

Rabelais, François, 25
Race, 147–50, 302–5
Racism, 11, 12, 230–37, 269–70
Ranke, Leopold, 7, 8, 156–59
Rationalism, 3
Reagan administration, 356
Reason: African, 268–69; disorder into
order through, 56; disturbances of,
55–56; unity produced through, 54–55
Rebuilding Russia (Solzhenitsyn), 9,
169–75
Rechtsstaat concept, 6
Reflections on the Philosophy of the
History of Mankind (Herder), 4, 48–57
Reflections on the Revolution in France
(Burke), 8, 134–42
Regionalism, 327
Religion, 151–52, 182; Acton's views
rooted in, 6; and allegiance to state,
7; as basis of civil society, 139;
colonization and, 272; condition of
society dependent on spiritual life,
174; consecration of state, 141; as
consoling force, 62; fundamentalism,
364–65; in India, 250–51; Islamic
government, 260–67; Muslim unity,
255–59; natural order fulfilled
through, 63–64; necessity for, 9; Pan-
Islamic militancy, 13; toleration and,
329, 330–31

Renan, Ernest, 7, 8, 143–55, 228, 334
Renner, Karl, 166
Republicanism: nationalism and, 334–35
Resurrection of the Negro, The
(Garvey), 15, 302–5
Revolution: Burke's attacks on
legitimacy of, 8; cultural evolution
vs., 8; and extension of rights, 88;
Islamic, 265; Maoist theory of, 347;
national principle in, 111; national
theory and end of doctrine of, 117–18;
theory of nations as auxiliary of, 110;
as upsurge of consciousness, 272
Revolution of 1848, 165–66, 167, 201,
228
Ricardo, David, 188
Right of Nations to Self-Determination,
The (Lenin), 11, 208–14
Rights: citizens' vs. cultural, 5;
conservatives' rejection of abstract
notions of, 7; duty and, 72;
education and, 89–90; extension
through revolution, 88; individual
and community compared, 88–89; in
Islam, 261; material improvements
and, 90–91; unfulfillment of, 87;
U.S. constitutional, 288
Rights of Man, 87
Roman Empire, 143–44
Romans: German resistance to, 67–68
Romer, Ole, 51
Rousseau, Jean-Jacques, 3–4, 22–34
Ruling class; political qualifications of,
122–23
Russia, 169–75, 204–6, 208–14, 306–8
Russian Revolution, 243, 347

Sandinistas, 356
Schelling, Friedrich, 162
Scientific revolution, 3
Second International, 347
Self-determination: Leninist conception
of, 208–14; right of nations to,
198–207
Selfishness: of nations, 312–14
Self-preservation: state and, 22
Senghor, Léopold Sédar, 12, 13–14,
268–73, 279
Separatist movements, 328–29
Sieyès, Emmanuel Joseph, 3, 4, 35–37
Slavery, 25–26, 51–52; religion and, 62;
U.S. Constitution and, 288, 289

Smith, Anthony, 1
Social compact, 22–23
Social contract: Burke's affirmation of, 141–42; confederation, 23; harm and protection, 23–24; sovereign guarantees and, 24
Social integration, 336–37
Socialism: African, 268–73; democracy and, 187; fascist opposition to, 224, 227; international division of labor, 188; migration and immigration, 189; nationalism and, 9–11, 346–48; nationality and historical conditions, 200; nationality principle realized under, 189–90; nation and community under, 185; nation defined under, 183–84; organization of economy, 188–89; and "right of nations" concept, 199; transition to, 186; World War I and, 346–47. *See also* Capitalism; Class; Working class
Social order: freedom and, 22
Social self-preservation: state and, 22
Social wealth: and conditions of working class, 87–88; rights and, 90–91
Society: changing of, 356–57; as contract, 141–42
Socrates, 83
Solidarity (Polish movement), 351
Solzhenitsyn, Aleksandr, 7, 9, 169–75
Sorel, Georges, 12
Soul: nation as, 153–55
Sovereign: as body politic component, 23; duty toward people, 40; expansion of power, 27–28; peace and warfare and, 26–30; popular sovereignty concept, 335; power and losses and gains of, 29; regulation to serve interests of, 108; resolution of disputes between, 28; social contract guarantees regarding, 24
Soviet Union, 169–75
Sparmann (explorer), 51
Spirit: freedom as substance of, 82; heroic impulse and, 84; in history, 79–80; history as process of self-discovery of, 84; knowledge as ultimate aim of, 80–81; of nation as development of principle, 82–83
Spiritual life, 219; African socialism and, 273; condition of society dependent on, 174; fascism and, 222–23. *See also* Religion
Spiritual principle: nation as, 153–55
Springer, R., 192, 193, 195
Stability: as primary political concern, 9
Stalin, Joseph, 2, 10, 192–97, 347
State: as actuality of concrete freedom, 71; aims of, 65; as body politic component, 23; breakup of blocs, 357–58; citizens as co-legislative members of, 40; citizenship and political membership in, 335–36; consecration by religious establishment of, 141; content of patriotism and, 74; contract of, 141–42; corporative, 11; cosmopolitanist-nationalist polarity regarding, 349; and democracy in unified Europe, 336–39; difference between nationality and, 114–16; as economic region, 187; embodiment of will in, 6; eternal continuance and, 65; as external necessity and higher authority, 71–72; fascism conception of, 224–25; fascist, 12; fear of world, 353–54; federation of nations compared with, 61; government of dependencies by, 103–6; growth of economic function of, 367–68; Hegel's definition of, 84–85; as historical object, 85; inability to provide basic functions, 351; inherent contradictions of, 355; international right, 38–44; Islamic, 260–67; Jewish, 125–31; left and nation-state, 346–48; and love of fatherland, 66–67; Marx's conception of, 346–47; as means to higher eternal purpose, 68–69; Mill's notion of nation vs., 6; minority secession and, 288–89; national cultures within multinational, 10; nationalism and, 1; nationality and forms of, 112–13; nationality as basis of political capacity in, 116; national state as norm under capitalism, 210; nation not synonymous with, 312; nation-state and, 345–46; natural products as artifacts of, 39; natural roots of, 60; natural to social passage, 24; past and future of nation-state, 333–36; peace and right

of, 41–42; political way of life in
modern, 342; property and, 136–37;
relations with each other, 77; religion
and allegiance to, 7; religious
toleration enforced by, 330–31; right
against own subjects, 39; rights
actualized in will, 76; rights against
unjust enemy, 42–43; self-
perpetuation of, 354–55; social self-
preservation and, 22; sovereignty and
absoluteness of, 76; substantial
welfare of, 76–77; tendency of
national movements toward, 209;
treaties and self-interest of, 312–13;
universal interest as end of, 74;
universal union of, 43–44; warfare as
right of, 40–41; world law and,
352–54. See also Colonialism;
Government; Imperialism; Nation
States General (assembly), 43
Sturm und Drang movement, 4
Sully, Maximilien, 30
Sun Yat-sen, 12–13, 240–47
System integration, 336–37

Third Estate, 4, 35–37
Third World, 16; capitalist
modernization and democratic regimes
emerging in, 337; national liberation
movements in (see National
liberation movements). See also
Colonialism; Imperialism
"Three Principles of the People" (Sun
Yat-sen), 12–13, 240–47
Trade: community and, 44–45;
international harmony and, 4;
international ideas disseminated
through, 3; peace and, 29
Trade unions: Nazi attack on, 235. See
also Socialism; Working class
"Trans-National America" (Bourne),
15, 292–301
Treaties, 76; state self-interest and,
312–13
Tribalism, 16, 322–32
Trotsky, Leon, 304, 347
Turkey, 241
Tyrrell, George, 314

United Nations, 354
United States: Anglo-Saxon
predominance in, 294–96;
constitutional union, 286–91;
dynamics of assimilation in, 294–95;
failure of melting pot, 292, 298;
immigration, 293–94; native
"American" culture, 297–98;
reassessment of meaning of
Americanism, 292–93; return of
immigrants from, 299–300; World
War I entry of, 241–42, 308
Universal Negro Improvement
Association, 302–5
Utopianism: national rights as, 201–3

Vergniaud, Pierre-Victurnien, 110
Victoria (queen of England), 304
Violence: anticolonialism and necessity
for, 281; as cleansing force, 283;
colonial rule and, 277, 279–80,
282–83. See also Revolution; Warfare
Voltaire, François, 304

Wakefield, Edward, 105
Walzer, Michael, 16, 17, 322–32, 342
Warfare, 11; ethical moment in, 75;
fascist exultation of, 226;
international right and, 38; moral
redemptiveness of, 318; national
consciousness and, 317–18; nation
strengthened through, 12; pursuit of
rights through, 46; and retention of
possibility of peace, 77; as right of
state, 40–41; Saint-Pierre's peace
project, 26–30; unharmonized will
resulting in, 76
Washington, George, 304, 312
Weber, Max, 5, 6–7, 119–24
"What Is a Nation?" (Renan), 8,
143–55
What Is the Third Estate? (Sieyès), 4,
35–37
Wilson, Woodrow, 2, 14, 15, 242,
306–11
Wittelsbachs, 109
Wordsworth, William, 163
Working class: alliance with
bourgeoisie, 11; in Germany, 121–24;
national differences between, 181;
nation not constituted by, 184; Nazi
opposition to trade unions, 235;
particularistic identities and, 347;
principal task of, 212; rights not
attained, 87; socialist consciousness

of, 186; solidarity, 212–13; unity of, 210. *See also* Bourgeoisie; Class; Class struggle; Socialism

World Court, 354

World law. *See* International law

World War I, 241–42, 308; imperialism and, 243; socialist movement and, 346–47

Wretched of the Earth, The (Fanon), 14, 274–83

Xenophobia, 364–65

Yazid, 261

Zionism, 7, 125–31, 206